A... ...he Law of the United Nations

This work aims at filling a gap in the existing legal literature by presenting a compact, concise but nevertheless panoramic view of the law of the United Nations. Today the organisation is at the centre of all multilateral international relations and impossible to avoid. The many facets of international life, and its multiple actors, whether States, corporations, NGOs or individuals, come within its powerful, sometimes distorting, gravitational pull. And of course the UN Charter is a foundational document without which modern international law cannot be properly understood.

In spite of its importance, this pre-eminent world political organisation is poorly understood by the general public, and the extent and variety of its activities is not widely appreciated. Even lawyers generally possess insufficient knowledge of the way its legal institutions operate. Assessments of the organisation and judgements about its achievements are consequently frequently distorted.

This work is aimed especially at remedying these deficiencies of public and legal understanding, but also at presenting the organisation as a coherent system of values and integrated action. Thus the book presents an overarching view of the significance of the UN organisation in general, the history of its origins in the League of Nations, the aims and principles of the Charter, governmental agencies, members of the Organisation, the non-use of violence and collective security, the peaceful settlement of disputes, and the question of amendments to the Charter.

This work will be suitable for students of law and international relations, as well as scholars and those interested in the work and organisation of the United Nations.

An Introduction to the Law of the United Nations

Robert Kolb

Translated by
Katherine Del Mar

·HART·
PUBLISHING

OXFORD AND PORTLAND, OREGON
2010

Published in North America (US and Canada) by
Hart Publishing
c/o International Specialized Book Services
920 NE 58th Avenue, Suite 300
Portland, OR 97213-3786
USA
Tel: +1 503 287 3093 or toll-free: (1) 800 944 6190
Fax: +1 503 280 8832
E-mail: orders@isbs.com
Website: http://www.isbs.com

Hart Publishing Ltd, 16C Worcester Place, Oxford, OX1 2JW
Telephone: +44 (0)1865 517530 Fax: +44 (0)1865 510710
E-mail: mail@hartpub.co.uk
Website: http://www.hartpub.co.uk

British Library Cataloguing in Publication Data
Data Available

ISBN: 978-1-84113-937-1

Typeset by Hope Services, Abingdon
Printed and bound in Great Britain by
TJ International Ltd, Padstow, Cornwall

Preface

This book was first published in French in 2007 by the Swiss publishing house Helbing & Lichtenhahn under the title *Introduction au droit des Nations Unies*. Its main aim was to provide a readable and concise introduction to the legal aspects of the functioning of the United Nations (UN). A sketch of a historical perspective was added in order to situate the salient features of the UN and of its work in a historical context. The motivation for writing this book was the lack of proper teaching materials on UN law. Existing materials in French were either too sketchy or descriptive, or too detailed and technical. The point of this study was thus not to produce yet another publication presenting the world organisation in general, even if some degree of overlapping with such generic information is practically unavoidable.

The main structure of the French version of this book, very aptly translated by Katherine Del Mar, teaching and research assistant at the Law Faculty of the University of Geneva, was essentially maintained. However, some additions and omissions have been made. In particular, the section containing an outlook on the Swiss participation in the UN during the first five years of its membership in the original French version has been omitted here. It was not sufficiently relevant for non-Swiss readers to warrant its inclusion in the present publication. In contrast, some issues that were addressed in this omitted section are relevant, such as a discussion about the new Human Rights Council, and these have been included.

This book is mainly intended to provide a helpful explanation for students of international law or any lay reader interested in world affairs. As an introduction, it is deliberately geared towards a first acquaintance with the subject matter. There is no detailed treatment of the various topics, nor any encyclopaedic coverage of the numerous and tedious details of the UN system. A strict selection of topics has been made and I have not feared to leave gaps where I thought the issues were too benign to require further explanation. Moreover, the text is largely free of footnotes and technical details. It rather attempts to offer an overview of the scope and principles in the legal functioning of the UN system. The perspective chosen is thus a sweeping view from a mountain peak; a sort of bird's eye view of the valley below like the views one can see from the Swiss Jura mountains of Lake Geneva, where I go hiking in summer. It is not the perspective of a fully-fledged treatise or reference work. Some fuller coverage of topics may be included in future editions of the book, if they ever happen to see the light of day.

Contents

Abbreviations

Table of Cases

Table of International Instruments

Table of Resolutions

1

Sketch of the Evolution of the Idea
for a World Organisation

§ 1 Idea of a World Organisation before the Twentieth Century

Reflecting upon the historical development of the world organisation, we encounter one of the many paradoxes in history. When international organisations were first envisioned in the modern era they were intended to be strong and effective. Later, when they came into being they were found to be fraught with weaknesses and fault lines. The core reason for this lies in the sovereignty of the State. This concept was still emerging in the Middle Ages; it has become consolidated in modern times. Sovereignty is the counterpart of international organisation. The stronger the concept or perception of one, the weaker the concept or perception of the other.

Following the late Middle Ages and before modern times, the idea of organising Christian society in Europe was characterised by three notable features: the Utopian quality of such an organisation; the essentially political character of such an organisation and the quest for an organisation that had clear powers to sanction and coerce.

—*Utopia*. Following the Middle Ages and before modern times, Europe was experiencing the progressive dissolution of imperial unity, and at the same time a foundational consolidation of independent and sovereign States that possessed mutually exclusive powers over their own territories. The motto was *rex imperator* in *regno suo*, the king is emperor of his kingdom. The engine behind this historical evolution was both centrifugal and centripetal: dissolution at the universal level and consolidation at the State level. Europe was now hostile to the idea of unity, which had been so strong in the Middle Ages. Unity in the medieval world was centred on the unity of God: *unus est enim Pater vester* (but your Father is one); *omnia naturalia unum reducuntur* (all things flow from the one). From this the following political conclusion was drawn: *unus princeps totius universi* (one is the Prince of the whole Universe). The idea of 'Roman peace' meant that many associated the notion of 'empire' with peace. The maxim was: *pax in universitate* (peace in universal unity). The universal monarchy endowed with political authority could arbitrate disagreements among peoples and could thus be viewed as the creator of order. Defendants of this idea were Engelbert d'Admont, Henry VII,[1] and later, Dante. Conversely, dissolution of imperial unity entailed the impossibility, even theoretical, of binding arbitrating disputes between

---

[1] *Universi homines distincti regnis et provinciis sub uno principe moderata, in pacis ac unitatis augmenta susciperet* (Humanity scattered in different kingdoms and provinces arbitrated by one prince, in order to realise peace and unity).

States that were now independent of one another. The modern world was anarchical in the strict sense of the term. Each sovereign State possessed its own and exclusive foreign policy; each possessed its own modern army which could be used as a powerful instrument of foreign policy. The idea of a universal organisation thus quickly became a Utopia. Dante, in his De Monarchia, lamented the imperial unity of ancient times: 'Oh Humanity! How many storms and scourges, how many shipwrecks must befall you before you become a monster with many heads'.[2] The Tower of Babel had succeeded Noah's Arc.

—*Politics*. Medieval world organisation was conceived as being a perpetual defensive alliance against any would-be aggressors. Such an organisation could also serve an offensive function in the recuperation of holy lands from infidels. The concept of a world organisation was thus, in modern words, literally 'political'. There was no interest in creating an organisation that would perform technical, humanitarian or social functions. Rather, interest lay in creating an organisation that would go right to the heart of the most serious matter facing shared existence, namely the maintenance of peace. The first steps towards the creation of a world organisation were thus quite ambitious: they marched straight ahead, leaving practical and smaller issues aside.

—*Sanction*. Medieval ideas for a world organisation were all based on the idea of a strong confederation, endowed with incisive decision-making powers on the basis of a majority vote and capable of imposing sanctions (military, if need be) against any recalcitrant entity. Arbitration of disputes would be obligatory. The arbitral award would be binding. To the extent it would not be spontaneously complied with, the recalcitrant State could be summoned to implement the award; at the end of the process, sanction would be applied.

These three features of medieval ideas for a world organisation proved to be late attempts of clinging to the crumbling ruins of the ancient idea of an empire that was already in the process of disintegration. Once the empire had collapsed, one searched for an *Ersatz*. However, these attempts were doomed to failure because they were out of touch with the important historical shift at the time. The world was marching towards new principles under the banner of pluralism, sovereignty, empiricism, the State and later, nationalism. The universalists had had their time. They would only be reborn in the nineteenth century.

§ 2 Examples of Drafts

Among the doctrinal ideas for a world organisation that emerged during this period, mention may be made to those of Pierre Dubois (fourteenth century), Georges de Podiebrad (fifteenth century), Emeric Crucé (seventeenth century), Sully ('Gran Dessein d'une Republique Chrétienne', seventeenth century), William Penn (seventeenth century) Jeremy Bentham (eighteenth century) and the Abby of St Pierre (eighteenth century).[3]

---

[2] Dante, *De Monarchia* (1313) book I, ch XVI.
[3] For more details, see L Ledermann, *Les précurseurs de l'organisation* internationale (Neuchâtel, 1945). See also, in this vein, B Boutros-Ghali, 'Un précurseur de l'Organisation internationale: Al Kawakibi' (1960) 16 *Revue égyptienne de droit international* 15ff.

Special mention must be made of Immanuel Kant and his work entitled 'Toward Perpetual Peace' of 1795. Kant situates his reflections in the context of the classical divide between the state of nature and the civil state, between the reign of force and that of law. War is a sign of the state of nature. It evinces the fact that there are no legal sanctions among nations; that law can be twisted to the will of each sovereign State without any legal authority restricting the State's actions; and finally that there is thus a false semblance of law. War is dominating international relations. Thus, the civil state, namely the state of peace, does not exist between nations; it must first be instituted. While reason dictates that the institutional solution is a world State, this is not what peoples want or accept. Consequently, in the absence of a better solution, it is necessary to advocate for a federation of free States—a 'society of nations'—as an alliance for perpetual peace. Peace treaties must be avoided at all costs because while they can bring an end to a current war, they do not end all wars. Thus, their provisions lay the groundwork for the next conflict. The closer this federation of sovereign States approaches universality, the closer it comes to attaining perpetual peace. Kant does not address the precise powers of such a society. However, in light of his general theory of law and his specific criticism of Grotius' conception of international law, it appears that according to Kant such a society would have coercive powers. It thus transpires that Kant is a direct precursor to the League of Nations, established in 1919.

§ 3 Modern World Organisations

In the nineteenth century, when the first world organisations were created, there was a complete reversal of the three features of the medieval conception of such an entity. The world organisation was *created*, its functions covered the domain of *functional cooperation* (non-political activities) and it was imbued with the idea of *cooperation among free sovereign States* without the power of coercion. The modern 'cooperation-organisation' thus succeeded the older 'sanction-organisation', which had, however, remained a paper project. The solidarity among peoples and States in the nineteenth century in the administrative and technical domains could no longer be reasonably shirked. It called for practical solutions. The postal system, the telegraph system, the weights and measures system, the management of literary works, the administration of rivers that traversed the territories of many States, all demanded regulation and administration at the international level. How could one send and receive letters abroad but on the international level? How could one send a telegraph to the ends of the earth? How could a shared river system be rationally managed? The result was the budding of administrative unions (universal postal union, international telegraph union, union of weights and measures, union of literary and artistic works, etc) and international river commissions (for the Rhine, Danube, Oder, Escaut, etc).

Cooperation in political matters—like the maintenance of peace—had not yet found fertile soil in which to grow. It struck at the entrenched idea of each nation having its own, inalienable, vital interests.[4] Only a catastrophe could stimulate the

---

[4] As C de Visscher wrote in *Théories et réalités en droit international public* 4th edn (Paris, 1970) 112: 'In the State, it is the vital interests, the most highly political, that produce the most supreme solidarities. The

necessary changes in old habits and narrow minds. The First World War can thus be said to have shaken the world to its core. Modern war was no longer the limited war of the past, fought between two professional armies. It was total war, fought with tenacity and fanaticism, with highly powerful, destructive weapons and impacting on all civil society. [The situation was aptly described by Maurice Bourquin: '[War has become a cataclysm] that leaves only ruin behind in its wake, where the victorious and the vanquished, belligerents and those who are neutral, struggle in the same failure, in the same anguish'.[5]]The maintenance of peace, therefore, suddenly appeared in a new light: it began to be perceived as a collective interest of primary importance. Once war had become a blight, it was necessary to attempt to erect barriers surrounding it so that it might be avoided, or at least occur less often. At best, war was seen as nothing more than a way of ending war: *the war to end all wars*, as was claimed for the First World War. Thus, the wind had changed. It was not the diplomats and members of the armed forces, but rather the people and the elite, such as the American president Woodrow Wilson, who would draw back the curtains on this new era. The United States of America in particular, through their president, had the honour of being the catalysing force behind the creation of the first great political world organisation, the League of Nations. The Utopia of yesterday had become a reality. Through the League of Nations the old medieval thread of a world organisation that was centred on political matters and had some power to coerce and sanction, was again taken up. Was it the first step towards a process of political integration, as some thought at the time? Or was it a hybrid entity, imbued with sovereignty and orientated more toward the soothing beaches of voluntary cooperation, rather than the embryo of a world government? History provides the answer: it was the latter rather than the former.

Some examination of the history of the League of Nations as a precursor to the United Nations is necessary to fully understand this second entity. The Charter of the latter refers on all points to the Covenant of the former, either to reproduce some parts unaltered, or to develop other parts in order to improve their weaknesses, or finally to completely repel certain parts as not having stood the test of experience. To have studied the United Nations without having studied the League of Nations is not to have studied in depth. All answers to the 'why' in the Charter are found in the Covenant.

inverse is true for the international community. There are minor solidarities in relation to economic or technical matters, for example; but the closer one approaches vital questions, such as the maintenance of peace or war, the less the community exercises action over its members; the solidarities weaken in proportion to the size of the perils that threaten; those that do exist in this area concern the traditional domain, the nation. Men do not contest, with reason, the existence of supranational values; in the order of action, they obey only national imperatives' (unofficial translation).

[5] M Bourquin, 'Le problème de la sécurité internationale' (1934) 49(3) RCADI (Collected Courses of the Hague Academy of International Law) 475 (unofficial translation).

2

From the League of Nations to the United Nations

§ 4 Historical Importance of the League of Nations

The League of Nations marked a decisive step in history. It signalled the beginnings of the political world organisation, the rising of the curtains, with the excitement of a premiere. The organisation had become indispensable in 1919 due to the level of technical and political interdependence that the world had reached at the time. A world without such an organisation would have been unimaginable in the twentieth century.[1] The experience of the League was rich and varied; it had successes as well as failures. The role of a 'first attempt' in a great human adventure is its most profound essence. In any event, it is too short-sighted to view the League as merely a 'failure' because it did not succeed in maintaining peace, its principal aim. This failure was due to the bad will of its most important members and its inability to act at a difficult period in time. Rich and decisive lessons may nevertheless be learned even from this disappointing page in League history. Thus, it was not a wasted experience. It allowed the United Nations (UN) to get off to a running start by avoiding the errors of its novice predecessor.

§ 5 Genetic Code of the League of Nations: the Transformation of War

The League of Nations is the fruit of the profound transformation of war. It was a child of the total war of the twentieth century that replaced the limited war of the

---

[1] As has been noted, 'It would be quite arbitrary to pass decisive and definitive judgment over the [United Nations] Organization which, if it were to disappear, would be replaced by another of the same type': C Chaumont, *L'Organisation des Nations Unies* 6th edn (Paris, Les Cours de droit, 1968) 125 (unofficial translation). Or again, 'Throughout its twenty years of existence the Covenant system has been attacked and ridiculed by nationalist press organs, and by many individuals holding positions of power in the service of their countries. They had condemned it as an unrealistic appeal to the sentiment of the ignorant masses. They had frustrated its efforts, grudged its successes, and rejoiced its failures; they had created doubt and confusion in the minds of many who had at first believed in it; and they had watched it go down in an inglorious defeat. And now the victorious nations showed themselves resolved to repeat the experiment. With some differences, indeed, but differences that were small compared with the resemblances, they set up once more a world-wide organization for collective security. In its purposes and principles, its institutions and its methods, the United Nations bears at every point the mark of the experience of the League': FP Walters, *A History of the League of Nations* (London; New York; Toronto, 1960) 812.

eighteenth century. More specifically, the League was devoted to the effort to fight this new form of warfare and to maintain peace. In what ways was modern warfare different from ancient warfare? Herewith the four most salient aspects:[2]

—*Nationalism.* In the old days, war was fought between two professional armies led by their kings and composed of professional soldiers. It was played out on battlefields between professional armies of limited size in order to resolve a dispute or to conquer territory. It ordinarily posed no direct threat to the lives of people. Civilians were largely strangers to these 'princely duels'; they were spared because they did not identify with the cause of their prince, nor did they participate in hostilities. War was thus limited overall and violence circumscribed; it could nevertheless cause injury to civilians in the form of famine and illness, siege warfare or blockade. Furthermore, wars were of short duration. The emergence of the principle of nationality changed this state of affairs. The nation took up arms to fight for a collective cause, for vital interests, for survival; people fought to carve out a place for themselves in the world. Huge armies were assembled by conscription and individuals were indoctrinated through propaganda into the national cause. Consequently, war was brutalised on the ideological level and also due to the fact that the conscripted members of a side were not professional and trained soldiers, unlike the members of the old royal armies. It was a period in which the *levée en masse*, volunteer fighters, and resistance movements emerged.
—*Technical revolution.* Up until the nineteenth century war had been conducted by technical means of limited destructive capacity: canons, firearms, bayonets, even earlier, the catapult. The nineteenth and twentieth centuries revolutionised the destructive power of weapons. New bombs had an infinitely superior destructive power over old cannon balls. Aviation, first used in the First World War, was capable of quickly releasing large quantities of firepower over the whole of the enemy's territory, creating hell in villages and built-up areas. The final addition to this weaponry evolution was the nuclear weapon, capable of annihilating all life on earth. Modern war is thus characterised by the destruction it causes, incomparably greater than previous wars.
—*Industrialisation.* The nineteenth century was the century of industrialisation. This changed the way war was conducted. During the eighteenth century and earlier, a State was victorious in battle because of the quality and training of its soldiers. At the beginning of the nineteenth century, a State came away victorious essentially because of the number of fighters at its disposal (*levée en masse*). From the second half of the nineteenth century onwards, victory has largely depended on the economic power and resources that a belligerent can use in furtherance of the war effort. Infrastructure (railway lines etc), access to resources (steel, etc), the economic production of goods in factories that could be used in war (all types of tools, etc), form integral elements of success in war. The entire national society contributes to the war effort, either directly at the front, or indirectly in the area of production. The civilian in the factory contributes just as much to the war as the soldier at the front. The effect of this evolution is that the opposing belligerent attacks industrial centres

---

[2] On the first three of these aspects, see F Bugnion, *Le Comité international de la Croix-Rouge et la protection des victimes de la guerre* 2nd edn (Genève, 1994) 827ff.

precisely because they contribute to the war effort. The result is that civilians have become a direct and frequent target in modern warfare. There is now no limit to destruction: it is total war. The entire territory of the enemy is like one, sole, military objective designed to sustain destructive attacks.

—*Interdependence*. Modern warfare produces more devastating effects by reason of the interdependence of the modern world in economic, financial, commercial and political matters. Third parties, notably neutral parties, are directly affected by war. Their commerce industry is affected by the measures taken by belligerents in attempting to block the supply of goods that could contribute to the war effort of their enemy. Seizure of goods, lists of contraband and measures taken by belligerents, all affect neutral parties. Industrialisation of the territories of third parties to the conflict thus has the same effect as it does within a belligerent State: all goods are susceptible to serving a remote military purpose and thus to being seized. Thus, neutral parties suffer as a result of war. War provokes general impoverishment that adds to the destruction already havocked by the fighting alone.

These different aspects of the evolution of war combine in highlighting the necessity of suppressing modern warfare. Modern war has become too destructive of social life to be countenanced. Rather, general interest indicates that it has to be suppressed as much as practically feasible. Consequently, law and international politics have the responsibility of creating the institutional framework for peace. This is a radical change of paradigm. The League of Nations bears the hallmarks of that effort.

§ 6 Fundamental Pillars of the Covenant of the League of Nations

The League of Nations is based on four fundamental pillars that all are directed towards the principal task of the organisation: the maintenance of peace.

—*No general prohibition of war*. The Covenant contains no general prohibition of war. It only prohibits certain enumerated wars, set out as a series of special provisions. This creates a certain amount of complexity in the legal regime, because each specific prohibition also corresponds to a freedom *a contrario*: all wars that are not expressly prohibited remain lawful. It is for this reason that we speak of 'fissures' (in French) or gaps in the Covenant that a series of complementary texts tried to fill from 1919 onwards. The Covenant was thus not able to fulfil the great plan of establishing a general prohibition of war or the use of force. Smaller States were in favour of such a general prohibition, because they had nothing to gain and everything to lose from individual uses of force. However, the great powers held the opposite view and refused to renounce this essential attribute of their power. Such a position is understandable at that time, when the world was dominated by the concept of sovereignty and a strong feeling of insecurity prevailed. The Covenant was a stopover on the journey towards a general prohibition; it was a break that allowed time for reflection, time to take a deep breath and to measure the distance already travelled.

—*War as a social wrong*. War is stigmatised by the Covenant as a wrong that affects the interests of all League members. It is a matter that no longer falls within the exclusive domestic jurisdiction of States, but is rather an *erga omnes* interest. All States must therefore cooperate to maintain peace and punish aggression. Peace is a common interest, a community matter, an issue pregnant with solidarity. Thus, article 11 § 1 of the Covenant provides that any war or threat of war, whether immediately affecting any of the members of the League or not, is a matter of concern to all its members. Article 16 of the Covenant adds: 'Should any Member of the League resort to war in disregard of its covenants under [the Covenant], it shall ipso facto be deemed to have committed an act of war against all other Members of the League'. International solidarity is thus two-fold: (1) War is a matter of concern for the League of Nations, even if it concerns a non-member—namely, it is a matter that affects the international community as a whole; and (2) war between members of the League is war among all members of the League. This second limb calls for a system of collective security. The spiritual scope of these new principals could not be overestimated.

—*No war without a settlement of disputes procedure*. The essential outcome of the Covenant system is the following general principle: no member State should have recourse to war without a prior examination of the conflict by an international organ. Resort to war can only be the result of a failure in a prior dispute settlement procedure. In all other cases, war is prohibited and constitutes a type of aggression (war by surprise). The Covenant does not make mandatory the actual settlement of the dispute between the litigants, for example, the proposal of settlement by a mediator or by the League Council (conversely, the judgment of the Permanent Court of International Justice (PCIJ) or the award of an arbitration tribunal would be mandatory for the parties to the dispute if they elected such a judicial body for the settlement of their dispute). The Covenant only makes resort to such a dispute settlement procedure a necessary precondition for a resort to war. The obligation is not one of substance, but one of procedure. Article 12 of the Covenant thus provides: 'The Members of the League agree that, if there should arise between them any dispute likely to lead to a rupture they will submit the matter either to arbitration or judicial settlement or to enquiry by the Council'. If a dispute is not submitted to a judicial body, the jurisdiction of the Council becomes mandatory (article 15 § 1); but the Council cannot impose a solution on the merits, it can only recommend a solution (article 15 § 3). If the Council is able to decide unanimously on the solution to be given to the dispute (not counting the votes of the parties to the dispute), resort to war is prohibited against the party conforming itself to the recommendations of the Council (article 15 § 6). Conversely, if the Council cannot decide unanimously on the solution to be given to the dispute (without counting the votes of the parties to the dispute), each one of these parties can resort to war after a period of three months from the Council's report (article 15 § 7 in combination with article 12 § 1). Thus, in the absence of precise and adequate a priori criteria for the illegality of war (just causes), the Covenant concerns itself with the organisation of a procedure for the peaceful settlement of disputes. A failure to use these procedures becomes the specific criterion of illegality as regards the resort to war.

The optimistic logic of the Covenant is that a war stalled is a war avoided. This notion of delaying war, taken from the Bryan Treaties and pacifist movements, is reproduced in article 12 § 1 of the Covenant.[3] The importance of the Covenant is thus to stop war breaking out by trying to resolve the dispute beforehand. The Covenant takes a gamble that each day that passes without war, buys time for the tempers of the two sides to cool and for a reasonable solution to be found. Playing with time is, therefore, not a bad thing in the logic of the Covenant; on the contrary, it is a good thing. This prophylactic logic is at the heart of the League system. Therefore, sanctions for violations of the Covenant's provisions, namely in cases of aggression, are not addressed in any depth. Sovereignty and optimism alike brushed away the development of a sanction system.

—*Guarantee of territorial status quo*. Territory has always been *par excellence* the subject of disputes among States and the most immediate cause of preceding wars. The Covenant takes a position on the use and conservation of the territory of each member and stipulates that a State must be able to use its territory free from any threats and without despoliation. The corollary of this right is the obligation of other States not to use force to interfere with this territorial possession. Wars to conquer territory are thus a second type of wars of aggression under the Covenant (wars of conquest). However, all problems stem from determining what territory belongs to whom at any given moment. What is the critical date for determining territorial possession? According to the Covenant, the crucial date is the establishment of the Treaty of Versailles. It is this link between territorial possession and the victorious States of 1919 that will be the principal basis of disputes from unhappy States in the short history of the League of Nations.[4] These States will contest the content of article 10 of the Covenant, which clothes this territorial freeze in legal terms. This fundamental provision provides as follows: 'The Members of the League undertake to respect and preserve as against external aggression the territorial integrity and existing political independence of all Members of the League. In case of any such aggression or in case of any threat or danger of such aggression the Council shall advise upon the means by which this obligation shall be fulfilled'. Under the Covenant, this freeze on territory against any use of force is complete. The only admissible 'exception' (although not strictly an exception) is to permit a State to change the status of its territory by peaceful means. Article 19 of the Covenant was supposed to play an important role in this respect,[5] which practice proved was not the case.[6]

---

[3] 'The Members of the League agree that, if there should arise between them any dispute likely to lead to a rupture they will submit the matter either to arbitration or judicial settlement or to enquiry by the Council, and they agree in no case to resort to war until three months after the award by the arbitrators or the judicial decision, or the report by the Council. In any case under this article the award of the arbitrators or the judicial decision shall be made within a reasonable time, and the report of the Council shall be made within six months after the submission of the dispute'.

[4] See, eg, C Schmitt, *Die Kernfrage des Völkerbundes* (Berlin, 1926).

[5] The text of article 19 of the Covenant reads as follows: 'The Assembly may from time to time advise the reconsideration by Members of the League of treaties which have become inapplicable and the consideration of international conditions whose continuance might endanger the peace of the world'.

[6] It was sufficient for those powers that were satisfied with the 1919 settlement not to consent to modify the status of their territories for the peaceful regulation to fail. The problem with the League of Nations was that it was inextricably linked to the European territorial settlement that was viciously refuted by some powers.

§ 7 Provisions of the Covenant

Following an analysis of the principles of the Covenant, let us mention its most important rules:

—*Preamble*: ideological manifesto of the Covenant: restrictions on war, respect for justice and law, cooperation among nations.
—*Article 5*: the principle of unanimous voting with only (rare) exceptions in other parts of the Covenant, for example in article 15 § 6. This highlights another funda-mental principle of the Covenant: equality of States.
—*Articles 8–9*: disarmament.
—*Articles 10–16*: collective security system
—*Article 10*: guarantee of the territorial integrity and political independence of members. This provision guarantees non-aggression as non-interference with territory.
—*Article 11*: war as a collective interest of the League and all of its members, regardless of the location or parties to the war.
—*Article 12*: obligation to peacefully settle disputes with a view to preventing a rupture of peace.
—*Articles 13–14*: settlement of legal disputes by arbitration or by the Permanent Court of International Justice to be established by the League.
—*Article 15*: settlement of political disputes, or other disputes not submitted to arbitration or to the Court, by the League of Nations Council or Assembly.
—*Article 16*: sanctions against any State that resorts to war in violation of the provisions of the Covenant.
—*Article 18*: rules concerning the publishing and registering of treaties with the League of Nations. This is the fulfilment of point number 1 of the famous Fourteen Points of 8 January 1918 drafted by President Wilson as a model for future peace. Point 1 was designed to combat secret diplomacy.
—*Article 19*: proposals for the reconsideration of treaties by the Assembly that have become inapplicable or dangerous for the maintenance of peace. This provision is designed to temper the principle of territorial status quo under article 10 of the Covenant.
—*Article 22*: institution of the system of international mandates over territories that were separated from the defeated Austrian-Hungarian, German and Ottoman empires.
—*Article 23*: functional cooperation in the fight against crime (treatment of women, trafficking of opium, etc), in the maintenance of communications, in sanitary and hygiene measures, in humanitarian progress, etc. All these matters were considered as 'non-political' under the Covenant regime.

§ 8 Similarities between the League of Nations and the United Nations

The League of Nations and the United Nations share more in common than their differences, even though the United Nations had the advantage of hindsight to modify some of the League's mechanisms. The most important similarities are the following:

—*Organic structure*. An Assembly, a limited Council acting as an executive organ, a Secretariat, a Court of Justice.

—*Push for universal membership*. The push for universal membership occurred in both organisations after initial discriminate phases where victorious States were reluctant to extend membership to previous enemy States.

—*Aims and principles*. The maintenance of peace and functional cooperation among States; disarmament, peaceful settlement of disputes, collective security, respect for international law, humanitarian causes. In general the ideology is international, that is, directed towards an ideal equality among peoples, the mitigating of the use of force and free cooperation among States.

—*Respect for the sovereignty of State members*. The League of Nations maintains the unanimity-voting rule, which amounts to giving each State the right to veto. Equality of sovereignty is thus preserved as no State can impose a decision against the will of others, although such an approach seriously hampers efficiency. The League of Nations, like the United Nations, is not a super-State. Under the United Nations system, article 2 § 1, of the Charter proclaims the sovereign equality of State members. Respect for sovereignty is also reflected in the provisions of both the Covenant and Charter that address issues falling within the exclusive domestic jurisdiction of States, article 15 § 8 and article 2 § 7, respectively. This notion has today lost a considerable part of its raison d'être in the practice of the United Nations.[7]

§ 9 Differences between the League of Nations and the United Nations

There are also a number of differences between the two organisations:

—*Membership*. Membership never attained universality or even near universality in the League. This fact considerably limited the work that could be achieved. Sanctions, for example, can never be crowned with success unless they also involve or apply to important powers. The United States of America was never a member of the League of Nations, the USSR was only a member between 1934 and 1939, Germany from 1926 to 1933 and Italy from 1920 to 1937. In the United Nations, universality of membership was not only sought, it was expected. Upon the entry of Switzerland into the organisation in 2002, universality was achieved.

—*Degree of contextualisation of peace*. The Covenant is based on a very simple and direct system for maintaining peace. Peace is sought in the settlement of disputes; it is a procedural device. The Charter enlarges its horizon and erects a number of different barriers to protect peace. It envisages stabilising economic and social conditions that promote the progress of peoples; it provides for the peaceful settlement of disputes; it assembles a powerful system for maintaining peace through emergency coercive measures taken by the Security Council. The system of the Charter is thus richer, multi-causal and more diverse than the Covenant system.

—*Criteria for the triggering of collective security measures*. Under the Covenant, the maintenance of peace is essentially triggered by a violation of one of its provisions,

---

[7] See below, ch 7, § 60.

namely, respect for territorial integrity as provided for under article 10, or the obligation to peacefully settle disputes under article 12. The Covenant thus links measures to maintain the peace with violations of international law. The optic changes under the Charter. The concept of a 'threat to the peace' is the keystone to collective action (article 39 of the Charter). It is more supple, more malleable and more discretionary. A political judgement under the Charter takes the place of legal assessment under the Covenant. The place of international law in the system of the Charter is consequently less omnipresent.

—*Role of the great powers.* Under the Covenant, extreme equality among members is constitutionally consecrated by the unanimity-voting procedure (article 5 § 1).The general right to veto that results ensures protection and accords real political weight to small and medium-sized powers. Under the Charter, the great powers have more say. Their supremacy is guaranteed by the predominant role assigned to the Security Council in all settlement of dispute measures, in the maintenance of peace and by exclusive veto power (article 27 § 3).

—*Unanimity/majority.* Under the Covenant, unanimity is the base rule (article 5 § 1). Under the Charter, the majority vote carries. It is generally a simple majority, sometimes qualified and usually taken on the basis of those members 'present and voting' (articles 18, 27, 67 and 89). Whereas there is a general veto right under the Covenant, the veto right under the Charter only applies to non-procedural matters before the Security Council and only to the five great powers expressly mentioned in article 23 (United States of America, Russia [formerly USSR], China, United Kingdom and France).

—*Permanence of executive organs.* The organ that provides for the settlement of disputes and for collective security action must be able to meet at any moment in order to adopt emergency measures. However, right from its very beginning, the League of Nations Council was not a permanent organ. Even worse, from 1928 onwards, it only met for three ordinary sessions a year.[8] Delegates were not always represented on these occasions; some had to travel from afar to meet in Geneva; on arrival, some delegates lacked information and additional time was lost in collecting it. Measures taken by the League of Nations in response to acts of aggression were thus always too late. In comparison, the Security Council at the United Nations is a permanent organ. Delegations must be based in New York in order to be called into session at any moment. Furthermore, they are kept constantly updated about crises that interest the Security Council.

—*Assembly distinguished from the Council.* Under the Covenant, the Assembly and the Council had much the same features. The Assembly did not control the Council. Each could be seized of 'any matter within the sphere of action of the League or affecting the peace of the world' (articles 3 § 3 and 4 § 4). As an organ of limited size, the Council enjoyed a certain priority when addressing disputes and crises, but it did not have any exclusivity over these matters. The Assembly dealt with a number of crises, such as Manchuria in 1931. A rule that was often applied was that the organ first seized of the matter had priority until such time as the matter was referred to the other organ. This partition of powers was rather vague and did not assist in the work of the two League organs and even contributed to a certain dilution of responsibility: one

---

[8] Before 1928 there were four ordinary session per year.

could always pass the buck. It should further be noted that the composition of the Council grew steadily larger until it became a sort of mini-Assembly, thereby also contributing to dilute responsibilities. The non-permanent members of the Council became 6 in 1922, 9 in 1926, 10 in 1933 and 11 in 1936.

Under the Charter, the distinction between the Assembly and the Council is clear. The Council has priority over any 'measures' concerning the maintenance of peace. This priority is referred to three times in the Charter: article 24 § 1 recalls the primary responsibility of the Security Council for the maintenance of peace and security. Article 11 § 2 affirms that the General Assembly may discuss any questions relating to the maintenance of peace and security, but specifies that any question on which action is necessary must be referred to the Security Council. Lastly, article 12 § 1 stipulates that while the Security Council is exercising its functions in respect of any dispute or situation, the General Assembly cannot make any recommendation with regard to that dispute or situation. Therefore, while the General Assembly can discuss a situation, it cannot take a position. Moreover, the composition of the Council is limited. The number of non-permanent members has only been altered once when the number of six members as originally provided in 1945 was increased to ten on 1 January 1966.

—*Importance of functional cooperation.* The Charter attributes greater importance than the Covenant to the cooperation among States in economic, social, technical and humanitarian matters. The logic of the Charter is that peace will not be effectively maintained without addressing the deep causes of conflicts. A global project of cooperation among sovereign States distinguishes the regime of the Charter from the more limited view of this end in the Covenant.

§ 10 Mechanisms in the Decline of the League of Nations

The League of Nations was caught up in a political storm from which it could not shield itself. This was due to a lack of proper means and to Member States that progressively preferred to return to the 'realist' policies of alliances or neutrality. These States turned their backs on the Covenant that had not fulfilled their highest hopes of security and cooperation. The weaknesses of the Covenant pushed them towards taking their security into their own hands. The attitudes of these States precipitated the fall of the organisation and the accumulated dangers. To not apply the collective security system in a world where certain States advocated the use of force was to send the message that bellicose adventures could be undertaken without risk. It was in fact to start the march towards war. It is perhaps useful to set out, in successive steps, how each of the Covenant's modest 'teeth' were pulled out one by one, leaving a gaping toothless void.

—*Article 10.* This provision contains a small covenant of non-aggression by guaranteeing the territorial integrity and political independence of League members. It was progressively interpreted as only containing a moral obligation that entailed no direct sanctions if violated. Only the procedure for settling disputes under Articles 12–15 was considered as a way of determining an aggressor State and applying the sanctions under Article 16.

—*Article 11*. This provision provides that war is a social wrong that concerns society as a whole, regardless of where it takes place or who are the belligerents. According to a rapport in 1927 by the Belgian delegate, Louis de Brouckère,[9] this provision could serve as a basis for preventative action by the League. The League could take action on the basis of recommendations or decisions before a dispute had crystallised and independent of the rigid mechanism contained under article 15, or sanctions that are imposed after a rupture of the peace under article 16. In this way, measures of mutual assistance could have been organised, for example, on a much broader basis than *ex post facto* sanctions when strictly interpreted. The League could also have taken action with respect to the drawing up of boundaries, incursions into territories by foreign groups, the application of treaties, minorities, etc.[10] However, these extraordinary powers of the League were emasculated by the following practice: States members considered that the rule concerning strict unanimity contained in article 5 § 1 applied to this article. Thus, the votes of the States concerned by the measures to be taken were to be computed when deciding. Any contrary vote in the Council would stymie any decision. Actually, in the context of preventive measures, it is not possible to always determine a dispute in the strict sense, nor consequently the parties to such a dispute. The Council could be faced with a situation of tension without clearly delineated claims or parties to such claims. However, to require the agreement of all States, including those involved in the dispute or tension, was to effectively sterilise any action taken. In the context of article 11, even the votes of the aggressor States had to be counted for taking any measure against it—one can imagine the result![11]

—*Article 15*. This provision concerns the manner in which the Council (or Assembly) must resolve the disputes that have been submitted for their consideration. However, this provision became used more often not in order to resolve a dispute *before* it broke out, but to try to resolve the dispute between the parties *after* the events had already unfolded. The Council thus met only once the conflict was underway and when the *fait accompli* had already been established. Can one imagine that a predator State, having obtained or in the process of obtaining the spoils, would wish to follow the courteous suggestions of the Geneva institution? It was in this way that the Council responded to the crises in Corfu (1923), Manchuria (1931) and Ethiopia (1935). The aggressors kept the League busy with delaying tactics comprised of ingenious quibbles.

—*Article 16*. This provision deals with sanctions against an aggressor State that has resorted to war in violation of the obligations it assumed under the Covenant. The content of the article is already problematic because the drafters of the Covenant generally chose to ground the Covenant on the goodwill of governments and public opinion, rather than in sanctions, strictly speaking. Article 16 was almost completely scuttled by the way in which it was interpreted in the course of the first Assemblies. According to these interpretations, each determination of an act of

[9] League of Nations Document, A. 14 1927 V, 60ff. The pertinent passages concerning article 11 are reproduced in JM Yepes and P da Silva, *Commentaires théorique et pratique du Pacte de la Société des Nations et des Statuts de l'Union panamericaine* vol II (Paris, 1935) 4–6.

[10] J Ray, *Commentaire du Pacte de la Société des Nations selon la politique et la jurisprudence des organes de la Société* (Paris, 1930) 379.

[11] *Cf* Walters, above n 1 at 477–78.

aggression and all measures taken by the League in the form of sanctions depend exclusively on individual and voluntary decisions of each State member. Consequently, in interpretative Resolution 4 of 4 October 1921, it is affirmed that 'it is for the different members of the League to determine if there was a breach of the Covenant'.[12] The Council could not impose its own unitary vision. It was thus sufficient for a State to affirm (by virtue of its sovereignty) that in its opinion there was not an aggression in a particular case for refusing to apply any sanctions. Absent unanimity, the aggression would thus go practically unchecked. This mistake was not committed in the Charter; the world had learnt from the League experience.

—*Article 19.* This provision provides for reconsideration by the Assembly of treaties that have become inapplicable and international conditions whose continuance might endanger the peace of the world. The Assembly could not make any decisions, by virtue of the strict unanimity rule of article 5 § 1 that applies to article 19, but it could at least suggest solutions. In the shadow of the Treaty of Versailles, any application of this provision was scuttled by State members, like France, who feared opening the floodgates up to demands for reconsiderations. Thus, the Assembly did not hesitate in declaring article 19 inadmissible simply because a claimant State had requested a 'revision' of the treaty even though the Assembly only had the power to 'recommend' a revision. Article 19 was finally only invoked in two situations, each marked by failure: Bolivia/Chile concerning the revision of the Peace Treaty of 1904 (1920) (it is in respect to this case that the Assembly had resort to the procedural subterfuge discussed above); China/great powers enjoying concessions on its territory (1925).[13]

§ 11 Reasons for the Failure of the League of Nations

What were the principal reasons for the failure of the League of Nations? There are many, the differing importance of which is the subject of historical debates. Some failures are of a political character, whereas others are more legal in nature. The League

---

[12] The anarchic scope of this procedure is so apparent that it was thought useful to temper it in a way that did not alter the substance of the provision. It was clear that the Council or the Assembly could at least direct or clarify the opinion of State members and, in a word, that the League organs were able to give their non-binding opinion on matters. However, the conditions of the exercise of this power were not clarified: what would be the exact value of taking a position? Following what voting procedure would this position be adopted—following the unanimity rule under article 5 § 1, or by following the modified unanimity rule under article 15 § 6 (where the votes of the parties to the dispute are not counted)? During the Italian–Ethiopian conflict, the only conflict in relation to which sanctions were adopted by the League, the problem was resolved by a procedural subterfuge. During the Council session, its members determined that Italy was the aggressor State. This opinion was then brought to the attention of the Assembly, where the members also expressed their individual opinions on the issue. Their silence was interpreted as acquiescing to the position taken by the Council. Thus 'the individualistic solution won out, tempered [. . .] by the atmosphere of a collective debate': M Bourquin, *Vers une nouvelle Société des Nations* (Neuchâtel, 1945) 175 (unofficial translation). Thereafter, a sanctions committee was created outside the League; it was the common organ of the States having agreed to the sanctions. The experience ended in failure, since the French and British governments were not interested in a defeat of Italy. They still had the idea that Italy should be involved in their policies directed against Germany.

[13] See the summary in H Mosler, 'The International Society as a Legal Community' (1974) 140(4) *RCADI* 295ff.

of Nations experiment was not destined for failure despite what many would like to think. In a more favourable political environment and with members that were more inclined to respect its principles, the League of Nations could have been a successful experiment that continued to grow. It was the widespread instability that followed the First World War and the betrayal of the League by its most important members that propelled it into the chasm from which it was only able to climb out by passing on its experience to the United Nations. Here are some reasons for the decay of the League.

—*Disproportion between ambitions and means*. In a troubled world, the League took on tasks of enormous proportions, not least the maintenance of peace; its work attempted to cover extensive ground, from the settlement of disputes to functional cooperation, in a world of great turmoil; and it had to carry out this work with trivial means compared with the enormity of its tasks. The budget of the organisation was small and contributing members often did not pay their contributions on time. The budget oscillated between 27 and 32 million Swiss francs per year, or roughly US$5–6 million. Such an amount did not even correspond to the budget of a large European city. The legal means of action were likewise insufficient. In particular, the principle of unanimity paralysed League action. Contained by this unanimity requirement, League organs were able to have recourse to procedural expedients that allowed them to postpone sensitive solutions or they could establish commissions that won them time, or they could render unanimous but heavily comprised decisions that lacked any weight. Disrepute of the organisation flowed from these effects of the unanimity rule. However, a more flexible unanimity rule would not necessarily have mitigated these problems: in the absence of members' goodwill, no voting rule could produce miracles. Even on a vote of simply majority, decisions that were subsequently not implemented would not be of any use. These difficulties bring to light a marked feature of the Covenant: the trust placed in the goodwill of League members and the weight of public opinion. It is on these foundations that the Covenant constructs solutions. States are given space in which to find agreement with one another, if they so wish. However, the real problem is not resolved because where there is goodwill, League mechanisms are not decisive, and in the absence of goodwill, they prove inadequate.

—*Weakening by partial membership*. The League of Nations lacked *leadership* by world powers, notably the United States of America. The United States' Senate rejected the proposed admission of the country to the organisation by President Wilson. Nothing could be achieved by a political world organisation without the collaboration of the great powers of the era. The League could not be efficient without the support of the powers. It was consequently paralysed in the absence of some of them; all its essential measures were incomplete and one-sided and consequently did not achieve the purposes for which they were designed. For example, sanctions against a recalcitrant State were unsuccessful without the full force of *leadership* from the great powers behind them. Without this participation from the great powers, sanctions had no chance of success. In such a situation, sanctions were detrimental to the sanctioning States that suffered commercial loss and were the subject of political attacks as a result. On the other hand, States outside the League system benefited commercially from sanctions because they could enter the markets

abandoned by the sanctioning States. The sanctions imposed against Italy demonstrated this in a very concrete way.[14]

—*Relationship with the Treaty of Versailles and other peace treaties*. The Covenant of
the League of Nations was conceived as the first part of the Treaty of Versailles and
other peace treaties that were concluded at the end of the First World War.[15] The
original League members were the allied, associated or neutral States, not including
the vanquished States. The latter could request subsequent admission to the League
if they fulfilled certain conditions and following assessment of their application for
admission by the League Assembly. The League was regarded in a bad light right
from the start because of this discriminatory admission procedure. The tie between
the Covenant and peace treaties also cast criticism on it. Defeated States perceived
the League as an alliance that institutionalised the advantages secured by States that
had won the war. These privileges notably included the territorial status quo, perceived by them as a great injustice. It was easy for the vanquished States to consider
that the Covenant kept them in a state of humility or *capitis deminutio*.[16] In international relations, there is nothing more sensitive than State honour with respect to how
a State is treated and the prestige that it enjoys. The activities of the League should
have dispelled these fears, being so clearly advantageous to the vanquished States of
yesterday when compared with the conference of (the allied) ambassadors. However,
the League was burdened with such a heavy psychological handicap, that it spent the
rest of its short life trying to free itself from this weight. This handicap was aggravated by the nationalist sentiments of European peoples in the inter-war period. The
liquidation of the past established a heavy hypothesis of future undertakings. Well-
known protests against the order established by the Treaty of Versailles and other
peace treaties[17] occurred in Germany,[18] Austria, Italy and Hungary.

—*Disrepute of the League in diplomatic, political and traditional military circles*. For the
former elite, the League was a sentimental, unrealistic idea that required no support
on their part. The principal supporter of the League was supposed to be public

[14] On the Ethiopian crisis, see Walters, above n 1 at 623ff.

[15] See H Kelsen (ed), 'The Separation of the Covenant of the League of Nations from the Peace Treaties'
in *The World Crisis* (London; New York; Toronto, Graduate Institute of International Studies, 1938) 133ff.
President Wilson insisted on this link between the Covenant and peace treaties. In this way, he had hoped to
make the peace treaties more acceptable.

[16] As noted by JG Guerrero, *L'ordre international—Hier, aujourd'hui, demain* (Neuchatel, 1945) 57: 'From
its birth, the League attracted animosity and mistrust in people who already felt profoundly humiliated by
the conditions set out in the peace treaties, and who believed that the League of Nations was created in order
to consecrate their defeat and to maintain the recent territorial acquisitions by their adversaries' (unofficial
translation).

[17] P Renouvin, *Histoire des relations internationals Vol VII, Les crises du XXe siècle, Se 1914 à 1929* (Paris,
1957) 154ff; M Baumont, *La faillite de la paix (1918–1939)* vol 2; 5th edn, vol 2 (1967–68).

[18] See Schmitt, *Die Kernfrage des Völkerbundes*, above n 4. See also, C Bilfinger, *Der Völkerbund als
Instrument britischer Machtpolitik* (Berlin, 1940). Or even: A Hold-Ferneck, *Lehrbuch des Völkerrechts* Vol
1 (Leipzig, 1930) 236. For an overview, *cf* CM Kimmich, *Germany and the League of Nations* (Chicago,
1976). For a more complete bibliography of German–League of Nations relations, *cf* VY Ghebali, *Manuel
bibliographique sur la Société des Nations* vol III (Genève, United Nations, 1980) 751; 175ff and 812ff, 520ff.
The link with peace treaties was even stigmatised by authors who were not hostile to the League of Nations,
in evocative terms. *Cf*, eg, A von Freytagh-Loringhoven, *Die Satzung des Völkerbundes* (Berlin, 1926) 22–23:
'Das grosse zentrale Problem des VB bleibt trotz aller Fortentwicklung seine Bindung an die Pariser
Verträge. Sie prägt seinem Wesen und seiner Wirksamkeit den Stempel auf. Sie ist es, die alle anderen ihm
obliegenden Aufgaben ausser der Aufrechterhaltung dieser Verträge in den Hintergrund drängt und ihre
Lösung hindert. Sie ist es, die seine Fortbildung zu einer wirklichen Gemeinschaft der Staaten unmöglich
macht . . .'

opinion. Politicians and diplomats, as well as members of the armed forces, were men who still thought in nineteenth-century terms. They did not believe in the ability of the League to succeed. Right-wing nationalist groups hated internationalism and the ideal of cooperation among States on the basis of equality. Pacifist and left-wing groups were opposed to the League because they objected to its links with the war. The capacity of the League to impose military sanctions (article 16 of the Covenant) was enough to make the organisation odious to them; it was accused of attempting to prevent war by making war. The League was thus attacked from all directions. It was abandoned by its cowardly friends and attacked with conviction by its enemies. Its activities never ceased to be under fire from friend and foe alike.

—*World upheavals.* The world in the 1920s and 1930s was full of upheavals of extraordinary magnitude. The tormented world of the twentieth century took over from the old world of the nineteenth century. Reference may be made here to nationalist irredentism and aggressive nationalism; communist revolution and subversion; war reparations and the Treaty of Versailles; social revolution brought about by mechanisation; the desire on the part of some nations (Germany, Italy, Japan), disadvantaged by the unfavourable repartition of war booty, to carve out a place for themselves; the economic crisis following the 1929 stock market crash; post-war hyperinflation that crushed the middle classes in a number of countries, traditionally of a moderate political persuasion; etc. What this foaming world required was a strong hand and a clear political vision. The Covenant did not provide responses at this level. It was not designed to provide a world government. Whatever it was, it could not respond to these types of crises. The predictions of those who knew most were inadequate in this period of rapid transformation and rude shocks.

—*Lack of leadership by the pillars of the League of Nations.* In the absence of United States' membership, the League of Nations found itself in the hands of two great European powers, guarantors of the Treaty of Versailles: France and the United Kingdom. Both would fail in their historical mission. France embarked on a policy in favour of excess sanctions against Germany, fearful of falling victim to it once again. The United Kingdom hastened to return to a policy of non-entanglement attached to the old idea of balance of power in continental Europe. Above all, it did not want to be bound by obligations of automatic mutual assistance (non-entanglement). In relation to the collective security system, for which these two States were the guardians and essential protagonists, the League followed an increasing practice of appeasement: Vilna (Polish aggression in 1920); Corfu (Italian aggression in 1923); Manchuria (Japanese aggression in 1931); Ethiopia (Italian aggression in 1935); *Rheinland* (German aggression in 1936, under the terms of the Locarno Agreement of 1925); *Anschluss* (1938); Munich (1938) and the Italian aggression against Albania in 1939 were the hallmarks of this practice of renunciation. The League failed to act, not because of the unwillingness on the part of small and medium-sized States that were remarkably loyal to the Covenant, but essentially because of the two founding States.[19]

---

[19] For a scathing critique of this policy, see Emile Giraud, former League employee, in his book *La nullité de la politique internationale de grandes démocraties: l'échec de la Société des Nations (1919–1939)* (Paris, 1948).

§ 12 Outcome

Following the evolutions discussed above, one witnessed the weakening of the collective security system under the Covenant. The abandonment of League mechanisms first occurred in 1935, following the failure of the League to impose effective sanctions against Italy. States returned to the old policy of forming specific alliances or remaining neutral.[20] 'Save yourself' and 'everyone for himself' were the mottos that thenceforth prevailed; *in fuga salus*! The League of Nations did not, however, fade into nothingness. The abandonment of the system of collective security was accompanied by the parallel development of functional cooperation in the areas of health, economics and technical matters, which bloomed in the last years of the Geneva experiment. This reorientation of the organisation was acknowledged through the release of the Bruce Report, named after the Australian delegate.[21] However, this development was never formally accepted due to the outbreak of war. The Bruce Report nevertheless greatly inspired the Dumbarton Oaks proposals for the establishment of the United Nations.

If we take the sum total of all League of Nations matters, two considerations come to light. First, there was a 'failure' of the League's political activities (maintenance of the peace) and a 'success' of its functional activities (hygiene, technical, social, humanitarian, financial and economic matters).[22] Secondly, the political failure of the League is not its own, nor should the remarkably devoted and competent Secretariat bear any blame. The League was betrayed by its members, in particular by the great powers. It was thus, in the words of Sir Winston Churchill, 'a failure of the nations of the League more so than a failure of the League of Nations'. Of course, it is not possible to completely disassociate the two from one another, as the failure is ultimately also that of the organisation. In any event, it should never be forgotten that in an organisation of cooperation that lacks any powers of coercion, it is the State members which hold the decisive powers. A large part of the glory of the success of the League is owed to them; but a large part of the responsibility for its failure likewise falls to them.

---

[20] In relation to Switzerland, see in particular the report of 2 December 1935 by the Federal Council to the Federal Assembly concerning the application of article 16 of the Covenant of the League of Nations in the Italian–Ethiopian conflict and the report of 3 June 1938 by the Federal Council concerning Swiss neutrality in the context of the League of Nations.

[21] VY Ghebali, *La Société des Nations et la réforme Bruce, 1939–1940* (Genève, 1970).

[22] See M Marbeau, *La Société des Nations* (Paris, 2001), 47ff, 81ff. According to Bourquin, *Vers une nouvelle Société des Nations*, above n 17 at 95: 'We often forget that the League of Nations achieved considerable progress in finding a solution to a problem. The memory of its failures casts the positive results it achieved, and the merits of the procedure that it left at the disposition of its members, in the shadows. There had been at least an organic system that for the first time functioned in this area. Despite some defaults and lacunae, the general conception seemed perfectly healthy' (unofficial translation).

3

The Establishment of the
United Nations Organisation[1]

§ 13 Dumbarton Oaks/Yalta

The League of Nations experience demonstrated that a political organisation at the universal level was indispensable in responding to the needs of an ever-increasingly interdependent humanity. This was the case not only on a functional level (social, economic, humanitarian, cultural cooperation, etc), but on the so-called political level (the maintenance of peace, disarmament, etc). The need for a universal forum had become incontrovertible for the work of peace and the progress demanded by different pockets of humanity. For this reason, the re-establishment of a similar organisation was one of the aims of the Allies that arose out of the Second World War and that was elaborated in the Declaration by the United Nations on 1 January 1942. A more precise elaboration of this idea was penned by the ministers of foreign affairs from the United States of America, United Kingdom and USSR, in the Moscow Declaration of 30 October 1943. Article 4 of this Declaration emphasises 'the necessity of establishing at the earliest practicable date a general international organization, based on the principle of the sovereign equality of all peace-loving states, and open to membership by all such states, large and small, for the maintenance of international peace and security'.

A closer examination of the structure and the principles of this new organization was undertaken at the quadripartite conference at Dumbarton Oaks from August to October 1944. Grouping first the United States, the United Kingdom and the USSR, the conference was later opened up to China. This meeting gave rise to the Dumbarton Oaks Proposals, which constituted the primary basis for discussions concerning the new Charter. The Proposals were a characteristic product of the great powers and were heavily criticised at the time by representatives of medium and small powers on this basis. Some more progressive States and authors also criticised the Proposals for embodying too many of the past errors of the former League. The Dumbarton Oaks Proposals were finalised by the Yalta Agreement of 11 February 1945. This agreement notably specified that each of the five powers permanently sitting in the Security Council would enjoy a veto power. It was also agreed that an inter-State conference in San Francisco would be convened before the adoption of the Charter of the new organisation.

---

[1] See E Luard, *A History of the United Nations* vol I (London, 1982) 17ff; WG Grewe and DE Khan, 'Drafting History' in B Simma (ed), *The Charter of the United Nations: A Commentary* vol I, 2nd edn (Oxford; New York, OUP, 2002) 1ff.

§ 14 San Francisco

The countries invited to this conference were those that had fought under the banner of the United Nations during the war or were 'those that had declared war upon the enemy before 1 March 1945', with the addition of Denmark. The San Francisco conference took place from 25 April to 25 June 1945. During the arduous negotiations it was the small and medium-sized powers that struggled to be heard. The result was a series of settlements, arbitrated by the official committee of the five great powers. The position of the smaller powers was weakened by the conference voting rules, according to which the propositions contained in the Dumbarton Oaks and Yalta drafts could only be reversed by a majority of two-thirds of the voting States present. Rules that were strongly criticised by the smaller States, such as the five permanent members' right to veto any amendment to the Charter (articles 108–09), could thus be maintained despite the contrary wishes of the majority of States. In relation to the system of collective security, which is at the heart of the Charter, the small and medium powers accepted, in the absence of an alternative, the predominance of the five powers over others in the Security Council. They nevertheless tried to increase their representation in this organ. In order to save the collective security mechanism contained in the Act of Chapultepec (1945), the Latin American countries insisted on the inclusion of regional systems of collective security. This resulted in article 51 of the Charter, which reserved the inherent right to exercise individual or collective self-defence and Chapter VIII of the Charter, in particular article 53, which foresees regional security systems allowed to use force in cases where the authority of the Security Council is first obtained. The smaller States also insisted on a strengthening of the powers of the Assembly. They wished to attribute a number of powers to this organ, particularly in relation to international security and the conferral of a more extensive power of discussion. However, the small and medium-sized powers only obtained marginal, although not negligible, concessions in this respect. The formula according to which the Assembly 'may discuss any questions or any matters within the scope of the present Charter or relating to the powers and functions of any organs provided for in the present Charter' (article 10) is notable in this respect. In a similar vein, all propositions relating to judicial control of the political acts of the Council were rejected. Here, again, one finds traces of the predominance of the great powers and the more political rather than judicial approach of the Charter compared with the Covenant of the League of Nations. Legal formalism was considered suspect because of the association made with the paralysis of the League. Thankfully, however, the Latin American States secured the inclusion of the clause 'in conformity with the principles of justice and international law' in article 1 § 1 of the Charter, in the context of the settlement of disputes. In effect, no rule is durable, nor serves peace, if it is founded on injustice, opportunism and political interests. The Munich Agreement is historical evidence of this.

In sum, the Charter turns out to be mainly a product of the great allied powers, namely the *Big Three* (United States of America, United Kingdom and USSR), toned down on some points by amendments pushed through by small and medium powers at the San Francisco conference. It is perhaps difficult to imagine how the Charter could have come about otherwise, in light of the vital importance of an agreement among the great powers and the divergence of existing interests.

4

Phases in the History of the United Nations

§ 15 The Four Historical Phases of the United Nations

All living organisms go through different stages in life. They experience both pros-
perous times and difficult moments; calm and stormier periods. From a bird's eye view
of these different life stages amassed together, it is possible to categorise by historical
periods the different phases of an institution that are marked by the predominance of
certain, distinct characteristics. In the history of the United Nations, four such phases
may be distinguished:[1]

First Phase: Predominance of the West; Disunion of the
Great Powers (1945–55)

The United Nations was established, above all, in order to maintain peace through the
united action of the great powers in the Security Council. To this end, the organisation
needed armed forces at its disposal to respond to acts of aggression; it had to be able
to adopt binding decisions by a majority vote and not on the basis of unanimity; it also
needed to engage as many States as possible in its work and thus move towards a universality of its membership. The Cold War parlayed these hopes. Instead of being a
forum for dialogue and cooperation, the United Nations become a battle ground of
mistrust and propaganda. The Security Council was almost completely blocked by the
USSR's excessive use of the veto in an organ it found to be dominated by the West. The
immediate effect of this was the paralysis of almost all Security Council action.
Consequently, States took security matters into their own hands, leading to a re-
emergence of the importance of individual and collective measures of self-defence.
From an institutional perspective, two consequences emerged. First, a number of
problems concerning international peace were addressed elsewhere than the United
Nations: the Berlin talks about Germany (1954); the Geneva Conference on Korea and
Indochina (1954); the Vienna negotiations concerning the status of Trieste (1954–55),
etc. It was only from 1960 onwards that the Security Council was again seized of international crises: Congo (1960); Cuba (1962); Cyprus (1962); Dominican Republic
(1965); the Israeli–Arab war (1967), etc. Secondly, the Western majority in the United

---

[1] See P Gerbert (with the collaboration of V-Y Ghébali and MR Mouton) *Le rêve d'un ordre mondial—
de la SDN à l'ONU* (Paris, 1996).

Nations tried to find a way of strengthening the role of the General Assembly by circumventing the Security Council. In terms of law, this was an attempt to overcome the paralysis of the Soviet veto by ensuring a minimum amount of UN action; in political terms, it was also an attempt to isolate the USSR and to find a way around the permanent blackmail of its veto. General Assembly Resolution 377 (V) ('Uniting for Peace', 1950) is one of the most emblematic signs of this tendency. The paralysis of the Security Council also resulted in an extension of the Secretary-General's powers, a development that was instigated by Dag Hammarkjöld towards the end of the 1950s. Ideological rivalries meant that problems that were discussed in the UN made little advancements. Consequently, the issue of admission of new member States to the United Nations was sidelined for many years; and similarly, discussions concerning the regulation of armaments made little progress. In conclusion, the United Nations was a mirror refection of a divided and blocked world. The Western majority tried to impose solutions, but did not have the power to overcome this division and the resistance of the communist States.

Second Phase: The UN and the Third World; Decolonisation (1955–65)

The Geneva meeting of the great powers in 1955 was followed by a smooth change within the United Nations and an era of 'peaceful cooperation' was ushered in. Politically, international affairs were dominated by a new problem: the attainment of independence of colonised territories. The United Nations supported decolonisation and the equality of peoples. Following the admission of new decolonised States, the majorities in the United Nations rapidly changed. Western States suddenly found themselves in a minority. Third World States now dominated the organisation. The consequences of this shift were four-fold. First, the membership of the United Nations doubled in ten years. With the growing number of actors, international cooperation became more difficult because of the supplementary ideological divide and also because of the absence of a leading group of States in the heterogeneous Third World bloc. Secondly, the priorities of United Nations activities changed: the new majority made decolonisation, human rights and peoples' rights, assistance in development, etc the dominant themes. Socio-economic topics coloured discussions. Thirdly, the United Nations was for the first time dominated by a majority of weak States. The powerful States in international relations (Western States) considered the Third World bloc to be irresponsible and excessive. The majority was no longer on their side, but on the side of the 'have nots'. The new majority exercised the only power it had, namely that of numbers: it did not hesitate to press through resolutions in the General Assembly that it dominated, against the wishes of the Western States. Numerous redistribution claims were made in relation to rich countries, which in turn alienated the organisation and particularly the Assembly. The political radicalism of some newly decolonised States aggravated this effect. Fourthly, the increase of United Nations devices to address equal geographic distribution and to respond to the new tasks of the organisation, including peacekeeping operations, created a financial deficit. This quickly became an acute financial crisis.

Third Phase: The Crisis and Marginalisation of the UN (1966–89)

From 1965 onwards the role of the UN was reduced due to a number of causes: failure to maintain peace and thus return of member States to alliances and individual security; the inability of the organisation to resolve causes of conflicts (Cashmere, Vietnam, Afghanistan, Iran, Iraq, etc); the crisis in development aid; the socialist ideology by the majority Third World that alienated an important faction of Western States; the multilateralism crisis in the acute disagreements between the Western States and the Third World (North–South conflict); the loss of impetus of decolonisation and the necessity to search for new policies; the increase in incantatory resolutions that had little effect; the marginalisation of the Economic and Social Council (ECOSOC) by the General Assembly, the Group of Seven (G7) and the United Nations Conference on Trade and Development (UNCTAD); the negotiations on limiting nuclear armaments that occurred outside the United Nations; the increase in staff and the mounting bureaucracy; the arrears of contributions from member States and the acute financial crisis; the loss of general prestige; the assault by the Reagan administration and neo-conservatives against the United Nations (accused of double standards; an excessive politicisation of functional cooperation; hostility towards the economy and the market; the excessive hold of the USSR over the Secretariat and the enlargement of the its structures. These criticisms, excessively inflated, were not always devoid of foundation). All these and other factors explained the decline and the gloom into which the organisation sank. However, the organisation remained during this phase a reflection of the real world. Each majority in the organisation imposed its views; Western States had also done this when they held the majority in the General Assembly in the first decade of its existence. It would not be correct to consider that the organisation was necessarily progressing well when the Western majority was able to impose its views and less well when another majority did the same. In both cases, the organisation reflects the state of things in the world and the concerns of the majority of States that make it up at any point in time. The crucial issue is rather to understand that the majority, at any one time, must seek out the cooperation of the minority if it wants to achieve useful and durable work; the imposition of non-obligatory resolutions by an unsupported majority only give the illusion of victory.

Fourth Phase: Renewal (1989–. . .)

A new phase of cooperation was ushered in with the collapse of socialist States in eastern Europe and the recoil of militant ideologies of planned State economies of Third World States. The Third World lost a great deal of its influence: the rivalry between East and West no longer served as a springboard; the fall in prices of primary materials plunged these States into an increasing economic crisis. The West, and in particular Anglo-Saxon countries, once again dominated the organisation. This phase is marked by a vast array of events. First, the revamping of the system of collective security during the Gulf War (1990–91), then the misadventures in Kosovo (1999),

Afghanistan (2001) and Iraq (2003), each representing a return to a particular type of unilateralism. Secondly, the noticeable tendency to discuss and to manage international conflicts within the framework of the United Nations and not outside. Successes that were achieved demonstrated that the organisation was not doomed to failure: Iran/Iraq (1988); the United Nations mission in Central America, Nicaragua, (1989–99), Guatemala (1990s) and in Cambodia (1989–91), etc. Moreover, there was an explosion in the number of classic, mixed and robust peace operations undertaken, finally dispelling the vagary and accompanying debates surrounding these operations since 1960. Thirdly, serious reforms of the institutional structure of the organisation were undertaken by Boutros Boutros-Ghali and Kofi Annan. These reforms sought to simplify the organisation chart; to make better use of financial and human resources; to reduce staff numbers (that consequently fell from 9000 to 7300); to increase transparency and external control in order to address corruption (thankfully quite marginal in the United Nations system); and even more extensive reform plans for the General Assembly and the Security Council. This reform process has still not ended. Fourthly, the organisation has significant hold in economic and social matters through the World Bank, the International Monetary Fund and the World Trade Organisation (OMC), even if its role is controversial in this respect. The UNCTAD has, however, declined. Fifthly, the organisation has achieved universalism: there is no reason these days for a State to remain outside the framework of the organisation. Switzerland consequently became a member on 10 September 2002.

In conclusion, the United Nations is not a world government and should not be measured by such an unrealistic idea. Judged with respect to international relations, its role has never been greater than today. All significant issues are addressed at least partially within one of the branches of the United Nations (international security, settlement of disputes, environment, human rights, disarmament, resources, economic changes, shifts in migration, natural disasters, global warming, etc). The United Nations exists alongside other organs with which it must cooperate and with which it exercises a complex form of world governance.

General Layout of the Charter

§ 16 Structure of the Charter

The Charter of the United Nations is composed of the following parts:

—*Preamble, Chapter I (articles 1–2)*: aims and principles of the Charter. This part consists of a sort of ideological or philosophical manifesto.

—*Chapter II (articles 3–6)*: membership, including admission to the organisation and expulsion from it.

—*Chapters III, IV, V, X, XIII, XIV, XV (articles 7, 9–22, 23–32, 61–72, 86–91, 92–96, 97–101)*: principal organs of the organisation, namely: the General Assembly, the Security Council, the Economic and Social Council, the Trusteeship Council, the International Court of Justice and the Secretariat. The functions of these organs are set out in the mentioned articles.

—*Chapter VI (articles 33–38)*: peaceful settlement of disputes. This is a domain where both the General Assembly and the Security Council exercise joint functions. Consequently, it could not be split into the chapters dealing with these two organs respectively.

—*Chapter VII (articles 39–51)*: measures in the case of aggression, breach of the peace, or threat to the peace. This part covers collective security, the masterpiece of the Charter. The importance of the matters covered account for the need of a separate chapter in the Charter.

—*Chapter VIII (articles 52–54)*: regional agreements and their role in the settlement of disputes and the maintenance of peace. This part follows on from Chapters VI and VII: the Charter strives to make room for regional systems but at the same time to co-ordinate their activities in the settlement of disputes and principally in the maintenance of peace in a way that does not undermine the universal system. A developed regional system existed in 1945 in Latin America.

—*Chapter IX (articles 55–60)*: economic and social cooperation, including cultural, technical and humanitarian (human rights) cooperation. This is the domain of the former 'functional cooperation'. The Charter considers this to be an important area of action, as peace cannot be achieved if the deep causes of wrongs and thus of instability are not eradicated. Cooperation in the Charter's design serves to soften destabilising inequalities and to build bridges of understanding rendering breaches of the peace more difficult.

—*Chapter XI (articles 73–74)*: declaration regarding non-self-governing territories (colonies). The small States succeeded in extorting from the colonial powers a certain number of engagements including the obligation to promote the prosperity of indigenous populations. A degree of control held by the United Nations developed in practice on the basis of a broad interpretation of the obligation to transmit information under article 73, letter e). This chapter has become obsolete following the wave of decolonisation that brought an end to colonialism.

—*Chapter XII (articles 75–85)*: international trusteeship system. This system was established in 1945 in order to supervise the 11 trust territories that were placed under the administration of seven States. This part mainly concerns the former mandates of the League of Nations under article 22 of the Covenant. The aim was to progressively lead towards independence those territories placed under the transitory administration of a power acting under the control of the United Nations.

—*Chapter XVI to XIX (articles 102–111)*: provisions concerning transitional security arrangements, amendments to the Charter, ratification and signature. Of particular note is article 102, which provides for the registration of every international agreement that is concluded by a member with the United Nations treaty service and of great importance, article 103, which provides that in the event of a conflict between the obligations of the members of the United Nations under the Charter and other obligations, their obligations under the Charter shall prevail.

These chapters of the Charter require deeper examination. This is undertaken in the sections that follow.

Ideological Manifesto of the Charter: Peace, Cooperation and the Rights of the Human Person

§ 17 General Outline

The closely linked Preamble and article 1 set out the aims of the Charter and the organisation. The supreme aim is the maintenance of peace: all other aims are directed towards this goal. The Charter opens with the following proclamation, loaded with meaning and with a rare dramatic flourish: 'We the peoples of the United Nations determined to save succeeding generations from the scourge of war, which twice in our lifetime has brought untold sorrow to mankind' (Preamble, § 1). Following which the other aims are listed:

—*Preamble, § 2*: to reaffirm faith in fundamental human rights, in the dignity and worth of the human person. This was a historical breakthrough, because human rights had previously fallen within the domestic jurisdiction of each State. Following this domestic jurisdiction thesis, each State could previously oppose any international action for the protection of the human person, at least where its own citizens were concerned. Human rights issues were the exclusive concern of each State and were not the 'business' of other States. The Charter reversed this state of affairs. In many ways this reversal was a reaction to the atrocities committed by the Axis powers, both before and during the war. The text provides as follows: 'to reaffirm faith in fundamental human rights, in the dignity and worth of the human person, in the equal rights of men and women and of nations large and small'. The term '*re*affirm' refers to earlier declarations made by the United Nations during the war, and not to the state of international law before the war.

—*Preamble, § 3*: respect for international law and justice, terms taken from the Preamble of the League of Nations on the insistence of Latin American States. The text reads as follows: 'to establish conditions under which justice and respect for the obligations arising from treaties and other sources of international law can be maintained'.

—*Preamble, § 4*: to promote social and economic progress, a concern that carried over from the League of Nations experience and in particular the Bruce report that was drafted towards the very end of the life of the Geneva organisation. This aim is concerned with fighting the deep causes of conflicts between nations and peoples. The text reads accordingly: 'to promote social progress and better standards of life in larger freedom'.

The mirror reflections of these general aims are then set out in the second part of the Preamble:

> [to] practice tolerance and live together in peace with one another as good neighbours, and to unite our strength to maintain international peace and security, and to ensure, by the acceptance of principles and the institution of methods, that armed force shall not be used, save in the common interest, and to employ international machinery for the promotion of the economic and social advancement of all peoples.

Article 1 reiterates these aims and ends with the luxury of greater detail:[1] maintenance of peace by collective measures and the settlement of disputes (§ 1); development of friendly relations among States (§ 2) and international cooperation (§3–4).

§ 18 'Negative' Peace and 'Positive' Peace

All the functions and finalities of the Charter are hierarchically structured in relation to one another: all are directed towards the aim of all aims, the maintenance of peace. The Charter is not, however, an instrument of radical pacifism. It foresees the use of force for self-defence (article 51), for measures taken by the Security Council to maintain and re-establish peace (article 42) and even measures that could be undertaken against former enemy States outside the Security Council (article 53 § 1 and 2, article 107). Nevertheless, war was considered a wrong that must be eradicated *as much as possible*. In order to do so, the Charter employs a multi-step strategy. The lesson that had been learned from the experience of the Covenant of the League of Nations was that an approach that concentrated solely on the settlement of disputes (carrying eventual sanctions) was not sufficient. Nor is the Charter concerned only with what may be called 'negative' peace, namely the absence of armed confrontations on the ground. Of course if armed conflict were to erupt, the first task of the world organisation would be to ensure that weapons fall silent, that a ceasefire is secured and that the belligerents return—as far as is possible—to their *status quo ante* while the dispute is settled by a peaceful procedure. This is one of the principal functions of the Security Council. However, to foresee a 'fire-fighter' when destructive elements have already been unleashed is not enough. This role must be encompassed in collective action towards what may be termed 'positive' peace, namely the ensemble of structural measures that address the deep causes of conflicts, which re-establish the trust breached and which promote international cooperation between nations. It is only in such a favourable

---

[1] 'The Purposes of the United Nations are: 1. To maintain international peace and security, and to that end: to take effective collective measures for the prevention and removal of threats to the peace, and for the suppression of acts of aggression or other breaches of the peace, and to bring about by peaceful means, and in conformity with the principles of justice and international law adjustment or settlement of international disputes or situations which might lead to a breach of the peace; 2. To develop friendly relations among nations based on respect for the principle of equal rights and self-determination of peoples, and to take other appropriate measures to strengthen universal peace; 3. To achieve international cooperation in solving international problems of an economic, social, cultural or humanitarian character, and in promoting and encouraging respect for human rights and for fundamental freedoms for all without distinction as to race, sex, language, or religion; and 4. To be a centre for harmonizing the action of nations in the attainment of these common ends'.

climate and environment, as material as it is intellectual, that prophylactic efforts to secure long-term peace will find success. Thus, to the 'fire-fighter' must be added the 'gardener'. In other words, the Charter attempts to employ a strategy of sustainable peace that responds to the urgency of conflicts when they erupt and that also addresses their deeper causes. It is a strategy of successive layers or barriers in fighting for the maintenance of the peace. The conception, according to which the UN system is erected on the maxim that 'peace comes before justice' is thus only partially true. It is expressing a truth in situations of urgency, when the Security Council confronts an outbreak of violence in the role of a 'fire-fighter'; it is insufficiently grasping the essence of things when the UN attempts to address deep causes as more or less diligent 'gardeners'.[2] Two essential steps in the area of maintenance of peace may be distinguished:

—*The domain of negative peace.* It is a question here of repressing, *ambulando*, a war or another major disturbance that is on the verge of breaching the peace. The measures respond to emergencies bracketing out the substantive disagreements among states. The sole goal is at this stage to stop the fighting. The 'fire-fighter' takes precedence over the 'gardener'. To succeed in this task, the Charter confers on the Security Council considerable powers: it may decide to undertake coercive measures, including the use of force, which are binding on State members of the organisation.[3] By interpreting broadly the term 'threat to the peace', the Council may extend its domain of activity and act far beyond authorising classical collective security measures against cases of aggression. This is what occurred in the 1990s when the Council, basing itself on collective security, intervened in internal armed conflicts or in internal disturbances in order to address humanitarian crises and/or to establish criminal justice systems. Despite its importance and its fame, Chapter VII is, however, not truly situated at the centre of the Charter structure. It comes only at the very end of the long string of preceding measures to maintain peace. It is both the hope and gamble of the Charter that it will not be necessary to have recourse to the extraordinary powers of the Council because the measures that the United Nations will undertake to address the deep causes of conflicts and disputes will not necessitate its frequent use. International life following 1945 has not seen this hope fulfilled.

—*The domain of positive peace*: This domain is composed of three areas that are closely related to one another.

First, the peaceful settlement of disputes, which performs a function of direct prevention of conflicts. It not possible to efficiently prevent recourse to violent measures unless those who are subject to the law have alternative means with which to settle their disputes and to remedy their rights. No State will permit another to violate with impunity its rights over a long period, or to take advantage of the fact that there is no peaceful settlement of dispute procedure in place. It is not possible to maintain the peace without settling the disputes. In order for States to relinquish any recourse to

---

[2] *Iustitia procurat pacem et iniuria bellum* (justice brings peace and injustice brings war): Ramon Lull, *Liber Proverbiorum* (c 1296) pars III, cap. L, § III.

[3] This does not mean, of course, that a State will be obliged to participate in any military response; deprived of military contingents under art 43 of the Charter, the Council only has the power to authorise such uses of force.

coercion or a use of force in their international relations, they must have access to peaceful settlement procedures that are as efficient as possible and that provide some guarantee of justice, thereby doing away with the need to resort to *self-help*. The peaceful settlement of disputes is thus indissoluble from the maintenance of peace, as well as the realisation of justice. It is when international law began to concern itself with the maintenance of peace, that is, at the beginning of the twentieth century, that the peaceful settlement of disputes progressively constituted a legal area of specialisation. Previously it had been an ignored area: international law only dealt with diplomacy and war. If a dispute arose, diplomatic discussions could take place; if an agreement was reached, it could be made the object of a transaction (treaty); if not, the claiming State could resort to war to redress the wrong it had allegedly suffered. When the use of force was not yet prohibited and disputes could be settled that way, there was no need for a chapter on settlement of disputes in international law. The solution of disputes was a point of fact or of policy rather than a point of law. Since the beginning of the twentieth century, mention is made of the peaceful settlement of disputes in direct relation to rules that seek to limit the use of force. The interrelationship of both is thus stressed. This is the case, for example, in the famous Briand-Kellogg Pact of 1928. Article 1 concerns the prohibition to resort to war as an instrument of national policy, whereas article 2 sets out the obligation to peacefully settle disputes. The peaceful settlement of disputes and the non-use of force appear alongside one another again in the Charter under articles 2 § 3 and 2 § 4 respectively.

Secondly, the development of friendly relations; the maintenance of neighbourly relations; the culture of peaceful dispositions. Here the function of preventing war occurs at a deeper level than the peaceful settlement of disputes. Whereas in the latter case a conflict has already crystallised and attempts are made to settle the dispute before it takes on proportions capable of disturbing social order, here the concern is to address cultural and relational inequalities in order to promote harmony among peoples and thus avoid, insofar as is reasonable, the crystallisation of conflicts. The settlement area attempts to solve existing disputes; the friendly relations limb attempts to prevent disputes from arising. It is useful to recall the famous statement contained in the Preamble of the Constitutive Act of UNESCO (1945):

> That since wars begin in the minds of men, it is in the minds of men that the defences of peace must be constructed; That ignorance of each other's ways and lives has been a common cause, throughout the history of mankind, of that suspicion and mistrust between the peoples of the world through which their differences have all too often broken into war.

Prolonged education; elimination of partial and heinous views about other peoples contained in schoolbooks; efforts to understand the positions and needs of others; exchanges between peoples; all the measures that build mutual confidence; all these are factors that contribute to greater international harmony and thus lessen the likelihood of war. Moreover, when trust and confidence increase among people, not only do disputes tend to erupt less frequently, but those that do, or those which already exist, will be solved with much greater ease and rapidity. Most of the long-term international disputes, stubbornly maintained on the agenda of international affairs, owe their prolonged life to a deep-seated distrust between the concerned States and peoples. Confidence-building measures are thus of the essence for any serious effort to resolve international disputes and ultimately to keep the peace.

Thirdly, international cooperation for economic and social progress. This domain addresses the deepest causes of conflicts, those that are found in the material aspects of relative wealth, access to resources, the growing gap between rich and poor, widespread and systematic violations of human rights, humiliation ushering in extremism, domination of some by others, etc. Article 55 of the Charter sets itself a highly ambitious programme in these respects:

> With a view to the *creation* of conditions of stability and well-being which are necessary for peaceful and friendly relations among nations based on respect for the principle of equal rights and self-determination of peoples, the United Nations shall promote:
>
> > higher standards of living, full *employment*, and conditions of economic and social progress and development;
> >
> > solutions of international economic, social, health, and related problems; and international cultural and educational cooperation; and
>
> universal respect and fundamental freedoms for all without distinction as to race, sex, language, or religion.

§ 19 Problem of Inadequate Means

The means given to the United Nations in its various areas of activity are in inverse proportion to the depth of the layer that is being addressed: coercive measures, the most efficient response, are only allocated to the organisation in the very last response, when the Security Council must undertake emergency measures in order to maintain or re-establish the peace; non-coercive measures (recommendations), based on persuasion and good faith, are undertaken in the preventative domain of the settlement of disputes and international cooperation, but remain more often than not unheeded and ineffective. States do not wish to grant the organisation greater powers in areas that still fall largely within their domestic jurisdiction, as evinced by article 2 § 7. This may be fully understandable. Further, in relation to cooperation among States, coercion could not be of great avail; in this context, nothing can compensate for the goodwill of States. The spirit of benevolence and openness of others cannot be ordered by a command; coercive persuasion, open threat or military power, conversely, could impose cessation of hostilities by injunction of a ceasefire. All structural problems concerning the world organisation stem from these two issues. Powers and competencies that are in principle efficient, are conferred on the organisation only when it is too late; adequate powers and competencies are denied while there is still time to act. A passing observer thus has the impression that there is a persistent discrepancy: he considers the action of the UN to address the causes of problems as being inadequate (since it is almost invisible and only recommendatory); at the same time he has a feeling of failure when effective measures are taken because the wound laid open to the organisation has already become infected. Two criticisms are thus warranted: the failure to prevent; and the inability to effectively treat a gaping wound that has become complicated to treat after being infected. However, as has been indicated above, such an awesome result is the nature of things. The United Nations is not a super-State; it can only act through the powers that States attribute it with. The efficiency of its action must thus be measured in exact relation to its powers and the material measures that are at its disposal. It is, nevertheless, clear that the United Nations remains a *dramatis persona*, whose role is to bear the weight of all the sins of humanity, while attempting with moderate success to raise spirits and to progress along better paths.

§ 20 Political Ideology of the United Nations

In short, is there a political ideology of the United Nations? The following passage appears to provide a clear, prudent answer, even though it dates from the Cold War period and is consequently somewhat restrictive:

> If it is hardly possible to link the Charter to one of the ideologies that exist in the world, one will find in this instrument some statements of principles that denote the existence of a political philosophy, in its broadest sense: 'faith in fundamental human rights, in the dignity and worth of the human person, in the equal rights of men and women', 'maintenance of justice', 'social progress', 'better standards of life in larger freedom', 'self-determination of peoples', the 'principle of sovereign equality', the notion of 'peaceful States', the 'political aspirations of peoples', the 'progressive development of free political institutions' are all concepts present in the Charter. It is evident that one may find in these concepts a certain way of thinking that resembles what is habitually called democratic thought. However the United Nations Organization now groups together all States in the world, and represents all forms of civilisation and all political and social regimes. Thus the only ideal that is really characteristic here is the ideal of international coexistence and cooperation: it is about bringing together, through the work of peace and progress, different parts of humanity.[4]

Whatever it may be, the ideological basis of the United Nations is to be found in the values and aims set out in the Preamble, article 1 and article 2 of the Charter.

---

[4] Unofficial translation from C Chaumont, *L'Organisation des Nations Unies* 6th edn (Paris, Les Cours de droit, 1968) 14–15.

7

Fundamental Principles of the Charter

§ 21 Article 2 of the Charter

Article 2 is one of the most important provisions of the Charter. It lists the principles on which the activities of the United Nations are based. These principles apply not only to member States of the organisation, but to its organs. Some of its rules apply also to all the States outside its institutional ambit, under the cover of customary international law. Article 2 provides as follows:

1. *The Organization and its Members, in pursuit of the Purposes stated in Article 1, shall act in accordance with the following Principles.*
2. *The Organization is based on the principle of the sovereign equality of all its Members.*
3. *All Members, in order to ensure to all of them the rights and benefits resulting from membership, shall fulfil in good faith the obligations assumed by them in accordance with the present Charter.*
4. *All Members shall settle their international disputes by peaceful means in such a manner that international peace and security, and justice, are not endangered.*
5. *All Members shall refrain in their international relations from the threat or use of force against the territorial integrity or political independence of any state, or in any other manner inconsistent with the Purposes of the United Nations.*
6. *All Members shall give the United Nations every assistance in any action it takes in accordance with the present Charter, and shall refrain from giving assistance to any state against which the United Nations is taking preventive or enforcement action.*
7. *The Organization shall ensure that states which are not Members of the United Nations act in accordance with these Principles so far as may be necessary for the maintenance of international peace and security.*
8. *Nothing contained in the present Charter shall authorize the United Nations to intervene in matters which are essentially within the domestic jurisdiction of any state or shall require the Members to submit such matters to settlement under the present Charter; but this principle shall not prejudice the application of enforcement measures under Chapter VII.*

These principles were reproduced and developed in General Assembly Resolution 2625 (XXV) of 1970, entitled 'Declaration on Principles of International Law concerning Friendly Relations and Cooperation among States in accordance with the Charter of the United Nations'. This resolution is an authentic interpretation of the Charter by all United Nations State members. It was adopted unanimously. The resolution clarifies and develops the principles contained in article 2 and includes new principles that arose out of United Nations practice between 1945 and 1970.

§ 22 Evolution from 'Classical' International Law to 'Modern' International Law

The principles contained in article 2 represent fundamental norms that guide all United Nations organs' activities. They also provide a measure of what is required of member States. They equally address, as mentioned, relations within the organisation, as well as those outside it. In fact, article 2 constitutes a small summary of modern international law, as opposed to what is called classic international law. Classic international law existed from the eighteenth century at least until 1919 (Covenant of the League of Nations). It eventually came to an end on the renunciation of war as an instrument of international politics (Paris Pact or Briand-Kellogg Pact of 1928). Some authors consider classic international law to have continued up until 1945 when the Charter came into existence. In what ways does modern international law differ from classic international law?

—*Classic international law: co–existence and predation.* At the height of its influence in the eighteenth and nineteenth centuries, classic international law was a very idiosyncratic and paradoxical law. It was made of two different strands inextricably sewn together: co-existence and predation. In the absence of sufficiently strongly felt common values deriving from humanity as a whole or from the community of States, international law attempted essentially to de-limit and ensure the areas of activities individually undertaken by each sovereign State: protection of its territorial integrity, its domain of essentially domestic questions, its freedoms and its uncontrollable will. Territory, diplomacy and war were its strong points. The subjective rights of States were found at the zenith of their power. Cooperation among States was at once voluntary and embryonic. At the same time, this law was so highly protective of the political and territorial integrity of each State, it was also strewn with antidotes that greatly mitigated the pre-eminence of State sovereignty. In other words, it was also a law characterised by predation. It permitted, for example, with a simple declaration of war, to move from a state of peace to a state of war. This entailed an abandonment of guarantees of territorial integrity and political independence usually enjoyed by States. Each State was able to freely decide to go to war: States had a free *jus ad bellum* that was an inalienable feature of State sovereignty, and which could be imposed on other States. In fact, it was a political device of powerful States exercised to the detriment of the weak: *vae victis, vae neutris* . . . A traditional corollary of this right of war was the power to annex conquered territory. The partition of Poland was thus not a manifestly illegal act from the historically legal point of view, if one puts aside any potentially applicable treaty commitments. Further, many parts of the world were considered territories that could be annexed through colonisation and the three-fold conception of humanity as civilised peoples, barbarians and savage peoples.[1] Lastly, even in peaceful times, intervention by powerful States in the affairs of smaller States was allowed. The great European powers, that gathered at conferences such as the nineteenth century Pentarchy (United Kingdom, France, Austria–Hungary, Prussia and Russia; later with Italy) governed European affairs.[2] In total, classic international law was a law based on the inequality of States, on unequal treaties, on the free use of force, on colonialism

---

[1] See J Lorimer, *The Institutes of the Law of Nations* vol I (Edinburgh, 1883) 101.

[2] See, among others, K Wolfke, *Great and Small Powers in International Law from 1814 to 1920, From the Pre-History of the United Nations* (Wroclav, 1961).

and the absence of legal devices such as the peaceful settlement of disputes or a developed body of law on the responsibility of States for violations of law.

Classic international law is calculated on the realism model. Unable to domesticate the power of sovereignty, law accommodated this feature up to the point of placing it in a paradoxical relationship with other legal features. This meant that classic law was essentially a servant, the 'valet' of States. It is thus not surprising that violations of this law were not often raised, because such a law was easy to 'obey'. It was based on the will of States and permitted almost every action: *quod fieris, ipsum valet*. It lacked normative density and did not try to go far beyond the merely observable, i.e. the facts of power. It mainly provided States with the means to do what they wished (for example, conclude treaties, exchange diplomatic missions) rather than limiting any of their actions (for example, through rules on the non-use of force, on duties to cooperate, etc). It was orientated towards a positivist model of law. In sum, it represented an enormous synchronism of highly varied and often axiomatically contradictory norms, as was the case in the context of the respect for territorial sovereignty.

—*Modern international law: coexistence, cooperation and community values.* Modern international law turned its back on the weaknesses of classic international law. True, it is a law that did not abandon the idea of co-existence among States that were sometimes reserved, prudent and hostile towards one another. However, it added to this minimal layer of international law supplementary layers of great importance that changed the very fabric of inter-State relations. These new layers were *cooperation* and *community values*. Modern international law tried to stabilise relations among States and to place them in a crucible of equality, order, justice and peace, namely those community values that were considered indispensable to a good life for all humanity, *sub specie humanitatis*. It thus transcends the interests of individual States and the idolatry of their subjective rights. It is an assertive law that challenges inequality, intervention in the internal affairs of States and use of force; it promotes the peaceful settlement of disputes, international cooperation human rights and decolonisation. It is also a law that responds to common threats against humanity: nuclear weapons; the destruction of the environment; humanitarian causes; inequality of wealth; the political life of peoples. Through each of these aspects, modern international law became somewhat messianic. It turned its back on blind conformity and the obsession with the practice of fact. It sought to free itself from the over-empowering will of States that was not compatible with the new approach towards higher values and those of States taken individually. Positivism was attacked for providing an all too weak and insufficient basis for international law. Modern law also became increasingly dense from the normative perspective. The number of norms and the precision of their injunctions were increasing. This also meant that international law was more strongly devoted to what should be and went beyond the state of things as they were. Modern international law did not limit itself to providing States with devices for them to do as they wished, but wanted to limit and orchestrate the powers of each State in light of a superior aim, common to all. This approach called for the reference to an 'international community' higher than States taken individually, notwithstanding the weaknesses this diffuse entity could bear in fact. That is to say that modern international law became at least partially the 'master' of States and ceased being the simple servant. Consequently, the violation of law now becomes a crucial issue because such a messianic law is clearly not easy to 'obey'. The way was paved for a doctrine of compulsory settlement of disputes and for a law of State responsibility, these two branches of the law emerging at the turn of the nineteenth to the twentieth century and developing in the League of Nations period.

An extensive catalogue of modern law, as described above, is set out in article 2 of the Charter. This article alone constitutes an extremely concise summary of modern international law as it had developed in the new era of the United Nations. Its importance can hardly be overestimated, particularly from a legal point of view. The Charter has on all these aspects decisively influenced and shaped international customary law. In this context, the Charter is much more than a simple treaty. In a certain sense, it is undoubtedly an international constitution since its normative contents are placed at the heart of the international law of today. In particular, the Charter does not add a treaty-based particular law to the former general law; rather, it modifies the general law itself. The Charter is thus a source that has a two-fold effect: (1) it casts the old body of law in a new light and provides a new reading of this ensemble of rules (for example, on the non-intervention in internal affairs, national independence, etc); (2) it abrogates the old rules of international incompatible with its injunctions (for example, on the power to resort to war). In legal terms, the Charter is both a source of interpretation and a source of abrogation. It is a paramount source and an important staple of modern international law.

It is useful to consider in closer detail some of the more important principles contained in article 2 of the Charter and in Resolution 2625.

A. Article 2 § 1: Sovereign Equality

§ 23 Contribution of Resolution 2625

This principle has a number of different facets that are graphically explained in Resolution 2625 as follows:

> All States enjoy sovereign equality. They have equal rights and duties and are equal members of the international community, notwithstanding differences of an economic, social, political or other nature.

In particular, sovereign equality includes the following elements:
States are judicially equal;

  a. Each State enjoys the rights inherent in full sovereignty;
  b. Each State has the duty to respect the personality of other States;
  c. The territorial integrity and political independence of the State are inviolable;
  d. Each State has the right freely to choose and develop its political, social, economic and cultural systems;
  e. Each State has the duty to comply fully and in good faith with its international obligations and to live in peace with other States.

§ 24 Content of the Principle

The Charter is based on the sovereign equality of States. Legally speaking, this rule has the following meaning:

—Each State enjoys the set of rights and duties defined by general international law; the conditions for effectively exercising those rights and duties may clearly vary according to power. The point here is formal not material equality. This formal equality may be altered by agreements freely entered into. The fact that material equality is not attainable (and would not even be useful) does not devalue formal equality. The fact that every State enjoys certain rights and status, such as, for example, the power to conclude treaties, to exchange diplomatic missions, to seize the International Court of Justice (ICJ), is clearly an asset that States cherish to the highest degree. It is a large part of a State's prestige. See § 25.

—The right of each State to enjoy inherent rights of sovereignty without diminution such as protectorates, semi-independent States, etc. Under modern international law, there remains only one state of things: the sovereign State; not a plurality of statuses in degrees of foreign influence.

—The obligation to respect the personality and the rights of other States: principle of mutual respect of rights.

—The right of each State to choose and to freely develop its political, social, economic and cultural system, free from intervention in its internal affairs by other States. As the Court affirmed in the case of *Military and Paramilitary Activities in and against Nicaragua* (Merits, 1986): '[the principle of non-intervention in internal affairs] forbids all State or groups of States to intervene directly or indirectly in internal or external affairs of other States. A prohibited intervention must accordingly be one bearing on matters in which each State is permitted, by the principle of State sovereignty, to decide freely. One of these is the choice of a political, economic, social and cultural system, and the formulation of foreign policy. Intervention is wrongful when is uses methods of coercion in regard to such choices, which must remain free ones'.[3]

—The equality of States regardless of economic, social, political or other differences; no socio-economic or political choice of a State entails a loss of equality in the relations with other States.

§ 25 Equality in Law and Equality in Fact

The equality provided for in § 1 is a legal and not a factual equality . States are unequal with respect to their power, wealth, culture, political orientation, etc. Paragraph 1 modestly tries *not to add* legal inequalities to such equalities that already exist. First, a State should not be discriminated against on the basis of the particular status it has been given. The aim is to address old notions like protectorate, slave States, colonies

---

[3] *Military and Paramilitary Activities in and against Nicaragua* (Merits) [1986] ICJ Rep, § 205.

and other States of limited sovereignty. Secondly, the equality rule does not mean that all States have, at every point in time, the same obligations and rights. The point is rather that they have an equal entitlement to acquire rights and be subjected to obligations. States may undertake a variety of different rights and obligations in specific treaties that they choose to conclude. These will not be the same as treaty obligations that other States have agreed to. Equality in law thus essentially refers to general international law which is universally applicable[4] and not to specific treaty-based obligations that have been freely entered into. The latter limit the sovereignty of contracting States (while also being an expression of sovereignty as they are freely entered into) and change the amount of obligations and rights of a State. Thirdly, the legal equality rule among States is not a *jus cogens* rule from which States cannot derogate by agreement, except if such an agreement leads to a decreased status that is as such incompatible with modern international law. However, for example, a voting power modulated with respect to the responsibilities of each State (financial and military contributions for the re-establishment of peace, etc) is perfectly possible. This is the case with respect to the big international financial institutions such as the World Bank and even the Security Council by virtue of article 27 § 3 of the Charter.

The fight for more equality in fact, rather than simply in law, was for a long time the weapon of choice for the so-called Third World States, for example with respect to attempts to establish a 'new economic world order' based on a particular form of North–South solidarity. These attempts were not crowned with success. The current trend has moved away from the solutions characterised in the relevant 1970s resolutions to a more pronounced form of neo-liberalism.

§ 26 Equality as a Principle of Structure and Content

Sovereign equality of States is at the same time a structural principle and one of content. As a structural principle—in which concrete rights and obligations are not contained—it reflects a horizontal distribution of power in international society composed of sovereign States juxtaposed to one another. There is no superior power than States that can legislate, execute or pass judgement for them or against them. These constitutional functions continue to be exercised by States. At the international level, they cannot be undertaken except by a competent State delegation, the original holders of such powers. These powers thus remain essentially enclosed in unities that are States; international society is deficient in this respect, as it is largely deprived of its own law-making, law-enforcing and law-determining agencies. It is a society that is highly decentralised, leading to a claim of 'anarchy' in international relations. Sovereignty remains plural and creates clashes; there is a law that attempts to appease

---

[4] Even such customary rules of international law may not actually, but only potentially, apply equally to all States. Thus, for example, only when a State possesses or acquires a coastline will the rights and duties with regard to the territorial area apply to it, not if it remains a land-locked State. Here too, it is the *entitlement* to enjoy these rights or to have these obligations imposed which is equal. Conversely, there are also rules of general international law which apply actually and not only potentially to all States at all moments. Equality here extends to the concrete legal position, to the actual rights and duties. Such is the case, for example, for the non-use of force rule.

and regulate these conflicts—international law—but there is no supranational sovereignty that can forcefully impose order, or insist on the execution of obligations by States, or indeed create laws. It is in this way that the principle of equality reflects the special structure of international society. As a principle of content, however, sovereign equality aims to protect each State, as discussed further above.

§ 27 Sovereignty Encased in Equality

It should be noted that the Charter uses the expression 'sovereign equality' (article 2 § 1). The word 'sovereignty', often used in international relations, does not appear alone; it is wrapped up in a parcel with another concept that blunts and domesticates its otherwise sharp and potentially wild effect. The Charter thus ideologically repudiates any acceptance of 'absolute sovereignty', insofar as this concept existed in earlier times: the all-powerful 'I, the sovereign', without any limits on what 'I' decides, even for the use of armed force. The Charter blunts this concept and binds it with another in a common and shared space. The international community-orientation of modern international law, as has already been discussed, adds strength to that idea of 'relative sovereignty'. Sovereignty is thus encased in the chains of equality: the sovereignty of one State is opposed and conceptually coordinated with the sovereignty of others on the footing of equality. Sovereignty is thus placed before a mirror of reciprocity. Consequently, modern sovereignty is necessarily a relative notion, as the rights of one State must be coordinated with those of others. An infinite projection of 'I, the sovereign', without taking account of the equal claims of other States, is no longer imaginable. The sovereign rights of States end where the sovereign rights of others begin. Is this not the same principle of law that is found in Kant or Rousseau and in the 1789 French Declaration of the Rights of Man and of the Citizen?[5] Equality here becomes the sword and the symbol of the beginnings of international civil society no longer cast under the old and exclusive shadow of the state of nature, that had imposed no limits on sovereignty. Sovereignty is Hobbes; equality is Kant; through 'sovereign equality under the law', Kant rolls back Hobbes.

B. Article 2 § 2: Fulfilment of Obligations in Good Faith

§ 28 Aim of the Provision

The importance of respecting a promise made is recalled in § 2: *pacta sunt servanda*. This is a founding principal of public international law, both classic and modern. No society could function and guarantee peace if the pledged word became meaningless.

---

[5] See, J-J Rousseau, *Contrat social* (1762) book I, 8, 9; CL Montesquieu, *De l'esprit des lois* (1748) book XI, 3;. E Kant, *Über den Gemeinspruch* (1793) ch 2; JG Fichte, *Grundlage des Naturrechts* (1796) ch 8; French Declaration of the Rights of the Citizen (1789) art 4.

After sovereign equality of members, sovereignty is thus tempered a second time by a principle that immediately follows in the Charter: the obligation to respect the law and to execute obligations, in a spirit of justice and propriety. The Charter thus moves away from a former deplorable practice of considering treaties to be 'mere scraps of paper', a term used the first time by German Chancellor Bethmann-Hollweg to describe his contempt for international treaties following Britain's declaration of war after Germany violated Belgium's neutrality. This expression inspired and was taken up by the State dignitaries of the Axis forces. Consequently, following the war, many insisted on the necessity of reaffirming the 'sanctity' of treaties and more generally of the rules of international law.[6] This is the purpose of article 2 § 2.

§ 29 Internal and External Scope of the Obligation to Fulfil Obligations

Paragraph 2 applies with respect to the execution of obligations under the Charter by member States and by United Nations organs, as well as by member States in their legal obligations outside the Charter. Consequently, § 2 has a two-fold scope: it applies with respect to the inner functioning of the United Nations (*Innenwirkung*: organs and State members in their relations within the organisation) and it applies outside this framework (*Aussenwirkung*: State relations outside the organisation, in international society in general). The Charter brings together these two strands and almost fuses them together.

§ 30 Limits of the Requirement to Respect Commitments

The obligation to respect obligations is not absolute. It is a principle of law rather than a legal rule without exceptions. It is manifestly fair and necessary in society that obligations are upheld. Further, international society lacks legislation in the strict meaning of the term. States are not subject to a superior power. In such a social environment, the rule *pacta sunt servanda* has a heightened importance. Indeed, a significant part of law is created by 'agreements' and not by 'laws'; thus respect for obligations freely entered into is even more essential for a minimal degree of stability in social and legal relations. However, the obligation to respect a promise only exists *within the boundaries of law*. No legal order requires obligations to be respected in all circumstances. On the contrary, it is acknowledged that in varying circumstances a legal subject may free itself of certain obligations. Examples that may be cited in this respect include cases of coercion, error, fraud, corruption; a fundamental change of circumstances (*clausula rebus sic stantibus*: where external events radically transform the extent of obligations to be performed, the duty of implementation could stop); response to violations of obligations by another (*inadimplendi non est adimplendum*: he

---

[6] See, eg, JM Yepes, *Philosophie du panaméricanisme et organisation de la* paix, (Neuchatel, 1945) 266ff. This author subsequently played an important role in the inclusion of § 2 in art 2 of the Charter. See R Kolb, *La bonne foi en droit international public* (Paris, 2000) 504.

who does not respect his obligations cannot expect others to respect theirs; reciprocity, reprisals); the outbreak of war; in some cases State succession (the clean slate thesis); material impossibility of execution; in some cases state of necessity; obligations that are contrary to rules of public order (immoral agreements or agreements threatening fundamental values, for example treaties organising aggression); etc. It should be noted that these exceptions to the obligation to respect undertakings are themselves subject to other exceptions. Thus, the principle of *inadimplendi* does not apply to some obligations of a humanitarian character (article 60 § 5 of the Vienna Convention on the Law of Treaties, 1969). For example, if a belligerent has unlawfully maltreated prisoners of war under its control, this does not mean that the adverse belligerent can respond by unlawfully treating the prisoners of war that it has under its control. There are, in effect, absolute obligations on which reciprocity has no bearing. In conclusion, it is evident that the legal order is complex. It is only in this crucible of interrelated obligations, at one particular moment in time and with respect to a particular society, that the general principle to respect obligations takes form. As a principle of law, morals and social order, it is beyond doubt; as a specific rule, the international legal order, as any other legal order, defines its place in relation to the complex array of other rules.

§ 31 Meaning of the Epithet 'in Good Faith'

The epithet 'in good faith' is an additional element to the general duty to respect obligations undertaken. It is not a hollow expression, since it has its own meaning in all legal orders based on Roman law; in Anglo-Saxon orders, the concept of good faith does not traditionally form a part of the legal regime as such but is reflected in the obligation to 'reasonably' interpret obligations. Good faith thus represents the manner in which an obligation should be executed. Substantively, § 2 reflects the old custom that general rules of international law (custom) and specific rules of international law (treaties) must be reasonably interpreted, ie, interpreted in good faith, taking into account the common interests of the many different legal subjects. Treaties, as is sometimes said, represent equal law and must be reasonably interpreted and in accordance with the standard of reciprocal trust (*jus aequum*). The purpose of this reasonableness rule is not to ensure that obligations are executed in accordance with morally correct intentions. Law only rarely concerns the moral intentions and incentives of action. Rather, the principle requires that the execution of a rule occurs without using a purely textual interpretation to avoid the spirit of its content. Hence, for example, it would be contrary to good faith to claim that Declaration IV (2) 1899, to 'Abstain from the Use of Projectiles the Sole Object of Which is the Diffusion of Asphyxiating or Deleterious Gases' meant that only dispersion of gas by *projectiles* was prohibited, whereas the dispersion of gas from *cylinders* was still allowed.[7] The wording of a provision was used in this case to undermine the spirit of the text. If an armistice were concluded for

---

[7] This was the argument of Germany: see the case of *Krupp* (1948) *Trials of War Criminals before the Nuremberg Military Tribunals under Control Council Law No 10* vol XI (Washington, 1950) 1376.

'thirty days', it would likewise be clinging to a literal interpretation with a view to destroying the aim and spirit of the undertaking to attack the opposing forces within these thirty days, but at night time.[8] Such a performance of the obligation would be contrary to good faith.

§ 32 Concrete Roles of the Rule contained in § 2

The good faith requirement contained in § 2 may notably play three legal roles:[9]

—*Aid in interpretation.* Two interpretative functions may be mentioned here: (1) the primacy of the spirit on the literal wording of a text. This is a particularly important aspect of a 'constitutional' instrument like the Charter that operates to facilitate governmental functions; (2) the reminder to member States that they must use a certain degree of restraint and manifest some loyalty to the organisation and its common goals when independently interpreting their obligations under the Charter. There is a duty in such cases to take into account the views of the organisation's organs and other members, without overly exaggerating the State's individual position.

—*Reinforcement of the duty to cooperate.* Good faith requires, for example, that attention and respect are paid to the resolutions of the organisation, even if they are only recommendations. Further, good faith serves too as a basis for developing the duty of cooperation within the framework of the organisation, for example in the area of coordinating sanctions adopted by its organs, or the management of the consequences of denunciation of a headquarters agreement with a State.[10]

—*Limitation of the discretionary powers of United Nations organs.* This is a potential application of the good faith requirement that has not yet been used in the practice of the United Nations, but could be of use in the future. If one wishes to limit the discretionary powers of the United Nations—in particular, the Security Council—it would be possible to refer to the principle of good faith contained in § 2 and to develop concrete applications flowing from this legal principle. The Security Council could thus be required, on the basis of the general requirement to act in good faith, to respect in a more explicit manner the rules of proportionality and necessity in its decisions, for example, as to sanctions; to act in a less selective manner in relation to

---

[8] See P Belli, *De re militari et de bello tractatus* (1563) para I, cap. III Carnegie Classics edn (Oxford, 1936) 139–40, in the English translation.

[9] Resolution 2625 mentions the following, rather generic, aspects:

'Every State has the duty to fulfil in good faith the obligations assumed by it in accordance with the Charter of the United Nations.

Every State has the duty to fulfil in good faith its obligations under the generally recognized principles and rules of international law.

Every State has the duty to fulfil in good faith its obligations under international agreements valid under the generally recognized principles and rules of international law.

Where obligations arising under international agreements are in conflict with the obligations of Members of the United Nations under the Charter of the United Nations, the obligations under the Charter shall prevail'.

[10] See, the *Interpretation of the Agreement of 25 March 1951 between the WHO and Egypt* (Advisory Opinion) [1980] ICJ Rep 93ff.

certain fundamental areas of the law (principle of estoppel or *venire contra factum proprum*, for example in the protection of human rights); to guarantee a certain equality of treatment in cases in accordance with the rule of law; etc. The above mentioned rules of necessity and proportionality, pre-eminence of law and equality, all stem to some degree from the overarching principle of good faith or could at least be related to it. The principle is thus very malleable as a basis for developing the obligations contained in the Charter. It could serve as a legal basis for a quasi-legislative function, when required by concrete social and political needs.

C. Article 2 § 3: Peaceful Settlement of Disputes

§ 33 Link between Settlement of Disputes and the Non-use of Force

The peaceful settlement of disputes is in direct relation to the principle of the non-use of force. Hence § 3 and § 4 of article 2 appear consequentially and keep intact the umbilical cord that connects them. Nevertheless, these two principles, united in a functional perspective, differ from one another in an analytical perspective. If they are in some respects the opposite sides of the same coin, they are not so in all respects.

The link between the peaceful settlement of disputes and the principle of the non-use of force is two-fold: on the one hand it is a static relationship, and on the other, a dynamic one. First, with respect to its static quality, § 3 directly provides that all international disputes must be settled by peaceful means; it thereby indirectly implies that force must not be used. Secondly, with respect to its dynamic quality, § 3 contains a condition of efficiency in relation to § 4. The use of force cannot be efficiently banned in practice unless injured States see another course of action, other than coercion, at their disposal in order to address the purported violations.[11] The degree of efficiency of the peaceful settlement of disputes is thus to a large extent an indicator of the practical chances of avoiding recourse to force. These two aspects explain why the two principles are inextricably linked in the framework of modern international law. They are both directed towards the same basic aim: the maintenance of peace. Hence, in articles 12 to 16 of the Covenant of the League of Nations, these two principles are closely interlinked; the same is the case in the Geneva Protocol of 1924, or in the Paris Pact of 1928; and finally the same close relationship exists in the Charter, in § 3 and § 4 of article 2, as well as in Chapters VI and VII.

§ 34 Autonomy of the Settlement of Disputes in Relation to the Non-use of Force

The link between the peaceful settlement of disputes and the non-use of force is only, however, one aspect of this relationship. Indeed, the characteristics and legal facets of

---

[11] See H Grotius, *De jure belli ac Pacis* (1626) book II, ch 1, no 1: 'Ac plane quot actionum forensium sunt fontes, totidem sunt belli: nam ubi iudicia deficient incipit bellum' (in English: 'The grounds of war are as numerous as those of judicial actions. For where the power of law ceases, there war begins').

the principle of the peaceful settlement of disputes differ from those of the prohibition of the use of force.

First, article 2, § 3, is limited to 'disputes'. The concept connotes the idea that there is a conflict of views between two or more subjects concerning a clearly defined object.[12] However, there are 'situations' in international society where there is no clearly defined object crystallising a dispute in the narrow sense. For example, 'tension' among two or more States does not does necessarily have a defined 'object'. Rather, it is a general antagonism of values and of policies, as was the case between the two superpowers during the Cold War. In such situations, any direct or indirect contact between the States concerned can cause international friction. Occasionally such friction leads to a defined dispute, as was the case with the missile crisis in Cuba (1962). Moreover, the non-use of force rule has a broader scope of application than the peaceful settlement of disputes. Indeed, the non-use of force generally applies in inter-State relations and not only in specific cases of clearly crystallised legal or political disputes. The 'dispute' is thus only one of many situations to which the principle of the non-use of force applies.

Secondly, the principle of the peaceful settlement of disputes is not confined to a simple rejection of violent means to settle disputes. Indeed, it imposes a legal duty to attempt to settle a given dispute. When the principle of the peaceful settlement of disputes is examined in light of the principle of the non-use of force, it is evident that stress is laid on the term 'peaceful': the *peaceful* settlement of disputes. Read in the context of only the peaceful settlement of disputes, stress seems rather to be laid on the term 'settlement': peaceful *settlement* of disputes. Indeed, it has been claimed that article 2 § 3 provides a duty to try to peacefully settle a crystallised dispute that may otherwise endanger world peace.

Thirdly, the settlement of disputes is grounded on an idea of positive peace, meaning a strategy for peace over a medium or long-term period. It is consequently not limited to maintaining peace in the short-term, for instance by applying emergency measures, or sending military forces. Thus, article 2 § 3 includes the expression: 'in such a manner that international peace and security, *and justice*, are not endangered' (emphasis added). There would be no medium or long-term peace if the settlement of a dispute were not based on justice. In contrast, short-term measures are, and must, often be based on the practical maxim, grounded on negative peace: 'peace before justice'. This is the role of Chapter VII of the Charter. It provides the basis for emergency measures to be taken in order to avoid or to end hostilities. Once hostilities have erupted, there is no time to chart the causes of the conflict and to fairly settle the dispute in the first place; there is a need to act immediately by imposing necessary measures, and this task falls to the Security Council. Once a ceasefire has been obtained, the settlement-limb will feature more prominently again. This is the role of Chapter VI. Negative peace here vacates its place for positive peace. In order to maintain peace over a longer term, every unjust and iniquitous measure is counterproductive because such measures contain the seeds of future conflicts. The maxim to apply is thus: 'peace through justice'. This is what is recalled in § 3. It is, however, recognised that in concrete cases efforts often fall short of this ideal. Opinions will differ as to

---

[12] As the Permanent Court of International Justice held in the case of *Mavrommatis* [1924] PCIJ Rep Series A No 2, 11: 'a [a] dispute in a disagreement on a point of law or fact, a conflict of legal view or interests between two persons'.' See below, § 39.

what is the just solution in any particular case. There will be disappointment if the solution does not conform to a particular view. This is not, however, the point that is being made in § 3. Rather, the Charter recalls the *endeavour* to be undertaken if the goal is to ensure long-term peace. The better this warning is heeded, the better the concrete work undertaken can achieve its peaceful purpose, and vice versa. It is thus a wise suggestion that the Charter makes. It is for governments and people within a State to choose whether to follow this advice or not. History will judge their actions.

§ 35 Contribution of Resolution 2625

Resolution 2625 places emphasis on the following facets of the peaceful settlement of disputes–principle:

> Every State shall settle its international disputes with other States by peaceful means in such a manner that international peace and security and justice are not endangered.

> States shall accordingly seek early and just settlement of their international disputes by negotiation, inquiry, mediation, conciliation, arbitration, judicial settlement, resort to regional agencies or arrangements or other peaceful means of their choice. In seeking such a settlement the parties shall agree upon such peaceful means as may be appropriate to the circumstances and nature of the dispute.

> The parties to a dispute have the duty, in the event of failure to reach a solution by any one of the above peaceful means, to continue to seek a settlement of the dispute by other peaceful means agreed upon by them.

> States parties to an international dispute, as well as other States shall refrain from any action which may aggravate the Situation so as to endanger the maintenance of international peace and security, and shall act in accordance with the purposes and principles of the United Nations.

> International disputes shall be settled on the basis of the Sovereign equality of States and in accordance with the Principle of free choice of means. Recourse to, or acceptance of, a settlement procedure freely agreed to by States with regard to existing or future disputes to which they are parties shall not be regarded as incompatible with sovereign equality.

> Nothing in the foregoing paragraphs prejudices or derogates from the applicable provisions of the Charter, in particular those relating to the pacific settlement of international disputes.

§ 36 Types of Disputes Envisaged in the Charter

The Charter envisages three different types of disputes. The legal response differs with respect to each type.

First, there are purely local disputes that are not at the level of endangering goodwill among nations. Of course, it is often difficult to draw the line between these disagreements and more serious disputes. Indeed, an insignificant dispute even between friendly States may, if it is not settled and becomes prolonged, irritate and sometimes poison relations between them. However, the fact remains that the Charter does not concern itself with purely interior disputes (like, for example, the dispute between Jura and Bern in the 1970s and 1980s, in Switzerland), or disputes of a purely technical nature between States still enjoying friendly relations, or venial disputes. These disputes do not reach the level of social gravity required to trigger intervention from the world organisation. Interpretation of this category of disputes is made in a restrictive manner: only strictly venial conflicts are not covered. The fact that the Charter is not concerned with this type of dispute can be evinced *a contrario* from article 33 § 1, which sets down the scope of application of Chapter VI: 'The parties to a dispute, the continuance of which is likely to endanger the maintenance of international peace and security . . .'; if a dispute does not reach that level of intensity, the United Nations organs shall not envisage to take measures as those mentioned in Chapter VI.

Secondly, there are disputes 'the continuance of which [are] likely to endanger the maintenance of international peace and security' (article 33 § 1). There exists no direct threat to peace in such cases; an armed conflict is not on the verge of erupting. However, if the situation is left unaddressed, the symptoms currently present could worsen and it could develop into something that might, in the future, endanger world peace. There is in this respect an application of a domino or 'chain of events' theory to the inoffensive dispute of today that is easy to address, which could, following the occurrence of increasingly serious and cascading unforeseen events, become an acute and difficult one to treat tomorrow. In the optic of positive peace, the Charter thus engages in trying to settle such conflicts. It is in some respects a form of 'early warning'. The Charter provides the parties with the means of resolving their conflict with the aid of United Nations organs. The instrument of action for these organs is the power to make a recommendation to the parties concerning the best way with which to settle their dispute. The parties are then free to accept or to reject the propositions that have been made; they only become binding once accepted by the parties.

Thirdly, there are disputes that immediately threaten peace: the wound has here become infected; earlier attempts to treat it have not been successful. Hence immediate intervention using the coercive measures of Chapter VII may be necessary or advisable. Such a response is not a settlement of a dispute, but merely measures that are taken in order to ensure that peace is not breached, or if this is already the case, that it is re-established. The peaceful settlement of such acute conflicts nevertheless raises an important problem. If reliance is made solely on coercive measures (if they are adopted), without treating the causes of the conflict, peace will likely be threatened again in the future as a result of the same dispute having remained unresolved. Chapter VI must thus remain pertinent alongside Chapter VII. Consequently, Chapter VI applies both to conflicts 'the continuance of which [are] likely to endanger the maintenance of international peace' (article 33 § 1) and to 'any threat to the peace, breach of the peace, or act of aggression' (article 39). The former contains a fortiori the latter. The expression contained in article 39 to 'maintain or restore international peace and security' can only be ensured in the medium and long run by application of Chapter VI measures. Clearly, the Security Council did not receive a mandate to impose a solution of a dispute by virtue of its Chapter VII powers. This Chapter is limited to emergency measures, which, because of their urgency, are granted mandatory force (article 25). At the same time, the Security Council may continue its mediation work by virtue of Chapter VI, even with respect to an urgent situation falling under Chapter VII. Article 39 makes this clear when it provides that the Security Council '. . . shall make recommendations, or decide . . .' within the context of Chapter VII. The power of the Council to recommend includes, but is not limited to, the settlement of disputes under Chapter VI. This means that the Council can continue its diplomatic action to settle a dispute through non-binding recommendations while also adopting sanctions or other measures under Chapter VII. The transition from Chapter VI to Chapter VII has the aim of giving the Council additional powers according to the latter Chapter, but not of removing its vested powers under Chapter VI; these are carried across. It would be absurd to remove the diplomatic powers of the Council because it is now acting under Chapter VII. The whole range of political action must remain at the disposal of the Council if its political action is to remain meaningful, comprehensive and flexibly situation-oriented. The paramount aim is to find the most appropriate solution for each situation. In order to achieve this aim, Chapters VI and VII of the Charter must be flexibly interconnected.

§ 37 Requirement to Look for a Solution to a Dispute?

Modern international law stipulates that States have an obligation to try to peacefully settle their disputes when these are disputes falling into the categories of 2 or 3 defined above, namely when their prolongation may endanger international peace and security (article 33) and a fortiori when they directly threaten or have breached peace (article 39). Article 2 § 3 states in no uncertain terms that 'All Members *shall* settle their disputes by peaceful means' (emphasis added). Resolution 2625 is no less clear when it provides with respect to each of its first three paragraphs of the heading that States 'shall . . .'. However, care should be taken not to misinterpret the exact meaning of this obligation: it is largely a 'soft obligation' that entails no sanction for its non-respect. There are three aspects of this obligation that require explanation.

First, practice does not impose any sanctions in the case of contravention. In such situations, the United Nations continues with its diplomatic efforts in order to try to stimulate progress and to eliminate obstacles. Sanctions would make no sense in this context. They would place the targeted State under a negative spotlight and provoke its hostility, thus making a constructive outcome even more difficult to achieve. It is only possible to sanction a State that has persistently and grossly violated its obligations under the Charter, including the obligation to negotiate. Member States could then decide, at a particular moment, to place a ban on the recalcitrant State. This was the case, for example, with South Africa in relation to the Namibia mandate and the policy of apartheid in the 1970s and 1980s. This ban did, however, not go so far as to exclude the State from the organisation under article 6 of the Charter.

Secondly, the obligation to look for a peaceful solution to a dispute is only an obligation of means, not of results. Efforts must be made to settle the dispute, but there is no obligation to reach an agreement on a proposed solution. Indeed, whether a government consents to a proposed solution, especially if it accepts its rights being compromised, is a matter of free choice. The requirement to 'try' to settle the dispute is therefore heavily qualified by the non-existence of an obligation to 'conclude'. This, however, does not detract from the obligation itself. The path to follow, that is, persistent attempts to settle the dispute made in a constructive spirit, is a value in and of itself. It indicates the only possible course to follow in order to progress in addressing and finally solving the problem. A dispute can only really be solved if all the parties to it can finally live with the solution adopted; it is thus essential that all the possible ways to reach such a common understanding are explored until the time is ripe for a final settlement. This last step can often only be reached through a series of intermediate steps spread out in time; the final settlement will thus often be the result of a series of partial settlements and confidence-building measures. Even if settlement proposals are rejected time and time again, they nevertheless serve to open up new discussions at any stage on a higher and clearer level of understanding of the true issues. Such proposals thus assist in achieving a satisfactory solution more easily. The just settlement of disputes is a complex matter of long duration. Impatience must therefore be overcome, because a conflict settled without the real consent of the parties, or the peoples, will neither be a solid compromise nor a lasting solution.

Thirdly, the obligation to look for a settlement is qualified by the principle 'free choice of means'. Not only are States free to decide whether or not to consent to a particular proposed outcome, but they are also free to choose the way in which they would like the dispute to be peacefully settled. There is thus a double consent required from States in order to settle disputes: (1) the means to use; (2) the solution on the merits, except if the means chosen is a judicial procedure or the parties have agreed to accept the decision rendered by a non-judicial third party to the dispute. The principle of free choice of means is covered in Resolution 2625: 'International disputes shall be settled on the basis of the Sovereign equality of States and in accordance with the Principle of free choice of means. Recourse to, or acceptance of, a settlement procedure freely agreed to by States with regard to existing or future disputes to which they are parties shall not be regarded as incompatible with sovereign equality'. General Assembly Resolution 37/10 on the settlement of disputes between States, also known as the Manila Declaration (1982), insists on the same principle in operative paragraph 3. This principle protects the sovereignty of the disagreeing States.

Indeed, the means chosen to settle a dispute considerably influences the merits. It is not the same thing to negotiate, to accept a process of mediation, or to present opposing arguments before a judge. Consequently, in a disagreement between a powerful State and a weaker State, the former may prefer to directly negotiate an outcome whereas the latter would like to avoid this at all costs. The powerful State could put considerable pressure on a weaker State in the context of direct negotiations that the weak State may ultimately not be able to resist. The weaker State would thus prefer that the matter is addressed in a multilateral forum or that control over the proceedings are exercised by third States in order to counterbalance its weakness and to limit the amount of concessions it may otherwise be forced to make. It may also be advantageous for a weak State to choose a judicial procedure in which the unequal powers of the two parties are almost completely erased during the proceedings which strictly conform to the principle of equality before the law. The case between Nicaragua and the United States of America is an example. The ICJ did not hesitate in condemning the United States of America, finding in favour of Nicaragua on the main thrust of the matters raised. This said, many States have also hidden behind the principle of 'free choice of means' in order to avoid usefully cooperating in the settlement of a dispute. Although designed to protect the sovereignty of States and legitimate concerns over the proper way to tackle a dispute, the principle has thus also been used to sabotage any attempt to make progress in the settlement. In this way, the principle has been used to undermine Chapter VI of the Charter. It has impeded United Nations organs—that have deferred too often to the will of any single party to the dispute—in initiating settlement solutions in accordance with the Charter. Attempts have been made to minimise the potential obstacles that the free choice of means can create by arguing that it is not a real principle and that it only exists in practice but not law.[13] However, it must be acknowledged, without any illusion, that the free choice of means has operated as a principle in practice, where it has also frustrated much goodwill.[14]

D. From Article 2 § 3 to Chapter VI of the Charter: UN Contribution to the Peaceful Settlement of Disputes

§ 38 General Aspects of Chapter VI

Article 2 § 3 provides a reference to Chapter VI, which sets out the practical conclusions of the former provision. Article 2 § 3 proclaims the principle of the peaceful settlement of disputes through justice; Chapter VI positively sets out the different ways of settling disputes. The two series of provisions thus complement one another, Chapter VI being a concretisation of article 2 § 3. How is Chapter VI structured? There are three distinct levels the sum of which constitutes a framework for this important Chapter in the grand design of the Charter: (1) the scope of application of Chapter VI; (2) the referral of a situation or dispute (what entity can bring a dispute or situation to the attention of UN organs?); and (3) the substantial powers of United Nations organs. These three points are positioned in a logical chain.

§ 39 Scope of Application

Three different aspects may be examined in this respect.

—'*Dispute or situation*'. According to the applicable provisions, Chapter VI covers all disputes or situations. Article 33, which concerns the means of settling *disputes*, concentrates logically on 'disputes' only and makes no mention of 'situations'. In contrast, article 34 refers to disputes alongside situations. Consequently, Chapter VI does not limit itself to settling already defined disputes. Its preventative function is greater: it also aims to get rid of international tensions and crises in the form of 'situations' that have not yet ripened into disputes where claims and counterclaims are neatly opposed one to another. Under the guise of 'situations', United Nations organs have the right to institute preventative action before a dispute crystallises, with the aim that

---

[13] See AA Cançado Trinidade, 'International Law for Humankind: Towards a New Jus Gentium' (2005) 317 *RCADI* 211.

[14] See the particularly clear explanation: E Jiménez de Aréchaga, 'International Law in the Past Third of a Century' (1978) 159 (1) *RCADI* 143ff.

it should not crystallise. They may, for example, investigate any situation or dispute the continuance of which is likely to endanger the maintenance of international peace and security (article 34). The Charter thus distinguishes between the treatment of disputes (last link in the chain of preventative action under Chapter VI) from the treatment of all symptoms of tensions (the first link in the Chapter VI chain of preventative action). Disputes are consequently dealt with in articles 33, 37 and 38, whereas disputes and situations are alternatively covered in articles 34, 35 and 36.

The issue is how to distinguish between these two stages. What is a dispute? What is a situation? A 'dispute' is not a term defined by the Charter. It has, however, been given quite a clear definition in the jurisprudence of the ICJ when applying the law. Reference may be made here to a pioneer 1924 case of *Mavrommatis* before the Permanent Court of International Justice (PCIJ), the predecessor to the current Court, which provided as follows: '[a] dispute in a disagreement on a point of law or fact, a conflict of legal view or interests between two persons'.[15] Only a few retouches of this definition are necessary for the purpose of Chapter VI disputes. First, the disagreement may be on a point of law, fact or policy. Secondly, the disagreement may encompass more than two persons. What constitutes a dispute is thus essentially the fact that the opposing positions of parties on a particular point are clearly defined. One party makes a complaint that is opposed by the other. Conversely, a 'situation', which is also not defined in the Charter, has a broader meaning that can be determined with reference to its function and purpose. United Nations organs should not be prevented from investigating a tense atmosphere that arises between two States even if no clearly defined dispute has yet crystallised. On the contrary, they must preferably take action before a dispute has crystallised, otherwise, it becomes more difficult to address the disagreement. Once the parties have become entrenched in their respective positions, once the dispute has crystallised and thus created friction and distrust between the parties, it will be significantly more difficult to treat the disagreement with any chance of rapid success. Early action is thus most indicated if the seeds of social disturbances are to be neutralised at lowest cost. Moreover, organs of international institutions cannot depend on the subjective attitude of the parties with respect to their capacity to determine more or less quickly their dispute. The concept of 'situations' gives them some leeway to address an international tension at the moment they think most fit and according to the greatest possible flexibility.

United Nations practice is not, however, really concerned about these subtle theoretical distinctions made in the Charter between disputes and situations. Having the competence to address 'all' that is considered as endangering the maintenance of peace and harmony among States, there is no need to get caught up in the refined discussions on the proper meaning of such distinctions. Further, it would be not be difficult to flesh out a situation to a dispute by simply articulating, mentally or in writing, the positions taken by the parties. This procedural subterfuge would allow situations to be considered as disputes and thus to give some answer as to the merits of the disagreement according to articles 36 or 37 of the Charter. Thus, the United Nations organs treated the Indo–Pakistan controversy concerning the territories of Jammu and Cashmere as a dispute, even though India wanted to classify it as a situation in order to limit the influence of the United Nations (1956–58).

[15] *Mavrommatis*, above n 11 at 11.

—*Internal affairs of a State*. Article 2 § 7 provides that no provision in the Charter authorises the United Nations to intervene in matters which are essentially within the domestic jurisdiction of a State, nor may it require member States to submit such matters to a settlement of dispute procedure. An exception only holds for emergency measures under Chapter VII. Article 2 § 7 was a political concession for some States including the United States of America and the USSR, which would not otherwise have agreed to ratify the Charter. It is, however, apparent that if the situation or dispute may endanger international peace in the sense of article 33, the competence of the United Nations would be triggered. It was never the intention that an issue that potentially threatens the peace would remain within the internal affairs of States. On the contrary, the Charter provides for an *erga omnes* interest in such a situation or dispute through the powers contained in Chapter VI. States cannot claim that the powers afforded to the United Nations in Chapter VI are not triggered because, according to them, the dispute in question is an internal affair. The question is rather framed in the opposite terms: if the dispute or situation may endanger international peace, then it is no longer a matter that falls purely within the internal affairs of a State. The criterion for determining an affair falling within the domestic jurisdiction of a State thus does not add anything to the definition of a disagreement likely to endanger international peace and security. Moreover, this limit on affairs falling within the domestic jurisdiction of States has been largely removed in the practice of the United Nations. The organisation examined a whole host of different situations in the broad perspective of whether they constituted a potential threat to peace, without any consideration of whether they constituted the internal affairs of a State. The long series of cases began with an examination of the 'situation' in Spain, which arose because of the Franco government, an extreme case because if the limitation concerning the internal affairs of States had any effect it would certainly have applied to this situation.[16]

—'. . . *the continuance of which is likely to endanger the maintenance of international peace*'. This substantive criterion is at the same time the most important in the definition of the scope of application of Chapter VI, and also the most difficult to determine. A vague measure is proposed, based on a prognostic that has few existing facts to refer to in order to make an objective determination. Consequently, the criterion proposed here is an essentially political appreciation made on a discretionary basis. In this type of situation, the question of 'who' determines whether the condition is fulfilled largely determines the 'how'. Compared with article 39 ('existence of any threat to the peace'), the necessary level to be reached is lower here. The determination to be made is thus one that falls within the domain of preventative action. The fundamental idea is that the seriousness of a conflict must justify international intervention. This seriousness is reached when the tension or misunderstanding has become a 'matter of international concern'. In this perspective the expression 'the continuance . . .' must be read in three ways. First, venial and purely local conflicts between States that maintain friendly relations are excluded. These disputes must be dealt with at a local level because the very fact of elevating them to an international level and submitting the disagreement to an international forum could amplify the issue into something that it is currently not. Secondly, the

[16] For the practice of the first years of the UN, see the comprehensive analysis in MS Rajan, *United Nations and Domestic Jurisdiction* (Bombay; Calcutta; Madras, 1958) 145ff.

criterion is functional: is it reasonable to try to settle the dispute by one of the means provided in Chapter VI? If this is the case, the United Nations organs will consider the standard 'the continuance . . .' for imposing such means to have been reached. Thirdly, the criterion refers to political will: do the United Nations organs want to undertake such political action in order to try to settle the dispute or to ease the situation? If this is the case, then United Nations organs will similarly consider the standard to have been reached. These three aspects may be in perfect agreement; but each offers a distinct perspective about which it is useful to be aware.

Analytically, the seriousness of the conflict depends on a series of contextual criteria that need to be considered on a case by case basis with the political savvy of a seasoned government official, rather than boxed-in objective criteria. The relevant factors for such a consideration are the following: (1) the exact object of the disagreement, for example, political tensions that could spill over into other areas or to third States; (2) the past relations between the States concerned, that could influence hypotheses about the current situation; and (3) the way in which one or other State parties to the disagreement try to defend their interests, for example in an aggressive or not very constructive manner, that creates a bad climate and that can only benefit from intervention by third impartial parties etc. The distinction with a 'threat to the peace' contained in article 39 is one of gradation and largely depends on what the United Nations organs, and in particular the Security Council, want to do. Do they consider that there is still time to settle the dispute and thus for making proposals concerning the means with which to do this? If so, then the course of action set out in Chapter VI will be followed and the conflict qualified as falling under article 33. Do they consider that there is no more time to reconcile adverse opinions, but that the seriousness of the situation demands coercive measures to be taken and sanctions to be imposed? If so, the conflict will be qualified as falling within the ambit of article 39 and thus as a matter to be dealt with under Chapter VII. The two standards are equally discretionary and are thus ultimately essentially functional. In conclusion, it may be noted that the standard contained in article 33 is not grounded on a concept of positive peace (all deep causes of the conflict), nor on a concept of negative peace (that only addresses the direct threats of war). Rather, it is a standard situated between the two, being a form of preventative action. It is the role for the midfielders of the United Nations football team, persons situated between the defence (economic and social action) and attack (Chapter VII measures). Whoever happens to be interested in football knows about the importance of the midfield.

§ 40 Referral of a Situation or Dispute

What entity can bring a situation or dispute to the attention of the United Nations organs and ask that it be addressed? Article 35 of the Charter responds in a very liberal way. This article grants a right to every member of the United Nations and, under more restrictive conditions, to every non-member State to refer matters to United Nations organs. In addition, United Nations organs can seize themselves of a matter for consideration, formally through the request of any member sitting in them.

A number of articles may be mentioned in this respect: article 11 § 2 (General Assembly) and articles 33 § 2, 34, 36, 37 § 2 (Security Council). The Secretary-General also plays an important political role under article 99 of the Charter. According to this article, the Secretary-General may bring to the attention of the Security Council any matter which, in his opinion, may threaten the maintenance of international peace and security. Thus, with respect to the settlement of disputes, the Charter tries to cast the net as wide as possible and avoid blocking any means of bringing a situation or dispute to the attention of a United Nations organ. The Charter thereby sets up a form of *actio popularis* in favour of all States, members and non-members. These categories will now be examined in more detail:

—*Any Member of the United Nations (article 35 § 1)*: 'Any Member of the United Nations may bring any dispute, or any situation of the nature referred to in Article 34, to the attention of the Security Council or of the General Assembly'. The Security Council (or the Assembly) is thus provided with the means for bringing a situation or dispute to its own attention. The Council is composed of State representatives. If one member of the Security Council wishes to include a matter on the agenda of the day, this necessarily implies that a State member brings the matter to the Council's attention. A case where such a procedure was followed was in the dispute between the USSR and Iran (1946) arising from an Iranian complaint against the stationing of Russian troops on its territory.[17] It should be noted that members of the Security Council may, but are not obliged, to bring such matters to the attention of the Council; a State is free not to do so. In some instances, referring a matter to the Council may not be considered useful by the parties to a disagreement, and they may even claim that it is a form of 'intervention' in their internal affairs (even if this cannot legally be qualified as such). Indeed, referring a matter to the Council could prove to be a poor diplomatic choice: for example, in the Cold War period, it could have meant casting a specific contention into the tensions then prevailing in the Security Council and thus to contaminate a dispute previously localised. To give more weight to a referral, States may rally together to give a collective request for a matter to be considered by a United Nations organ. There is rich practice in this respect, as evinced in the following cases: India and Australia referred the dispute arising from the decolonisation of Indonesia and the Netherlands (1947) to the Council; United States of America, Norway, Portugal and the United Kingdom referred the dispute between Cambodia and Vietnam, following military intervention by the latter (1979) to the Council; Mexico and Norway referred the dispute between Iran and Iraq (1980) to the Council; a group of non-aligned States referred the situation in Namibia (1985) to the Council, etc.

—*A State which is not a Member of the United Nations (article 35 § 2)*: 'A state which is not a Member of the United Nations may bring to the attention of the Security Council or of the General Assembly any dispute to which it is a party if it accepts in advance, for the purposes of the dispute, the obligations of pacific settlement provided in the present Charter'. The conditions for referring a matter to the Council or Assembly for this category of States are more rigid: (1) only disputes, and not situations, may be the subject of a referral; (2) the State making the referral must be a party to the dispute; and (3) the State making the referral must first accept the obligations

---

[17] See 33rd meeting of the Security Council, first year.

of peaceful settlement under the Charter. The scope of the *actio popularis* is thus here restricted. These restrictions, not very consonant to the finality of Chapter VI, which is to settle disputes as largely as possible, are explained by historical considerations that influenced the drafters of the Charter. To give non-member States the same referral rights as member States would have meant giving former enemy States the right to refer any matter to United Nations organs, including a claim for reparation of alleged harm with respect to the post-war liquidation. It was also thought that a former enemy State would try to refer matters to the Security Council with the sole aim of discrediting United Nations action, without any tangible risk for the referring State itself. It was these types of concerns that led to the limitations contained in § 2, in contrast to § 1.[18] The equality of a non-member States with respect to member States under § 2 is, however, assured in a settlement of dispute procedure. In practice, provision § 2 has become largely inapplicable as there are currently hardly any non-member States. Further, even if there were such non-member State, there will always be member States that would be ideologically affiliated with any non-member States and that would bring a matter to the Council's attention, under the more favourable conditions of § 1, on their behalf. Between 1946 and 1980 when there was a considerable number of non-member States, there were only four cases where provision § 2 was applied. Thus, for instance, in 1983, South Korea referred the shooting down of an airliner by the USSR to the Council, when it was not a member at the time.[19]

—*General Assembly (article 35 § 3)*: Article 11 § 3, reads as follows: 'The General Assembly may call the attention of the Security Council to situations which are likely to endanger international peace and security'. This power of the Assembly has been frequently used, for example, in Resolution 181 (1947) on Palestine; in Resolution 1596 (1961), concerning the situation in Namibia, etc. The Assembly must defer to the Security Council because the Charter provides that the Council and not the Assembly will take concrete action. The division of powers roughly means that the Council acts and the Assembly discusses. However, the Assembly also has its own powers to act in the context of the settlement of disputes, as can be evinced from the terms of Chapter VI.

—*Secretary–General (article 99)*: Article 99 reads as follows: 'The Secretary-General may bring to the attention of the Security Council any matter which in his opinion may threaten the maintenance of international peace and security'. The term 'matter' encompasses 'disputes' and 'situations' mentioned in article 34. This article has been frequently applied in practice, for example, Cyprus (1947), Congo (1960), hostage crisis in Tehran (1979), etc.

§ 41 Action

The powers exercised by United Nations organs under Chapter VI are almost exclusively limited to recommendations of the solution to be adopted with respect to a particular

---

[18] See LM Goodrich and E Hambro, *Charter of the United Nations, Commentary and* Documents 2nd edn (London, 1949) 252–53; also the 3rd edn of the same text, with the collaboration of AP Simons (New York; London, 1969) 275–76.

[19] It became a member in 1991.

dispute or situation. These may be procedural recommendations (the means to be used to settle a dispute: article 36 § 1) or they may concern the merits (article 37 § 2). More precisely, the Security Council (or the Assembly) can exercise the following functions:

—*Establish the facts (article 34)*: It may be useful or even necessary to determine the facts in a more exact manner before recommending the precise action to be taken or before adopting a decision. Article 34 allows the Council to initiate an investigation if needed. This investigation may be either general or specific. A *general investigation* aims to determine disputed or unclear facts arising from situations or disputes under either Chapter VI or Chapter VII. The establishment of facts serves to provide a basis for Council action, either a recommendation or a decision about the dispute or situation. Such an investigation took place in 1977 in the context of the attacks by mercenaries in Benin. A *specific investigation* aims to clarify certain factual elements allowing the Council to determine whether the dispute or situation is of such gravity as to fall under article 33, namely whether the continuance of the disagreement may endanger international peace and security. The establishment of a fact in this context has the goal of clarifying the scope of application of article 33. In practice these two forms of investigation are often difficult to distinguish, as an investigation can cover both stages. Practice shows that investigations often have rather broad finalities and have been undertaken in flexible ways. Reference may be made to Resolution 4 (1946): did the Franco regime endanger peace?; Resolution 15 (1946): was the Greek civil war a threat to the peace?; Resolution 132 (1959): was the infiltration of guerrillas in Laos a threat to the peace? etc. In 1983 an investigation was referred to the Secretary-General on the mass poisoning in the Arab territory occupied by Israel.[20] Questions concerning an investigation are often treated as non-procedural questions and are therefore subject to veto under article 27 § 3 of the Charter. However, a veto may be overcome by the creation of an investigative commission as a subsidiary organ by virtue of articles 22 or 29, as this would amount to only a procedural question (articles 22 and 29 fall under the heading 'procedure'). Nevertheless, the question of whether these subsidiary organs then undertake an investigation in the sense of article 34 remains controversial.

Does the investigation impose obligations on member States? Does the decision of the Security Council to investigate legally impose any obligations on them? Must they allow the investigative mission sent by the Security Council to have access to their territory? The question was raised in the case concerning the Greek civil war (from 1946 onwards), where communist States neighbouring Greece (Albania, Bulgaria and Yugoslavia) refused to cooperate with the Commission of Investigation. It was argued that the powers exercised under Chapter VI of the Charter were only of a recommending nature, leaving it to each State to decide whether or not to cooperate; the other side invoked articles 2 § 5 and 25 of the Charter and argued that all 'decisions' of the Security Council (and setting up a fact-finding body is a decision) were of a binding nature and obliged States to cooperate with the action taken to put them in practice.

It is impossible to provide one stand-alone answer to these questions concerning the legal nature of an investigation. Rather, two cases in point should be distinguished. If

---

[20] UNSC Presidential Statement UN Doc S/PRST 15680 (1983).

the Council opts for an investigation in the context of Chapter VII, this choice will be wrapped in the binding nature of a mandatory decision. Article 34 could then be regarded as part of the exercise of a Chapter VII power. This presupposes that the Council has already qualified the situation under article 39, namely that there is a threat to the peace, a breach of the peace or an act of aggression. The Council must be able to take all necessary action to put into practice the sanctions and measures provided under Chapter VII. Without the correct information, the measures taken may be seriously inadequate. The Council thus enjoys an implicit power to engage in mandatory investigation under Chapter VII. Either it is considered that there is an unwritten power to investigate under Chapter VII, or this power is directly attached to article 34. The result is the same in both cases: the decision adopted under Chapter VII imposes an obligation on all State members.

However, if the Council appoints a commission of investigation under Chapter VI of the Charter, the commission will not have been established in a legally binding manner,[21] and State members consequently only have limited obligations in relation to its work. Member States will not be required to provide a commission with militarily sensitive information, nor would they have to allow the commission access to their territories. While the Charter limits State sovereignty in some important ways, it also clearly affirms it. Further, State practice offers no basis for claiming that there is a general power of the Council to order investigations in contravention of the aforementioned points relating to sensitive information or opening of territory. However, there is nevertheless a duty to take notice of a commission and to cooperate with it—with the exception of the two aforementioned points—in carrying out its mission, notably when established under article 34. If the Security Council can properly exercise its powers under Chapter VI only when benefiting from the insights of the commission's work, the duty of cooperation of member States is defined. The *establishment* of a commission is action that has been taken and not simply a prospective recommendation. Member States must demonstrate solidarity to the organisation in order to allow it to exercise its functions and they are required by virtue of articles 2 § 2 and 2 § 5 of the Charter to act in good faith and give the organisation all assistance in all its actions taken under the Charter. Lastly, it is noted that in addition to subsidiary organs, the General Assembly can itself establish commissions of investigation. This is an implicit power of the Assembly, that flows directly or indirectly from articles 22 and 14 of the Charter. The aforementioned comments concerning the 'binding' nature of investigations with respect to the Security Council applies mutatis mutandis to the investigations established by the Assembly.

—*Adopt substantial recommendations concerning the dispute or situation.* The Security Council has a discretionary power to decide if it wishes to make a recommendation on the merits of a dispute or a situation, or if it does not wish to do so. The wording of the relevant provisions is clear: 'The Security Council may . . .' (article 36 and 38); 'If the Security Council deems . . .' (article 37, § 2). If a matter is referred to the Security Council in a regular manner according to article 35, the Security Council must be convened; but it is not obliged to act by adopting a recommendation. It may

---

[21] A considerable number of authors, notably in the early years of the United Nations, claimed that an investigation under article 34 of the Charter would be binding on States members: *cf*, eg, H Kelsen 'The Settlement of Disputes by the Security Council' (1948) 2 *International Law Quarterly* 185; E Jiménez de Aréchaga, 'Le traitement des diiférends internationaux par le Conseil de sécruité' (1954) 85(1) *RCADI* 45–46.

in fact determine that the making of a recommendation would be premature in a particular case. The first debate that concretely takes place concerns whether the case should be included on the agenda of the day. This debate turns on a question of procedure that is not subject to the veto (article 27 § 2). States often oppose the inclusion of a case on the business of the day because they fear the bad press and the domino effect of action once the matter has been referred to the Council. It is easy for a matter to be included on the agenda, but much more difficult to have it removed. Once a matter is included on the agenda, the Council will decide whether to recommend an investigation, a particular means of settling the dispute, a solution on the merits on the basis of political criteria or a sequence of such means, one after the other. There is differing practice; it varies with respect to the political criteria at play. If the Council decides to make a recommendation on the dispute, it has three options:

a. *Article 33 § 2: general incitement to the parties to peacefully settle the dispute by the means of their choice.* The Security Council recalls here the principal duty of parties to a look for a solution to their dispute and the means of their choice, as mentioned in § 1 of article 33. The means of settling a disagreement are not however specified in such resolutions. The Security Council is merely providing a general reminder, not a specific recommendation. However, the Council is also demonstrating to the parties that it remains seized of the matter and incites them to make progress. Once States are aware that an international organ is watching them and may adopt more incisive measures in the case of stagnation in talks, the goodwill to make progress may be stimulated. An example of an application of article 33 § 2 is the first phase of the Indonesian dispute (1947) where the United Nations allowed direct negotiations to take place between the Netherlands and the Republic of Indonesia. Similarly, the parties to the Falklands/Malvinas dispute were called on to find a 'diplomatic solution' to the crisis in Resolution 502 (1982).

b. *Article 36 § 1 and § 3*: specific invitation to the parties to resolve disputes or analogous situations (namely those threatening the maintenance of peace) by a particular method (article 36, § 1). This is appropriate action to be taken if the parties have been unable during the first phase to reach a suitable settlement of the dispute. The principle of the 'free choice of means' may be an obstacle to reaching a compromise if the parties not only disagree on the merits, but also on the means. The Council can thus try to unblock the stand-off by recommending a particular means. Thus, in the conflict between Israel and Syria, the Council recommended that the questions concerning an armistice in 1948 be submitted to the armistice commission: Resolution 93 (1951). Article 36 § 3 recalls that the Security Council should consider that legal disputes should as a general rule be referred by the parties to the ICJ, the principal judicial organ of the United Nations. The Court is at the disposal of States that wish to judicially settle their dispute. It is regretful that the Council has only once made this type of recommendation—that was followed in this instance—in the Corfu Channel case between the United Kingdom and Albania, in 1947. Frequently, the Council does not refer parties to a dispute to a pre-established means or organ, but is rather in the habit of creating its own subsidiary organs to deal with the conflict. This was the case, for example, with the creation of the Commission of good offices designed to ease the India–Pakistan conflict: Resolution 47 (1948).

c. *Article 37: recommendation on the terms of the concrete settlement (article 37 § 2)*. This provision was included in the Charter in the San Francisco conference, that is to say, at a relatively late stage.[22] It recognises the role of the Security Council as a mediator or counsellor. Under article 37 § 2 the Council can recommend particular terms of settlement on the merits of the dispute. At the same time, article 37 § 2 tries to erect certain barriers against overly bold Council action. There are in principle two conditions: (1) that the continuation of the dispute appears, in fact, to threaten the maintenance of peace; and (2) that one of the parties to the dispute has seized the Council (§ 1). Further, the same § 1 seems to consider that all means of settlement in article 33 have already been exhausted. However, practice has overcome all of these obstacles: indeed, the Council has given a very broad interpretation to article 37. Thus, for example, it is sufficient that *any* State seizes the Council. This means, as has already been seen, that the Council can refer a matter to itself and then recommend a solution to the merits. The range of the *actio popularis* has here been extended. Legally, this means that § 2 of article 37 has become separated from the provisions in § 1 of the same article. This broad manner of reading the article is certainly appropriate for a mediator function. Action of the Council would not be of sufficient usefulness if it were limited to recalling the general duty to settle a dispute or to recommending a particular means of doing so. The sovereignty of member States is sufficiently protected by the fact that the Council can only adopt recommendations, not decisions. The terms of settlement proposed by the Council must not be in conformity with international law applicable to the parties to the dispute: the Council may propose political compromises, solutions which it deems 'just' (article 1 § 1) or 'appropriate' (article 37 § 2). In other words, the Council has not to apply the strict law but can recommend transactional solutions.

Council practice with respect to article 37 is rich, but its successes are mixed. One of the first applications of article 37 took place in relation to the second phase of the Indonesian dispute in 1949, following the failure of a procedure based on good offices. A number of resolutions taken under article 37 have recommended terms of settlement: for example, Resolutions 47, 80, 91 and 122 (1948–57) in relation to the India–Pakistan conflict and among others the recommendation for a plebiscite controlled by the United Nations; Resolution 138 (1960) on the reparation of Israel to Argentina for the violation of the latter's territorial integrity concerning the abduction of Adolf Eichmann; Resolution 242 (1967) on the Israeli–Arab conflict, with its principle of 'land for peace'; Resolution 637 (1989) that approved the peace agreement, the democratisation and reconciliation in Guatemala; Resolution 731 (1992), principle of cooperation of Libya to determine those responsible for the terrorist attack at Lockerbie, etc. The voting procedure for these recommendations is for non-procedural questions and thus the veto applies (article 27, § 3).

Article 38, which provides as follows, 'Without prejudice to the provisions of Articles 33 to 37, the Security Council may, if all parties to any dispute so request, make recommendations to the parties with a view to a pacific settlement of the dispute', has never been applied. This article does not add much to the powers already set

---

[22] See UNCIO vol 12, 181.

out in article 37. Formally, it differs from article 37 in that it does not require that the dispute submitted to the Council be likely to endanger international peace and security. Under article 38, the Council may undertake any mediation function entrusted to it by the parties to the dispute. However, if the words 'likely to endanger international peace and security' contained in article 37 are interpreted broadly, there is no reason to use article 38 instead of article 37. Moreover, the Council never bothered to enter into such subtle distinctions and legal interpretations. Article 38 provides that the Council may make recommendations at the request of parties to a disagreement. In these cases, where the parties agree to Council action, the Council may take all kinds of action; it is not even limited to recommendations if the States in dispute agree to provide it with additional powers. According to the terms of an agreement, the Council could thus eventually establish a binding solution for the parties. However, this would be outside the ambit of article 38 under which the Council can only make recommendations (Chapter VI). In fact, article 38 has remained dead letter, with the exception of a proposal for its application by the United States of America and Columbia in relation to the dispute between India and Pakistan (1948). It has been reabsorbed into article 37, which has in turn been broadly interpreted. If the parties to the dispute agree to remove the case from the Security Council (or the Assembly) its competence under article 38 would cease, but not its competence under article 37, § 2, or 34 or 36. Article 38 is just useful for recalling that the Council can engage in action for the settlement of disputes as a mediator whenever the parties wish, even apart from the potential of a dispute to endanger international peace.

The General Assembly possesses in the area of the settlement of disputes more or less the same powers as the Security Council. Article 14 of the Charter is the *sedes materiae* of the Assembly's powers:[23] it states that the Assembly 'may recommend measures for the peaceful adjustment of any situation . . . which it deems likely to impair the general welfare or friendly relations among nations . . .'. This expression is sufficiently broad to encompass the powers conferred on the Council in articles 33, § 2, 34, 36, 37 and 38. This result may seem surprising, as a generic expression contained in article 14 has replaced and in fact doubles the specific powers under Chapter VI. The practice of the General Assembly, however, demonstrates that this reading of the Charter corresponds to reality. The Assembly has thus made recommendations to canvass the reunification of the two Koreas (Resolution 2516, 1969), to support the peace process in Central America (Resolution 47/118, 1992) and in the complex context of the Israeli–Arab conflict (for example, Resolution 45/68, 1990). Sometimes Resolution 377 (V) of 1950, called the 'Dean Acheson Resolution',[24] provides the basis for Assembly action when meeting in an extraordinary session. Solutions have thus also been recommended in response to acute crises: Hungary (1956), Suez (1956), India/Pakistan (1971), Afghanistan (1980), Bosnia (1992), etc when the Council was not able to exercise its principal responsibility for the maintenance of peace due to stalemates caused by the exercise of the right to veto.

---

[23] This article was also included at a late stage in the Charter during the San Francisco conference, when the medium and small powers insisted on reinforcing the role of the General Assembly: *cf* E Luard, *A History of the United Nations* vol I (London, 1982) 55.

[24] On this Resolution, see below § 58.

§ 42 Outcome

If we take the sum of the experiences with respect to the settlement of disputes under Chapter VI, it must be concluded that United Nations action has situated itself between what the political environment and the strong attachment of States to sovereignty has permitted. It must be recalled here that in dispute settlement questions international organs can only persuade, and not coerce; act by recommendation, not by decision. They cannot thus be held accountable for not succeeding when they do not have at their disposal the means to do so. It must also be understood that States are sometimes quite obstinate when they are parties to a dispute. Are we ourselves more sensible in such situations? United Nations action in this area does not deserve either indignation in too extreme a form, nor excessive optimism. Chapter VI, above all, is situated between the heavens and hell: on earth.

The initial idea was that United Nations organs, by virtue of their prestige, would be able to spur on progress in the settlement of disputes by providing new decisive stimulus, particularly when the parties were blocked by temporary insurmountable difficulties. The Council was considered here to be the chief instigator of such action: the great powers in the framework of the Security Council would be able to help, by formidable persuasion, to put things back on track and letting the parties direct themselves to their final destination. However, an often too important deference was paid to respecting the sovereignty of the parties, notably through the principle of 'free choice of means'. This had the effect of undermining the system. The United Nations organs were not always sufficiently able to effectively stimulate action from the parties in such situations, particularly when this required hurrying the parties, gently pushing them from behind, outmanoeuvring their delaying tactics.

Nevertheless, United Nations action in this area of the settlement of disputes exists and is in abundance. Not all was a failure. What in fact would amount to a 'failure' in this context? In cases of frictions, tensions or disputes, societal action is always necessary in the broadest sense of the term; it must always try to find solutions to the disagreements it faces. These arise whether we like it or not and we cannot refuse to address them because this will be fraught with difficulty or hazard. Failure to provide an immediate solution to the conflict is consequently only relative, because the aim is not simply to find an *immediate* solution to a conflict. Immediate settlement cannot, therefore, be the measure of success or failure. Partial solutions realised today can serve tomorrow as a new point of departure: work must progress in steps and proceed stage by stage. A settlement is often the result of prolonged efforts and has progressively ripened between the parties from both problems and solutions. The intervention of United Nations organs can have the effect of clarifying and crystallising the respective positions of the parties, thereby making it easier to determine the problems and the obstacles; of understanding the position of the other States; and of envisaging practical solutions. An understanding of the problems to be addressed and of the possible solutions is the first but decisive step towards finding a solution. Once a final solution has been found it is easy to forget the many abandoned proposals left along the way that nevertheless contributed to the final success. Many United Nations good offices and mediators have advanced suggestions that have played an important, yet often unacknowledged and invisible, part in the final solution of the dispute. Further, the prophylactic function exercised by the United Nations in this area should also be recalled, as without such collective intervention the situation may have continued to degenerate; violence might have become more frequent and more serious. These reasons already amply justify the work of the United Nations in this area. In the imperfect world in which we live, we must arm ourselves with patience and perseverance—values that are unfortunately not worth much to some busy, ignorant and occasionally pretentious modern Western citizens. May we recall the good offices used in the Cuba missile crisis (1962), Vietnam (1965–71), between India and Pakistan (1965–71), between Cambodia and Thailand (1961–68), the mediation in Palestine (1947–49), in Cyprus (1964) and in the Middle East (1967)? The United Nations responses to these very serious and violent situations contributed to their containment, first by delaying and preventing violence, secondly by maintaining contact between the parties and ultimately by finding often very practical, even if partial, solutions to pressing problems. Nor should it be forgotten that the United Nations system deals only with disputes having certain gravity. In these cases it is much more difficult to achieve success. If the United Nations could concentrate only on venial disputes where the reciprocal goodwill of the parties allows steering quickly in the havens of mutually satisfactory solutions, the picture would be different. But the United Nations are really useful only for the first type of disputes; the second ones can easily be settled by the parties themselves, having recourse to the means recalled in article 33 § 1 of the Charter.

The settlement of disputes necessitates constant action undertaken in goodwill and perseverance. It requires faith, courage, patience, discretion, tact and an understanding of cultures, history and the particular situation or dispute in question. Results are unspectacular, but this does make them any less important. Chapter VI above all rests on the maxim of the 'necessary being made possible as much as is feasible'; or of the partial and miraculous taming of the outraged, self-righteous and stubborn Screws. It is imperative to understand the exact parameters and complexity of the work of the United Nations in these areas before passing judgement.

E. Article 2 § 4: Prohibition of the Use of Force

§ 43 General Aspects

Article 2 § 4 is a response to the radical transformation of war.[25] In the twentieth century war has become more and more 'total'. Such total or at least heavily destructive war cannot be accepted as a means of action or of settlement of disputes in inter-State relations. The price that such war places on humanity as a whole, including neutral parties, is indeed too great. Moreover, the reign of anarchic violence is no way to ensure justice; the law of the jungle where the stronger prevails over the weaker starts to be considered, at a certain moment of social history, as an intolerable state of affairs. In any society where community values and a minimal conception of the common weal start to emerge, the condemnation of war becomes essential. To leave States free to exercise their *jus ad bellum* amounts to condemning international society to

---

[25] See above, ch 2, § 5.

living under the constant threat of destruction. No progress in civilisation could be achieved as long as the threat of such modern war cast its shadow over the international society. Social and cultural progress is conditioned on the existence of a state of peace. Living standards, economic and social progress, cultural cooperation, human rights, are all premised on the existence of peace, in the absence of which such functional progress is impossible.

These are the fundamental reasons that drove the States meeting in San Francisco to try to almost completely 'outlaw' individual uses of force by States or by self-proclaimed coalitions. It was certainly a tough bet. The drafters of the Charter were aware that they would strike at traditional habits and that they would be making a frontal attack on the most uncontrollable asset of State sovereignty, that of 'high politics'. Nevertheless, even if the prohibition would be difficult to impose in practice, the rule would nevertheless be priceless. It would saddle the violator of the rule with an enormous burden of justifying its actions. Sometimes it would forestall a violation and be able to deflect reality towards its injunction. This ambivalent reality of the rule, torn between its fundamental importance as a rule and the difficulty of being imposed in fact, is a hallmark of many fundamental principles of common life. The prohibition of force is certainly an example of such an elementary rule.

§ 44 Prohibition of Force and its Exceptions

Article 2 § 4 provides as follows: 'All Members shall refrain in their international relations from the threat or use of force against the territorial integrity or political independence of any state, or in any manner inconsistent with the Purposes of the United Nations'. The new rule contained in article 2 § 4 of the Charter generally prohibited the use of force by States, with some exceptions set out in that instrument, or possibly developed subsequently in customary international law. Conversely, all rules of customary law anterior to the Charter that were incompatible with the new prohibition were abrogated. The Charter provides three exceptions to the prohibition of the use of force. One of these exceptions is no longer applicable today, as it has become obsolete: articles 53 and 107 relating to former enemy States. Another is not a real exception, as it is situated on a different level from that of prohibition; it does not address itself to member States, but to an organ of the United Nations: articles 39 and following, setting out the powers of the Security Council. Practice has, however, almost always referred to it as an 'exception'. Lastly, the remaining major and essential exception is article 51, relating to self-defence against an armed attack.

—*Self- defence (article 51)*. Herewith the text of this essential provision: 'Nothing in the present Charter shall impair the inherent right of individual or collective self-defence if an armed attack occurs against a Member of the United Nations, until the Security Council has taken measures necessary to maintain international peace and security. Measures taken by Members in the exercise of this right of self-defence shall be immediately reported to the Security Council and shall not in any way affect the authority and responsibility of the Security Council under the present Charter to take at any time such action as it deems necessary in order to maintain or restore international peace and security'. In view of the importance of this exception, its contents will be examined in greater detail in separate sections.[26]

—*Provisions concerning former enemy States.* Article 53, § 1, provides that: 'no enforcement action shall be taken under regional arrangements or by regional agencies without the authorization of the Security Council, with the exception of measures against any enemy state, as defined in paragraph 2 of this Article, provided for pursuant to Article 107 or in regional arrangements directed against renewal of aggressive policy on the part of any such state, until such time as the Organization may, on request of the Governments concerned, be charged with the responsibility for preventing further aggression by such a state'. Article 107 stipulates: 'Nothing in the present Charter shall invalidate or preclude action, in relation to any state which during the Second World War has been an enemy of any signatory to the present Charter, taken or authorized as a result of that war by the Governments having responsibility for such action'. Articles 53 and 107 concern former enemy States from the Second World War and permit the allied States, victorious in the war, to take unilateral measures (that is, outside the framework of a Security Council decision) by force in case of a resurgence of belligerent spirit in the vanquished States. Article 106 adds that while awaiting the entry into force of the special agreements mentioned in article 43, the allied States could take all action that was necessary to maintain international peace and security. Nowhere in the Charter is it made more clear that it was first and foremost an instrument for the victorious States in the war and not yet a constitution for the international community.

These provisions concerning former enemy States are now legally and practically obsolete. By joining the United Nations, these former enemy States acquired all the rights and obligations of members. Discrimination against them can no longer be justified. Further, the conditions contained in article 4 concerning the admission of new members, provides that these must be 'peaceful' States. By admitting a State, the United Nations recognises, at least implicitly, that it is a peaceful State. Admission to the United Nations thus definitively ends the *capitis deminuito* of certain States following the war.[27] Article 106 had also only a temporary scope of application and must now be considered to be obsolete. It was linked with articles 53 § 1 and 107. It could not be claimed today that ex-Ally States (or their successors) have a right to use force outside the framework of the Security Council because of the agreements provided in article 43 of the Charter, to which article 106 makes reference and have still not been concluded. In conclusion, these articles only constituted temporary exceptions to the prohibition of the use of force, and they no longer apply.

—*Coercive military action following an authorisation from the Security Council (or eventually the General Assembly).* Chapter VII, which will be examined separately, covers this type of action.[28] This so-called 'exception' means that the Security Council can

---

[26] See below, §§ 47–49.

[27] This is the reason why the report of the committee of experts appointed by the United Nations Secretary-General proposed deleting those passages of the Charter that refer to former enemy States (with the condition that the abrogation would be formulated in such a way so as not to retroactively question measures taken): UN Doc A/59/565 (2 December 2004) § 298. A condition with respect to non-retroactivity is legally useless as an abrogation has *ex nunc* effects.

[28] See below, §§ 50–60.

decide to use force. According to the practice of the United Nations it can expressly authorise one or more States to use such force, under Chapter VII of the Charter, whereby these States will not then be in violation of article 2 § 4 of the Charter. In one sense, this does not amount to a real exception, as the prohibition in article 2 § 4 is only addressed to States acting in their individual capacity and not the Security Council as an organ of an international institution. Collective action is situated on a different level from that of individual action; article 2 § 4 addresses itself to 'individuals' and not the 'police'. Nevertheless, since the Council 'authorises' member States to use force on its behalf instead of having recourse to a United Nations army, which has never existed, the mandated States refer to Chapter VII in order to justify their action as not being in contravention of article 2 § 4. At this inter-State level, the authorisation of the Council functionally operates as an exception to article 2 § 4. This result flows from the fact that the Charter does not provide action by State members under the cover of a Security Council authorisation. What the Charter provided in its text was the use of force by military contingents placed at the direct disposal of the United Nations Security Council and acting on its own behalf. Thus, in a broader sense these authorisations refer back the enforcement action to the level of States and hence constitute, at this level, an exception to article 2 § 4. This exception, not however provided in the Charter, has been developed through a legally consolidated subsequent practice of the United Nations membership.

§ 45 Developments of Article 2 § 4 contained in Resolution 2625

Resolution 2625 has significantly developed the wording of article 2 § 4, in the following way:

Every State has the duty to refrain in its international relations from the threat or use of force against the territorial integrity or political independence of any State, or in any other manner inconsistent with the purposes of the United Nations. Such a threat or use of force constitutes a violation of international law and the Charter of the United Nations and shall never be employed as a means of settling international issues.

A war of aggression constitutes a crime against the peace, for which there is responsibility under international law.

In accordance with the purposes and principles of the United Nations, States have the duty to refrain from propaganda for wars of aggression.

Every State has the duty to refrain from the threat or use of force to violate the existing international boundaries of another State or as a means of solving international disputes, including territorial disputes and problems concerning frontiers of States.

Every State likewise has the duty to refrain from the threat or use of force to violate international lines of demarcation, such as armistice lines, established by or pursuant to an international agreement to which it is a party or which it is otherwise bound to respect. Nothing in the foregoing shall be construed as prejudicing the positions of the parties concerned with regard to the status and effects of such lines under their special regimes or as affecting their temporary character.

States have a duty to refrain from acts of reprisal involving the use of force.

Every State has the duty to refrain from any forcible action which deprives peoples referred to in the elaboration of the principle of equal rights and self-determination of their right to self-determination and freedom and independence.

Every State has the duty to refrain from organizing or encouraging the organization of irregular forces or armed bands including mercenaries, for incursion into the territory of another State.

Every State has the duty to refrain from organizing, instigating, assisting or participating in acts of civil strife or terrorist acts in another State or acquiescing in organized activities within its territory directed towards the commission of such acts, when the acts referred to in the present paragraph involve a threat or use of force.

The territory of a State shall not be the object of military occupation resulting from the use of force in contravention of the provisions of the Charter. The territory of a State shall not be the object of acquisition by another State resulting from the threat or use of force. No territorial acquisition resulting from the threat or use of force shall be recognized as legal. Nothing in the foregoing shall be construed as affecting:

a. Provisions of the Charter or any international agreement prior to the Charter regime and valid under international law; or
b. The powers of the Security Council under the Charter.

All States shall pursue in good faith negotiations for the early conclusion of a universal treaty on general and complete disarmament under effective international control and strive to adopt appropriate measures to reduce international tensions and strengthen confidence among States.

All States shall comply in good faith with their obligations under the generally recognized principles and rules of international law with respect to the maintenance of international peace and security, and shall endeavour to make the United Nations security system based on the Charter more effective.

Nothing in the foregoing paragraphs shall be construed as enlarging or diminishing in any way the scope of the provisions of the Charter concerning cases in which the use of force is lawful.

§ 46 Analysis of Article 2 § 4

Article 2 § 4 raises essentially the following points:

—*Customary status.* Article 2 § 4 reflects universal customary international law. This universal customary law binds all States in the world. The prohibition of the use of force does not therefore constitute only a treaty-based rule, applicable between States that have ratified or adhered to the Charter. It binds all States in the world by the fact that it reflects international customary law that has been universally accepted. This provision of the Charter thus has a double scope of application: as a treaty-rule under the Charter; and as a customary rule, both under international law. Violations of the rule do not automatically weaken or erase its customary status. As long as States justify their violations by exceptions recognised in law, for example by claiming to be exercising legitimate self-defence, this amounts to a reinforcement of the rule rather than a weakening of it. Indeed, arguing by exception (however hypocritically) demonstrates that States recognise the rule. The ICJ has recognised the customary character of the principle contained in article 2 § 4: *Military and Paramilitary Activities in and against Nicaragua* (Merits, 1986), § 292.

—*Addressees of the rule.* Article 2 § 4 is addressed to State members. It obliges them not to use force against 'any State' and not only against 'member' States. The scope of the obligation is thus *erga omnes*. In other words, third States directly benefit from the rule contained in the Charter, independently from its customary law status (this is an exception to the ordinary principle of privity of contract). The rule is clearly perceived as a rule of public order, as a fundamental principle of international law, from which all must benefit. It echoes former article 11 of the Covenant of the League of Nations.

—*'Force'.* Contrary to preceding texts, for example the League of Nations Covenant of 1919 or the Paris Pact (Briand-Kellogg) of 1928, the Charter avoids the term 'war' and instead uses the term 'force'. The term 'force' is legally broader than 'war'. Force refers to a simple fact whereas war refers to a complex legal status. A state of war between two States traditionally means in effect that there are great-scale hostilities accompanied by an intention to make war, ie, an *animus belligerendi*. This is ordinarily expressed by a declaration of war. A prohibition of only war opens up many loopholes in the fight against violence in international relations. It allows States to militarily intervene on a foreign State without finding themselves in a state of war, notably in the absence of their intention to be in such a state. A State could thus argue that its actions only amount to 'armed intervention', an 'armed reprisal' or a 'police operation' (forcible measures short of war).[29] Force could thus be used without being unlawful, since only the recourse to war is prohibited and not the recourse to force. It is these types of legal escapes that the Charter wanted to try to stop by introducing the term 'force'. Force is the sense of article 2, § 4, refers simply to the fact of physical coercion, of effective hostilities. The causes and the exact legal status of the use of force are not pertinent for the law of the Charter.[30]

[29] On these measures, which were much discussed in the inter-war period, see M Bourquin, 'Règles générales du droit de la paix' (1931) 35(1) *RCADI* 224; N Politis, 'Les représailles entre Etats membres de la S.d.N.' (1924) 31 *RGDIP* 5ff; A Guani, 'Les mesures de coercition entre membres de la Société des Nations' (1924) 31 *RGDIP* 285ff; L Cavaré, 'Quelques notions générales sur l'occupation pacifique' (1924) 31 *RGDIP* 339ff; C de Visscher, 'L'interprétation du Pacte au lendemain du différend italo-grec' (1924) 5 *RDILC* 377ff; R Erich, 'Quelques observations sur les mesures de coercition "pacifiques" ' (1926) 4 *Revue de droit international, de sciences diplomatiques, politiques et sociales (Sottile)* 16ff; G Tenekidès, 'L'évolution de l'idée de mesures coercitives et la Société des Nations' (1926) 7 *RDILC* 398ff; B de l'Hôpital, *Des moyens de coercition autres que la guerre entre membres de la Société des Nations* (Paris, 1926); N Petrascu, *Les mesures de contrainte internationale qui ne sont pas la guerre entre Etats membres de la Société des Nations* (Paris, publisher, 1927); JLL Brierly, 'International Law and Resort to Armed Force' (1932) 4 *Cambridge Law Journal* 308ff; AE Hindmarsh, *Force in Peace. Force Short of War in International Relations* (Cambridge, MA, 1933); E Borchard, ' "War" and "Peace" ' (1933) 27 *AJIL* 114ff; J Fischer Williams, *Some Aspects of the Covenant of the League of Nations* (London, 1934) 292ff; H Lauterpacht, ' "Resort to War" and the Interpretation of the Covenant during the Manchurian Dispute' (1934) 28 *AJIL* 43ff; Q Wright, 'The Test of Aggression in the Italo–Ethiopian War' (1926) 30 *AJIL* 45ff; S Séferiadès, 'La question des représailles armées en temps de paix, en l'état actuel du droit des gens' (1936) 17 *RDILC* 139ff; PM Brown, 'Undeclared Wars' (1939) 33 *AJIL* 538–541; ES Colbert, *Retaliation in International Law* (New York, 1948) 60ff; I Brownlie, *International Law and the Use of Force by States* (Oxford, 1963) 26ff, 59–60; J Zourek, *L'interdiction de l'emploi de la force en droit international* (Genève, 1974) 34–37; J Gardam, *Necessity, Proportionality and the Use of Force by States* (Cambridge, 2004) 46–49.

[30] Reference may be made to a parallel branch, the law of armed conflicts, where the Geneva Conventions of 1949 provide, and apply to (among other situations) 'international armed conflicts' between the High Contracting Parties (article 2 § 1 common to the four Conventions). What is significant here, again, is the use of force and not the presence of a state of war. The main concern that led to this change in the law was similar to that which underlay the inclusion of article 2 § 4: to ensure application of the rules of international humanitarian law without any lacuna.

—'*Armed' force*: According to the leading interpretation, article 2 § 4 only covers armed force. This removes from the scope of application political or economic coercion. These forms of coercion only come into play with respect to the rule concerning the prohibition of intervening in the internal affairs of other States.[31] There is no general prohibition against some degree of political or economic pressure, except in extreme cases. In another respect, the rule has to be broadly interpreted. According to a justified interpretation, the term 'armed force' (military forces and weapons) should encompass all forms of 'physical force'. The concept of a weapon is indeed relative. It is possible to use many different objects as weapons. The essential point is that the result is one of physical coercion analogous to armed coercion. Consequently, diverse forms of behaviour may be covered by article 2 § 4. First, explosive weapons or weapons of propulsion, like bombs and projectiles, are manifestly covered. Secondly, weapons that are not of an explosive nature, like biological weapons, would be covered. Thirdly, particular methods such as the ignition of a fire, the opening of dams, the release of radioactive material, cyber-terrorism (attacks against computer systems that control nuclear centres, dams, etc). Fourthly, there is a whole series of more doubtful uses of physical 'force'. For example, spy missions gave rise to discussion when the USSR accused the United States of America of having unlawfully (and physically) entered its airspace during the 1950s. In these last cases, however, there is not a comparable effect to a military use of force; thus there would be no violation of article 2 § 4, but rather a violation of the territorial integrity of the aggrieved State. Similar reasoning can be held for the arrest of ships on the high seas or for abduction or other law-enforcement actions of minor intensity.

—*Threat of use of force*. Due to the gravity that force represents, the Charter also prohibits the preparatory act, namely the threat of force. There are several reasons for this prohibition. First, powerful States may easily obtain the equivalent results to those of a use of force by simply threatening to use force. It would be questionable, both legally and politically, to allow a State to act with impunity by using threats to achieve the same result as by using force. Moreover, what sense would there be in permitting the threat when the content of the threat is prohibited, ie, when the threat could never be realised, since that would constitute a use of force? Secondly, a threat of force constitutes a very serious risk for peace. States that make such threats may eventually have recourse to force for the sake of their credibility. A threatened State may succumb to a threat, or it may not. In this latter case, a State that has threatened another may feel obliged to use violence unless it wishes to lose all its credibility in the future. By prohibiting the threat of force, the Charter tries to avoid these unwelcome results. Thirdly, the Charter attempts to foster international cooperation and peaceful relations among States. How could it accept behaviour blatantly opposed to these aims? How could it tolerate a course of conduct that directly poisons international relations? Whatever the reasons of the prohibition, it is nevertheless not easy to define the term 'threat'. It certainly covers 'any blatant and direct threat [of force] in order to obtain concessions'.[32] However a purely objective vision is not sufficient. To it must be added a perspective that takes into account the level of a threat necessary to affect a *particular* State having regard, for example, to its

---

[31] See in this respect, *Nicaragua* case, above n 3, § 228.

[32] See O Schachter, 'International Law in Theory and Practice: General Course of Public International Law' 178 *RCADI* 1982-V, 139.

weakness, or its particular dependence on the threatening State. Moreover, one has to bear in mind that all threats to use force are not prohibited. The threat to use force is only unlawful if the force threatened would be unlawful to use. There is here a 'principle of parallelism'. Hence, it is unlawful to threaten to use force to annex territory or to impose certain economic or political policies on another State, in violation of the principle of non-intervention. Conversely, it is not unlawful to threaten to use force in order to use self-defence against an act of aggression or if the Security Council has conferred a mandate on a State under Chapter VII. Similarly, a general policy of dissuasion of States, which is based on a threat to use force in certain circumstances, is not contrary to the Charter, insofar as it respects the rules contained therein. It may not be clear if the use of force threatened will conform with the rules of international law; but if the threat is not blatantly contrary to international law, the presumption is that a State threatening to use force will conform with the requirements of international law. Thus, for example, a State may threaten to use force and indicate that it will lobby for an authorisation of the Security Council. Such a threat must not be unlawful, if it can be understood as not relinquishing the requirement for prior authorisation of the Council. The principle of parallelism referred to has been recalled by the ICJ in the advisory opinion on *Legality of the Threat or Use of Nuclear Weapons* (UNGA, 1996).[33] The opinion of authors who argue that a threat is lawful if it supports recognised rules or even the aims of the United Nations Charter, must however be rejected.[34] What matters is only whether the use of force threatened, if the threat is carried through, would itself be unlawful under article 2 § 4 of the Charter.

—*'Indirect' force.* The use of indirect force is covered by article 2 § 4: see § 8 to § 9 of Resolution 2625, under the heading of the prohibition to use force. This would amount to organising irregular armed forces or armed groups in view of unlawfully entering the territory of another State; or providing assistance to such forces or groups; or organising and participating in acts of terrorism on the territory of another State.[35] The problems in this respect concern evidence of such State involvement.

—*'In their international relations'.* The prohibition formulated in article 2 § 4 only applies to international relations, meaning between subjects of international law. The relevant international relations are here the relations between States, since only States traditionally possess armies and engage in uses of force. Attacks by private groups not sponsored by States (indirect uses of force, see the point above) are in principle not uses of force in the sense of the Charter, but rather criminal action calling for suppression by means of criminal law devices. The prohibition of the Charter presupposes in any event inter-border relations. This means that it does not apply within the borders of a State during a civil war. All States have the right to use force to defeat an insurgency; conversely, insurgency is not prohibited. An internal conflict may, however, become internationalised, by for example the proclamation of independence (secession) as was the case in Slovenia and Croatia with respect to the former Yugoslavia. If this independence is effective, meaning the new power is factually independent from the former central power and this independence is internationally recognised, by for example its admission to the United Nations, then the new subject

---

[33] *Legality of the Threat or Use of Nuclear Weapons* (Advisory Opinion) [1996] ICJ Rep 246, § 47.
[34] R Sadurska, 'Threats of Force' (1988) 83 *AJIL* 260.
[35] See the *Nicaragua* case, above n 3, § 228.

is protected by article 2 § 4. If the armed conflict between an old State and a secessionist entity continues, there is not yet effective independence. Consequently, the protection afforded by article 2 § 4, does not yet apply, unless the international community prematurely recognises the independence of the entity as an independent State (with the corollary protection of article 2 § 4). This was the case for Bosnia-Herzegovina. The problem often boils down to determining when such an armed conflict has ended. According to the leading doctrine, it suffices that there is a general end of hostilities, namely a general armistice or a definitive surrender. From this moment onwards, the law of armed conflicts ceases to apply and the law applicable during peacetime becomes operational. Article 2 § 4 thus applies.

Article 2 § 4 protects both stabilised borders and de facto regimes (entities possessing all the qualities of a State but not recognised as such by the international community, ie, the overwhelming majority of States). Stabilised borders may take the form of demarcation lines and armistice lines, or other lines inherited from the end of hostilities. These are borders that are recognised by agreement or de facto, or which are stabilised without any ulterior resistance (principle of effectiveness). This is the case, for example, with the armistice line at 38° latitude that marks the border between the two Koreas. Resolution 2625 (1970) is explicit in this regard: 'Every State likewise has the duty to refrain from the threat or use of force to violate international lines of demarcation, such as armistice lines, established by or pursuant to an international agreement to which it is a party or which it is otherwise bound to respect' (§ 5, under the prohibition of the use of force). Further, the same Resolution recalls that 'Every State has the duty to refrain from the threat or use of force to violate the existing international boundaries of another State or as a means of solving international disputes, including territorial disputes and problems concerning frontiers of States' (§ 4, under the prohibition of the use of force). This second hypothesis covers cases where a State claims that it has not violated the prohibition of the use of force because the territory it evaded belonged to it in law, even though at the moment of attack was controlled by another State. These two legal aspects are largely the two sides of the same coin: one concerns the line that demarcates a border with another State, the other concerns the foreign territory that lies just beyond; the first does not exist without the other, except in the case of islands. These rules were applied by the Ethiopia/Eritrea Arbitral Commission in the *Jus Ad Bellum* decision rendered in 2005. Eritrea claimed that it had not violated article 2 § 4 of the Charter because the territories that it militarily invaded lawfully belonged to it. The Commission recalled that force cannot be used to settle disputes, including territorial disputes, and reproduced the above quoted passes from Resolution 2625 (§ 4). The Commission added an argument of legal policy. Territorial disputes, it held, are frequent. To allow an exception to the prohibition of the use of force in such disagreements 'would create a large and dangerous hole in a fundamental rule of international law'.[36]

—*Problem of the last twenty-three words.* Article 2 § 4 concludes with the end of a phrase that has given rise to very divergent interpretations. The end of the phrase consists of exactly twenty-three words in English (twenty-four in French), which are the following: '. . . against the territorial integrity or political independence of any

---

[36] *Jus ad Bellum* Award, *Ethiopia's Claims 1–8*, decision of 19 December 2005, § 10. The decision is available on the website of the Permanent Court of Arbitration: www.pca.cpa.org.

state, or in any other manner inconsistent with the Purposes of the United Nations'. Some authors have interpreted this part of the article as containing an exception to the prohibition formulated at the beginning of the article. Thus only force that is employed with a certain finality would be prohibited, namely force that aims to violate the territorial integrity or political independence of a State, or the purposes of the Charter. All other uses of force that do not have such a finality would be *a contrario* lawful: for example, the force used for the purposes of humanitarian intervention, emergency operations to save nationals abroad in mortal danger, military operations that aim to disarm dangerous States, etc. An understanding of what would be compatible with the finalities would be made by each State individually. The result of such an argument is that article 2 § 4 contains not an absolute prohibition (apart from self-defence and Security Council authorisations), but only a limited teleological prohibition. There are traces of this argument in State practice, even recently, for example in the pleadings before the ICJ.[37] This argument was already made in the Suez case of 1956. It was claimed, in this context, that the Franco–British operation was in accordance with the purposes of the Charter because it would have provided a sanction for the violation of international law, a purpose not inconsistent with the United Nations Charter.[38] The majority of authors and States reject this interpretation based on two principal arguments. First, the *travaux préparatoires* demonstrate that the last twenty-three words were inserted following a proposal by Australia (and some other States), not to weaken the prohibition by inserting a proviso, but rather to reinforce the prohibition by linking it explicitly to territorial integrity, political independence and the purposes of the United Nations. The Australian idea was to stress the prohibition by providing examples of what its violation would lead to: namely to infringe territorial integrity, political independence, the purposes of the United Nations. The argument was: the use of force must be prohibited *because* it leads to violations of territorial integrity, political independence and the purposes of the United Nations. If this 'because' had been textually included, the subsequent doubt would not have arisen. Secondly, there is an argument relative to the practical effects. If the permission interpretation is retained, the scope of article 2 § 4 would be dramatically reduced because each State could claim subjectively and/or objectively that the effects required by the last twenty-three words of article 2 § 4 had not occurred and thus their actions were not unlawful. With notions as broad as 'purposes of the United Nations' (peace, settlement of disputes, cooperation, human rights, international law, bettering the standards of living, democracy, disarmament, etc) the freedom to use force would be practically unlimited. A good pretext could always be found: it could suffice to claim that a use of force was undertaken in order to further peace, the settlement of a dispute, better cooperation by regime change, human rights, democracy, etc. However, the finality of article 2 § 4 itself, which is to expropriate the use of force from States, would be entirely lost. Article 2 § 4 is aimed at the maintenance of international peace, not merely to proscribe unjust force subjectively appreciated. In relation to this general aim of article 2 § 4, it can be stated that all uses of force would violate the territorial integrity and political independence of States and the purposes of the Charter, the first of which is to

---

[37] See below under humanitarian intervention, no 120, b.
[38] *Cf* S Bastid, 'L'action militaire franco–britannique en Egypte et le droit des Nations Unies' in *Mélanges G Gidel* (Paris, 1961) 49ff; J Stone, *Aggression and World Order* (London, 1958) 94ff.

maintain peace. Article 2 § 4 imposes an 'absolute' prohibition. Real and eventual exceptions must be found elsewhere, in article 51, and possibly in customary international law, but not within article 2 § 4 itself. This provision contains a clear and unambiguous principle: States may not use force.

§ 47 Self-defence

Article 51, quoted above, provides each State with a right to exercise self-defence. This provision has held a significant place in international practice since 1945. In a world full of uncertainty, some States—notably powerful States—looked for a measure that would permit them to find a way around the rigid prohibition contained in article 2 § 4. They found the sole recognised exception in article 51, which they then tried to enlarge as much as possible. In contrast, small and medium-sized States have generally insisted on a strict interpretation of article 51. They have nothing to gain in a world where force is surreptitiously reinstalled.

The Charter structures this right to legitimate self-defence in quite a strict manner in order not to open the door to liberal uses of force, proscribed by article 2 § 4. Self-defence in the Charter is limited in four ways:

1. *It is reactive and non-anticipatory*. There must be an armed attack ('aggression armée' in the French text) before a State can resort to a use of force. An armed attack is in principle an objective fact, observable from the ground. It was thus hoped that this would limit anticipatory abuses of uses of force and all forms of preventive wars.
2. *It is inter-mediatory.* The attacked States defends itself or with the help of other States that come to its assistance whilst the Security Council—being immediately informed of the armed attack—has not yet taken efficient collective security measures.
3. *It is subordinate*. Once the Security Council, by virtue of its powers under Chapter VII, has taken the necessary measures, these take priority over all exercises of individual or collective self-defence. The measures taken by the Security Council shall take precedence over decentralised action, about which the Charter is wary.
4. *It is exceptional.* As an exception to the principle of non-use of force enshrined in article 2 § 4, self-defence would have to be interpreted narrowly. *Exceptiones sunt strictae interpretationis.*

In the reality of the post-1945 world, these conditions have not been respected with sufficient precision. In practice, some powerful States have enlarged self-defence to encompass anticipatory action in the context of immediate threats; the use of force even in cases of non-territorial attacks (acts of terrorism, attacks against citizens abroad, drug trafficking); forcible actions disconnected from the timing of the armed attack being armed reprisals rather than self-defence; admission of uses of force also against non-State armed groups deprived of their own territory (terrorist groups, militias) etc. This is not the place to discuss at length the substance of self-defence.[39]

---

[39] For more details, see R Kolb, *Ius contra bellum, Le droit international relatif au maintien de la paix* 2nd edn (Basel;Bruxelles, 2009) 273ff.

One single condition may be examined in detail in this context. It is the material condition: what is an armed attack in the context of article 51?

§ 48 Main Condition for the Exercise of Legitimate Defence: (Prior) Armed Attack

According to the wording of article 51, the legal qualification linked to establishing a right to exercise self-defence is the (prior) existence of an armed attack. The French text is slightly different and less precise; it refers to an 'agression armée'.[40] The term 'attack' used in the English text correctly describes the triggering mechanism. It is of no concern that the attack amounted to an act of armed 'aggression' according to the legal definition of the term. Rather, what is important is that the attack was of a certain level of intensity in the degree of force used. Like the distinction between war and force, the triggering mechanism of article 51 is not referring to a particular legal status (like 'war' or 'aggression'), but simply to the observable facts on the ground.[41] The principle is about responding to violence with violence: *vim vi repellere*. The fact that the expression 'agression armée' is included in the French version of the text stems from imprecise translation rather than a voluntary decision, as evinced by the subsequent practice of States confirmed in the text of the NATO Treaty (1949). In the French version of article 5 of this instrument, dealing with collective self-defence, the term 'attaque armée' is included instead of 'agression armée'.

An armed attack ('agression armée') is not defined anywhere in the Charter. The ICJ, in the *Case concerning the military and paramilitary activities in and against Nicaragua* (1986), found that there was general agreement on the nature of acts which can be considered to constitute armed attacks. The Court limited itself to providing two examples: action by regular armed forces across an international border and indirect aggression by an armed group sent by another State, without going into a deeper analysis.[42] To clarify the term 'armed attack' in article 51, reference may be made to the definition of 'aggression' in United Nations General Assembly Resolution 3314 (1974). Of course both terms do not completely overlap. The definition in article 51 covers 'armed attacks', whereas the definition in the Resolution defines 'aggression' in strict legal terms. However, most actions which may be defined as aggression under the Resolution may a fortiori be defined as an armed attack and thus fall within the ambit of article 51. Hence the argument *ejusdem generis* for moving from the Resolution to article 51: forcible acts of the same level of gravity as those enumerated in the Resolution must also be covered by article 51.

Article 3 of Resolution 3314 enumerates those cases qualified as aggression. Herewith the content of that article. Cases of armed aggression are:

---

[40] Art 51 was lately inserted in the drafts of the Charter, at the San Francisco stage. Due to time constraints, the text of the English and French versions was not fully harmonised.

[41] This is why we prefer the term 'armed attack'.

[42] At § 195.

1. *Invasion of territory, bombardment, blockade* (a) to (c). These actions correspond to traditional military warfare in an attack leading to a full-fledged war or armed conflict.
2. *An attack by the armed forces of a States on the land, sea or air forces, or marine and air fleets of another State* (d). This consists of, for example, armed attacks against navy vessels on the high sea or on a large part of the merchant fleet. The wording of (d) does not include nationals abroad. If such individuals are attacked, there is not according to the Resolution an armed aggression against the national State of the individuals concerned.
3. *Violation of agreement of the sending State with respect to armed forces stationed within the territory of another, notably the extension of their presence beyond the termination of the agreement* (e). Violations of these agreements must be of a seriousness equivalent to an invasion. Minor violations will be neither an aggression nor an armed attack. In relation to the termination of the agreement, the obligation to leave the territory is unconditional. It cannot be claimed that the agreement was unlawfully terminated by the receiving State. This would trigger a settlement of dispute procedure, but it does not authorise the State to leave its armed forces stationed on the territory. Otherwise, this would open the door to obvious abuses manifestly contrary to the sovereignty of the receiving State. In the context of (e), the State first using force will be in self-defence.
4. *The action of a State in allowing its territory, which it has placed at the disposal of another States, to be used by that other State for perpetrating an act of aggression against a third States* (f). Here there is complicity between two States. In such a case, both States are aggressors. This provision only envisages the voluntary placing at disposal territory for another State; it does not cover the case of insufficient prevention against acts of hostilities with respect to the other States. However, such cases may be difficult to distinguish in reality.
5. *Sending by or on behalf of a State of armed bands, groups, irregulars or mercenaries, which carry out acts of armed force against another State of such gravity as to amount to the acts listed above, or its substantial involvement therein* (g). This is a category of 'indirect aggression' by intervening irregulars.[43] The most acute problem in this category is to determine the level of engagement which must be reached for the acts of armed groups or irregulars to be attributable to it. This is a problem that continues to be debated. In order to make the acts of the irregulars attributable to a State, that State must exercise complete control over these irregulars (that then become a de facto organ of the State), or effective control is exercised over the individuals to whom a specific mandate in given (control by instruction).[44] Alternatively a State may acquiesce ex post to the acts of private persons. The standards applied by the ICJ are thus relatively high and strict, even though attempts to lower this standard are not lacking.[45]

There remains the important question of when the armed attack begins and when it ends—thus triggering or terminating the right of self-defence. There have traditionally

---

[43] See *Nicaragua* case, above n 3, § 195.

[44] See *Application of the Convention on the Prevention and Punishment of the Crime of Genocide* (*Bosnia and Herzegovina v Serbia and Montenegro*) [2007] ICJ Rep § 390ff, 396ff.

[45] See, eg, A Cassese, 'The Nicaragua and Tadic Tests Revisited in the Light of the ICJ Judgment on Genocide in Bosnia' (2007) 18 *EJIL* 649ff.

been some differing views on these questions, in particular between the Anglo-Saxon and the Continental States. The first continue to perceive self-defence as a sort of 'right of necessity', allowing vital interests of the State in situations of overwhelming urgency to be protected. The second define self-defence more narrowly as a use of force to repel an ongoing armed attack on territory or on quasi-territorial positions such as warships at sea. Modern international law, as manifested in the Charter, is closer to the second than to the first conception. It attempts to restrict the right to use force rather than enlarging it

For the beginning of an armed attack, four situations can be distinguished: (i) *Reactive self-defence*: the armed attack has occurred, its effects have already unfolded, for example, a bombardment has taken place. (ii) *Interceptive self-defence*: the armed attack has started since an irrevocable course of action has begun, even if the effect of the attack has not yet occurred (eg a missile has been launched, but it has not yet struck its target). If a fleet sails towards the target, the time frame expands; interceptive self-defence moves towards anticipatory self-defence. In such cases, proper and reliable intelligence becomes all the more crucial. (iii) *Anticipatory self-defence*: the armed attack has not yet been launched, but it is imminent. (iv) *Preventive or Pre-emptive self-defence*: there is no foreseeable armed attack, but there is a window of opportunity to strike first in order to avert future threats. Reactive and interceptive self-defence are compatible with the Charter. However, interceptive self-defence should be allowed only in situations of clear imminence. Preventive self-defence is manifestly incompatible with the Charter since it does away with the key criterion of an armed attack. Preventive action under the Charter is the province of the Security Council. Allowing preventive self-defence would be tantamount to reinstall the *jus ad bellum* of States as it existed in the nineteenth century. Anticipatory self-defence remains very controversial, albeit it has been viewed somewhat more generously since the 11th September attacks. On one side are those who claim that it would be unjust and impractical to ask a State to be a 'sitting duck' awaiting the imminent strike and thus possibly putting itself at a military disadvantage with respect to the aggressor State. Moreover, it is claimed that in an era of weapons of mass destruction such a course could be suicidal. The law cannot be interpreted as a 'suicide pact'. On the other hand, the arguments are that the text of the Charter is clear ('if an armed attack occurs ...'); that pretexts and abuses would otherwise flourish, blurring the line between self-defence and veiled aggression and opening the gates of power politics; that in practice references to anticipatory self-defence are extremely rare, which shows the discomfort of States in the face of such a dangerous argument; that the Charter reserves action in cases of threats (imminent or not) to the Security Council only; that there is a signifi-cant risk that there is a significant risk that a State will misjudge whether an attack is imminent, particularly where another State displays provocative military power stop-ping short of any real intention to initiate hostilities, thus potentially allowing two States to accidentally stumble into war; and that it is difficult to give a clear and objec-tive meaning to rules such as necessity and proportionality in self-defence in the absence of a real attack. All these arguments, both for and against, carry weight. It would seem that the law cannot properly respond to such borderline situations. The better course is thus to maintain the prohibition of anticipatory attacks, but to be ready to assess the facts on a case-by-case basis and to refrain from condemning a State which manifestly exercises anticipatory self-defence *bona fide* and with an objectively proper justification. It must be added that the International Court of Justice, in the *Military and Paramilitary Activities in and Against Nicaragua* (merits, 1986, § 140) and in the *Armed Activities* (*Democratic Republic of Congo v Uganda*, 2005, § 143) cases left the question of anticipatory self-defence undecided. However, the whole reasoning of the Court in both cases is predicated upon the requirement of a prior armed attack.

For the termination of the armed attack (and thus of self-defence) the legal position differs according to the type of attack: (i) The attack is a single, isolated act, such as a bombardment. Here, the response of the attacked State must be immediate in order to avoid sliding into prohibited armed reprisals, which would amount not to defence but retaliation and intimidation. 'Immediacy' must obviously be understood as the grant of the necessary and reasonable time for preparation according to the circumstances. (ii) The attack stretches in time, such as through the occupation of a territory. The right of self-defence here extends to the moment of cessation of the attack, namely the occupation.

§ 49 Level of Intensity of the Armed Attack under Article 51

Following one line of argument, the level of intensity required should be relatively low because a State should not be required to remain passive if there is force being used against it. According to this reading, it would not be realistic or fair to consider that a State must take a beating without being allowed to respond with force, simply because the level of intensity of the armed attack is not sufficiently high and consequently, the State cannot exercise self-defence. The principal value to be protected is, in this conception, the vital defence interests of the State. Thus, according to Yoram Dinstein, an attack need not be 'large-scale, direct, and important'; even a border incident would suffice if there is an exchange of fire. Article 51 only excludes 'trivial incidents'.[46] Following, the dominant criterion of self-defence is not the level of intensity of the armed attack, but rather proportionality: the legitimacy of the response depends on the fact that it does not exceed the intensity of the attack.

According to another line of argument, a higher level of intensity must be required in order not to open the door to individual uses of force with its stream of abuse and escalation. According to this reading, the spirit of the Charter demands quite a strict approach when it comes to recognising individual uses of force. The principal value for this line of argument is the international community's interest in peace. Accordingly, there must be a use of force of a relatively high degree of intensity and having substantial effects in order to permit the exercise of self-defence. Anything less and the aggrieved State must endure the attack without responding with force. The only lawful response would have to be a peaceful one, for example, referring the matter to the Security Council. The aggrieved State is thereby making a sacrifice to the international community and to the maintenance of peace. This is the view of authors such as A Randelzhofer.[47]

---

[46] See Y Dinstein, *War, Aggression and Self–Defence* 3rd edn (Cambridge, 2001) 173ff.

[47] A Randelzhofer, 'Article 51' in B Simma (ed), *The Charter of the United Nations: A Commentary* vol I, 2nd edn (Oxford; New York, 2002) 790–91.

How should these different approaches be evaluated? First, it must be stressed that there is no one single level of required intensity. Some acts constitute *eo ipso* an armed aggression, for example, to open fire on a navy vessel at sea. The different categories listed in article 3 of Resolution 1344 (1974) are thus a list of different *leges speciales*, having their own level of intensity. Outside these enumerated examples, there remains the case of direct use of force. In this context, the level cannot be too elevated or it would open the 'justice gap', as highlighted by some authors. At the same time, the level cannot be too low as it would open the 'violence gap' as others argue. The only valuable abstract criterion that exists is to say that there must be a use of force with a minimum degree of consistency and danger. This is a criterion situated half-way between 'trivial' and 'substantial'. The armed attack must therefore be understood as forming part of a pattern of violence against a State rather than sporadic acts with low levels of intensity (unless these are constantly repeated, accumulating their effect). It is not possible to more precise in the abstract.

The ICJ has never clarified the exact level of violence that distinguishes the use of force under article 2 § 4 from an armed attack under article 51. However, the Court has always insisted on the fact that all uses of force are prohibited under article 2 § 4 but not all these uses are automatically armed attacks triggering the application of article 51. There is thus a gap between articles 2 § 4 and 51. The Court makes an axiological choice, based on the text of the Charter. The reason for this choice is to raise the triggering requirement for uses of force in international relations. The relevant comments of the Court are found in the cases of *Military and Paramilitary Activities in and against Nicaragua* (1986) (§ 191) and *Oil Platforms* (2003) (§ 51). The Arbitral Commission established by Ethiopia and Eritrea also insisted that 'localized border encounters between small infantry units, even those involving the loss of life, do not constitute an armed attack for the purposes of the Charter',[48] particularly when the border is not delimited. The Commission held that Eritrea did not have a right to exercise self-defence, even though border incidents had occurred. These incidents lacked any intention of being a more generalised attack on the part of Ethiopia. Consequently, the massive Eritrean invasion on Ethiopian territory was incorrectly undertaken in the absence of an armed attack as required by article 51 of the Charter and Eritrea's actions were moreover disproportionate. The Commission thus provides us with some material concerning the criterion of 'trivial incidents'.

F. From Article 2 § 4 to Chapter VII: The Maintenance of Peace through Collective Security

§ 50 General Aspects

The Charter is not an instrument based on pacifism. It allows for the use of force but tries to link it with some form of community control. If the Charter tries to 'expropriate' the

---

[48] *Jus Ad Bellum* Award, above n 35, *Ethiopia's Claims 1–8*, decision of 19 December 2005, § 11. Available on the website of the Permanent Court of Arbitration: www.pca–cpa.org.

right to use unilateral force, except in the case of self-defence, it transfers the use of legitimate violence, indispensable in any organised society, to an organ that represents the international community as a whole. This organ is the Security Council. Its principal activity is 'collective security'. What is collective security? It has three aspects. First, it turns on a *casus foederis vel garantiae*;[49] that is, the reasons for intervening through collective measures, or the use of force, are determined in advance. Secondly, the determination of whether to intervene based on this *casus* is entrusted exclusively to a common organ. One sole organ representing the group as a whole qualifies a situation in order to determine whether the conditions of the *casus* have been met or not. Thirdly, the solidarity of all members of the system against the State targeted by the measures taken or with sanctions adopted by the organ representing the group as a whole. The collective security mechanism is thus 'all for one and one for all'. All State parties to the collective security system are obliged to unite against the States endangering or breaching the peace in the eyes of the organ charged with qualifying the situation and to cooperate with executing the measures or sanctions adopted against this same State. A collective security system is universal when the organ that enjoys the decision-making powers represents the international community as a whole. The ideal form of collective security is one that is universal. Regional systems of collective security risk degenerating into specific alliances often dominated by the most powerful State in the region. These alliances are then often orientated towards concurrent alliance systems (for example, NATO, the Warsaw Security Pact) and often in fact increase international tension, whilst sometimes temporarily reinforcing regional security. Regional systems of collective security were traditionally regional alliances for collective self-defence (see, for example, the Panamerican system of the inter-war period and up to the Act of Chapultepec of 1945). Their scope of action was very narrow, as the *casus foederis* here was simply armed aggression. Today, regional systems have much broader missions in the area of the maintenance of regional peace. Their relationships with the universal system of the United Nations have thus at once become more challenging and more complex.

The Charter defines the *casus garantiae* in rather broad terms. It not only refers to aggression or an armed attack, as in the case of self-defence in article 51. The collective organ, unlike States acting for individual interests and on an individual basis, is granted much broader foundations for its action. It notably also covers preventative action. The Charter does not fear abuse in this respect, as it does when individual State action is at stake. In the view of its drafters, any abuse is here cushioned by competing political views within the Council that must reach a consensus of nine votes in favour in order for the collective security mechanism to be triggered. Article 39 thus defines the *casus* of the Charter in the following terms: 'The Security Council shall determine the existence of any threat to the peace, breach of the peace, or act of aggression and shall make recommendations, or decide what measures shall be taken in accordance with Articles 41 and 42, to maintain or restore international peace and security'. This is the way in which Chapter VII of the Charter opens.

---

[49] *Casus foederis* refers to alliances; *casus garantiae* to collective security systems. Thus, the latter term is to be preferred when dealing with the United Nations system of collective security.

§ 51 General Layout of Chapter VII

What is the general layout of Chapter VII?

—*Article 39*: definition of situations in relation to which action under Chapter VII may be taken.
—*Article 40*: binding or non-binding provisional measures taken while the Council is examining the merits (for example, requiring a ceasefire). These measures may be binding if the Council so decides; in case of doubt, they will probably be held to be non-binding. This article was applied, for example, in the cases of Indonesia and Palestine in 1947.
—*Articles 41 and 42*: coercive measures and/or sanctions taken against a State than threatens the peace, has breached the peace or is an aggressor. These sanctions or measures may be non-military (article 41) or military (article 42). The Council may adopt measures that go beyond what would traditionally considered to be 'sanctions' (for the violation of the law), for example the creation of a criminal tribunal.
—*Articles 43 to 47*: the process and substantive devices for the establishment of a military force under the command of the United Nations.
—*Articles 48 and 49*: the binding character of measures taken by State members and the duty of mutual assistance in order to put them into practice. These provisions have to be read in conjunction with articles 2 § 5 and 25 of the Charter.
—*Article 50*: the process to address economic problems for member States arising from sanctions imposed by the Council.
—*Article 51*: the relationship between collective security and individual or collective self-defence.

In order to understand the spirit and operation of Chapter VII, a number of its aspects will be examined in closer detail.

§ 52 Dominating Idea of a Strong Executive

The main idea of Chapter VII is that the Security Council must be a strong executive that is capable of ensuring respect and able to effectively maintain peace. It must thus be an organ that 'has teeth' and not like the Council of the League of Nations that lacked powers for taking effective action and was humiliated by the arrogance of aggressor States sure of their impunity. In Chapter VII, the Charter does not therefore shy away from taking away from States elements of their sovereignty in a way never before seen. The experience of the League of Nations may be credited to a great measure for this development.

The considerable power enjoyed by the Security Council derives from three fundamental choices that were made.

First, the *absence of any meaningful legal limitations* on the exercise of Security Council action. The only real barrier to collective action is the need for consensus of the five permanent members and some support by the non-permanent members. This is a purely political condition. If there is agreement between the P5 States (and a majority in the Council, which is usually the case of the five permanent members are in agreement), the Council has the green light. There are no legal hoops through which the Council must jump, except a general requirement to act in accordance with the aims and purposes of the Charter, excessively malleable, in article 24 § 2.

Secondly, the *discretionary character* of almost all the powers conferred on the Security Council. The discretion enjoyed by the Council is evident throughout Chapter VII: for example, at the gates to Chapter VII, in the hazy standard of 'threat to the peace' (article 39); in the freedom to adopt binding or non-binding provisional measures at the Council's choice (article 40); in its discretion whether to adopt measures/sanctions or not; and whether to adopt a recommendation or a decision (both possibilities are granted in article 39); concerning the types of non-military measures, where the Council is not constrained by the type of measures listed in article 41; on the choice of adopting non-military or military measures, etc.

Thirdly, the Security Council, unlike the Council of the League of Nations, is a *permanent organ*. This means that its members are permanently based in New York. Consequently, a meeting of the Council can be convoked at any time and with little delay, at the very early stages of a crisis. This change was effected following the experience of the League of Nations, characterised by its considerable delays in gathering the Council round its session table in Geneva.[50]

The Charter thus provides a system based on the idea of some form of world federalism that is limited to the urgent needs of maintaining international peace.

§ 53 Article 39: The Keystone to the System

All action under Chapter VII presupposes a qualification by the Council of a situation that must, in its eyes, represent a 'threat to the peace, a breach of the peace or an act of aggression'.[51] The qualification 'act of aggression' is a concept that is rarely used by the Council. Why target for no compelling reason a State and limit the margins of diplomatic manoeuvre by designating it as an aggressor? Indeed, there is no need to qualify an act as an 'act of aggression' in order for the Council to take action under Chapter VII. The three concepts 'act of aggression', 'breach of the peace' and 'threat to the peace' are alternatives. Contrary to the concept of aggression, the 'breach of the peace' is a statement of fact: there are hostilities on the ground; this is sufficient to trigger that concept. In this respect, unlike aggression, the Council is not directly taking a position on the respective culpability of the States concerned (except perhaps

---

[50] The result was as follows: 'Nothing was ready at the beginning of the session, and measures were sought to cover this embarrassing situation. For example, a rapporteur or a Committee was asked to prepare a draft of a resolution. In reality, what was asked to do was to negotiate with the most interested and influential delegates in order to draft a text that they could all agree upon. But how could men who are not magicians accomplish such a miracle? In relation to the most serious, complex and sensitive international situations, would one think States to find a collective response in a matter of days or weeks?': M Bourquin, *Vers une nouvelle Société des Nations* (Neuchatel, 1945) 103ff, 176 (unofficial translation).

[51] With only some rare exceptions, notably the removal of sanctions decided under Chapter VII. This decision operates by virtue of the same Chapter VII but presuppose that the threat to the peace now no longer exists.

implicitly, like in the case of Kuwait, 1990). The Council limits itself to making a state-ment of fact, namely that hostilities are ongoing. Lastly, there is the concept of 'threat to the peace'. This concept can be approached from three different but related angles: the first objective, the second mixed objective–subjective, the third subjective. First, objectively, this concept refers to an immediate threat of inter-State hostilities such as preparations to go to war, transfer of troops, war rhetoric, etc. Secondly, the concept can also refer to the existence of tension about an, even minor, object between two States that have difficult, if not explosive, relations. A small border incident could be of great concern if it occurs between India and Pakistan, whereas it would be of less importance if it occurred between France and Germany today. Thirdly, in a subjective way, the concept finally opens the door to the use of discretionary powers by the Council.[52] A threat to the peace is that what the Council considers it to be, ideally taking into account the views and concerns of the international community about a certain state of affairs. The powers conceded to the Council in this subjective layer pave the way for an approach of international governance. In the 1990s, the Council was often faced with a collective will to act in situations that were deplorable from the humanitarian or political point of view. This overwhelming will of a somewhat diffuse international community prompted the Council to qualify the situation as constitut-ing a threat to the peace. It was not the threat to the peace which pushed the Council to act; it was the collective will of action which made the Council qualify a situation as a threat to the peace. This was the path to follow in order to be in a position to exer-cise the legal power of taking binding measures. Gradually, the Council has come to be regarded as an organ of some sort of world governance. As the only organ able to act with binding force and to impose measures of member States, a number of its actions aim at echoing 'fundamental values of the international community', or at least of the political majority of the day. In this way, the International Criminal Tribunal for the former Yugoslavia was established (Resolution 808, 1993) in order to respond to grave violations of international humanitarian law and human rights law; usurper governments that provoked refugee crises were sanctioned (Haiti, Resolution 875, 1993); repression of civilian populations was sanctioned and assistance to these populations was organised (Iraq, Resolution 688, 1991); the extradition of terrorists and the fight against terrorism occurred (Libya, Resolution 748, 1992; Resolution 1373 and others), etc. The hyperactivity of the Council did not stop after 11 September 2001. If the Council has at times been less willing to authorise the use of force, it has continued with rhythmical regularity to take other measures (fight against terrorism, disarmament, respect for human rights and international humanitarian law in non-international armed conflicts, etc).

The power to qualify a situation under article 39 is not one that the Security Council can delegate to States. It is a power that only it, alone, can use. The Charter grants it to the Security Council with respect to its composition and its function within the United Nations organisation (thus the grant is *intuitu personae*). The Council is not, however, precluded from delegating its power to the General Assembly and the Assembly could exercise residually this type of power by making simple recommenda-tions. Resolution 377 (V) could constitute the basis of this delegation of power. This

---

[52] On this discretionary power and its limits, see the case of *Tadic*, International Criminal Tribunal for the former Yugoslavia, Appeals Chamber, judgment of 1995, § 31ff.

transfer of power would not imply a decentralisation of the collective measures. The initiation of action remains in the hands of a collective organ of the United Nations. There is thus no reason to exclude the Council from passing this power to the General Assembly, which the final words of article 12 § 1 seem to allow. Does this mean, however, that the Council could also delegate to the General Assembly the power to make a binding decision on its behalf to the effect that there is a threat to the peace or a breach of the peace or eventually an aggression? This is not an easy issue. The response depends on a preliminary determination as to whether and to what extent an organ can exercise some powers that were ad hoc conferred on it, without any conferral of such powers under the Charter itself. It is recognised that States may attribute their decision-making powers to the General Assembly in matters that interest them. It is not, however, clear whether the Council can delegate its decision-making power since the Charter may oblige the Council itself to exercise that power. The question requires greater examination than can be provided here. It might be ventured that if the Charter does not exclude such a transfer of power, it could be considered to be lawful, but only for a specific case and not as a general grant of power. Conversely, it might be argued that a power conceded *intuitu personae* cannot be lawfully delegated at all.

§ 54 Articles 41 and 42: Considerable Powers of the Council

Once a qualification under article 39 has been made, the Council can adopt measures and sanctions that aim to maintain or re-establish international peace and security. These powers are highly discretionary. With the enlarging of the *casus garantiae* to a whole host of different situations that do not constitute a traditional threat to the peace—such as civil wars, human rights and international humanitarian law violations, extreme suffering of civilian populations due to famine and the collapse of States structures—it follows that the scope of measures to respond to such situations under articles 41 and 42 would also be expanded. Here, again, the decision as to which measures to take is a decision that can only be made by the Security Council. It is a power that cannot be delegated or left to member States. However, putting such measures and sanctions into practice can and must be exercised by State members. The organisation does not have the means to do this itself. A separate analysis of articles 41 and 42 is warranted at this juncture.

§ 55 Article 41

This article covers binding, non-military, measures that the Council can adopt. The text of the article provides as follows:

> The Security Council may decide what measures not involving the use of armed force are to be employed to give effect to its decisions, and it may call upon the Members of the United Nations to apply such measures. These may include complete or partial interruption of

economic relations and of rail, sea, air, postal, telegraphic, radio, and other means of communication, and the severance of diplomatic relations.

In its text, the article provides notably that such measures may include interruption of communications of all types with the sanctioned State, with humanitarian exceptions, as practice has shown.[53] Such sanctions are often adopted. The oldest example in the United Nations law is South Rhodesia (Resolution 232, 1966).[54] Similarly, the Council has often imposed arms embargos (Somalia, Liberia, Haiti, Angola, Sierra Leone, etc) or restricted commerce on petroleum (Haiti), or on certain goods (for example, diamonds: Angola, Sierra Leone).

However, the Council is not limited to imposing only these types of measures. Others can also be imposed under article 41[55] as long as they do not overstep the boundaries of the very discretionary powers of the Council and they are not of a military nature: (1) the creation of the ad hoc criminal tribunals (former Yugoslavia, Resolution 808, 1993; Rwanda, Resolution 955, 1994; Lebanon, Resolution 1757, 2007); temporary administrations on territories such as East Timor and Kosovo (for East Timor, Resolution 1272, 1999; for Kosovo, Resolution 1244, 1999); quasi-legislative measures, for example, in the fight against terrorism (for example, the famous Resolution 1373)[56] or weapons of mass destruction (Resolution 1540). All binding non-military measures that the Council may adopt are covered by article 41; it operates as a residual clause.

According to an interpretation of article 41, the Council can also take such measures in response to violations of fundamental rules of international law, even if there is no real threat to the peace. The sanction of international law would be a case of a 'threat against the peace' construed in legal terms. This approach corresponds to the extensive practice of article 39 followed in the 1990s. Alternatively, the UN could avail themselves of a power to adopt counter-measures under general international law, when the norm of international law having been violated had an *erga ownes* nature. However, the sanction of the law entrusted to a political organ remains selective, as it is practised on a case by case basis and unevenly. Moreover, the measures adopted under article 41 can be combined with an authorisation from the Security Council to member States of the United Nations in order to ensure their respect by the use of force. Article 42 measures, centred on the use of force, are here used to ensure compliance with the peaceful measures adopted under article 41. We could thus speak of an 'article 41½' of the Charter. Thus, article 42 can serve not only to sanction the State having threatened or breached the peace; it can also serve as an instrument to lend effectiveness to article 41 measures against the States not complying with these measures.

Are there specific limits to the action of the Security Council under article 41? For us, there are two.

First, the Council cannot *legislate*. The Council is not a legislative organ. It is an executive organ of limited State representation. No organ is less appropriate for the

---

[53] See DL Tehindrazanarivelo, *Les sanctions des Nations Unies et leurs effets secondaires* (Paris, 2005) 137ff.

[54] See V Gowlland–Debbas, *Collective Responses to Illegal Acts in International Law, United Nations Action in the Question of Southern Rhodesia* (Dordrecht, 1990); PM Eisemann, *Les sanctions contre la Rhodésie* (Paris, 1972).

[55] Alternatively, the idea of unwritten rules under Chapter VII could be retained.

[56] See also Resolutions 1377 (2001); 1438 (2002); 1440 (2002); 1450 (2002); 1452 (2002), etc.

task of legislation. The grant of such powers would be analogous on the domestic level to saying that the chief of police had the power to legislate. The Council can of course adopt emergency measures in order to maintain order, but these measures can only be localised, limited in time and directly related to the functions of an executive. It is self-evident that, for example, the Council can adopt rules governing the United Nations forces stationed in Kosovo. These acts, however, remain within its domain of activities within the United Nations as they concern the organisation's own forces in the field. Such measures do not impose general obligations on State members. Recent anti-terrorism measures adopted by the Council have, however, verged on creating an international legislation in the proper sense of the term. As legislation, they are of a doubtful legal quality. Nevertheless, the widespread (if sometimes grudging) acceptance of these measures by member States may be considered as a seal of approval for the exceptional legality of these Council acts in this particular case of emergency.

Secondly, the Security Council cannot *settle disputes* by mandatory decisions under Chapter VII. The settlement of disputes is provided in Chapter VI under which the Council only disposes of powers of recommendation. The Council cannot, therefore, undermine this clear stipulation by imposing Chapter VII measures in order to settle a dispute according to its own preferences, through a solution which may reflect a political compromise. The Munich Agreement of 1938 could not have taken place within the framework of the Charter of the United Nations. An exception to this limitation to Council powers in the settlement of disputes might eventually be conceded, if there is a legal dispute that the Council qualifies as a situation threatening the peace. The Council could attempt to oblige the parties to settle the dispute before the ICJ. The resolution of the Security Council would constitute the basis for the Court's jurisdiction. This would be action at the very brink of United Nations legality, which perhaps even oversteps this mark. If quite improbable on the facts, such action would legally not be unimaginable today,[57] particularly as there are no rule of law objections to such a course: the law would be applied in the context of a procedure that guarantees procedural fairness.[58] There would, however, have to be an exception in such a case to the consensual jurisdiction of the Court, whereby all parties before the Court must have agreed to its jurisdiction. This principle of consent has, however, developed in the jurisprudence of the Court. It is not based on the Court's Statute where the exercise of non-consensual jurisdiction remains at least possible. Article 36 § 1 of the Statute states that the Court has jurisdiction in all cases that the parties refer to it 'and all matters specifically provided for in the Charter of the United Nations . . .' This last phrase could, if one wished, be interpreted in the above mentioned way, even though the word 'specifically' remains problematic.

In sum, the real limits to the measures that the Security Council can impose are grounded on the rule of law.

---

[57] Even if the idea of such a binding resolution of the Security Council as establishing the jurisdiction of the Court was rejected at the San Francisco Conference. See M Bourquin, 'Pouvoir scientifique et droit international' (1947) 70(1) *RCADI* 387.

[58] In this vein, see C Tomuschat, 'Article 36' in A Zimmermann, C Tomuschat and K Oellers–Frahm (eds), *The Statute of the International Court of Justic,: A Commentary* (Oxford, OUP, 2006) 617, MN 45. And see already Kelsen, 'The Settlement of Disputes by the Security Council', above n 20 at 213.

§ 56 Article 42

This article concerns the coercive military measures that the Council may adopt. The text of the article reads as follows:

> Should the Security Council consider that measures provided for in Article 41 would be inadequate or have proved to be inadequate, it may take such action by air, sea, or land forces as may be necessary to maintain or restore international peace and security. Such action may include demonstrations, blockade, and other operations by air, sea, or land forces of Members of the United Nations.

This is the heart of collective security. Military force may be used against the aggressor and any recalcitrant State targeted by the Security Council. It is the ultimate sanction of the Charter. Article 42 is closely linked to the two provisions preceding and following it: articles 41 and article 43.

First, article 41. According to the text of article 42, the Security Council enjoys a discretionary power to try to address the situation by imposing peaceful measures (article 41), or to move immediately to imposing military measures (article 42). Political prudence demands that the principles of necessity, progressiveness and proportionality, are taken into account. Generally, less strong, less risky, less onerous measures should first be tried. However, everything turns on the Security Council's consideration of the situation. The Charter does not impose any limits in this respect; in its eyes the executive must be strong and unconstrained by rigid rules. Thus, article 42 provides that the Council may consider that the measures under article 41 would be inadequate, without having tried them, and pass directly to military measures under article 42.

Following, article 43. The original idea of the Charter was that military action decided to be taken by virtue of article 42, would then be carried out by military forces placed under the command of the Council. Everything would be centralised: the decision qualifying the situation under article 39; the impulsion of action under 42; and the carrying out of such action on the ground under article 43. Article 43 thus provided the means by which the Council could put into practice the measures decided under article 42. Article 42 provides the rules of the game, the football rules; article 43 provides the ball with which to play. However, article 43 has never been operational. The Cold War quickly buried any hope that member States, notably the most powerful States, would place contingents of armed forces at the disposal of the Security Council. Arm the United Nations with a formidable military force? Lose control over one's armed forces placed at the disposal of a foreign super-State? Share one's armed forces with others with whom one has little sympathy? From the USSR perspective, to allow a Western dominated armed force, in addition to a Western dominated organisation? All this explains why article 43 has remained dormant even after the end of the Cold War.[59] The legal significance of this fact is that the United Nations found itself incapacitated to exercise the coercive military action provided under article 42. Lacking its own military forces, it could not go into battle. 'How many armed contingents has the Vatican got at its disposal?' Stalin ironically asked. And how many armed contingents has the United Nations got? one could add.

---

[59] On the concrete stumbling blocks, see Luard, *A History of the United Nations* vol I, above n 22 at 98ff.

In order not to leave the United Nations in completely incapabale of contributing to the principal finality for which it was created, a system of substitution was quickly devised. It was perfected during the 1990s. If the United Nations did not possess armed forces, the member States certainly did. Thus, the United Nations could authorise (or grant a mandate to) States willing to execute by military force the decisions adopted by the Council. There would thus be a collective decision that the situation satisfies the requirements of article 39 and that it is appropriate to use force; and there would then be a decentralised execution of this decision on the ground by those States ready to act. Nevertheless, a dangerous element of decentralisation was thenceforward instilled in the system. States would on the one hand act in the name of the Council, but could on the other hand act in their own interests and following their own agendas. The collective finalities of the United Nations could thus be used as a mask behind which States could hide their real motives. However, the choice between complete inaction and imperfect action was made; the United Nations chose the lesser of the two evils. Under this new system of authorisations to use force on behalf of the United Nations, decentralised action as an exercise of collective security began to look very much like a form of collective self-defence. The *casus garantiae*, which is the basis of authorised action by the Council, remained, however, broader as the *casus foederis* of collective self-defence. Indeed, the Council can authorise action far beyond the restrictive scope of responding to an armed attack under article 51. The Council can authorise an action to 're-establish the peace in the region'. This notion encompasses much more than the simple power to counter an adverse attack, which is the only right conceded in an exercise of self-defence. This new approach to military action authorised by the Security Council was not generally accepted at first. Some States, notably the USSR, saw it as a way of circumvention of article 42 and thus in a blatant violation of the text of the Charter. It thought that decentralised action could not take the place of the system established at San Francisco without a formal revision of the Charter text. Form the 1970s onwards these controversies died down. The decentralised solution was definitively established as a general practice in the 1990s.

In summary, it may be said that an argument about preservation of the strictly collective character of military action from the beginning to the end of an operation lost to a counter-argument based on the effectiveness of the Charter: it is better to act beyond what the Charter text provided, than not to act at all and thus to condemn the UN to increasing irrelevancy in the area of international peace, which is the main function of the organisation. The ICJ appeared, in the 1962 opinion of *Certain Expenses*, to lend support for the latter argument. In the different context of consensual peacekeeping operations, the Court used an argument of effectiveness to support its flexible interpretation of the Charter: 'Moreover, an argument which insists that all measures taken for the maintenance of international peace and security must be financed through agreement concluded under Article 43, would seem to exclude the possibility that the Security Council might act under some other Article of the Charter. The Court cannot accept so limited a view of the powers of the Security Council under the Charter. It cannot be said that the Charter has left the Security Council important in the face of an emergency situation when agreements under Article 43 have not been concluded.'[60] If this interpretation based on effectiveness is followed, articles 42 and

---

[60] *Certain Expenses of the United Nations* (Advisory Opinion) [1962] ICJ Rep 167.

43 read together only provide for one measure among many according to which the Council can use force. There remain other measures at the Council's disposal, according to the doctrine of implied powers. In other terms, the Council could look for other balls for the football match, other than the leaked one proposed by article 43.

§ 57 Sanctions Committees

The Security Council cannot be in charge of the daily administration of all the sanctions that it imposes. The number of sanctions imposed, as well as the need to manage them on a day to day basis, does not permit this. For example, the sanctions programme of 'Oil for Food' established for Iraq required detailed control of transactions, management of blocked accounts in which the funds from the sale of Iraqi petrol were deposited, the granting of importation licences, etc. The Security Council thus created a 'Sanctions Committee' to exercise these administrative tasks. This committee forms part of a consistent practice dating back to the management of the sanctions adopted against South Rhodesia in 1966. Today, there exist more than ten Sanctions Committees.[61] The composition of these committees corresponds to that of the Council; they are thus 'committees of the whole'. However, the representation in the committees is diplomatically of a lower level. The committees constitute, from the legal point of view, a subsidiary organ of the Council. They are created by virtue of the powers conferred on the Council under article 29 of the Charter.

The principal task of the Committees is to take care of the administration of sanctions. To accomplish this mission, they examine the reports of the Secretary-General and member States concerning how such sanctions are to be put into practice. Further, the committees have a decision-making power for all questions concerning their execution. They also have the power to submit recommendations in order to make the sanctions more effective. Committees cannot make decisions that would alter the substance of the sanctions; they cannot make sweeping political decisions. Questions of this nature must be deferred to the Security Council.

The problems that these Committees have encountered in practice are of the following order: (1) the lack of transparency since the Committees function behind closed doors; (2) the lack of synergy between the Committees, each having a tendency not to coordinate with one another; this leads to heterogeneous, even unequal, results; and (3) the need to better target sanctions in order not to affect the civilian populations ('smart sanctions', 'intelligent sanctions'). There remains a general problem of a political nature. Sometimes certain States have blocked the ordinary functioning of the Committee in its daily management of sanctions in order to increase political pressure on the sanctioned State. Hence, in the case of Iraq, the United States of America and the United Kingdom at certain moments delayed granting importation licences for

---

[61] These are (state of affairs at the end of 2008): (1) Somalia (Resolution 751, 1992); (2) Rwanda (Resolution 918, 1994); (3) Sierra Leone (Resolution 1132, 1997); (4) Al-Qaida / Taliban (Resolution 1267, 1999); (5) fight against terrorism (Resolution 1373, 2001); (6) Iraq (Resolution 1518, 2003); (7) Liberia (Resolution 1521, 2003); (8) Democratic Republic of Congo (Resolution 1533, 2004); (9) Non-proliferation of nuclear, chemical and biological weapons (Resolution 1540, 2004); (10) Ivory Coast (Resolution 1572, 2004); (11) Sudan (Resolution 1591, 2005); (12) terrorist attacks in Lebanon (Resolution 1636, 2005); (13) People's Democratic Republic of Korea (Resolution 1718, 2006); (14) Iran (Resolution 1737, 2006).

certain types of foodstuffs and medical material, although such grants were authorised by the agreement 'Oil for Food', in order to exert additional pressure on Iraq. To overcome these weaknesses, a list of goods where the agreement of the Committee is established in advance has been elaborated.

§ 58 Residual Powers of the General Assembly: Resolution 377 (V) of 1950, 'Dean Acheson'

May only the Security Council authorise the use of force? It is uncontroversial that the Council is the only entity that can 'decide' to use force; but is it the only entity that can 'authorise' (ie, recommend) its use?

This question created a deadlock of opinion in the Council during the Korean crisis of 1950. The Council had responded to the aggression by North Korea (People's Democratic Republic of Korea) against South Korea (Republic of Korea) on 25 June 1950, taking advantage of the absence of the Soviet delegate who had boycotted the Council sessions because of a dispute concerning the legitimate representation of China in the Council.[62] As soon as the USSR became aware of the activities of the Council in its absence, it decided to return to its seat and blocked any further action by the exercise of its veto power. The problem became acute when the question arose if the UN forces should pursue the military operation north to the 38th parallel. The initial resolution of the Security Council had provided only for repelling the aggression; marching into the territory of North Korea in order to implement the UN plan for reunification of the Korean State needed some additional legal justification. A new resolution authorising such action could not be obtained in the Security Council because of the Soviet veto. Western States, and in particular the United States of America, responded by trying to mobilise the General Assembly into taking action against North Korea. Western States argued that while the General Assembly could not adopt binding measures, it could nevertheless exercise its right to recommend such measures. The recommendation would then have the effect of legitimatising the proposed military action. It was in this vein that on 3 November 1950, the General Assembly adopted Resolution 377 (V) entitled 'Uniting for Peace', also known as the 'Dean Acheson Resolution', named after the United States Secretary of State and Foreign Affairs at the time who had set in motion the initiative.

What are the contents of this Resolution?[63] In the case of inaction of the Security Council caused by a veto, namely, where the Council does not exercise its primary responsibility for the maintenance of peace,[64] the General Assembly may be convoked

---

[62] USSR was absent from the Council between 13 January 1950 and 1 August 1950.

[63] Herewith an extract of the relevant part of the Resolution, § 1: 'Resolves that if the Security Council, because of lack of unanimity of the permanent members, fails to exercise its primary responsibility for the maintenance of international peace and security in any case where there appears to be a threat to the peace, breach of the peace, or act of aggression, the General Assembly shall consider the matter immediately with a view to making appropriate recommendations to Members for collective measures, including in the case of a breach of the peace or act of aggression the use of armed force when necessary, to maintain or restore international peace and security'.

[64] Care must be taken in the use of implicit ideological arguments when referring to the Security Council being 'blocked'. Why do we only speak of the Council being 'blocked' when Russia, China, or even

in an extraordinary session following a simple procedural vote of the Council (a vote that consequently is not subject to the veto) that provides that the Council deletes the matter from its agenda, or that it refers the matter to the General Assembly. This would in turn open the way for State members to convene in accordance with article 9 (b), of the internal regulations of the Assembly in an extraordinary session. The emergency Assembly would then be able to adopt a recommendation, including one that recommended the use of force. The Charter permits the Assembly to adopt recommendations and to address all questions that fall within the scope of the powers of the organisation, including the maintenance of peace (article 11).[65] By removing the matter of its agenda or turning it over to the Assembly, the Council moreover eliminates the stumbling block of article 12, § 1, which reads: 'While the Security Council is exercising in respect of any dispute or situation the functions assigned to it in the present Charter, the General Assembly shall not make any recommendation with regard to that dispute or situation unless the Security Council so requests'. The recommendation of the Assembly would then lend legitimacy to the exercise of collective self-defence, or in any event have legally permissive effects. No member of the United Nations would incur responsibility for a wrongful act when carrying out the recommendation.

The adoption of the Resolution initially gave rise to bitter and epic debates.[66] The USSR and socialist States, that held a minority position in the organisation and deeply attached to the protection afforded by the veto power, argued that the Resolution was illegal. In accordance with the Charter of the United Nations, the Security Council had absolute priority for every sanctioning *action*, and in particular for military action. The Assembly can only generally discuss a question, not recommend a specific action. The Charter under article 11 § 2 protects the exclusive prerogatives of the Council to sanction or take any other form of concrete action.[67] The aim was obviously to safeguard the effectiveness of the Soviet veto. On the other side, Western States argued that the resolution was lawful. According to this argument, the Council only had 'primary responsibility' and not exclusive responsibility, for the maintenance of peace and security. The term 'primary' contained in article 24 § 1 of the Charter implies that there is also a secondary, subsidiary responsibility: that of the Assembly. With respect to Article 11 § 2, this provision only refers to coercive measures or action and not to

France threaten to use or indeed do use their veto powers, a right conferred by the Charter? Why can we not imagine a 'blocked' Council that focuses negatively on other Council members? Why do we not speak of the Council being 'blocked' when the United States exercises its veto power? After all, the United States is the State after the USSR that has had most recourse to the veto power. A 'blocked' Council is thus an ideological qualification that attempts to distinguish good vetoes from bad ones. In this vein, Chaumont was right when he wrote: 'It is not at all the case that the Council only exercises its functions when it passes effective resolutions. It can just as well be argued that the Council exercises its functions by the simple fact that it examined a situation and that after examining the situation it has not taken action, it has not adopted a resolution': C Chaumont, *Conceptions en vigueur à l'époque contemporaine sur la souveraineté et la sécurité internationale* (IHEI course, Paris, 1952–53) 31 (unofficial translation). This does not mean to say that the exercise of the power of veto (particularly when this becomes very repetitive) cannot be misused. Such misuse (abuse of rights) is a fair assessment of the behaviour of the USSR during the 1950s.

[65] See art 10 of the Charter.

[66] See LB Sohn, *Cases on United Nations Law* (Cambridge, MA, 1967) 474ff. For a historical and political summary, see A Fontaine, *Histoire de la guerre froide*, vol II, (Paris, 1967) 24–25.

[67] The relevant phrase of this article provides as follows: 'Any such question [relating to the maintenance of international peace and security] on which action is necessary shall be referred to the Security Council by the General Assembly either before or after discussion'.

recommendations. Lastly, the flexible and broad interpretation best corresponds with the aims of the Charter since it provides an efficient response to breaches of the peace. The aim of this line of reasoning was to rob the veto of its radical blocking power. These two lines of arguments, one conservative and literal, the other progressive and teleological, represented masterpieces of legal argumentation conveyed with skill and with force. To which should preference be given?

The ICJ was able to provide some guidance on the question, although without alleviating all uncertainty. In the advisory opinion of *Certain Expenses* (1962), the Court adopted the flexible approach supported by Western States in the context of the establishment of peacekeeping forces. The Court held that no coercive action could be taken by the General Assembly. However, the peacekeeping force (UNEF in this instance) was the subject of an agreement between the parties to the dispute, namely the States on whose territory the forces were stationed (Egypt/Israel). Thus, no coercive action was at stake. According to the Court, the Council did not enjoy exclusive powers under the Charter to guarantee this sort of action between States and in relation to which the United Nations provided logistical support.[68] The question that manifestly remains is whether the Assembly may recommend a course of forcible action when the State concerned *does not consent* to such measures. To this question the Court gave no answer, since the facts did not compel it to consider the point. The Court only ruled out one thing: the Assembly could not *decide* to impose a concrete sanction, measure or action; however, this does not expressly exclude the possibility of the Assembly making a *recommendation* in that respect. In any event, the rule must be applied according to which it is presumed that action by an organ of the United Nations is taken in conformity with its powers (*intra vires*).[69]

In light of subsequent practice—and despite the fact that the legality of the resolution has continued to remain controversial[70]—it is possible to state today that such action would not be contrary to the Charter. Since 1950, practice demonstrates an acceptance for a larger role of the General Assembly. The Council has often referred disputes to the General Assembly, even though the latter did not recommend a use of force. Some instances of this practice include the Suez crisis (1956), where the USSR itself cited the Acheson Resolution as a ground; following the Soviet invasion of Hungary (1956); during the Congo crisis (1960); in the situation leading to the independence of Bangladesh (1971); or in case of the occupied Arab territories in 1982. The Acheson Resolution was also used for other purposes, such as to invite States to attend an international meeting on the application of the Fourth Geneva Convention, relative to the protection of civilians during armed conflicts, to the occupied Palestinian territories.[71] The resolution was even used to convoke extraordinary sessions of the General Assembly in relation to the Israeli occupied territories. This has been the case since 1997 where extraordinary sessions have been convoked year after

---

[68] Above n 59, in particular at 163–65.

[69] *Ibid*, 168.

[70] Those who oppose the validity of the resolution include: L di Qual, *Les effets des résolutions des Nations Unies* (Paris, 1971) 159ff; M Bourquin, *L'Etat souverain et l'organisation internationale* (New York, 1959) 94ff. In favour of validity were: FA Vallat, 'The General Assembly and the Security Council of the United Nations' (1952) 29 *BYIL* 94; P Manin, *L'oranisation des Nations Unies et le maintien de la paix* (Paris, LGDJ, 1971) 138ff.

[71] See Resolutions 10/3 and 10/9 of the 10th Extraordinary Session. On this process *cf* PY Fux and M Zambelli, 'Mise en œuvre de la Quatrième Convention de Genève dans les territoires Palestiniens occupées: historique d'un processus multilatérale (1997–2001)' in (2002) 84 *International Review of the Red Cross* 661ff.

year. Finally, a request for an advisory opinion of the ICJ on the *Legal Consequences of the Construction of a Wall in the Occupied Palestinian Territory* (2004) was handed down in such an emergency session.[72]

In conclusion, the resolution has been turned on its head with respect to the main idea of its original application. Whereas it was created in order to provide a power of recommendation for a use force in the absence of Council action, the resolution has only been applied and used in the practice of the United Nations to recommend peaceful measures undertaken by the Assembly in situations of emergency. This does not mean that a recommendation to use force would be contrary to the law of today. Rather, practice has not made use of the 'use of force' aspect of the resolution. It is used mainly today in order to convoke extraordinary sessions of the General Assembly. It is understandable that the Assembly will not recommend the use of force if the major military powers of the Security Council are not ready to accept it, since such a recommendation would then remain meaningless and even be dangerous. It is only in highly exceptional cases that a use of force flowing from the Acheson Resolution could provide a proper answer to a situation on the ground.

§ 59 Operations for the Maintenance of Peace

During the mid-1950s, Dag Hammarskjöld, the Secretary-General of the organisation, followed a proposal made by Lester Pearson, the Canadian Minister of Foreign Affairs at the time and made a case for a peacekeeping force that would physically separate the contending parties in the Suez war and thus help to de-escalate the tension in the region by allowing a progressive repatriation of the French and British armed forces.[73] Thus, the first operation for the maintenance of peace, the United Nations Emergency Force I (UNEF I), was created and deployed in 1956/1957.[74] The success of this initiative led to its repeat some 49 times between 1949 and 2000.[75] This practice gave rise to an international custom on peacekeeping operations of the United Nations. From 1965 onwards, the Special Committee on Peacekeeping Operations established norms to govern the activities of peacekeeping operations, including 'Status of forces agreement models'. These norms constituted regulation models relating to the status of the troops once they were posted to a particular territory. In relation to the concrete activities they could carry out on the ground, these were non-coercive measures situated between Chapters VI and VII of the Chapter. It is for this reason that some people speak of a 'Chapter VI½', following the words of Dag Hammarskjöld. Such operations can also simply be based on non-written law of the Charter that has developed from subsequent institutional custom.

In the first years, there have been essentially two different types of peacekeeping forces: (1) forces that are military observers (for example, the United Nations Military

---

[72] See, *Legal Consequences of the Construction of a Wall in the Occupied Palestinian Territory* (Advisory Opinion) [2004] ICJ Rep § 18ff.

[73] On the creation of this force, see WR Frye, *A United Nations Peace Force* (New York, 1957).

[74] Beforehand there had only been military observer missions, in, eg, Indonesia in 1947.

[75] For an overview of these operations, see M Bothe and T Dörschel, *United Nations Peacekeeping— A Documentary Introduction* (The Hague; London; Boston, 1999).

Observer Group in India and Pakistan, established in 1949 on the territory of Cashmere); and (2) peacekeeping forces that maintain a ceasefire line (for example, the UNEF I which ran from 1956 to 1967 and the United Nations Peacekeeping Force in Cyprus which remains in place since 1964, albeit this force had also a larger mandate, etc). These traditional operations for maintaining peace are based on a number of organisational principles. These principles have become crystallised in practice:

1. Forces are established by the Security Council (or exceptionally the General Assembly, basing itself of the 'Uniting for Peace' resolution like in the case of UNEF I which has remained the only force created by a General Assembly resolution). They are placed under the control of the Secretary-General, who is the real metronome behind their activities. He reports on their activities to the Security Council (or the Assembly). The forces are thus a subsidiary organ of either the Council or the Assembly.
2. The consent of the territorial State(s) concerned by the deployment of the forces is indispensable. Moreover if a permanent member of the Security Council were to oppose a particular operation, then it would not take place (except where the Assembly acts under the 'Uniting for Peace' Resolution). The consent of the territorial States may be withdrawn at any time. It would require all peacekeeping forces to immediately leave the territory. This occurred in relation to UNEF I when Egypt withdrew its consent on 1967. The UN can however try to exert some pressure on local government(s) in order to maintain the force and not to ask for its withdrawal. This happened during the Congo Operation (1960–1963).
3. Military personnel are provided by State members of the United Nations or by non-member States on a voluntary basis. Military personnel from the five permanent Council members do not take part in such operations (but logistic support or the participation of administrative personnel from such States is allowed).
4. Peacekeeping forces cannot use weapons, except in the case of self-defence, namely when they are attacked. Cases of uses of force outside exercises of self-defence were rare until 1990. They occurred in the Congo crisis in 1960, in order to oppose the secession of Katanga. Controversy had surrounded this use of force.
5. Peacekeeping forces do not interfere in the internal affairs of the host State. The mandate is limited to peacekeeping or observance missions.

As can be seen from these principles, the activities of traditional peacekeeping forces walk a fine line between Chapters VI and VII, articles 34 to 42, of the Charter. With the emergence of a robust form of peacekeeping in the 1990s, the limits between these two Chapters of the Charter are increasingly blurred.

Since the 1990s, a two-fold evolution has occurred.

In the first instance, there has been a noticeable increase in the number of tasks conferred on forces for the maintenance of peace. Often, these missions are not simply charged with monitoring a ceasefire between two conflicting parties, but they are required to take on civilian administrative tasks, to monitor the human rights situation, to distribute humanitarian aid, to supervise local elections, to arrest individuals and even to participate in 'nation building' activities. The number of activities that international peacekeeping forces must undertake in modern operations is impressive. Herewith some examples: mitigate tensions and stabilise the general situation; create order; supervise peace agreements; supervise the withdrawal of troops; watch over a ceasefire; supervise disarmament; secure roads, airports etc; de-mine; inspect demili-tarised zones; undertake inquiries into incidents; inform the public; track down an arrest war criminals; distribute health and humanitarian relief; rebuild infrastructure; supervise the movement of refugees; escort humanitarian convoys; run the civil admin-istration; organise and control elections and assist in the electoral process; train local police forces; ensure the running of local justice systems; create democratic institutions and strengthen the rule of law; ensure the protection of minorities; create the neces-sary conditions for economic development, etc. International forces have thus become partial or total substitutes for governments within a certain timespan. In other words, international organisations, through the personnel of State members at their disposal, temporarily assume the exercise of the prerogatives of a territorial sovereignty. Some critically refer to this phenomenon as a new form of 'international protectorates'. Such multifunctional operations have taken place for instance in Somalia, in the Central African Republic and in Angola.

In the second instance there has been an increase in the power of peacekeeping forces to use force, notably in order to implement the specific mission at hand. Often the peacekeeping force itself is authorised to use force. An example of such a 'robust peacekeeping' (or 'peace enforcement' operation) was the United Nations operation in Somalia II (UNOSOM II) in 1992. At other times it is other entities that have been sent to provide extra support for the peacekeeping forces that may resort to a use of force. For example, NATO received authorisation to intervene, including authorisation to use force, to support United Nations forces stationed in Bosnia-Herzegovina. Further, in the mid-1990s, the Security Council delegated its task of maintaining international peace and security to multinational forces that were not under the command of the United Nations. To do this, the Security Council chose to 'authorise' the use of force following the example of its practice under Chapter VII. Consequently, a centrifugal pull affected operations for the maintenance of peace. A degree of decentralisation and of privatisation has thus characterised these operations, which were previously thought to be firmly anchored to the collective crucible of the United Nations Security Council.[76] This was the case in 1995 concerning the mandate conferred in Resolution 1031 on the NATO-led Implementation Force (IFOR, Operation Joint Endeavour) in Bosnia and Herzegovina; and following with respect to the armed conflict situations in Albania (Resolution 1101, 1997); Central African Republic (Resolution 1125, 1997); Kosovo (Resolution 1244, 1999); East Timor (Resolution 1264, 1999); Afghanistan (Resolution 1368, 2001); the Ivory Coast (Resolution 1464, 2003); Liberia (Resolution 1497, 2003) and Haiti (Resolution 1529, 2004). Many peacekeeping forces were now established on the basis of Chapter VII of the Charter, such as the United Nations Protection Force for the former Yugoslavia (UNPROFOR).

In conclusion, there has been a slide from soft, consensual peacekeeping activities to a hard and coercive form of peacekeeping. These modern operations are more closely associated with Chapter VII of the Charter, making it tempting to speak of a 'Chapter VI½'. In such operations, the different components of peacekeeping and peace enforcement operations tend to be muddled. Traditional peacekeeping is based on two

---

[76] See J Cardona Llorens, 'Le maintien de la paix et recours à la force: entre l'autorisation des opérations de maintien de la paix et l'externalisation' in VIth meeting of the Faculty of Legal, Political and Social Sciences of Tunis, *Le droit international à la croisée des chemins* (Paris, 2004) 92ff.

axes: consent and buffer-zone logic. The new mechanism of peacekeeping or peace-enforcement is based on a decision of the Security Council (with the eventual consent of the parties concerned obtained through the exercise of numerous forms of pressure) and characterised by the variety and number of tasks performed by the forces. This evolution reflects the reality of a world which, following the Cold War, has seen a number of territories subjected to the aberrant power of States (failed States) and on which ethnic, political, social and economic conflicts have erupted. Often such territories have become ridden with armed criminal gangs. In such cases, classic peacekeeping operations are no longer an adequate response. An additional element of coercion is necessary to avoid the peacekeeping force itself becoming caught up in the chaos on the ground.

The problems that 'robust peacekeeping' has encountered are well known. These include the consequences of poorly planned operations, quickly decided in the smoke of momentary events; poorly coordinated forces on the ground lacking the necessary means to carry out their tasks; and ill defined tasks. The disappointment has often been in equal proportion to the magnified optimism invested in such operations following the end of the Cold War: UNOSOM II is an example in this respect. Calls to action are frequent in a world subject to so many crises and composed of many weak or failed States. However, there is a lack of adequate logistical and financial support for such needs. Moreover, the United Nations system, with its very limited means, cannot be the *Deus ex machina* for all the wrongs and crises in the world. The studied confusion surrounding consensual and coercive elements of the various operations adds to the lack of coherence. A clear definition and legal categorisation of such operations that are neither governed by an agreement with the host State, nor are peace enforcement measures in the strict sense of article 42, of the Charter is lacking. Practice proceeds on a case by case basis.

In some cases it may in fact be better not to intervene when the proposed operation lacks the necessary means to effectively address the situation on the ground and where the seriousness of the threat posed by armed factions is unclear. However, can intervention on the ground only occur when one is reasonably sure of its success? Would that not amount to abandoning many populations to their fate denying them possible help? Can the United Nations systematically put prudence above help?

§ 60 Outcome

Chapter VII has proven, to this day, to be a poorly-balanced chapter. It oscillates in a manic-depressive manner between phases of hypothermia, characterised by the short-circuiting of the Security Council (almost completely frozen during the Cold War), to phases of hypertension, characterised by extensive activities (almost a form of 'world governance' during the 1990s).[77] In the former case, States attempted to replace the Security Council with unilateral responses grounded on article 51 of the Charter, or to

---

[77] This was remarkably formulated by S Hoffmann, *Organisations internationales et pouvoirs politiques des Etats* (Paris, 1954) 269: the Security Council is omnipotent in cases of agreement by the great powers (especially the P5), whereas it is impotent in cases of disagreement of the great powers.

revitalise other organs of the United Nations like the General Assembly or the Secretary General. In relation to the latter case, there have been questions as to whether the Security Council had not abused its discretionary powers. Several voices have required stricter legal control, such as judicial control by the ICJ. The Council was perceived by some as acting in a too pronounced way in accordance with the particular policy of some of its members. It finally lost considerable credibility in the eyes of some member States. The organisation remains intact, but its prestige has been affected.

From 11 September 2001 onwards, other features of the Council complicated the fluctuations between hypothermia and hypertension. The Council remained remarkably active in the area of collective governance, attested by its bold activities in the areas of anti-terrorism and disarmament. On the other hand, it has experienced difficulties in its principal mission, that of deciding whether or not to use force in exercising its powers for collective security. In this respect, the United States of America, followed by other Western States, brandished the threat of intervening militarily if necessary without the assent of the Council. Iraq (2003) is the most emblematic example of this course. The United Nations was thus reduced to a walk-on role. If it did not grant the assent sought then it would be marginalised and branded as irrelevant; if it did assent it would be seen as a servant to one great power. If approval were not given, then it would have no other choice than to participate in the post-war management of the territory, in the form of a problematic transitory administration for which it would then depend on the goodwill of the powers having used force in contravention to its Charter. It is self-evident that control over all the essential questions would then be vested in the coalition forces while granting a secondary role to the United Nations for reasons of legitimacy-building. The organisation thus had to contend itself with sweeping up the crumbs in terms of management *jus post bellum* and not, as provided in the Charter, with the decision to use force (*jus ante bellum* and *jus ad bellum*) and all that follows. In addition, the organisation is required to take part in situations of occupation of territories by invading forces, in situations that are described by a non-negligible part of the UN membership as forms of neo-colonialism. The prestige of the organisation thus suffers. In Iraq, this loss of face was more serious for the United Nations than it was for the coalition forces, which after all only pay the price for the action in which they have engaged. Moreover, there remains the delicate problem of determining the extent to which the participation of the United Nations *post bellum* means an acceptance in fact or in law of the military action previously undertaken without its assent. Even though the organisation took great pains not to comment on this aspect, a number of Western commentators have argued that such participation amounts to a form of acquiescence. In the case of Iraq, this effect was almost achieved.[78] Consequently, the system of collective security experienced its last misadventure. Overall—to some extent analogously to the League of Nations where functional cooperation was successful but collective security ended in disaster—the United Nations is in a phase where Chapter VII works satisfactorily for all action not involving the use of force but remains ineffective in terms of action concerning the use of force (collective security in the narrow sense).

---

[78] See the strong criticisms from L Condorelli, 'Le Conseil de sécurité entre autoristion de la légitime défense et substitution de la sécurité collective. Remarques au sujet de la Résolution 1546' in Société française de droit internationale (ed), *Les métamorphoses de la sécurité collective, Journée franco–tunisienne* (Paris, 2005) 231ff.

Chapter VII is today more a basis for some form of world governance than a classi-cal system of collective security. The situation will, however, change. The misfortunes of any system of collective security are accompanied by a growth in violence and threats. This in turn induces the States to return to a more reasonably balanced collective system, based on the incontrovertible common management of crises. The movement from centralisation to decentralisation and back is never ending. It is the great fugal theme of collective security.

G. Article 2 § 7: Exclusive Domestic Jurisdiction and Non-intervention in Internal Affairs

§ 61 General Aspects

Article 2 § 7 covers two distinct aspects: (1) the principle of exclusive domestic jurisdic-tion concerning the relations of United Nations organs vis-à-vis member States; and (2) the principle of a non-intervention in the interval affairs in the relations between States, in conjunction with article 2 § 1. The first principle operates on a vertical level, whereas the second principle operates on a horizontal level. The practical value of these two principles also differs quite fundamentally.

—*Exclusive domestic jurisdiction.* The exclusive domestic jurisdiction of a State was reg-ulated by article 15 § 8 of the Covenant of the League of Nations. It was natural that when the United Nations was created, its strongly political character made some States concerned by its propensity to become involved in matters which States consid-ered to belong to the exclusive realm of their domestic politics and law. Would the organisation address issues of immigration, customs law and tax? Article 2 § 7 repro-duces in an enlarged version the restriction contained in the Covenant. Article 2, § 7, thus provides: 'Nothing contained in the present Charter shall authorize the United Nations to intervene in matters which are essentially within the domestic jurisdiction of any state or shall require the Members to submit such matters to settlement under the present Charter; but this principle shall not prejudice the application of enforce-ment measures under Chapter VII'. This text was supported by, among others, the United States of America and the USSR. One notable difference with the Covenant is that the Charter text does not restrict the concept to 'exclusive domestic jurisdiction' but enlarges it to areas 'essentially within the domestic jurisdiction'. Under the Covenant, the concept was qualitative; under the Charter it becomes quantitative; its application is thus further complicated.

The principle concerning domestic jurisdiction mainly serves a political and psycho-logical function. It attempts to delimit the powers of the organisation and those of the States. However, legally, the scope of the concept is very limited. Indeed, international organisations do not possess sovereignty that would allow them act as they please in all areas of international relations. The powers of organisations are those that have been attributed to them in their constituent charter. This is also referred to as the 'principle of speciality' (*principe de spécialité*). Either a power has not been attributed and an organisation cannot therefore exercise it (independently from the domestic jurisdiction of a States) or the power has been attributed and thus the organisation can exercise this power despite a claim that it would be acting within the domestic jurisdiction of a State. The principle concerning domestic jurisdiction perhaps requires that the organisation takes care when interpreting its attributed powers. Some degree of restriction would be required from it. However, the principle is not particularly strict: interpretations of an organisation's attributed powers to adapt to new needs (notably by the technique of implied powers or by accepted subsequent practice) would not be contrary to this principle.

United Nations practice, like other organisations, has showed that the principle on domestic jurisdiction has been in decline in an increasingly interdependent world and in relation to an organisation that has considerable powers attributed to it by the Charter in almost all areas, from security, to economic and social conditions, to human rights. What areas would fall within the essentially domestic jurisdiction of States and in relation to which the organisations could not discuss or adopt resolutions? In effect, practice has developed an opposing concept, a 'matter of international concern'. All matters that have international repercussions, that is, all matters that affect the rights and interests of other States, are considered matters that the organisation can discuss and about which it can pass resolutions (recommendations).[79] Consequently, from the very first year of its existence,[80] the United Nations discussed and adopted recommendations in relation to the Franco regime in Spain; the law governing the immigration of Soviet wives of diplomats; the rights of the Indian population in South Africa; the racial conflict in South Africa; issues related to atomic energy; issues linked to decolonisation (Algeria, Morocco, Tunisia), etc. This practice shows how the principle concerning domestic jurisdiction was cast aside at the very beginning of the life of the organisation. The principle was thus like a plant that never took root. Consequently the deadbolt securing matters of domestic jurisdiction was prised open in subsequent practice of the United Nations. To this bold range of material powers of the United Nations organs to discuss issues of international concern and to pass resolutions on them, there is a powerful brake outside the domestic jurisdiction issue: formally, these organs can only recommend a solution and not decide (except under Chapter VII powers of the Security Council). The formal limitation counterbalances the material boundlessness. The system of the Charter finds its proper point of equilibrium in this particular balance.

—*Principle of non-intervention inter-State.* Non-intervention concerns situations where coercion is exercised by one or more States against one or other States, in order to subordinate the exercise of the latter's sovereign rights to the will of the former. According to the definition of this principle, articulated by the ICJ in *Case concerning Military and Paramilitary Activities in and against Nicaragua* (Merits, 1986): 'the principle forbids all States or groups of States to intervene directly or

---

[79] Similarly, the 'chain of events' doctrine was also rejected. According to this argument, no essentially domestic matter should be included on the business of the day of the United Nations, nor in discussion or resolutions, etc because once United Nations action was taken, it would snowball into increasing and persistent pressure. The principle concerning domestic jurisdiction was supposed to prevent this chain of events occurring.

[80] For an excellent overview, see MS Rajan, *United Nations and Domestic Jurisdiction* (Bombay; Calcutta; Madras, 1958).

indirectly in internal or external affairs of other States. A prohibited intervention must accordingly be one bearing on matters in which each State is permitted, by the principle of State sovereignty, to decide freely. One of these is the choice of a political, economic, social and cultural system, and the formulation of foreign policy. Intervention is wrongful when it uses methods of coercion in regard to such choices, which must remain free ones'.[81] What amounts to intervention depends on the context and dependency of one State on another. Intervention was invoked with respect to Arab States when they attempted to influence European policy about Israel by imposing a petroleum embargo in 1970. Similarly, intervention may be argued to exist more easily than on average when a former colonised State confronts the former colonising State because of the particular dependencies. The most extreme form of intervention is the use of force or the threat of its use. In such a case, the prohibition on the use of force, as well as the principle of non-intervention may both be violated. There are also exceptional cases, defined in customary law, where the prohibited intervention is not based on the exertion of pressure. This is the case when a foreign State recognises prematurely the secession or control of part of another State's territory by rebels. The application of the principle of non-intervention in concrete cases often creates problems, because to some extent all foreign policies try to influence the policies of others in some way, by using weaker or stronger forms of pressure. Each application of pressure is, therefore, not prohibited; international relations cannot be conceived in a state of weightlessness. It is the excess pressure that must be sanctioned. In football, tackling and shoulder to shoulder plays are allowed; but tripping is not. The whole problem is to define the threshold of such excessive pressure. This cannot be done without some consideration of the particular features of each type of concrete relationship.

Resolution 2625 describes the content of the principle as follows:

> No State or group of States has the right to intervene, directly or indirectly, for any reason whatever, in the internal or external affairs of any other State. Consequently, armed intervention and all other forms of interference or attempted threats against the personality of the State or against its political, economic and cultural elements, are in violation of international law.

> No State may use or encourage the use of economic political or any other type of measures to coerce another State in order to obtain from it the subordination of the exercise of its sovereign rights and to secure from it advantages of any kind. Also, no State shall organize, assist, foment, finance, incite or tolerate subversive, terrorist or armed activities directed towards the violent overthrow of the regime of another State, or interfere in civil strife in another State.

> The use of force to deprive peoples of their national identity constitutes a violation of their inalienable rights and of the principle of non-intervention.

> Every State has an inalienable right to choose its political, economic, social and cultural systems, without interference in any form by another State.

> Nothing in the foregoing paragraphs shall be construed as reflecting the relevant provisions of the Charter relating to the maintenance of international peace and security.

Two other principles were added to the list of principles set out in article 2 of the Charter. They had emerged in the constitutional practice of the United Nations. These principles were then codified in Resolution 2625. They are addressed below in sections H and I.

---

[81] *Case concerning Military and Paramilitary Activities in and against Nicaragua*, above n 3, § 205.

H. Duty of State Cooperation

§ 62 Contribution of Resolution 2625

In relation to the duty of States to cooperate, Resolution 2625 provides as follows:

States have the duty to co-operate with one another, irrespective of the difference in their political, economic and social systems, in the various spheres of international relations, in order to maintain international peace and security and to promote international economic stability and progress, and general welfare of nations and international cooperation free from discrimination based on such differences.

To this end:

a. States shall cooperate with other States in the maintenance of international peace and security;
b. States shall co-operate in the promotion of universal respect for, and observance of, human rights and fundamental freedoms for all, and in the elimination of all forms of racial discrimination and all forms of religious intolerance;
c. States shall conduct their international relations in the economic, social, cultural, technical and trade fields in accordance with the principle of sovereign equality and non-intervention;
d. States Members of the United Nations have the duty to take joint and separate action in cooperation with the United Nations in accordance with the relevant provisions of the charter.
e. States should co-operate in the economic, social and cultural fields as well as in the field of science and technology and for the promotion of international cultural and educational progress. States should co-operate in the promotion of economic growth throughout the world, especially that of the developing countries.

Articles 55 and 56 of the Charter are the basis of these developments:

Article 55

With a view to the creation of conditions of stability and well-being which are necessary for peaceful and friendly relations among nations based on respect for the principle of equal rights and self-determination of peoples, the United Nations shall promote:

a. higher standards of living, full employment, and conditions of economic and social progress and development;
b. solutions of international economic, social, health, and related problems; and international cultural and educational cooperation; and
c. universal respect for, and observance of, human rights and fundamental freedoms for all without distinction as to race, sex, language, or religion.

Article 56

All Members pledge themselves to take joint and separate action in cooperation with the Organization for the achievement of the purposes set forth in Article 55.

The principle of inter-State cooperation is the *leitmotiv* of modern international law and the law of the United Nations in particular. Cooperation must confront the increasing number of matters of international concern among States and other actors in international life; it must also address the common dangers of humanity, such as global poverty, global warming or weapons of mass destruction. It is necessary in a world of growing inter-dependency; it corresponds to the image of a common response to growing challenges taken in solidarity with the individual and his or her fundamental needs. Simply put, it is indispensable in a world that is increasingly broken up into different States, as evinced by the number of States increasing from roughly 60 in 1945 to 192 in 2008.

There are some areas where States have a greater duty of cooperation than otherwise. The general duty to cooperate is thus reinforced in some areas by a special duty to cooperate, qualified *ratione materiae*. According to Resolution 2625, the areas that entail a special duty to cooperate are matters concerning peace and international security; the fundamental rights of the individual, including non-discrimination; cooperation of State members with the United Nations in matters over which it exercises power; and economic, social, cultural, scientific and technical cooperation (functional cooperation). The duty applies not only to State members, but insofar as the duty is a norm of general international law, it also encompasses all subjects of law, namely States, international organisations, insurgents, de facto regimes, the International Committee of the Red Cross, the Vatican, etc. Under international law, there are further matters defined in particular treaties where States have bound themselves to a special duty of cooperation, such as for example the negotiations for nuclear disarmament under article VI of the non-proliferation treaty;[82] or more generally in all *pacta de negotiando* or *de contrahendo*.

§ 63 Scope of the Obligation

It is uncontroversial that the duty to cooperate is a legally soft obligation. Even if a violation of this duty entailed a sanction, it could hardly be imposed. It would risk being counterproductive, as it would pin the sanctioned State in a corner and increase its resistance, rather than improving the situation. Cooperation requires goodwill and a readiness to take into account the other's position. The Charter may propose cooperation as a guiding star and a model for inter-State relations, but it cannot create a spirit of cooperation if one does not exist. This does not mean that the reference to the duty to cooperate in the Charter is useless or superfluous. It is recommended as a permanent goal towards which efforts must be channelled. In effect, in the complex world of today, each course of action depends ultimately on some form of cooperation among States. The lack of international cooperation both quantitatively and qualitatively, in a spirit of respect and mutual trust, is one of the emblems of the current crisis in the world.

I. Right of Self-determination of Peoples

§ 64 General Aspects

Resolution 2625 addresses the new law that arose out of the decolonisation process. Drafted in 1945, before the process of decolonisation had occurred, the Charter

---

[82] See the *Legality of the Threat or Use of Nuclear Weapons* (Opinion) [1996-I] ICJ Rep 226ff, 263–65.

limited itself to setting out a declaration regarding non-self-governing territories (Chapter XI). This declaration imposes certain obligations on colonial powers, while recognising colonial titles over territory. At the same time, some vague references to self-determination of peoples were made (articles 1 § 2 or 55 of the Charter). However, in the first years of the United Nations and particularly in the 1960s, the wind of decolonisation swept through international society. More and more States gained independence, often following armed struggles. They were admitted into the United Nations and filled out the rung of decolonised States. Thus, a strong current of decolonisation moved through the organisation. This current weakened old colonial powers, notably France and the United Kingdom, but also the Netherlands and Portugal. It was in the wake of decolonisation, that the principle of the right of self-determination of people found a place in modern international law. Indeed, at the beginning of its emergence in the United Nations, the principle was closely linked to decolonisation. This is demonstrated by General Assembly Resolutions 742 (VIII) of 1953, 1514 (XV) and 1541 (XV) of 1960. From here, the principle was taken up in other texts and then in jurisprudence. From a poorly defined political principle,[83] it has progressively been moving toward a legal principle. The principal steps in this journey are article 1 of the two United Nations Covenants on human rights of 1966 and the jurisprudence of the ICJ (*Namibia* case of 1971;[84] *Western Sahara* case of 1975;[85] and *East Timor* of 1995)[86]. In the latter case, the Court recognised the *erga omnes* character of the right: all States have a legal interest in ensuring respect of the principle, as the obligation is due the international community as a whole and not merely to the oppressed people. Lastly, domestic jurisprudence has assisted in developing the principle: one may refer to the Supreme Court of Canada's opinion on *Quebec*, 1998.[87]

§ 65 Content of Resolution 2625

Resolution 2625 sets out in the following terms the principles of self-determination of peoples:

> By virtue of the principle of equal rights and self-determination of peoples enshrined in the Charter of the United Nations, all peoples have the right freely to determine, without external interference, their political status and to pursue their economic, social and cultural development, and every States has the duty to respect this right in accordance with the provisions of the Charter.

> Every State has the duty to promote, through joint and separate action, realization of the principle of equal rights and self-determination of peoples, in accordance with the provisions

---

[83] The hostility of some authors towards the principle is understandable in this respect: see, eg, W Friedmann, 'General Course on Public International Law' (1969) 127(2) *RCADI* 185ff (the so-called principle of self-determination is a political principle to be interpreted by each States as it pleases; it has no legal content); M. Villey, *Leçons d'histoire de la philosophie du droit* 2nd edn (Paris, 1962) (the principle of self-determination is a pretext for violence, injustice and the oppression of minorities).

[84] *Legal Consequences for States of the Continued Presence of South Africa in Namibia (South-West Africa)* (Advisory Opinion) [1971] ICJ Rep 27ff.

[85] *Western Sahara* case (Advisory Opinion) [1975] ICJ Rep 25ff.

[86] *East Timor case* (Advisory Opinion) [1995] ICJ Rep 102, § 29.

[87] (1998) 37 *ILM* 1340ff.

of the Charter, and to render assistance to the United Nations in carrying out the responsibilities entrusted to it by the charter regarding the implementation of the principle, in order:

a. To promote friendly relations and cooperation among States; and
b. To bring a speedy end to colonialism, having due regard to the freely expressed will of the peoples concerned;

And bearing in mind that subjection of peoples to alien subjugation, domination and exploitation constitutes a violation of the principles, as well as a denial of fundamental human rights, and is contrary to the Charter.

Every State has the duty to promote through joint and separate action universal respect for and observance of human rights and fundamental freedoms in accordance with the Charter.

The establishment of a sovereign and independent States, the free association or integration with an independent State or the emergence into any other political status freely determined by a people constitute modes of implementing the right of self-determination by that peoples.

Every State has the duty to refrain from any forcible action which deprives peoples referred to above in the elaboration of the present principle of their right to self-determination and freedom and independence. In their actions against, and resistance to, such forcible action in pursuit of the exercise of their right to self-determination, such peoples are entitled to seek and to receive support in accordance with the purposes and principles of the Charter.

The territory of a colony or other Non-Self-Governing Territory has under the Charter a status separate and distinct from the territory of the State administering it; and such separate and distinct status under the Charter shall exist until the people of the colony or Non-Self-Governing Territory have exercised their right of self-determination in accordance with the Charter, and particularly its purposes and principles.

Nothing in the foregoing paragraphs shall be construed as authorizing or encouraging any action which would dismember or impair, totally or in part, the territorial integrity or political unity of sovereign and independent States conducting themselves in compliance with the principle of equal rights and self-determination of peoples as described above and thus possessed of a government representing the whole people belonging to the territory without distinction as to race, creed or colour.

Every State shall refrain from any action aimed at the partial or total disruption of the national unity and territorial integrity of any other State or country.

The tension that exists among several of these paragraphs reflects the complex and politically protean character of the principle. The last paragraph of the Resolution is thus in tension with a number of the preceding paragraphs. It is by contextual interpretation that the respective spheres of applications can be distinguished. International practice and doctrine have progressively clarified the subject to whom the principle applies and the practical consequences of its application.

§ 66 'People'

In the context of the norm on self-determination, 'people' is a legal term. According to practice, this term covers the following subjects:

1. *Colonised peoples* according to the general definition contained in Resolution 1541 and within colonial borders defined by the principle of *uti possedetis*. This principle

signifies that the administrative borders defined by the colonising power become international borders when the territory is decolonised. These borders can only be altered by agreement. Resolution 1541 provides in Principles IV and V that a colonial territory is that which is 'geographically separate and is distinct ethically and/or culturally from the country administering it' (Principle IV), particularly if there is a situation of subordination between the metropolitan State and the territory concerned (Principle V). A series of more precise criteria are found in Resolution 742 (VIII) of 1953. The United Nations often applies the salty water test: when the metropolitan territory is separated from the territory concerned by an ocean, then the latter is a colony. Colonisation belongs, for the time being, to the past.

2. *Peoples under foreign domination outside cases of colonisation.* In particular, this concerns occupied territories. An example would be the territories occupied by Israel.

3. *Peoples who have already established their own State.* The principle of self-determination has a protective application in this respect. Together with the principle of non-intervention in the internal affairs of States, the principle protects the independence and sovereignty of established States.

4. *Peoples in a divided State.* The principle signifies here the right of peoples who have been previously divided to be reunited. This right applied to Germany and remains pertinent in Korea.

5. *Groups of individuals suffering from systematic discrimination.* The permanent stigmatisation of a group can create solidarity within it and render impossible a common existence with the oppressing majority. This is the most problematic aspect of self-determination, particularly when it encompasses a right to secession. This category is usually taken from the following phrase contained in Resolution 2625:[88] all States must respect the territorial unity of States 'conducting themselves in compliance with the principle of equal rights and self-determination . . .'. *A contrario*, respect for the territorial integrity of a State not conducting itself in accordance with this principle seems not to be guaranteed in the same manner. Contrary to the preceding categories, 'people' is not defined in this instance. Law leaves the definition open. It is mainly through recognition by regional organisations and then the United Nations, that an initially vague group can attain the status of a people who have the right of self-determination. This process is here mainly political. Law limits itself to attaching certain legal consequences to a fact determined by multilateral international politics. It is not surprising that such instances of recognition are rare, with States being generally wary of creating dangerous precedents. Beyond cases of decolonisation, international organisations generally limit themselves to demanding respect for fundamental human rights within internationally recognised borders. Some limited cases may be cited in this vein: the right of self-determination of the Saharan people was recognised by the United Nations and the question is presently being discussed in relation to Kosovo.

---

[88] It is less well known that this interpretation was made by the Commission of Rapporteurs established by the Council of the League of Nations when setting out the merits of the Finnish–Swedish dispute concerning the Aland islands. On page 28 of the report submitted on 16 April 1921, the Commission stated as follows: 'The separation of a minority from the State to which it forms a part, and its incorporation with another State can only be envisaged as an extreme and exceptional solution when the State does not have the will nor the necessary power to apply just and efficient guarantees [in favour of minorities]' (unofficial translation). See AN Mandelstam, 'La conciliation internationale d'après le Pacte et la jurisprudence du Conseil de la Société des Nations'(1926) 14(4) *RCADI* 439.

§ 67 Limits to the Right to Self-determination

All other ethnic or social groups only possess minority rights and fundamental human rights. They do not enjoy a right to external self-determination, namely the right to freely choose their political status, including the right to secede. To hold otherwise would create anarchy in international relations. However, international law does not prohibit secession. If it is successful, a new State is established which other States may recognise. International law looks principally to the principle of effectiveness for determining the existence of a new State. An exception to the rule concerning effectiveness is where a new State has been created in violation of fundamental rules of international law, up to now the non-use of force, or a violation of the right of self-determination of peoples. Consequently, if a puppet State is created with the backing of a military regime (for example, Japanese Manchukuo in 1932), and/or as a screen for the violation of the principle of self-determination (for example, South African townships), State are under an obligation not to recognise the new entity. The principle of non-use of force, contained in article 2 § 4 of the Charter, applies only in inter-State relations. Violence emanating from an internal insurrection in an attempt to secede territory from the metropolitan State is thus not covered by this prohibition of the use of force. Secession for the creation of a new State is not contrary to the prohibition of the use of force in international relations. Hence, there is no obligation for existing States not to recognise the new State. International law simply treats the act as a fact. It may be questioned whether in a particular case secession would be prohibited by particular international law (treaties, binding resolutions, etc.). Such could be the case of Resolution 1244 (1999) recognising the territorial integrity of former Serbia and Montenegro, including the Kosovo territory. However, the better interpretation in this case is that the resolution concerned only the territorial integrity of Serbia towards third States (namely those conducting the armed operation against Serbia) and not a permanent international guarantee of the extension of Serbian territory at the critical date of 1999, upgraded with an immunity *sine die* against any secession coming from within the territory.

§ 68 Exercises of the Right to Self-determination

The exercise of the right of self-determination has two aspects: one protectionist; the other revolutionary. The principle of self-determination is thus both a 'reactionary' principle and a principle of 'movement'.

1. *Peoples who have already established their own State.* In relation to peoples who already constitute a State, the principle of self-determination refers to their constitutional autonomy, namely their freedom to choose their own political, economic, social and cultural system. This principle here converges with the principle of non-intervention in the internal affairs of States. Such an application of the principle of self-determination also protects a failed State and its people. Its territory could not be considered by other States to be *terra nullius* open to acquisitive occupation because of the collapse of its governmental structures. The absence of a government

means of course that one of the essential elements of the definition of a State is lacking. A State is defined in international law as the composition of four elements: territory, effective government, population and sovereignty. However, in the case of a failed State, international law maintains the legal fiction of the existence of the State to protect it from appropriation of its territory by others. Thus Somalia, the famous State in decline since 1992, has not become a State preyed upon by predator third States. This protective legal fiction is rooted amongst others in the principle of self-determination. A territory is not considered any more, as in the past, to be an abstract and lifeless object open to appropriation by anyone, but a piece of soil inextricably linked with the fate of the people inhabiting it.

2. *Peoples who have a right to external self-determination but who have not yet established their own State.* For colonised peoples, peoples dominated by a foreign State, or even peoples who suffer from discrimination but are recognised as units having a right of self-determination, the principle entails the following political options:

—become an independent and sovereign State;
—to freely associate or integrate with an independent State;
—choosing another status.

The United Nations has more readily recognised the creation of an independent State than an association or integration with an existing State, due to a concern that the choice made may not be a free one. In the great majority of cases, decolonised peoples have chosen independence or unification with a neighbouring State—with the exception of a number of Pacific islands that have preferred to be associated with the United States of America.

3. *Separated Peoples.* For separated peoples, self-determination means above all the over-arching right to be reunited, if so wished.

8

Membership of the United Nations
(Chapter II, articles 3–6)[1]

§ 69 Membership of States only

Only States may be members of the United Nations in accordance with articles 3–4 of
the Charter. The organisation is above all an 'inter-State club'. This does not mean that
the United Nations is not open to other entities. Simply, these entities have a different
legal status from that of a member. Thus, observers may participate in the work of the
organisation without enjoying a right to vote. Examples include national liberation
movements (for example, the famous cases of the Palestinian Liberation Organisation
and the South West African People's Organisation) and other international organisations (the European Union, the African Union, and other organisations affiliated with
the United Nations). There is also a growing number of non-governmental organisations (NGOs) working in the areas of human rights, social, cultural, technical, environ-
mental and other matters that are increasingly participating in the work of the organs
and at United Nations conferences. It is difficult to overestimate the role that these
NGOs have played in world conferences organised by the United Nations since 1991:
Rio Conference on Environment and Development (1992); Vienna World Conference
on Human Rights (1993); Cairo Conference on Population and Development (1994);
Copenhagen World Summit for Social Development (1995); Rome Conference for an
International Criminal Court (1998); Dunbar World Conference against Racism,
Racial Discrimination, Xenophobia and Related Intolerance (2001) etc. Outside the

---

[1] Herewith the relevant provisions:

Article 3: 'The original Members of the United Nations shall be the states which, having participated
in the United Nations Conference on International Organization at San Francisco, or having previously
signed the Declaration by United Nations of 1 January 1942, sign the present Charter and ratify it in
accordance with Article 110.'

Article 4: '1. Membership in the United Nations is open to all other peace-loving states which accept
the obligations contained in the present Charter and, in the judgment of the Organization, are able and
willing to carry out these obligations. 2. The admission of any such state to membership in the United
Nations will be effected by a decision of the General Assembly upon the recommendation of the
Security Council'.

Article 5: 'A Member of the United Nations against which preventative or enforcement action has been
taken by the Security Council may be suspended from the exercise of the rights and privileges of membership by the General Assembly upon the recommendation of the Security Council. The exercise of
these rights and privileges may be restored by the Security Council'.

Article 6: 'A Member of the United Nations which has persistently violated the Principles contained in
the present Charter may be expelled from the Organization by the General Assembly upon the recommendation of the Security Council'.

context of United Nations organised conferences, mention may be made of the Ottawa Conference on Anti-Personnel Mines (1997), an initiative of the Canadian government. This conference led to the adoption of the Convention on the Prohibition of the Use, Stockpiling, Production and Transfer of Anti-Personnel Mines and on their Destruction. The Convention and its contents would not have been imaginable without the decisive support of a large number of NGOs.

§ 70 Founding Members and Subsequently Admitted Members

The Charter draws the same distinction as the League of Nations Covenant between original members, those victorious in war and other States, notably the vanquished. The latter are eligible for admission into the organisation at a later date and according to stricter conditions than original members.

Article 3 of the Charter concerns original members: 'the states which, having participated in the United Nations Conference on International Organization at San Francisco, or having previously signed the Declaration by United Nations of 1 January 1942, sign the present Charter and ratify it in accordance with Article 110'. This is a remnant of 'Wartime United Nations'. The invitation at the San Francisco conference, where the aim was to get the organisation up and running, was addressed by the principal allies to those States that had signed the 'United Nations Declaration' (1942),[2] and other associated States that had or would declare war on Germany or other Axis powers before 1 March 1945. This latter requirement resulted in a series of States declaring last-minute war on Germany: Chile, Equator, Paraguay, Uruguay, Venezuela, Turkey, Egypt, Lebanon, Syria and Saudi Arabia. The invitation was also extended to Denmark even though the country was occupied by Germany at the time. In some cases the quality of the States admitted was dubious, for example, the Philippines and India (that were not yet independent) and Lebanon and Syria (occupied by Allied forces at the time on the basis of old mandates). Further, two Soviet republics, Ukraine and Byelorussia, were treated as States even though they did not have this status in international law. To this end, Stalin could attain a slightly less unfavourable numerical representation of communist States at the conference. The States that were represented at the conference, or those that had the right to be represented, are referred to as the 'original members' of the organisation by the Charter. By simply ratifying the Charter, these States automatically became members without having to fulfil any other requirements. Their letters of credit to become members were bestowed simply because of their association with the Allies during the war against the Axis powers. There were 51 founding and original members: the five great powers (United States of America, USSR, United Kingdom, France and China) and others including, for instance, Belgium, Brazil and Greece.[3]

Other States could subsequently be admitted to the United Nations according to the qualitative conditions enumerated in article 4 § 1: 'Membership in the United Nations

---

[2] These amounted to 47 States, which were all at war with the Axis powers. Fifty States participated in the San Francisco conference.

[3] For a complete overview, see JP Jacqué, 'Article 3' in JP Cot, A Pellet and M Forteau, (eds), *La Chartre des Nations Unies,: Commentaire article par particle* vol 1, 3rd edn (Paris, 2005) 512–15.

is open to all other peace-loving states which accept the obligations contained in the present Charter and, in the judgement of the Organization, are able and willing to carry out these obligations'. It is up to the founding members to determine whether these conditions have been fulfilled, according to article 4 § 2: 'The admission of any such state to membership in the United Nations will be effected by a decision of the General Assembly upon the recommendation of the Security Council'. The role of the Security Council in this respect reflects that the admission of ex-enemy States was a matter considered to affect peace and international security. It thus touched upon the prerogatives of the Council.

As can be seen, the logic of the United Nations was initially one of a semi-closed club not open to the vanquished States. However, unlike the League of Nations, the United Nations was not plagued by the differential treatment in the Charter made between original members and subsequently admitted members. This was due to two factors. First, unlike the Covenant, the provisions of the Charter were not linked to the contents of peace treaties concerning the division of territories; thus the Charter did not aggravate the division between members so palpable in the League of Nations. Secondly, the new political rearrangements of the Cold War were to take hold of the organisation and blur the membership distinction according to division lines inherited from the past war.

There are three requirements for non-original membership under article 4. Candidate States must be:

—*Peaceful States*. Every State that opposed the Axis powers in one way or another (even if it did not declare war against these powers) was considered to be a peaceful State. In addition, former enemy States could be admitted if they renounced the nationalist militarism that they had subscribed to during war. This is the meaning of the requirement of 'peaceful'.

—*Accepting of the Charter obligations*. In practice, this requirement amounts to a declaration by the candidate State of its willingness, made before the General Assembly.

—*Judged capable and willing to respect these obligations*. This requirement was problematic for neutral States and micro-States that could not adhere to all the obligations of the Charter, particularly in relation to international security, due to their limited position or resources. This inability could potentially constitute an obstacle to admission. The interpretation of the United Nations was that the policy of neutrality was not a reason for not admitting a particular State. In relation to micro-States, the organisation reserved the question over a longer period, resulting in late membership from entities such as Lichtenstein (18 September 1990), Monaco (28 May 1993) and San Marino (2 March 1992). These reservations were only lifted at the end of the East–West confrontation and during the new push toward universalism in the United Nations.

§ 71 From Discrimination to Universality

In the practice of the United Nations, the question of membership initially produced clashes between the superpowers. Each bloc, Western or communist, tried to maintain an equilibrium between the number of pro-Western States on one side and the number of communist States on the other, or to improve these numbers in its respective favour. This resulted in a deadlock. A superpower would only accept the admission of a new member supporting the other side if another candidate that supported its interests was admitted at the same time. The Cold War thus quickly dominated the admission procedure under article 4. This concern meant that the superpowers were inclined to accept packages of proposals for admission. The admission of one series of States was thus intrinsically linked to the admission of a host of other States that had to be accepted simultaneously and as a whole. The Assembly questioned the legality of these bulk admissions, because they inhibited an individual evaluation of each candidate State according to its respective merits, as foreseen in the Charter. The Assembly put the question to the International Court of Justice in a request for an advisory opinion on the matter. The Court held that the list of admission conditions listed under article 4 was exhaustive and had to be evaluated on a case by case basis. Therefore, State members were not free to add other conditions, particularly political ones (for example, package reciprocities), according to their own interests. Each State candidate had the right for its application to be evaluated on its own merits.[4] The political requirement of bulk admissions was thus condemned. The Court affirmed that article 4 provided for a legal regime governing admission: it created rights and obligations between State members and candidate States and bound the organisation to the rule of law. According to the Court, article 4 does not establish a mere political regime that may be manipulated by members in keeping with their diplomatic interests at any one time. Admission to the organisation is both a political and legal act; it is not only a discretionary political act. The opinion of the court, insofar as it is an advisory opinion, is not binding. The solution finally found in 1955 was that of a package deal whereby 16 States were admitted in bulk but their applications for admission were examined on an individual basis so as not to contradict the opinion of the Court. The recommendation for admission was in any event formulated as a package in order to impede the slightest attempt of a separate vote. The logic of the Cold War policy thus encroached to some extent on the, nevertheless excellent, opinion of the Court.

However, the period of decolonisation in the late 1950s marked a more liberal approach to membership. There was a new paradigm of universalism in the United Nations; the idea was that the organisation would group together all States in the world and thus become the centre *par excellence* of international cooperation and security. This was the vision supported initially by Secretary-General Trygve Lie, who slowly brought it to fruition. The umbilical cord with 'Wartime United Nations' and the legacy of war was thus cut and a new image of 'Peacetime United Nations' was erected on the foundations of a universal organisation. From this moment onwards article 4 lost its importance and was no longer a burning issue; its discriminatory conditions faded into the distance; admission increasingly became a pure formality. The Assembly began to admit members without careful analysis of a candidate's conformity with the not negligible admission requirements of article 4. The conditions for admission were progressively held to be fulfilled by a sort of irrefutable legal presumption. Practice thus modified the legal content of article 4.

---

[4] *Competence of the General Assembly for the Admission of a State to the United Nations (Article 4 of the Charter)* (Advisory Opinion) [1947–48] ICJ Rep 57ff.

§ 72 Admission Procedure

Article 4 § 2 provides that admission by the General Assembly follows a recommendation from the Security Council: 'The admission of any such state [fulfilling the conditions of § 1] to membership in the United Nations will be effected by a decision of the General Assembly upon the recommendation of the Security Council'. The Assembly has never voted against the application of a State recommended by the Security Council. However, in the early days of the atmosphere of Cold War politics and bloc divisions, the veto in the Council led some States to try to end the deadlock with the aid of ingenious legal constructions. Consequently, it was argued that a veto in the Council amounted to giving a 'negative' recommendation, but still a 'recommendation' of sorts, to the General Assembly. The Assembly could then vote on this (negative) recommendation and admit the candidate State by the required majority. It has thus been argued that article 4 § 2 simply provides that the Council will 'recommend' an application for admission to the General Assembly, not that this must necessarily be a positive recommendation. Thereafter, it was argued that on receiving a 'negative' recommendation, States in the General Assembly could treat it simply as a 'recommendation' about which they were free to vote and could even admit the State concerned. The International Court of Justice, in its advisory opinion of 1950 (*Competence of the General Assembly for the Admission of a State to the United Nations, Article 4 of the Charter*), refused to accept this somewhat fabricated interpretation by Western States.[5] The Court insisted on a teleological interpretation of the Charter, which manifestly required a favourable recommendation by the Council since otherwise the role of the latter would be nullified.[6] It was the intention of the Charter to install a right of decision of the Council *and* of the Assembly, in conjunction. The Western interpretation tried to downgrade the role of the Council to that of a mere preliminary and advisory function. This was not what was provided for by the Charter.

§ 73 Specific Issues

In the case of the secession of a State and in the absence of legal continuity between the new State and the predecessor State, the new State must apply for admission to the United Nations: 'a new State, a new admission' is the rule that applies. This was the situation, for example, for Bangladesh when it separated from Pakistan in 1974. It was also the case—following a lengthy debate as to whether it was a continuation of the former Socialist Federal Republic of Yugoslavia—for Serbia and Montenegro, which was considered to be a new State by the majority of the international community represented in

---

[5] All the efforts of Western States in the early years of the United Nations, dominated by the Cold War, were directed at trying to find a way around the Soviet veto. The USSR in turn, a minority in the organisation, attempted to limit as much as possible the influence of the Western States, and thus to direct all question to the Security Council where it enjoyed a veto power. The Western States, that held the majority, made every effort to increase the reach of the organisation. They tried to avoid using to the Security Council, blocked by the Soviet veto. One way to do this was to reconsider the powers of the General Assembly.

[6] *Competence of the General Assembly for the Admission of a State to the United Nations (Article 4 of the Charter)* [1950] ICJ Rep 4ff.

the United Nations. In contrast, Russia was considered to be the continuing State of the former USSR. The criteria for distinguishing between successor and continuing States are not completely defined by international law. Political considerations also play a significant role. The fundamental criterion is recognition by the majority of United Nations members of a State as continuing or successor State.[7] However, in cases of fusion or the incorporation of one State into another, a simple notification is sufficient and no admission procedure is necessary. This was the case for reunited Germany (1990), an example of incorporation; and also unified Yemen (1990), a case of fusion. The difference between incorporation and fusion is that in the case of incorporation the State that absorbs the other continues to exist, whereas in the case of fusion, the two (or more than two) predecessor States cease to exist on the creation of one new State. Logic would dictate that in the latter case a new application for admission would be required. However, the political preference is to allow the new entity to be a continuing State, as it has not fundamentally changed the profile of its predecessor States and remains, for example the political entity of 'Yemen' (prior to 1990, the Arab Republic of Yemen and the People's Democratic Republic of Yemen).[8] This course avoids the unnecessary complications of a new admission within the United Nations system.

The fiction of continuity of membership is sometimes applied in the case of a State that temporarily withdraws from the United Nations, as was the case with Indonesia between 1965 and 1966. When this State reintegrated back into the United Nations, its legal status during its absence was generously interpreted as having been a temporary suspension of its membership to avoid subjecting it to the humiliation of reapplying for admission. This was a sort of gift offered to the prodigal son, legally dubious, but politically astute. The approach in favour of a continuity of States rather than a break in their legal status (except in cases of secession) reflects the important place held by the guiding idea of universal membership in today's United Nations. Everything that tends to create gaps of membership is restrictively interpreted or not applied.

§ 74 Expulsion from the United Nations

Article 6 provides as follows: 'A Member of the United Nations which has persistently violated the Principles contained in the present Charter may be expelled from the organisation by the General Assembly on the recommendation of the Security Council.' Article 16 § 4 of the Covenant of the League of Nations stated as follows: 'Any Member of the League which has violated any covenant of the League may be declared to be no longer a Member of the League by a vote of the Council concurred in by the Representatives of all the other Members of the League represented thereon'. This latter provision was applied to the USSR in 1939 following its aggression against Finland. This response explains the hostility with which the USSR consequently regarded the Geneva organisation.

Article 6 provides a sanction of non-participation, of ostracising the excluded State, of banishment. The excluded State can no longer benefit from international cooperation

---

[7] On this point, see A Zimmermann, *Staatennachfolge in völkerrechtliche Verträge* (Berlin, 2000) 46ff.

[8] The General Assembly simply welcomed this fusion: UNGA Res 45/193 (21 December 1990).

and the contacts offered by the United Nations. In a closely interdependent world, this is not a negligible sanction. It would withhold benefits for violating and recalcitrant States. It could serve as a deterrent. But is it politically savvy? In effect, the sanction is quite ambiguous. In most cases the imposition of the sanction would be counterproductive, notably by an organisation that is based on cooperation and dialogue. Many different issues need here to be carefully taken into consideration. First, the State in question would find itself suddenly free of all its Charter obligations that previously weighed heavily on it. This result may be unwelcome and unwise. Secondly, all methods of persuasion and of exerting pressure on the wayward State, found within the United Nations system, would no longer be available. The League of Nations had this experience in relation to States that publicly denounced the Covenant: Germany, Italy and Japan. It is much easier to influence a State from within rather than outside the organisation. Moreover, the sanctioned State would turn against the organisation and make itself out to be a heroic defiant State 'alone against the world' that would doggedly become more distanced from the international community. Would such a course be wise? Thirdly, the organisation would itself suffer from any sanctioning measure. The further the United Nations moves away from universality, the more the organisation loses its influence and its raison d'etre. International cooperation requires the participation of all States. Fourthly, the expulsion of member States is often made on the basis of political criteria, according to the view of one or other changing majority. Tension in international relations could lead to the sanctioning mechanism being used to settle scores between opposing groups of States in the United Nations. That would hardly advance the matter.

In light of these considerations, it is understandable that the principle of universalism impacts significantly on the question of expelling a member. The United Nations thus does not expel a member even if there have been grave violations of obligations contained in the Charter. The United Nations is today perceived as a necessary world family. It is a mirror of the world, with its emotions, divided State interests and also violators of the law. Behind the States there are populations, innocent by definition. Can they be expelled? However, if article 6 has never been applied, it is not for want of trying. Attempts were made to expel States like Israel or South Africa. However, the Security Council has systematically refused to adopt a recommendation in this vein, on the basis of the arguments discussed above.

Article 6 requires, as a condition of expulsion, persistent violations of the principles of the Charter. Minor or isolated (yet grave) violations are thus not sufficient. What must be shown are manifest and prolonged violations and disregard; and a determination to continue the deviant practice. Further, the conduct must be in violation of the fundamental rules of the Charter, particularly the principles set out in article 2. A violation of just any rule of the Charter will thus not suffice. In the positive law of the Charter, expulsion is a last resort that is subject to stringent conditions. From the procedural point of view, a recommendation from the Security Council is required, just as it is required for the admission of a new member. The vote in the Security Council on a question of expulsion is not a procedural matter but an 'other' matter that falls within the ambit of article 27 § 3. The veto power thus applies.

At the San Francisco conference, the USSR insisted on the inclusion of article 6. As the USSR would have a veto power in the application of this article, it was thus assured of not having a repetition of its misadventure with the League of Nations that resulted in its expulsion from the organisation in 1939. In contrast, small and medium-sized

States, lead by Belgium, were not in favour of the inclusion of the provision. Their principal argument was that the suspension of rights (as provided in article 5) was a sufficient mechanism to address such situations.

A distinction must be made between the expulsion of a State and that of a government. In this vein, in Resolution 2758 (XXVI), the United Nations considered that the government of Taiwan was not any more to be regarded as the legitimate government of China. It determined that the government of the People's Republic of China was the legitimate government. It thus substitutes the communist delegation for the nationalist one in its organs. This declaration had been long delayed by Western countries which supported the nationalist rather than the communist government. The principle of effectiveness however clearly supported this new approach, if only in order to have represented within the United Nations the huge mass of the Chinese population. The fact that Taiwan did not become a separate member is linked to the consideration that there are not two Chinas but only one; the dispute is strictly limited to the question of who is the legitimate government. The People's Republic of China has also maintained pressure on Taiwan not to make any secessionist attempts. In this case, no membership question is at stake: China is and remains the member of the United Nations; the question is only about whom represents it at the United Nations.

§ 75 Withdrawal from the United Nations

The Covenant of the League of Nations permitted the voluntary withdrawal of a State from the League. Article 1 § 3 provided: 'Any Member of the League may, after two years' notice of its intention so to do, withdraw from the League, provided that all its international obligations and all its obligations under this Covenant shall have been fulfilled at the time of its withdrawal'. There is no analogous provision in the Charter. The experience of the Covenant showed that it was better not to expressly provide for the possibility of withdrawing from the organisation. To include such a provision would send States the signal that they were able to withdraw when they pleased ('heroically' in some cases) and thereby free themselves from the obligations they had assumed under the Charter. They would thereby deprive the organisation of the possibility of exerting any pressure over their actions, as the painful experience of the League had demonstrated. States that had intentionally planned to violate the international legal order had simply withdrawn from the League and blatantly pursued their aggressive policies.

At the San Francisco conference, the great powers nevertheless insisted uon implicitly allowing for the possibility of denunciation in the Charter. The United States of America argued that in some situations, for example, following an extensive amendment of the Charter decided by the required two-thirds majority, it would be unjust not to allow a State to denounce the Charter if it fundamentally disagreed with the new provisions. A compromise was found in not including any provision in the Charter, but recognising tacitly the implicit ability for denunciation.

Only one State has withdrawn for a period of one year and a half from the Organisation. From 20 January 1965 to 19 September 1966, Indonesia was not a member of the United Nations.[9] On the occasion of its return to the United Nations, the General Assembly accepted the interpretation of the Secretary-General that Indonesia had suspended its cooperation with the organisation but had not denounced its membership. Following, Indonesia was able to resume its full cooperation with the United Nations without having to apply for readmission.[10]

[9] The reason was mainly the Indonesian government's dissatisfaction with its regional rival, Malaysia, when the latter was elected as a non-permanent member to the Security Council: see the exchange of letters with the Secretary-General of the United Nations published in UN (ed), *Everyman's United Nations* 88th edn (New York, 1968) 144–45.

[10] *Repertory of Practice of United Nations Organs*, Supplement III, vol. I, § 29ff.

9

Organs of the United Nations:
Functions and Powers

§ 76 General Theory on the Powers of Organs of an International Organisation

The question of the powers of an international organisation is a matter of general international law. The relevant rules apply not only to the United Nations, but to a whole array of other entities that exercise international functions. These include inter-governmental organisations and international organs, such as an arbitral tribunal, a river commission or an international conference. The essential principle is that these entities may be distinguished from States because they *lack sovereignty*. Only States possess sovereignty. There is thus a legal presumption that States are omnipotent within the limits of international law: a power must not be specifically attributed to a State; the grant of powers is already implicit in the principle of sovereignty. Practically speaking, States thus possess a *jus actionis omnimodae*: they can legally perform any act authorised by international law without requiring any special authorisation. This presumption is reinforced on State territory where it is subject to a particularly power-ful interpretation: States can do anything they wish, within the limits of international law, on their territories, except insofar as their powers has been removed or otherwise altered by a rule of international law, either specific (contained in a treaty), or general (found in customary law, or in general principles of law). Thus, if a treaty provides a right of passage for foreign vessels in a canal situated on the territory of a State, this State cannot legally refuse such passage. However, if the powers of a State are not lim-ited in this way, then the State may either refuse or grant passage as it sees fit and in accordance with the conditions it chooses to apply. This ability to freely choose is a right that flows directly from territorial sovereignty. For extraterritorial action, the limits of international law are far more restrictive, especially if the territory of another State could be affected. It may even be said today that for such action a specific grant of powers by a rule of international law is necessary.

Unlike States, international organisations are not omnipotent in the sense previ-ously discussed. They may only exercise the powers that have been *conferred upon them* in their constituent document (principle of speciality). There must be an attribution of powers; there is no presumption of capacity to act. Whereas the presumption is that a State can do anything it wishes on its own territory, except where its powers are expressly limited, the presumption for international organisations is that they cannot do anything within their respective domains of activity without specific authorisation. A State possesses everything except that which is taken from it; an organisation does not possess anything, except that which it is given.

It must be noted that this very general description of the distribution of powers—that reflects the dominance of States—is only an approximation that must be nuanced to provide an accurate account of current positive law. The powers of international organisations rest on three complementary principles. These vary according to their nature and scope. This triad reflects the complex considerations at play in a highly interdependent and changing world. The work of international organisations in this environment is indeed increasingly important. They must adapt to the changing political climate in order to successfully undertake their assigned functions. Thus, some flexibility and progressiveness in the grant and exercise of powers becomes necessary. The three principles relating to the powers of international organisations are alternatives: powers may be conferred on an organisation in accordance with the first, second or the third principle. The three complementary principles are as follows:

—*Principle of speciality.* According to this principle, as we have seen, an international organisation only possesses conferred powers; it can only exercise those powers that are conferred on it in its constituent documents in order to accomplish its organisational aim. The limitation is two-fold in law: (1) only conferred powers may be exercised; (2) conferred powers may only be exercised for particular purposes, namely those assigned to the organisation in its specific area of activity. As the Court recalled in the case of *Legality of the Use by a State of Nuclear Weapons in Armed Conflicts* (WHO): 'The Court need hardly point out that international organizations are subjects of international law which do not, unlike States possess a general competence. International organizations are governed by the "principle of speciality", that is to say, they are invested by the States which create them with powers, the limits of which are a function of the common interests whose promotion those States entrust to them'.[1] These powers are consequently inherently limited. In principle, all non-conferred powers rest with the States members. The principle of speciality protects the sovereignty of State members. These tend to fear that the organisation they have created could become too autonomous in relation to them and pursue policies of which they disapprove.

—*Principle of implied powers.* The second principle is that of implied or implicit powers. The origin of this legal device is federal States, in particular the jurisprudence of the Supreme Court of the United States of America. Implied powers expand the tight corset sewn shut by the principle of speciality, which is poorly suited to respond to changes in the life of international organisations and their social surroundings. The principle of implied powers considers that some powers, even if not expressly contained in the constituent treaty, are implicitly conferred on the organisation where these powers are 'necessary' for the exercise of other powers, expressly conferred, or alternatively in the fulfilment of the organisation's aims. More succinctly, the organisation is presumed to have those powers that are necessary for it to accomplish its expressly conferred functions. If 'x' is to be done and 'y' is

---

[1] *Legality of the Use by a State of Nuclear Weapons in Armed Conflicts* (WHO) (Advisory Opinion) [1996] ICJ Rep 78, § 25. See also *Jurisdiction of the European Commission of the Danube* [1927] PCIJ Rep Series B No 14, 64: 'As the European Commission is not a State, but an international institution with a special purpose, it only has the functions bestowed upon it by the Definitive Statute with a view to the fulfilment of that purpose'.

necessary to do 'x', 'y' has been implicitly granted. There is an implication here of function to function, or aim to function (that is, aim to power). The core of the argument is thus a 'necessity' of a *sine qua non*-type: it is impossible to exercise an expressly conferred power or function without the implied one; 'x' cannot be performed without 'y'. The International Court of Justice (ICJ) developed this principle in the famous advisory opinion on *Reparation for injuries suffered in the service of the United Nations* (1949): 'Under international law, the Organization must be deemed to have those powers which, though not expressly provided in the Charter, are conferred upon it by necessary implication as being essential to the performance of its duties'.[2] Those who want to achieve the end result must also want the indispensable powers to achieve that result. An example is the provision of the Charter which provides that the United Nations, through the Secretary-General, shall employ staff, and that the paramount consideration in respect of such employment is the need to secure staff that demonstrate the highest standards of efficiency, competence and integrity (article 101). The express power (to employ qualified staff) necessarily implies an implicit power of the Secretary-General to enact staff regulations that specify the rights, obligations, privileges, allowances, appeals, etc. It is impossible to employ staff and engage them in work without administrative regulations. Moreover, an administrative tribunal to decide disputes between the UN and its staff must then be created. The implication here is that there are other implied functions within those express functions.

Implicit powers may operate in a narrow or broad manner. In the most narrow sense, they operate from one determined function or power to another determined function or power, where the link from one function to another is implicitly 'necessary' in the strictest interpretation of the term. The example above is an example in this respect: the capacity to employ staff and to guarantee their rights entails the implied power to adopt staff regulations. At the other end of the spectrum of implied powers are the broader conclusions from the aims of an organisation to its functions, namely the inference that a function is 'useful' or 'suitable' to an aim of the organisation and must thus considered to have been granted to it. The organisation may then promote such an aim and exercise powers in its respect. Operations for the maintenance of peace envisaged by the Secretary-General in the 1950s are undoubtedly suitable to promote the general and primary aim of the United Nations of international peace. Are they however 'necessary' to achieve this end? This may depend on both a historical and political context. This question was at the centre of debates in the advisory opinion of the Court in *Certain Expenses of the United Nations* (1962).[3] The Court considered these types of operations to be covered by the law of the Charter. To this end, the Court gave a dynamic and evolutionary reading of the text. Herewith the key considerations of the Court: 'When the Organization takes action which warrants the assertion that it was *appropriate* for the fulfilment of one of the stated *purposes* of the United Nations, the presumption is that such action is not *ultra vires* the Organization'.[4] The criteria thus changed three-fold with respect to the *Reparations* opinion: (1) the essential criterion is the

---

[2] *Reparation for injuries suffered in the service of the United Nations* (Advisory Opinion) [1949] ICJ Rep 182.

[3] *Certain Expenses of the United Nations* (Advisory Opinion) [1962] ICJ 151ff.

[4] [1962] ICJ Rep 168, emphasis added, except on *ultra vires*.

appropriateness of the action, a much broader concept than 'necessary' action. Many things may be appropriate; few may be called necessary. The extension of the powers of the organisation under the guise of appropriateness may thus be quite generous. (2) The units of measure for the implication are the *purposes* of the organisation and not the expressly conferred powers. Here again, the point of departure could easily lead to a considerable extension of powers. The Court provided that the United Nations had implied powers in this respect as the operations for the maintenance of peace served the paramount aim of the Charter, peace. However, an infinite amount of other things could also serve this purpose. Are they all impliedly conferred on the organisation? In this particular instance, it was possible to argue that the operations for maintaining peace were the only practical measure for the organisation, at this specific moment of its history, to take action on the ground in order to maintain peace. In an abstract perspective, these operations could seem simply appropriate to the aim; in a concrete perspective, they could appear to be necessary for giving some practical effect to the aim. Thus, in practice the implication of 'necessity' in order to fulfil the aim of the organisation could be considered to be met. (3) The Court provided that there is a *presumption of legality* of the acts of the organisation that applies particularly in relation to third parties outside the organisation. This presumption may be reversed according to the evidence produced. The reasoning of the Court, which has been criticised with the best of motives,[5] appears defensible with respect to the implied consent of most member States in the operations in question and the importance of these operations in a world brought to a standstill by the Cold War. These examples demonstrate the highly malleable character of implied powers, capable of addressing the changing needs in the constitutional and international political life.

Implied powers in the strict sense (by implication 'necessary') undoubtedly form part of the powers that are attributed to international organisations. They are the 'attributed' powers that follow from a slightly more sweeping reading of the text. Implied powers in the broad sense (by implication 'useful') are not attributed powers. They are the product of a teleological interpretation of the constituent instrument and propose a minor or significant development in the law. Thus, to avoid being ultra vires and in order to apply to all members of the organisation, such powers must enjoy substantial acceptance within the organisation from its members or at least be based on an ad hoc agreement among the participants in relation to a specific operation. Even then, financial issues in relation to the general budget can nevertheless still arise, as evinced by the *Certain Expenses* case.

Overall, four types of implication could thus be distinguished:

1) power/function→(necessity) power/function
2) aim→(necessity) power/function
3) power/function→(useful/appropriate) power/function.
4) aim→(useful/appropriate) power/function, this being the broadest form of implication.

In conclusion, the principle of implied powers operates to the benefit of an organisation and constitutes an extension of its powers. The principle limits the exercise of the sovereignty of member States.

---

[5] *Cf*, eg, R Bindschedler, 'La délimitation des compétences des Nations Unies' (1963) 108(1) *RCADI* 359ff.

—Principle of subsequent practice. Lastly, powers may be conferred on international organisations on the basis of the subsequent practice of their organs[6] and their State members. When the organs of an international organisation act in a particular way and States acquiesce to this practice, or at least do not oppose it, this practice becomes a rule of law. Subsequent practice may also modify the powers initially conferred on an organisation, by either enlarging or limiting them. A classic example is the 'affirmative vote' of the five permanent members of the Security Council, in accordance with article 27 § 3 of the Charter of the United Nations. Practice established that the Council could take a decision even if one or more of the five permanent members abstained from the voting process. The ICJ approved this practice in the advisory opinion on *Namibia* (1971)[7] and held that it represented a new rule of law. Other examples include Resolution 377 (V) which has been discussed above;[8] operations for maintaining peace that were originally opposed then accepted by State members; the extension of the powers of the Security Council under Chapter VII to encompass internal armed conflicts and humanitarian crises, etc. It might be worth asking when a practice has become sufficiently accepted and when, conversely, it rather constitutes the imposition of the will of the majority on the minority. The problem is similar to that of the 'general practice' required for the emergence of a norm of customary international law and need not be addressed here. Supposing that this problem is resolved then it appears clear that we are dealing with conferred powers. The organisation has a new power because State members (perhaps *nolens volens*, by absence of opposition) have granted it such a power. The difference between powers obtained through subsequent practice and formally granted powers is that the former are simply informally given.

—The organisation may also be granted *ad hoc powers*, conferred by agreement by some of its members in specific contexts. Consequently, two States may give the United Nations the mandate of setting up a joint bilateral armed force. Whether the organisation can exercise such powers ad hoc is a delicate question. It is not clear whether the organisation can cite such a ground as a basis for action where the necessary functions to do so are not provided for also in its constituent instrument. Certainly, the organisation cannot undertake the action in its own name, unless it

---

[6] Some have strongly opposed the contention that international organs can impose their subsequent practice on State members. According to this point of view, only the practice of States is relevant to law. International organs do not have any power to create or modify rules by their practice: *cf* P Spender, *Certain Expenses* case (Individual Opinion) [1962] ICJ Rep 187ff. This opinion is not confirmed by international practice. For the role of subsequent practice in international organisations, see the literature concerning this notion: eg, E Gordon 'The World Court and the Interpretation of Constitutive Treaties' (1965) 59 *AJIL* 826ff; S Engel, '"Living" International Constitutions and the World Court: The Subsequent Practice of International Organs under their Constituent Documents' (1967) 16 *ICLQ* 865ff; G Ress, 'Interpretation' in B Simma (ed), *The Charter of the United Nations: A Commentary* vol II, 2nd edn (Oxford; New York, OUP, 2002) 27ff, with a number of references. What counts in the end is that the international practice of organs is not opposed by a significant number of State members, ie, that there is general approval by members, demonstrated by a lack of complaints.

[7] *Legal Consequences for States of the Continued Presence of South Africa in Namibia (South-West Africa)* (Advisory Opinion) [1971] ICJ Rep 22, § 22: 'However, the proceedings of the Security Council extending over a long period supply abundant evidence that presidential rulings and the positions taken by members of the Council, in particular its permanent members, have consistently and uniformly interpreted the practice of voluntary abstention by a permanent member as not constituting a bar to the adoption of resolutions . . . This procedure . . . has been generally accepted by Members of the United Nations and evidences a general practice of that Organisation'.

[8] See above, ch 7, § 57.

falls within the general aims and functions of the organisation. In relation to the United Nations, its aims are so broad that it is difficult to imagine an ad hoc function conferred on the organisation that would not fall within the ambit of one of its general aims as set out in the Preamble and article 1 of the Charter. States that oppose a particular action on the part of the organisation can try to limit the action to being merely a 'service of the organisation' undertaken outside the constituent Charter (although not contrary to it). Thus, the effects, including the budgetary implications, will apply only to those States that were participating in the operation and not to members in general. The action of organisations and the legal bases for such action may consequently increase significantly. In such cases, however, the organisation is not granted a new general power, but rather undertakes a specific and delegated mission. On completion of such a mission, the delegation and ad hoc power previously conferred is removed. Overall, it appears that an organisation could accept such functions (or refuse them) according to a discretionary judgement when they are compatible with its aims and purposes, but that it must refuse them if they are not compatible with its aims and functions, unless the membership agrees to accept that function (the legal basis being then an agreement).

§ 77 Outline of the Principal Organs of the United Nations

The organisation is composed of both principal organs and subsidiary organs. The latter are attached to a principal organ on which they are established and depend. Article 7 of the Charter provides a general overview of these organs. First, according to § 1, there are six principal organs: 'a General Assembly, a Security Council, an Economic and Social Council, a Trusteeship Council, an International Court of Justice and a Secretariat'. Paragraph 2 recognises the general power of principal organs to create, according to their needs, subsidiary organs: 'Such subsidiary organs as may be found necessary may be established in accordance with the present Charter'.

The diagram on pp 122–3 illustrates the organic structure of the United Nations.

A. General Assembly

§ 78 General Aspects

Issues concerning the General Assembly are dealt with in Chapter IV of the Charter (articles 9–22). The Assembly is the plenary organ of the organisation within which each State is represented by (a maximum of) five delegates and enjoys a right to vote. Article 9 § 1 provides 'The General Assembly shall consist of all the Members of the United Nations'. To this, article 18 § 1 adds: 'Each member of the General Assembly shall have one vote'. It is sometimes said that the Assembly is the 'democratic' organ of the United Nations. This qualification requires some discussion. The Assembly is 'democratic' insofar as its membership is not limited to only certain members of the United Nations. It is also 'democratic' in the sense that each member has an equal right to vote, regardless of the size or the State, its resources or power. However, the term is inappropriate with respect to the representation of individuals in the Assembly. The Assembly is made up of States and not individuals elected by an electorate; it is composed of members of the executive of each State. Some represent governments that have never been subject to universal suffrage. The United Nations is a club of inter-State cooperation that represents only indirectly the peoples.

§ 79 Functions and Powers

The powers of the Assembly are specified in article 10 and following. Article 10 is the most important provision as it addresses the general powers of the Assembly:

> The General Assembly may discuss any questions or any matters within the scope of the present Charter or relating to the powers and functions of any organs provided for in the present Charter, and, except as provided in Article 12, may make recommendations to the Members of the United Nations or to the Security Council or to both on any such questions or matters.

The Assembly is the principal deliberative organ of the United Nations that determines the principal policies of the organisation and receives reports from all other organs that it examines and discusses. The Assembly is thus said to be 'omnipotent' within the United Nations. According to article 10, the Assembly can discuss any matters that fall within the scope of the United Nations. It can therefore discuss almost anything as the aims and powers of the organisation extend without clear limits to matters of peace and security, human rights, international cooperation, economic, social, cultural and humanitarian action, etc. All matters 'of international concern' may be addressed by the Assembly. In an interdependent world like our world today, this means that the Assembly may discuss almost anything, to the extent it has some international implications. Consequently, the Assembly is equally competent to address matters relating to indigenous populations as it is in considering the lawfulness of the use or threat of nuclear weapons. The extension of the Assembly's powers to cover discussions on 'any questions or any matters within the scope of the present Charter' was inserted in the San Francisco conference on the initiative of small and medium-sized States. They insisted on a reconsideration of the role of the Assembly with respect to that of the Council, which, in their opinion was too much in favour of the great powers, as proposed in the Dumbarton Oaks draft.[9]

The Assembly can discuss any question that falls within the scope of the United Nations and can make recommendations within the same, subject to the limitation imposed by article 12 § 1: 'While the Security Council is exercising in respect of any dispute or situation the functions assigned to it in the present Charter, the General Assembly shall not make any recommendation with regard to that dispute or situation unless the Security Council so requests'. Even in such a case, the Assembly can still *discuss* questions submitted to the Council. It must simply abstain from making a

---

[9] *Cf* E Luard, *A History of the United Nations* vol I (London, 1982) 54–56.

The United Nations System

Principal Organs

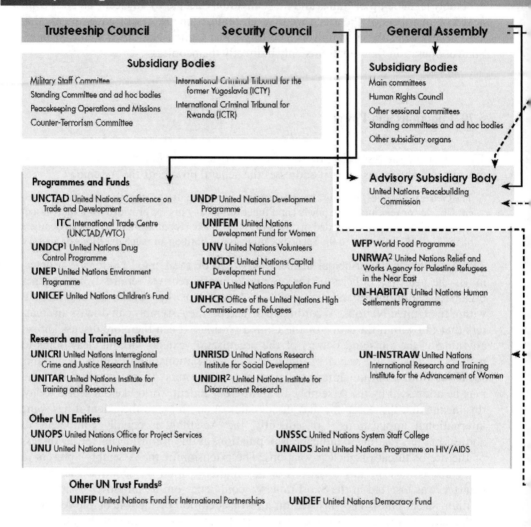

Trusteeship Council

Security Council

General Assembly

Subsidiary Bodies

Military Staff Committee

Standing Committee and ad hoc bodies

Peacekeeping Operations and Missions

Counter-Terrorism Committee

International Criminal Tribunal for the former Yugoslavia (ICTY)

International Criminal Tribunal for Rwanda (ICTR)

Subsidiary Bodies

Main committees

Human Rights Council

Other sessional committees

Standing committees and ad hoc bodies

Other subsidiary organs

Programmes and Funds

UNCTAD United Nations Conference on Trade and Development

   ITC International Trade Centre (UNCTAD/WTO)

UNDCP¹ United Nations Drug Control Programme

UNEP United Nations Environment Programme

UNICEF United Nations Children's Fund

UNDP United Nations Development Programme

   UNIFEM United Nations Development Fund for Women

   UNV United Nations Volunteers

   UNCDF United Nations Capital Development Fund

UNFPA United Nations Population Fund

UNHCR Office of the United Nations High Commissioner for Refugees

Advisory Subsidiary Body

United Nations Peacebuilding Commission

WFP World Food Programme

UNRWA² United Nations Relief and Works Agency for Palestine Refugees in the Near East

UN-HABITAT United Nations Human Settlements Programme

Research and Training Institutes

UNICRI United Nations Interregional Crime and Justice Research Institute

UNITAR United Nations Institute for Training and Research

UNRISD United Nations Research Institute for Social Development

UNIDIR² United Nations Institute for Disarmament Research

UN-INSTRAW United Nations International Research and Training Institute for the Advancement of Women

Other UN Entities

UNOPS United Nations Office for Project Services

UNU United Nations University

UNSSC United Nations System Staff College

UNAIDS Joint United Nations Programme on HIV/AIDS

Other UN Trust Funds⁸

UNFIP United Nations Fund for International Partnerships

UNDEF United Nations Democracy Fund

NOTES: Solid lines from a Principal Organ indicate a direct reporting relationship; dashes indicate a non-subsidiary relationship.

1 The UN Drug Control Programme is part of the UN Office on Drugs and Crime.
2 UNRWA and UNIDIR report only to the GA.
3 The United Ethics Office, the United Nations Ombudsman's Office, and the Chief Information Technology Officer report directly to the Secretary-General.
4 In an exceptional arrangement, the Under-Secretary-General for Field Support reports directly to the Under-Secretary-General for Peacekeeping Operations.
5 IAEA reports to the Security Council and the General Assembly (GA).
6 The CTBTO Prep Com and OPCW report to the GA.
7 Specialized agencies are autonomous organizations working with the UN and each other through the coordinating machinery of the ECOSOC at the intergovernmental level, and through the Chief Executives Board for coordination (CEB) at the inter-secretariat level.
8 UNFIP is an autonomous trust fund operated under the leadership of the United Nations Deputy Secretary-General. UNDEF's advisory board recommends funding proposals for approval by the Secretary-General.

Economic and Social Council

Functional Commissions

Commissions on:
  Narcotic Drugs
  Crime Prevention and Criminal Justice
  Science and Technology for
    Development
  Sustainable Development
  Status of Women
  Population and Development
Commission for Social Development
Statistical Commission

Regional Commissions

Economic Commission for Africa (ECA)

Economic Commission for Europe (ECE)

Economic Commission for Latin
  America and the Caribbean (ECLAC)

Economic and Social Commission for
  Asia and the Pacific (ESCAP)

Economic and Social Commission for
  Western Asia (ESCWA)

Other Bodies

Permanent Forum on Indigenous Issues

United Nations Forum on Forests

Sessional and standing committees

Expert, ad hoc and related bodies

Related Organizations

WTO World Trade Organization

IAEA[5] International Atomic Energy
  Agency

CTBTO Prep.Com[6] PrepCom for the
  Nuclear-Test-Ban Treaty Organization

OPCW[6] Organization for the
  Prohibition of Chemical Weapons

International Court of Justice

Specialized Agencies[7]

ILO International Labour
  Organization

FAO Food and Agriculture
  Organization of the United Nations

UNESCO United Nations
  Educational, Scientific and Cultural
  Organization

WHO World Health Organization

World Bank Group

  IBRD International Bank
    for Reconstruction and
    Development

  IDA International Development
    Association

  IFC International Finance
    Corporation

  MIGA Multilateral Investment
    Guarantee Agency

  ICSID International Centre for
    Settlement of Investment
    Disputes

IMF International Monetary Fund

ICAO International Civil Aviation
  Organization

IMO International Maritime
  Organization

ITU International Telecommunication
  Union

UPU Universal Postal Union

WMO World Meteorological
  Organization

WIPO World Intellectual Property
  Organization

IFAD International Fund for
  Agricultural Development

UNIDO United Nations Industrial
  Development Organization

UNWTO World Tourism
  Organization

Secretariat

Departments and Offices

OSG[3] Office of the
  Secretary-General

OIOS Office of Internal Oversight
  Services

OLA Office of Legal Affairs

DPA Department of Political Affairs

UNODA Office for Disarmament
  Affairs

DPKO Department of Peacekeeping
  Operations

DFS[4] Department of Field Support

OCHA Office for the Coordination
  of Humanitarian Affairs

DESA Department of Economic and
  Social Affairs

DGACM Department for General
  Assembly and Conference
  Management

DPI Department of Public Information

DM Department of Management

UN-OHRLLS Office of the High
  Representative for the Least
  Developed Countries, Landlocked
  Developing Countries and Small
  Island Developing States

OHCHR Office of the United
  Nations High Commissioner for
  Human Rights

UNODC United Nations Office on
  Drugs and Crime

DSS Department of Safety and
  Security

☙❧

UNOG UN Office at Geneva

UNOV UN Office at Vienna

UNON UN Office at Nairobi

Published by the United Nations
Department of Public Information

DPI/2470—07-49950—December 2007—3M

recommendation that would impede the free consideration and thus action of the Security Council (a limitation it did not always respect in practice). The activities of the Assembly are directed toward cooperation among States, discussion of common problems and the best way in which to address a problem from an international standpoint, namely, in consideration of the interests of all States in international society. This is not a negligible function.[10]

The Assembly is not, however, a legislator. It has neither the composition (non-elected members) nor the mandate (limited to the adoption of recommendations) for such a role. The Assembly may discuss and recommend; it may not decide. States have not renounced their legislative sovereignty; they have retained this completely. However, this does not mean that the Assembly can never 'decide' in a binding manner. It can insofar as States specifically conferred such a power, as occurred for example in 1947 in the peace treaty concluded with Italy concerning the Italian colonies in Africa. Annex XI of the treaty provides that in the case of a disagreement between the powers, the General Assembly can determine the fate of the territories. By virtue of this authorisation, the General Assembly was able, in a resolution passed on 2 December 1950, to integrate Eritrea to Ethiopia.[11] Above all, the Assembly can decide any internal question of the organisation for which the Charter has conferred it with the power to make definitive decisions. This is the case, for example, for budgetary questions (article 17). The Assembly may also apply binding injunctions to all its subsidiary organs, except those that have a judicial function and thus enjoy a degree of independence, such as administrative tribunals. The general rule of thumb is that outside the organisation, in relation to State members, the Assembly does not have any decision-making powers, whereas within the organisation, it does. The broad material powers of the Assembly (all questions falling within the scope of the Charter) are thus balanced by very limited formal powers of this organ, which can only make recommendations to States concerning questions not of a purely internal nature.

If a particular function is not expressly or impliedly attributed by the Charter to an organ other than the Assembly, it will be the Assembly which has to deal with it by virtue of the sweeping residual power-attribution under article 10 of the Charter. Thus, for example, when the League of Nations mandate over South-West Africa passed over from the League to the United Nations and South Africa refused to transform it into a trusteeship, the question arose as to what organ within the UN would receive and scrutinise the periodical reports due according to the mandatory power. Under the League it had been the Council and its Mandate Commission. No provision was made under the Charter, since it was not envisaged that a League mandate would survive. In the *International States of South West Africa* advisory opinion, the ICJ advised that this function of control was now vested in the General Assembly of the UN by virtue of its general power under article 10, failing any specific attribution of power to

---

[10] M Bourquin, *Vers une nouvelle Société des Nations* (Neuchâtel, 1945) 65 stresses the contribution of one of the rarely appreciated aspects of these common sessions: 'These meetings are useful. They serve to reduce, to a certain degree, areas of misunderstanding that divide peoples. The fact that international life is filled with misunderstandings, even in areas where there should logically be more understanding, governments often feel inhibited by mistrust without any basis, or apprehensions caused by ignorance. By bringing together the representatives of these governments, and making them work with one another in the pursuit of the same goals, the collective institution frees them of at least some of their prejudices' (unofficial translation).

[11] See V Coussirat-Coustère and PM Eisemann, *Répertoire de la jurisprudence arbitrale internationale*, vol III/1 (Dordrecht; Boston; London, 1991) 196–99.

another organ (ICJ, *Reports*, 1950, p 137).The principal functions of the Assembly are the following:

—To discuss and adopt recommendations on all questions falling within the scope of the United Nations (article 10);

—To consider general questions concerning the maintenance of peace and disarmament, and to discuss all questions in this context (article 11);[12]

—To initiate studies and make recommendations for the promotion of international cooperation in the political field as well as the codification and development of international law. To work toward the realisation of functional cooperation in human rights matters. In relation to the codification and development of international law, the Assembly established an important subsidiary organ, the International Law Commission, composed of expert jurists. The Commission prepares drafts of international treaties the adoption of which are often discussed during inter-State conferences. Important treaties have seen the light of day as a consequence, for example, on the law of the sea (1958), diplomatic and consular relations (1961, 1963), law of treaties (1969, 1986), etc (article 13);[13]

—To recommend, where required, solutions for the peaceful settlement of disputes or other situations of a nature likely to impair the general welfare or friendly relations among States (article 14);[14]

—To examine reports on the activities of the Security Council and other principal organs, as well as subsidiary organs in relation to which the Assembly may also provide instructions if required (article 15);[15]

[12] '1. The General Assembly may consider the general principles of cooperation in the maintenance of international peace and security, including the principles governing disarmament and the regulation of armaments, and may make recommendations with regard to such principles to the Members or to the Security Council or to both.

   2. The General Assembly may discuss any questions relating to the maintenance of international peace and security brought before it by any Member of the United Nations, or by the Security Council, or by a State which is not a Member of the United Nations in accordance with Article 35, paragraph 2, and except as provided in Article 12, may make recommendations with regard to any such questions to the state or states concerned or to the Security Council or to both. Any such question on which action is necessary shall be referred to the Security Council by the General Assembly either before or after the discussion.

   3. The General Assembly may call the attention of the Security Council to situations which are likely to endanger international peace and security.

   4. The powers of the General Assembly set forth in this Article shall not limit the general scope of Article 10'.

[13] '1. The General Assembly shall initiate studies and make recommendations for the purpose of:

   promoting international cooperation in the political field an encouraging the progressive development of international law and its codification;

   promoting international cooperation in the economic, social, cultural, educational and health fields, and assisting in the realisation of human rights and fundamental freedoms for all without distinction as to race, sex, language, or religion.

   2. The further responsibilities, functions and powers of the General Assembly with respect to matters mentioned in paragraph 1 (b) above are set forth in Chapters IX and X'.

[14] 'Subject to the provisions of article 12, the General Assembly may recommend measures for the peaceful adjustment of any situation, regardless of the origin, which it deems likely to impair the general welfare or friendly relations among nations, including situations resulting from a violation of the provisions of the present Charter setting forth the Purposes and Principles of the United Nations'.

[15] '1. The General Assembly shall receive and consider annual and special reports from the Security Council; these reports shall include an account of the measures that the Security Council has decided upon or taken to maintain international peace and security.

—To approve the budget of the organisation and determine the contributions of each State (article 17);[16]
—To elect non-permanent members to the Security Council as well as judges to the ICJ (article 23 § 1; article 4 of the Statute of the Court of Justice);
—To vote on the admission of new States to the organisation (article 4).

§ 80 Voting

The right to vote is regulated by article 18. Paragraph 1 provides the basic principle: each State has one vote. Formal equality thus prevails in the Assembly. The scrawny dwarves carry the same weight in the Assembly as the muscular giants. The difference in voting modalities is made according to the distinction between 'important questions' and 'other questions'. For 'important questions', a two-thirds majority of States present and voting is required; for 'other questions', a simple majority of present and voting States is sufficient. What are 'important questions'? The Charter provides a response in article 18 § 2: 'These questions shall include: recommendations with respect to the maintenance of peace and security, the election of non-permanent members of the Security Council, the election of members of the Trusteeship Council in accordance with paragraph 1 (c) of Article 86, the admission of new Members to the United Nations, the suspension of the rights and privileges of membership, the expulsion of Members, questions relating to the operation of the trusteeship system, and budgetary questions'. Further, a simple majority may decide to treat other questions as 'important questions'. These are then subjected to a two-thirds majority vote after having passed a vote of a simple majority on the preliminary question of whether to treat the questions as 'important'. This rule is provided in article 18 § 3: 'Decisions on other questions, including the determination of additional categories of questions to be decided by a two-thirds majority, shall be made by a majority of the members present and voting'.

There are also rules as to the quorum. First, a question may be debated if at least one third of the members are present. Second, a resolution may be adopted if a majority of the members are present. With regard to this question, reference may be made to Rule 67 of the 'Rules of Procedure of the General Assembly', last revised in 2000.

In practice, a significant number of resolutions of the General Assembly are adopted without any vote, by so-called consensus. Thus, in the absence of any objection, the resolution is deemed to have been adopted. Furthermore, practice indicates that it may be difficult to decide whether a subject falls under the heading of 'important questions' according to article 18, § 2. Thus, for example, violations of human rights may be regarded as 'social matters', in the vocabulary of the Charter, but also as an issue relating to (positive) peace. In many cases, the question is not of practical significance, since

---

2. The General Assembly shall receive and consider reports from the other organs of the United Nations'.

[16] '1. The General Assembly shall consider and approve the budget of the Organization.
2. The expenses of the Organization shall be borne by the Members as apportioned by the General Assembly.
3. The General Assembly shall consider and approve any financial and budgetary arrangements with specialized agencies referred to in Article 57 and shall examine the administrative budgets of such specialized agencies with a view to making recommendations to the agencies concerned'.

clearly a two thirds majority (or more) are able to vote for the resolution. In other cases, the President of the Assembly will state the required majority, but he may be overruled by simple majority. In some cases, the Assembly expressly determines that an agenda item is an 'important question', for example information on self-governing territories, the racial conflict in South Africa, the Tunisian and Moroccan questions in the wake of decolonisation, the draft convention on the political rights of women or the representation of China (in 1961). It is more often as a result of declaring a question as 'important' under § 2 than by making it important under § 3 that two third majorities have been imposed. The practice with respect to 'important' categories according to § 2 and 'important'categories according to § 3 has, at the end of the day, remained somewhat haphazard and dominated by ad hoc motives.

§ 81 Sessions

Ordinary sessions of the General Assembly commence in September in the United Nations New York premises and are of limited duration. Extraordinary sessions may be convoked at the request of the Security Council or by a simple majority of member States (article 20).[17] Resolution 377 (V) provides a supplementary mechanism, not regulated by the Charter, according to which extraordinary sessions of the Assembly may be convoked.[18]

§ 82 Subsidiary Organs

The Assembly may create subsidiary ad hoc or permanent organs.[19] Article 22 recalls the power already addressed in a general manner in article 7 § 2. This capacity is also an implied power of each principal organ. Article 22 reads as follows:[20] 'The General Assembly may establish such subsidiary organs as it deems necessary for the performance of its functions'. In its history, the Assembly has created more than 500 subsidiary organs. At any one moment, 60 subsidiary organs attached to the Assembly are functioning in parallel. From the 1990s onwards, the organisation has tried to simplify the organic structure which, with permanent additions, had become too complicated and resulted in the overlapping of activities among organs. The permanent subsidiary organs mainly consist of six committees that discuss the questions submitted to the General Assembly, and report back to the plenary:

[17] 'The General Assembly shall meet in regular annual sessions and in such special sessions as occasion may require. Special sessions shall be convoked by the Secretary-General at the request of the Security Council or of a majority of the Members of the United Nations'.

[18] See above, ch 7, § 57.

[19] An overview of the subsidiary organs of the United Nations is found in the *United Nations Juridical Yearbook*.

[20] In general, subsidiary organs may in turn create their own subsidiary organs, as was the case, eg, with the United Nations Conference on Trade and Development (UNCTAD) which created a number of commissions.

—First Committee: disarmament and international security questions
—Second Committee: economic and financial questions
—Third Committee: social, humanitarian and cultural questions
—Fourth Committee: special political and decolonisation questions
—Fifth Committee: administrative and budgetary questions
—Sixth Committee: primary forum for the consideration of legal questions (for exam-
   ple, discussions concerning drafts of international law codifications presented to the
   General Assembly by the International Law Commission and addressing all legal
   questions affecting the organisation). The Sixth Committee is peopled by interna-
   tional lawyers.

The majority of questions submitted to the Assembly are discussed in these themed
committees. Each committee has the same composition as the plenary Assembly, but
the delegates are experts in the particular area of speciality. Other permanent subsidiary organs include the International Law Commission, the new Human Rights
Council and the United Nations Administrative Tribunal. In relation to ad hoc and
temporary subsidiary organs, there is a whole host of different entities including the
Preparatory Commission for the International Criminal Court, which played a crucial
role in the drafting of the 1998 Rome Statute. This Commission existed from 1996 to
1998. The activities of the subsidiary organs are increasingly varied: information and
expert functions (the International Law Commission, Committees of procedure); the
elaboration of programmes and rules (United Nations Commission on International
Trade Law); technical assistance in a range of areas (United Nations Industrial
Development Organisation before 1985), etc. Generally, the Assembly controls the
subsidiary organs; it determines their powers and can modify them at any time; it has
the power to give them formal instructions and binding terms.

   The Assembly can create an organ and grant it powers that the Assembly itself does
not enjoy. Consequently, it does not always delegate its own powers to a subsidiary
organ. It can grant an organ functions that are directly entailed from the Charter. In
this vein, the Assembly created the United Nations Administrative Tribunal (UNAT)
as a subsidiary organ. The Tribunal has judicial independence. Its judgments may not
be reviewed by the Assembly; the Assembly cannot give the Tribunal directives in relation to its jurisprudence. The Assembly does not itself exercise judicial powers, but was
nevertheless able to create the UNAT. The ICJ accepted the creation of this organ in
its advisory opinion on *Effect of Awards of Compensation Made by the UNAT* (1954).
This capacity is grounded on the implicit powers of the Assembly found in Article 101
of the Charter:

> It would, in the opinion of the Court, hardly be consistent with the expressed aim of the char-
> ter to promote freedom and justice for individuals and the constant preoccupation of the
> United Nations Organization to promote this aim that it should afford no judicial or arbitral
> remedy to its own staff for the settlement of any disputes which may arise between it
> and them. In these circumstances, the Court finds that the power to establish a tribunal, to do
> justice as between the Organization and the staff members, was essential to ensure the effi-
> cient working of the Secretariat, and to give effect to the paramount consideration of secur-
> ing the highest standards of efficiency, competence and integrity. Capacity to do this arises by
> necessary intendment of the Charter.[21]

---

[21] *Effect of Awards of Compensation Made by the UNAT* (Advisory Opinion) [1954] ICJ Rep 57.

According to the Court, this power resides in the Assembly as principal organ of the organisation.[22] The example of the UNAT demonstrates that in exceptional cases there are no parallel activities exercised simultaneously by a principal organ and its subsidiary organ. Rather than there being a delegation of powers, the subsidiary organ is created directly from the basis of the Charter in accordance with the doctrine of implied powers. The same can be said for the criminal tribunals established by the Security Council under Chapter VII of the Charter.

§ 83 Human Rights Council

International human rights are recognised by the Charter of the United Nations in § 2 of the Preamble and in articles 1 § 3, 13 § 1 (b) and 55 (c). These rights are more concretely developed in the 1948 Universal Declaration on Human Rights, which is incorporated into General Assembly Resolution 217 and by the two 1966 Covenants on civil and political rights, and social, economic and cultural rights, respectively.

The branch of human rights law infiltrated public international law in 1945 as a response to the barbaric acts of the Axis powers. The old doctrine, according to which an individual was not a 'subject' properly so-called, but an 'object' of international law, was untenable in light of the shocking treatment of oppressed populations during the 1930s and 1940s under the yoke of authoritarian regimes. It also became evident that long-term peace was not attainable without the protection of fundamental human rights, at both the international and the internal level. Whereas Chapter VII of the Charter is imbued with the ideology of negative peace and the maxim that peace pre-vails over justice in the context of urgent measures, the other chapters of the Charter, in particular Chapters IX and X in which human rights feature prominently, focus on positive peace and the maxim that justice is a necessary condition of peace.

The Charter does not limit itself to simply expounding the international protection of human rights; it also institutionally reinforces these rights. The task of finding a concrete expression for the human rights mentioned in the Charter, as well as the task of ensuring that universal human rights are applied in practice, fell on a newly created organ, the Human Rights Commission.[23] Established in 1946, the Commission was a subsidiary organ of the United Nations Economic and Social Council (ECOSOC) and from 1973 comprised 53 governmental delegates. The Commission had three principal functions: (1) a normative role of 'standard setting', namely the elaboration of texts on the protection of human rights, like for example the 1966 Covenants, or the Declaration on the Protection of All Persons from Enforced Disappearance;[24] (2) a rather weak enforcement role: in order to put into practice human rights obligations of State members, the Commission established a number of mechanisms; the most well-known was Resolution 1503 of 1970 that established a procedure of confidential consultations with member States accused of grave and systematic violations of

---

[22] *Ibid*, 57–58.
[23] This organ should not be confused with the Human Rights Committee which is the supervisory organ created to ensure respect for the International Covenant on Civil and Political Rights of 1966.
[24] UNGA Res 47/133 (12 February 1993) UN Doc A/RES/47/133.

human rights; and (3) finally, a reporting system on specific subjects, that was supposed to create a sort of general monitoring system on sensitive questions, for example the status of women and children, respect for human rights during armed conflict, the human rights situation in some countries, etc. The Commission only had powers of recommendation, not decision-making powers. Consequently, its work was based on 'constructive dialogue' with State members. This earned the Commission accusations of ineffectiveness. However, this general complaint is only partially justified as it does not take into account the tasks entrusted and the means allocated to the Commission. An important aspect of understanding the functioning of the Commission is its composition. The Commission is comprised of governmental delegates, not independent experts, and thus it could only ever be a reflection of divided political wills. To criticise the political character of the Commission is also only partially justified. Its creators thought that an organ representing the will of world governments would have greater influence over the situation on the ground rather than an organ composed of independent experts that would not have leverage over anyone. The inevitable outcome of this gamble was the politicisation of the Commission's approach to human rights.

From 2000 onwards, a number of Western countries expressed their dissatisfaction with the work of the Commission. In their eyes it had discredited itself. They criticised, in particular, the political selectiveness of its activities where some countries such as Israel were regularly put under the spotlight whereas others that had the support of the Third World regularly escaped scrutiny. Similarly, they criticised the position of some States on the Commission that had little regard for human rights: could the cat be set loose among the pigeons? They also considered the practice of certain member States of the Commission, which had little respect for human rights, to be more orientated towards avoiding their own condemnation and those of their political allies, than promoting the human rights cause. Lastly, they claimed that human rights could not be adequately addressed by a subsidiary body of ECOSOC. In view of the importance of these rights in a modern world and in the absence of creating a new principal organ of the United Nations, an institutional change was necessary. The United Nations Secretary-General explored several possibilities in this respect and Switzerland also supported these reforms. As a consequence, the Human Rights Council was created on 15 March 2006,[25] and replaced the predecessor Commission.

Four main features of the new Council distinguish it from the old Commission:

—*Institutional change.* The Council is a subsidiary organ of the General Assembly, and not of ECOSOC. The greater importance of the General Assembly as the United Nations plenary organ reflects the significance of this institutional change. The Secretary-General had proposed to establish the Council as a new principal organ, but his recommendation was not heeded. This was principally because such a creation would have necessitated a formal revision of the Charter, entailing a cumbersome procedure fraught with pitfalls.

—*Membership change.* The Council is composed of 47 States that are elected by the General Assembly by a simple majority of votes for a term of 3 years, once renewable. A State must then wait one term before it can be re-elected to the Council. In order to be elected as a member, candidate States must 'uphold the highest standards'

---

[25] UNGA Res 60/251 (3 April 2006) UN Doc A/RES/60/251.

in human rights matters. This condition is a response to the express wish not to elect States to the Council that have little respect for human rights. At the same time, the resolution establishing the Council insists on 'equitable geographical distribution', with thirteen African seats, thirteen Asian seats, eight Latin American and Caribbean sears and 13 European seats (six for Eastern Europe and seven for Western Europe). However, the first elections resulted in States being elected that are by no means exempt from serious criticism of their human rights record. This was due to different understandings of human rights and the priorities between civil rights and collective rights and even more compellingly by the mandatory pluralist representation of States in the United Nations organ. Lastly, it should be noted that the General Assembly has the possibility to suspend a Council member by a vote of two-thirds majority for 'gross and systematic violations' of human rights. It is unlikely that the Assembly will have frequent recourse to this possibility, as it could easily contaminate the working relations and instigate a practice of settling scores.

—*Greater frequency and length of sessions.* The Council meets at least three times a year, for a minimum of 10 weeks in total. In addition, each member may propose holding emergency sessions. Such sessions take place if a third of the Council members vote in favour. It will be recalled that the European Union proposed that the Council should meet four to six time a year, thus for a minimum of 12 weeks. Experience, however, shows that the length alone of sessions is not a guarantee of efficiency and progress. It is the atmosphere in which sessions are conducted, rather than a measure of the lapse of time, which will make for productive sessions.

—*A new evaluation procedure (peer review).* The Council must evaluate respect for human rights obligations of all State members of the United Nations on the basis of cooperation, discussion and technical assistance, namely respect for the old principles of constructive dialogue. This is what is called the universal periodic review. Within one year after the holding of its first session, the Council can develop the modalities and time allocation for the universal periodic review mechanism (§ 5 (e) of the resolution cited above). This rule was established in Resolution 5/1 passed by the Council on 18 June 2007 and with a follow-up at its sixth session, 20th meeting, on 27 September 2007.[26] This series of reforms undeniably gives rise to legitimate hopes of progress. The political selectivity of the choice of candidates to be evaluated will in the future be less pronounced, although there is some squabbling over the chronological order in which these evaluations should proceed.

Additionally, particular functions of the Commission, such as the nomination of special rapporteurs, or the 1503 procedure, have been passed over to the new Council.

Legal commentators have generally given a cool reception to the reasons given for the handover from the old Commission to the new Council. Authors are essentially divided into three categories: one group defends the old Commission and consequently questions the impact of the new Council; another group considers the new Council to be much the same as the old Commission and the differences between the

---

[26] Decision 6/12. The text is available on the website of the United Nations: www.ohchr.org/EN/HRBodies/UPR/Pages/UPRmain.aspxhttp://www.ohchr.org/EN/HRBodies/UPR/Pages/UPRmain.aspx. For the first session of 2008, the following States will be examined: Morocco, South Africa, Tunisia, Algeria, Bahrain, India, Indonesia, the Philippines, Argentina, Equator, Brazil, the Netherlands, Finland, United Kingdom, Poland, Czech Republic (16 States, listed in the order of the appearance). The lists are established until the 12th session in 2011. See the abovementioned website for further details.

organs to be merely cosmetic. A third group of authors continue to reserve their judgement, but consider that the changes made are worthwhile.

—*Defenders of the old Commission.* In an article devoid of diplomatic niceties, a former employee of the United Nations has defended the old Commission against attacks of over-politicisation. He accuses Western countries of having followed an egoistic agenda by painting themselves in a favourable light and portraying the 'others' as human rights violators, as rogue States that are bent on politicising the organ.[27] He also highlights the work accomplished by the Commission, for example the adoption of the Universal Declaration in 1948, the Covenants in 1966 and various other conventions and protocols. Likewise, he notes the Commission's establishment of a number of important working groups on arbitrary detention, missing persons, the rights of indigenous peoples, internally-displaced persons, etc; and the nomination of special Rapporteurs on torture, extra-judicial executions, and religious intolerance.[28]

—*Sceptics who focus on the similarities between the two organs.* In a lively article,[29] one author stresses the strong resemblance between the Council and the old Commission. He notes that the problem of the politicisation of the organ has not been solved because it remains structurally-inbuilt: 'no institution, regardless of its nature, exists in a vacuum detached from its social environment'.[30] As the Council is composed of governmental delegates, its work inescapably amounts to political considerations in matters of human rights. Unlike a court, its business will not be centred on legal issues concerning human rights. According to this author, the first session of the Council has confirmed these concerns.

—*Those who reserve judgement.* Some authors[31] analyse, in straightforward terms, the transformation of the old Commission into the new Council, and argue that the Council at least brings a symbolic advantage, namely that of a 'fresh start'. The bitter disappointments and objections that the old Commission aroused might never have been overcome without such drastic institutional change. The new Council offers the collective imagination a clean slate and thus gives States fresh impetus to deal with human rights issues. These authors nevertheless stress that the measure for determining whether the institutional change has been worthwhile turns on the attitudes of its State members, as the Council is only the substance of what States make it.[32]

---

[27] A de Zayas, 'The New UN Human Rights Council was Let Down by the European Union' (2006) 1 *Current Concerns Express* 5–6. Herewith some extracts: 'If the Commission of Human Rights allegedly lost credibility in the last years, had the European Union states not contributed to it? I myself participated in the Commission's 2004 and 2005 sessions, when Guantanamo was on the agenda. The "good states" of the European Union then mightily politicized and brazenly applied double-standards. I remember the breathtaking cynicism of some European Union states and the shameful fact that all European Union states actually voted against the Guantanamo resolution, in order not to irritate their NATO ally and friend, the USA'. In a similar vein: 'Who is entitled to determine, who rogue states are? Are Libya, Saudi Arabia, North Korea, Iran the only rogue states? Or perhaps other states, too, which trample on international law, like Russia with its massacres and bombardments in Chechnya, the United States with its wars of aggression and crimes against humanity in Guantanamo, or Israel, which has been repeatedly condemned for a consistent pattern of grave violations of human rights by the UN Human Rights Committee and the UN Committee against torture?'.

[28] *Ibid*, 5.

[29] V Chetail, 'Le Conseil des droits de l'homme des Nations Unies : réformer pour ne rien changer?' in *Mélanges V. Y. Ghébali* (Bruxelles, 2007) 125ff (unofficial translation).

[30] *Ibid*, 164.

[31] N Ghanea, 'From UN Commission on Human Rights to UN Human Rights Council: One Step Forwards or Two Steps Sideways ?' (2006) 55 *ICLQ* 695ff.

[32] *Ibid*, 705.

The Council is largely a continuum of the Commission with some marginal improvements that could have been included in the rules governing the old organ. Of course, the institutional rebirth of the organ and the inclusion of the 'peer review' mechanism are commendable improvements. They are not, however, reforms that should be welcomed with pomp and ceremony. The honeymoon period of the symbolic new beginning soon ended. The first sessions of the Council, in which, *inter alia*, the situation in Darfur was discussed, revealed old divides. In an organ composed of government delegates, human rights cannot be addressed as they would in a court of law. How can questions like the detention of individuals in Guantanamo, or the treatment of Tibetans, be discussed in such an environment in a 'non-political manner'? Delegates are confronted with radically different world visions and competing policies in the consideration of highly sensitive issues. One must be aware that debates about human rights in this politically-constituted world organ turn on 'politics' in the most basic sense of the term, and not 'politics' in its noble understanding, as a socio-political vision of the world.

As neither the General Assembly nor any of its subsidiary organs have the power to make decisions, if the sails of soothing rhetoric are pierced, the only course to follow is that of 'constructive dialogue', prickly and fraught with pitfalls. It is thus by small, rather unspectacular, steps that progress in human rights issues is achieved. Even so, constructive dialogue requires a climate of goodwill and reciprocal trust, as well as considerable tact, understanding, patience and sometimes an acute understanding that the process with be long-drawn-out. If it remains possible to strongly censure *coram publico* a particular attitude, then this option should be the *ultima ratio* because it risks sterilising a State's will to cooperate, which is indispensable for addressing human rights issues. Further, at the macro-relational level, by inflaming international relations in general, States become irritated with one another and all progress is impeded. In an atmosphere saturated with emotions and threats, States are put on the defensive. In such an environment, constructive compromises are hard to come by in human rights matters, just as in disarmament or any other international matter.

In conclusion, the new Council has replaced the old Commission without any notable improvements because 'politics' remains at the core of its composition. The Council thus continues to reflect the emotions of an ideological world divided in the area of human rights. Just as the Commission did not deserve the excessive criticisms that it received, the Council does not deserve opprobrium for its work that merely reflects the realities of international life.

B. Security Council

§ 84 General Aspects

The composition, functions, powers and voting procedure of the Security Council are addressed in Chapter V (articles 23–32). Article 24 § 1 refers to the Security Council's principal attribution, namely its ability to take measures for the maintenance and re-establishment of international peace: 'In order to ensure prompt and effective action by the United Nations, its Members confer on the Security Council primary responsibility for the maintenance of international peace and security, and agree that in carrying out its duties under this responsibility the Security Council acts on their behalf'. Paragraph 2 establishes certain limits to the measures that the Security Council may take. These are of a generic character; overall, the idea of a strong executive that is not constrained by 'legalities' prevails. Herewith the content of § 2: 'In discharging these duties, the Security Council shall act in accordance with the Purposes and Principles of the United Nations. The specific powers granted to the Security Council for the discharge of these duties are laid down in Chapters VI, VII, VIII, and XII'. The principal functions of the Council according to the Charter are as follows:

—Measures for the maintenance and re-establishment of peace, including the decision to impose sanctions or measures of execution: article 24, article 39 and following.
—Power to investigate any situation that may give rise to a dispute (article 34); power to recommend appropriate measures for resolving a dispute or methods of adjustment (articles 36 and 37).
—Provide recommendations to the General Assembly concerning the appointment of the Secretary-General (article 97).
—Elect, together with the General Assembly, the judges of the ICJ (article 4 of the Statute of the ICJ).

The Council can be called into session at any moment; it is a permanent organ. That is to say, State delegates that are represented on the Council are required to be based in New York so that the Council can meet at any time, in case of a crisis. This requirement improves a weakness of the Council of the League of Nations, which in cases of crisis, first had to be convoked, with the results one can imagine.[33] This change implemented in the United Nations in response to the unfortunate experience of the League of Nations may seem quite innocuous to us today. However, in 1945 it aroused vehement opposition from the USSR, which feared giving the new organisation, dominated by Western States, too much power.

§ 85 Composition

The Security Council is composed of 15 member States,[34] including five permanent members that are expressly listed in the Charter and enjoy a veto power (China, the

---

[33] The Council of the League of Nations should have met once a crisis had erupted, but the Council could only meet days, and sometimes weeks, after such an event, due to the time taken for unprepared delegates to arrive from the ends of the earth. The remarks made by Bourquin, *Vers une nouvelle Société des Nations*, above n 10 at 103ff, 176, describe the result of such a practice: 'Nothing was ready at the beginning of the session, and measures were sought to cover this embarrassing situation. For example, a rapporteur or a Committee was asked to prepare a draft of a resolution. In reality, what was asked to be done was to negotiate with the most interested and influential delegates in order to draft a text that they could all agree upon. But how could men who are not magicians accomplish such a miracle? In relation to the most serious, complex and sensitive international situations, would one consider States to be able to find a collective response in a matter of days or weeks?' (unofficial translation).

[34] By an amendment to the Charter, adopted on 17 December 1963 and entered into force on 31 August 1965, the number of non-permanent members of the Security Council increased from 6 to 10, thereby increasing the total number of Security Council members from 11 to 15. See UNGA Res 1991 (XXVIII) (17 December 1963).

United States of America, France, the United Kingdom, and Russia). The ten non-permanent members are elected by the General Assembly for a period of two years. Article 23 § 1 provides:

> The Security Council shall consist of fifteen Members of the United Nations. The Republic of China, France, the Union of Soviet Socialist Republics, the United Kingdom of Great Britain and Northern Ireland, and the United States of America shall be permanent members of the Security Council. The General Assembly shall elect ten other Members of the United Nations to be non-permanent members of the Security Council, due regard being specially paid, in the first instance to the contribution of Members of the United Nations to the maintenance of international peace and security and to the other purposes of the Organization, and also to equitable geographical distribution.

This equal distribution of non-permanent seats has been made according to the following formula: 3 seats for Africa, 2 seats for Asia, 2 seats for Latin America, 2 for Western Europe and other States (South Africa, Australia, Canada, Israel, and New Zealand) and 1 seat for Eastern Europe. Article 23 § 3 stipulates that each member of the Security Council will have only one representative, in comparison to article 9 § 2 according to which in the General Assembly each State may have five representatives. The restrictive character of the Council is thus further protected. This provision does not exclude experts and assistants to the sole delegate at the Security Council.

§ 86 Voting

According to article 27 § 1 each State has one vote. For all 'procedural' questions, a decision is taken on a slightly qualified majority of 9 votes to 15 (article 27 § 2).[35] For all 'other questions' (substantive), the required majority is 9 votes to 15, including the 'affirmative' vote of the five permanent members (article 27 § 3).[36] This requirement has been interpreted in practice, diverging from the text, as meaning that no permanent member has voted against a proposition.[37] The abstention of a permanent member from the voting process does thus not affect the decision. The extent to which voluntary absence of a permanent member may be counted as abstention has remained controversial.

This 'affirmative' vote of permanent members (in practice: no negative vote, abstention does not affect the decision) expresses in legal terms the famous veto introduced by the three great powers at Yalta (USSR, United States of America, United Kingdom). Veto means in Latin 'I prohibit', 'I oppose'. This is the formula that the peoples' tribune in the ancient Republic of Rome would use to oppose decrees issued by the Senate, consuls or acts handed down by judges. The veto is a negative vote; but not all negative votes of one of the five permanent members are a veto. Use of the veto

---

[35] 'Decisions of the Security Council on procedural matters shall be made by an affirmative vote of nine members'.

[36] 'Decisions of the Security Council on all other matters shall be made by an affirmative vote of nine members including the concurring votes of the permanent members; provided that, in decisions under Chapter VI, and under paragraph 3 of Article 52, a party to a dispute shall abstain from voting'.

[37] *Legal Consequences for States of the Continued Presence of South Africa in Namibia (South-West Africa)* (Advisory Opinion), above n 7 at 22, § 22.

supposes that the decision of the Security Council could have been adopted if it were not applied, as there was a majority of 9 votes. It is in these situations that the negative vote of one of the five permanent members inhibits the decision from being adopted: this is where the 'I oppose' is voiced. However, when a decision has not been adopted because it falls short of the required majority, then the negative votes of the permanent members are not counted as veto. Thus, all negative votes by the permanent members are not necessarily a veto. The right to veto was not a novelty in 1945. The League of Nations applied the old rule of unanimity (article 5 § 1 of the Covenant). This meant that the right to veto could be exercised by all States, whether great powers or small entities. In 1945 the novelty consisted in restricting the exercise of the right to the five great powers and thereby depriving other States of the veto. Thus, a new type of discrimination was created, not a new right. In fact, in 1945, the choice was made to limit the exercise of the right rather than increase it.

The aim of the veto is not to give satisfaction to an old theory of justice according to which those who provide the most support for the measures taken (notably military sanctions) should have a reinforced vote, according to the maxim 'to the most responsible, the most rights'. According to such a theory, the vote of the great powers should count for more because of their support in the enforcement of sanctions by military action. However, the veto applies to much more than decisions to impose sanctions. It extends, for example, to the election of judges on the ICJ. The purpose of the veto is in fact a political concern. It is a way of ensuring the ongoing participation of the five great powers in the organisation by not allowing decisions to be made within the organisation with which they would fundamentally disapprove and which would give them cause to leave. For action in the area of security, the utility of the principle is particularly evident. To decide to impose sanctions (perhaps military) against a great power would amount to plunging the world into a third world war and would mark the end of the organisation. Such a prospect was simply not a practical possibility; it would surpass even the most extreme measures that the organisation could reasonably take; and it would entail gravest consequences for humanity under the maxim *fiat justitia pereat mundus*.

Initially, the veto was not considered to be a concession of any excessive gravity. It simply meant that it would be impossible to direct a measure *directly* against one of the permanent members, namely the USSR, the United States of America, the United Kingdom, France or China. The problem really arose during the Cold War, which polarised the world into two camps. From this moment on, the veto was used not only to protect the direct interests of the superpowers, but their *indirect* interests. Consequently, the veto was used to block any proposed action against an 'ally' of the superpowers regardless of who they were, or where they were situated in the world. As in the 1950s, every State was affiliated with one of the two sides,[38] Western or communist, thus every political situation, no matter where in the world it took place, was viewed through the lens of the Cold War. The exercise of the veto in this context thus completely paralysed the organisation. The fatal use (and abuse) of the veto power by the USSR, with such pronounced frequency, was symptomatic of the acute minority position in which it had found itself.

The Charter deliberately leaves two expressions vague: 'decisions on procedural matters' (article 27 § 2) and 'decisions on all other matters' (article 27 § 3). Articles 28

---

[38] The movement of the non-allied States only took hold from 1955 onwards.

to 30, falling under the title of 'procedure', typically cover procedural matters, such as the creation of a subsidiary organ or the establishment of internal regulations. Other such procedural matters include issues relating to the order of business (agenda items), an invitation for an entity to participate in Council proceedings, reference of a question to another meeting or session, requests to the Assembly for a recommendation and the convocation of extraordinary sessions of the Assembly (article 20). In contrast, recommendations or decisions under Chapters II, VI, VII, XIV and XV, typically concern non-procedural matters, such as a recommendation for the settlement of a dispute, sanctions against a State threatening international peace, recommendation for the admission of a new member, measures for the execution of a judgment of the ICJ or recommendation of a person for the position of Secretary-General.

One speaks of a 'double veto' to describe a prior decision on whether a matter is procedural or not within the meaning of articles 27 § 2 and 27 § 3. The Security Council (following an agreement among the great powers at the San Francisco conference), quickly determined that this preliminary decision concerning the nature of a matter was in and of itself subject to the veto, in all cases of doubt. Otherwise the protection of the veto could be easily bypassed in cases of doubt by holding that a question concerned a 'procedural matter' on a majority vote of nine members. As the practice of the Security Council shows, there has been much squabbling on whether a question is procedural or not 'in cases of doubt', this latter notion being also prone to extensive interpretations.

One speaks of the 'reverse veto' when a permanent member uses its right of veto to block the lifting of a sanction or a regime previously established. This opens up the possibility for abuse. If a resolution of the Council gives States a right to 'use all necessary means to re-establish international peace and security in the region' and this blank cheque is abused in practice, it is for the Council to limit the powers granted to State members, or to remove them. It is here, however, that the veto could be used by a permanent member to prevent the authorisation previously granted by the Council from being modified or removed. If it is the State abusing this authorisation, it would use the veto to its own benefit and to cover all its action. Without its individual agreement, the authorisation could not be modified. Thus, an authorisation (possibly a blank authorisation) can only be established collectively by a majority of nine; but it will be impossible to modify it without the agreement of every permanent member taken individually. This is one way of summarising what occurred in Iraq with respect to the United States of America and the United Kingdom during the 1990s, almost as though it constituted a law-free zone. In effect, these two States refused a modification with respect to the previously Council-granted authorisation and interpreted the resolutions in question in an excessively liberal and self-serving manner.

Lastly, it may be noted that article 27 § 3 sets out the requirement for obligatory abstention: '. . . provided that, in decisions under Chapter VI, and under paragraph 3 of Article 52, a party to a dispute shall abstain from voting.'[39] In relation to an attempt to settle a dispute under Chapter VI or VIII (settlement of a dispute through regional mechanisms), a party to the dispute that is represented on the Council must abstain from voting. This is an application of the maxim according to which no one can judge his or her own case: *nemo iudex in re sua*. Practice has lessened this obligation from the very first situation that was submitted to the Council, that of the stationing of Soviet

---

[39] See art 15 § 6 of the Covenant of the League of Nations.

forces in Iran (1946). The question of abstention was first formally raised in 1951, during the examination of the Palestinian question. Since then, one single precedent is uncontested: the abstention of Argentina in the case of *Eichmann* in 1960. However, the Council has always attempted to get around this obligation: by not clearly basing itself on Chapter VI (to which the rule applies) but rather, for example, basing itself on Chapter VII, article 40 (to which the rule does not apply); by not making it clear that there is a 'dispute' (to which the rule applies) but rather simply affirming the existence of a 'situation' (to which the rule does not apply); or, by not subjecting it to a formal vote (30 per cent of Council decisions are adopted without a vote). The last part of article 27 § 3, the obligation to abstain, has thus lost much of its reach in practice.[40]

§ 87 Council Measures

The Security Council may decide (Chapter VII; Chapter XIV, article 94) or recommend (Chapters VI, VII) measures within the fields of its competences. When it has the power to decide, as with Chapter VII, the Council is not obliged to do so and can either not make a decision, or limit itself to recommending a course of action: he who can do the most, can also do the least, *in maiore minus inest*. The Charter makes this clear in article 39, which opens the door on Chapter VII measures: 'The Security Council shall determine the existence of any threat to the peace, breach of the peace, or act of aggression and *shall make recommendations, or decide* what measures shall be taken in accordance with Articles 41 and 42, to maintain or restore international peace and security' (emphasis added). Therefore, even under powerful Chapter VII, the Council is not limited to only giving orders. It could also pursue a diplomatic course of action. Indeed, it would be absurd that on moving from Chapter VI to Chapter VII, which gives the Council a range of more powerful measures at its disposal, that it would in turn limit the measures to which the Council can resort.

The 'decisions' of the Council have binding force. Article 25 describes this effect as follows: 'The Members of the United Nations agree to accept and carry out the decisions of the Security Council in accordance with the present Charter'. Article 2 § 5 recalls the solidarity imposed on members in the execution of United Nations measures: 'All Members shall give the United Nations every assistance in any action it takes in accordance with the present Charter, and shall refrain from giving assistance to any state against which the United Nations is taking preventive or enforcement action'. Articles 48 and 49 reiterate this binding force of decisions adopted under Chapter VII and the duty to cooperate in implementation of the measures. Article 48 § 1 provides: 'The action required to carry out the decisions of the Security Council for the maintenance of international peace and security shall be taken by all the Members of the United Nations or by some of them, as the Security Council may determine'. Article 49 echoes article 2 § 5 and stipulates that the solidarity extends to direct relations between member States: 'The Members of the United Nations shall join in affording

---

[40] For an excellent and brief overview, see P Tavernier, 'Article 27' in JP Cot, A Pellet and M Forteau (eds), *La Charte des Nations Unies, Commentaire article par article* vol I, 3rd edn (Paris, Economica, 2005) 944–48.

mutual assistance in carrying out the measures decided upon by the Security Council'. This group of provisions is completed with the very important article 103: 'In the event of a conflict between the obligations of the Members of the United Nations under the present Charter and their obligations under any other international agreement, their obligations under the present Charter shall prevail'. Despite being situated in Chapter XVI, the primary aim of this provision is to ensure the efficiency of Council action under Chapter VII, even though its scope goes much beyond the fulfilment of this goal. No State can thus argue that it is impeded in the implementation of sanctions by conflicting obligations contained in other treaties (or indeed in customary international law). Article 103 is addressed in more detail below.[41]

It remains to be considered whether the Security Council can adopt binding decisions outside Chapter VII. The Charter undeniably provides decision-making powers outside Chapter VII, for example in article 94 § 2: 'If any party to a case fails to perform the obligations incumbent upon it under a judgment rendered by the Court, the other party may have recourse to the Security Council, which may, if it deems necessary, make recommendations *or decide* upon measures to be taken to give effect to the judgment' (emphasis added). The question that is often asked is whether the Council can also adopt binding decisions by basing itself simply on the general authorisation of aforementioned article 25. Does article 25 only refer to other Charter provisions that provide for binding decision-making powers of the Council? Is it a provision that contains a reference *intra legem*, meaning that when a particular provision of the Charter stipulates that the Council has the power to decide, that its decision is binding? Or, is a provision capable of creating a separate basis for the binding force of a decision? The ICJ, in its advisory opinion on *Namibia* in 1971,[42] held that the Council could exercise its coercive powers directly on the basis of article 25 each time that it manifested its will to act accordingly. The Court considered the basis of the binding character of any such decision of the Council to be contained in article 25 of the Charter that provides that 'the Members of the United Nations agree to accept and carry out the decisions of the Security Council in accordance with the present Charter'. This solution has been contested in legal doctrine and has not been taken up again in the practice of the Security Council. It remains a dormant option.

§ 88 Question of Security Council Reform

During recent years, discussions concerning the possible reform of the Security Council have moved steadily along. The United Nations continues to consider this question. The two principal aims of the current reform proposals are the following: (1) to increase the legitimacy of the Council through better representation; and (2) to increase the rule of law and transparency of the decision-making process within the Council.[43]

---

[41] Below, ch 10, § 105ff.

[42] *Legal Consequences for States of the Continued Presence of South Africa in Namibia (South-West Africa)* (Advisory Opinion), above n 7 at 52–54.

[43] See T Giegerich, 'A Fork in the Road—Constitutional Challenges, Chances and Lacunae of UN Reform' (2005) 48 *German Yearbook of International Law* 29ff.

—*Composition of the Council.* In relation to this first issue, discussions have turned on a possible increase of the number of State seats in the Council and a more equitable geographical distribution of seats. Some regions are currently over-represented (Europe) and others are under-represented (Africa). Initially, two reform models were proposed. The *first model* (model A), proposes a Council numbering 24 members, with six new permanent seats that do not have a right of veto and three new non-permanent seats for which representative States would not be eligible for re-election at the end of a cycle. Each region of the world would be represented by six States. There would not be inter-regional equality with respect to the number of permanent members/non-permanent members. The *second model* (model B) pro poses a Council composed of 24 States by the creation of eight new semi-permanent seats of four-year cycles and one seat of a two-year non-renewable cycle. Each region of the world would have six representatives.

Following, in 2005, new proposals were presented. According to *Model A*,[44] the Council should consist of 25 members, with six new permanent and four non-permanent seats. A geographic formula for the election of these seats is included in the text. It is also proposed that the new permanent members would not have a right of veto, but this could be the subject of a future reform. According to *Model B*,[45] it is also proposed to increase the number of members to 25 by electing 20 non-permanent members for two years and keeping the same number of permanent members. The criteria for the election of non-permanent members would be, according to this proposal, the contribution of candidate States to international peace and security and to the principal goals of the United Nations, while maintaining an equitable geographic distribution. The permanent members are invited to be parsimonious with their right of veto. According to a *Model C*,[46] the number of seats in the Council should be increased to 26, with 11 new seats distributed according to a specific distributive formula, mostly favourable for Africa. Among these new seats would be six new permanent seats and five non-permanent seats. The new permanent members would have a right of veto.

In order to adopt one of these models, or another proposal, an agreement for an amendment of the Charter would require a positive vote (or perhaps abstention would suffice) from the current five permanent members. According to article 108, these members have the right to veto any amendment of the Charter. As they are not inclined to weaken their influence in the Council and as it is difficult to choose the States that would have a seat at the Council (lobbies, pressure, as well as jealousy are in abundance), it is unlikely that reform will take place in the near future. It may also be questioned, in light of the League of Nations experience, whether enlargement of the Council is prudent and wise. The principal function of the Council is to adopt urgent measures in order to ensure peace. The restrictive and confidential character of the organ is necessary in this respect. A Council with many members would become a sort of mini-General Assembly and would lack coherence. The capacity of such an organ to quickly respond would be affected.

---

[44] See UNGA UN Doc A/59/L.64. States that support this proposition include France, Germany, Greece, Japan, Poland and Brazil.

[45] See UNGA UN Doc A/59/L.68. States that support this proposition include Argentina, Canada, Italy, Mexico, Spain and Turkey.

[46] See UNGA UN Doc A/59/L.67. This proposal emanated from African States.

With an increase in the number of States seated around the Council table, the sense of responsibility for each of these members would also be diluted. In all probability, the organ would progressively slide into conciliation or procrastination, rather than swift action.

There is agreement at the moment on only one point: the right of veto should not be extended to other States beyond those that currently enjoy it. Those that currently have a veto right are not going to relinquish it. There are, of course, proposals that aim to limit the veto right, but it is unlikely that these will be adopted. A proposal that was made in this vein and supported by Switzerland, was to require the permanent Council members to make a declaration in which they would morally undertake, in line with a code of conduct, not to use the veto right when a decision concerned questions of genocide or grave and systematic violations of human rights. However, the principal obstacle to United Nations action in such areas is not the veto. It is rather indifference, a lack of resources, the impossibility of being everywhere at once and political selectiveness. Further, any significant action (other than that which currently exists) directed against Russia with respect to Chechnya, or the United States of America with respect to Guantanamo, or other similar issues is unimaginable, even with veto reform. It is thus possible that a code of conduct for the Security Council is an illusion, despite what it may appear in abstract. Another proposition suggests introducing a deadline after which Security Council measures would be terminated if not renewed by a subsequent decision. This proposal aims to prevent abuses in relation to the 'reverse veto'. It is, however, unlikely that the permanent members would accept such a measure. It would be very useful, on the one hand, insofar as it prevented abuse, but it could, on the other hand, hinder the participation of States willing to commit military resources to respond to a call for action, as it would create uncertainty about the operation. A State that is willing to participate in such vast, costly and delicate operations would not do so without some guarantees of reasonable duration.

—*Rule of Law*. Proposals concerning this issue are made on two levels. They are still at an early stage. The first proposal is to include parliamentary input on the United Nations. Thus, it would not only be the executive of each State, but also national parliaments that would be represented in the General Assembly. For example, it was suggested that parliaments could be obliged to be integrated with their State representative in the Assembly; that committees charged with liaising between national parliaments and the General Assembly could be created; that national parliament could create a special commission that would debate questions concerning the United Nations, etc.

A second set of proposals suggests increasing the responsibility of the Council and the transparency of its decision-making process. These proposals include suggestions to provide a form of judicial control over Council decisions exercised by the ICJ; the organisation of a judicial referral to the ICJ on questions concerning the legality of Council decisions that come before a national court;[47] an attempt to force the Council to act in certain situations under the banner of the 'responsibility to protect human rights'; a desire to increase the transparency of the decision-making

---

[47] A national court would not determine the validity of Council actions but would refer this matter to the ICJ for its consideration and suspend, in the meantime, the proceedings at the national level.

process of the Council that currently takes place between members in corridors, etc. It is not impossible that some of these proposals will leave a mark on the law of the United Nations. They are likely to influence, at the very least, future interpretations of the Charter. With respect to their formal fate, it is difficult to say much. It seems fair to say that formal United Nations reforms are rare. This is not simply because of the stringent procedural rules governing amendments to the Charter, but it is also a matter of substance because overall the organisation does represent in its current form what States would wish it to be. States do not want a super-State any more than they want a highly efficient organisation that would weaken their influence. It is before this picture that the 'efficiency' of the organisation and reasonably possible reforms must be judged. The miraculous and dynamic Metamorphoses of Ovid are not within the realm of the United Nations.

C. Economic and Social Council

§ 89 Importance of 'Functional Cooperation'

The importance of functional cooperation in the fields of social, economic, humanitarian, health, cultural and technical areas was demonstrated by the League of Nations experience. Prior to the creation of the United Nations, in the late days of the League, the 'Bruce Plan' was the turning point in this evolution.[48] In 1945, functional cooperation was not considered to be a negligible measure in the promotion of peace and understanding among peoples. It is the old idea that commerce and exchanges between countries render war less common. This idea has since been developed. It is argued that if social, economic and other problems are left unchecked, disputes develop and eventually, armed conflicts. To address these questions is therefore an indirect contribution to keeping the peace in the medium and long run (conception of a positive peace). The same 'functional' logic prevailed in 1957 on the establishment of the European Economic Community (EEC). Rather than proposing directly a political unity of European peoples, the idea was to eliminate the causes of disagreements by functionally integrating Europe. The first part of such a progressive integration was the economy. Other areas then followed.

An obvious advantage of this area of the law is that it is based on voluntary cooperation among States. What voluntary cooperation does not possess in terms of coercive powers (which are in any event often of questionable efficiency), it nevertheless makes up for in the feeling of free choice it instils and that, in turn, assists in developing mutual goodwill among States. Consequently, even though such cooperation does not achieve any fast results because of the lengthy discussions that must take place and thus the modest steps that are made, it is able to address profound issues and achieve long-lasting results. It is of course difficult to determine the precise impact of the functional ideal in the maintenance of peace and understanding among peoples. It could, however, be claimed that such an approach often achieves more, and much more

---

[48] See above, ch 2, § 12.

lasting, results than more direct measures such as the settlement of disputes or the coercive measures taken under Chapter VII. Some lay commentators make the error of giving less credit to such quiet, invisible and humble measures that are less prominent in comparison to highly publicised measures like sanctions. However, the complex reality of international life rarely reflects this superficial view of things.

§ 90 Functions, Composition, Sessions, etc

The work of the Economic and Social Council (ECOSOC) is too great and too varied to reasonably be reduced to a complete overview. The Council was created as the principal organ to coordinate the economic, social, and other work of the United Nations, including its numerous affiliated organisations—World Health Organisation (WHO); United Nations Educational, Scientific and Cultural Organisation (UNESCO); Food and Agriculture Organisation (FAO); International Labour Organisation (ILO), etc. This task is referred to in article 62, which must be read in conjunction with articles 55 to 56 of the Charter.[49]

Article 62

1. The Economic and Social Council may make or initiate studies and reports with respect to international economic, social, cultural, educational, health, and related matters and may make recommendations with respect to any such matters to the General Assembly to the Members of the United Nations, and to the specialized agencies concerned.
2. It may make recommendations for the purpose of promoting respect for, and observance of, human rights and fundamental freedoms for all.
3. It may prepare draft conventions for submission to the General Assembly, with respect to matters falling within its competence.
4. It may call, in accordance with the rules prescribed by the United Nations, international conferences on matters falling within its competence.

ECOSOC shares its functions with the General Assembly. There is thus a voluntary overlapping of competences, with the Council however being the more specialised organ for this work. Article 60 provides to this end: 'Responsibility for the discharge of the functions of the organisation set forth in this Chapter shall be vested in the General Assembly and, under the authority of the General Assembly, in the Economic and Social Council, which shall have for this purpose the powers set forth in Chapter X'. Cooperation with affiliated organisations is provided in articles 57, 58, 63 and 64.

---

[49] Article 55: 'With a view to the creation of conditions of stability and well-being which are necessary for peaceful and friendly relations among nations based on respect for the principle of equal rights and self-determination of peoples, the United Nations shall promote:

higher standards of living, full employment, and conditions of economic and social progress and development;

solutions of international economic, social, health, and related problems; and international cultural and educational cooperation; and

universal respect for, and observance of, human rights and fundamental freedoms for all without distinction as to race, sex, language, or religion'.

Article 56: 'All Members pledge themselves to take joint and separate action in cooperation with the Organization for the achievement of the purposes set forth in Article 55'.

ECOSOC is composed of 54 government delegates from member States who are elected for terms of three years by the General Assembly (article 61 § 1). Voting in ECOSOC is based on a simple majority of the present and voting members, where each member has one vote.[50] The Council meets several times a year for brief sessions. The longest ordinary session takes place in July. ECOSOC has created a number of subsidiary organs, of which there are various types:

—*Thematic organs*. For example, the Commission for Social Development (CSocD); the Commission on Narcotic Drugs (CND); the Commission for Sustainable Development (CSD); the Commission on Crime Prevention and Criminal Justice; the Statistical Commission (CCPCJ); the former Commission on Human Rights (dissolved and replaced by the new Human Rights Council (HRC), that is directly relation to the General Assembly), etc. These organs often produce expert reports.
—*Regional organs*. For example, the Economic Commission for Africa (ECA); the Economic and Social Commission for Asia and the Pacific (ESCAP); the Economic Commission for Latin America and the Caribbean (ECLAC); the Economic and Social Commission for Western Africa (ESCWA).
—*Expert committees*. For example, the Committee on Energy and Natural Resources for Development.
—*Other*. For example, the United Nations Forum for Forests.

The ESC cooperates in a close way with a number of specialised institutions affiliated with the United Nations: ILO, WHO, UNESCO, FAO, etc. It consults with non-governmental organisations. More than 1600 of these organisations have a consultative status with the ESC.

In the last decades, the ESC has been somewhat marginalised by the work of the General Assembly, specialised institutions, and formerly also by UNCTAD.

D. Trusteeship Council

§ 91 Functions and Powers

The Trusteeship Council (TC) is provided for and its activities stipulated, in Chapter XIII, articles 86–91, in the Charter. This organ was established in 1945 to supervise 11 territories that were placed under trusteeship administered by seven States. The Charter sets out three categories of territories that may be placed under the trusteeship regime (article 77). First, there are territories held under mandate, namely colonial territories that have been detached from the defeated powers in the First World War (Austria-Hungary, Germany, the Ottoman Empire). These territories were placed under the supervision of Mandatory States. The League of Nations was kept informed of the territories under the charge of a Mandatory State in accordance with article 22 of the Covenant of the League of Nations. Secondly, there are the territories that were detached from former enemy States following the Second World War. This was only the case for Italian

---

[50] Article 67: '1. Each member of the Economic and Social Council shall have one vote. 2. Decisions of the Economic and Social Council shall be made by a majority of the members present and voting'.

Somalia. Thirdly, there are territories that could be voluntarily placed under the system by States responsible for their administration. This wish did occur only with respect to some Pacific islands, formally under a Japanese mandate, then occupied by the United States of America following their military activities in the region. The main duty imposed on States exercising tutelage of these territories is to 'promote . . . [the inhabitants of the trust territories] progressive development towards self-government or independence' (article 76 (b)). The exact functions of the TC are described in articles 87 and 88.[51]

Concretely, the following 11 territories were covered by the trusteeship regime:

—Togoland (United Kingdom), independence obtained in 1957, political regime: fusion with the Gold Coast, ie, Ghana.
—Somaliland (Italy), independence obtained in 1960, political regime: fusion with British Somaliland, Somalia.
—Togoland (France), independence obtained in 1960, political regime: creation of Togo.
—Cameroon (France), independence obtained in 1960, political regime: creation of Cameroon.
—Cameroon (United Kingdom), independence obtained in 1961, political regime: territories finally portioned between Nigeria and Cameroon.
—Tanganika (United Kingdom), independence obtained in 1961, political regime: creation of Tanzania; 1964, fusion with Zanzibar.
—Ruanda-Urundi (Belgian), independence obtained in 1962, political regime: separation between Rwanda and Burundi.
—Western Samoa (New Zealand), independence obtained in 1962, political regime: creation of Samoa.
—Nauru (Australia, New Zealand, United Kingdom), independence obtained in 1968, political regime: creation of Nauru.
—New Guinea (Australia), independence obtained in 1975, political regime: creation of Papua New Guinea, fusion with Papua.
—Pacific islands administered by the United States of America: (a) Micronesia, independent State in political union with the United States of America (1990); (b) the Marshall islands (1990); (c) the North Mariana Islands (commonwealth in political union with the United States of America, 1990); (d) Palau (independent State in political union with the United States of America, 1994).

Thus, in 1994, the last trust territory—Palau—obtained independence. Consequently, this part of the United Nations history has come to an end and Chapter XII has now become obsolete. The TC has suspended its work crowned with success; it could be removed from the Charter following a revision.

---

[51] Article 87: 'The General Assembly and, under its authority, the Trusteeship Council, in carrying out their functions, may:

consider reports submitted by the administering authority;

accept petitions and examine them in consultation with the administering authority;

provide for periodic visits to the respective trust territories at times agreed upon with the administering authority; and

take these and other actions in conformity with the terms of the trusteeship agreements'.

Article 88: 'The Trusteeship Council shall formulate a questionnaire on the political, economic, social, and educational advancement of the inhabitants of each trust territory, and the administering authority for each trust territory within the competence of the General Assembly shall make an annual report to the General Assembly upon the basis of such questionnaire'.

E. International Court of Justice

§ 92 General Aspects

The International Court of Justice (ICJ) is the principal judicial organ of the United Nations. Article 92 provides:

> The International Court of Justice shall be the principal judicial organ of the United Nations. It shall function in accordance with the annexed Statute, which is based upon the Statute of the Permanent Court of International Justice and forms an integral part of the present Charter.

The Court constitutes a central instrument in the settlement of disputes, mainly of a legal nature. The United Nations puts it at the disposal of and recommends it to States to settle their legal disagreements. The settlement of disputes is one of the primordial aims of the United Nations (see article 1 § 1). The more extensively disputes will be settled, the better international trust and cooperation will function and the better international peace will be maintained. The Court is thus available also to non-member States, in accordance with the conditions set out in article 35 of the Statute of the Court.[52] The United Nations does not want to close the door of the Court to any State willing to accept an adjudication of a legal dispute. The ICJ enjoys judicial independence. This is symbolised by the fact that the seat of the Court is in The Hague, remote from the political organs of the organisation. The Hague is a city with a tradition of being the location for arbitrations and peace conferences and where the Permanent Court of Arbitration is also based. It is not possible to include here an overview of the work of the Court; this however has been covered extensively in many public international law texts.[53]

§ 93 Functions and Jurisdiction

The functions of the Court are two-fold:

1. *Contentious function.* To settle inter-State disputes by decisions that are binding on the States parties to the case (articles 34ss, 59 of the Statute of the ICJ). The Court only has jurisdiction to hear a matter if the State parties to the dispute have consented to its jurisdiction, either by agreement (before or after the dispute has arisen) or by a unilateral declaration of acceptance of the Court's jurisdiction in accord-

---

[52] '1. The Court shall be open to the state parties to the present Statute.
    2. The conditions under which the Court shall be open to other states shall, subject to the special provisions contained in treaties in force, be laid down by the Security Council, but in no case shall such conditions place the parties in a position of inequality before the Court.
    3. When a state which is not a Member of the United Nations is a party to a case, the Court shall fix the amount which that party is to contribute towards the expenses of the Court. This provision shall not apply if the state is bearing a share of the expenses of the Court'.

[53] See, eg, MN Shaw, *International Law* 6th edn (Cambridge, CUP, 2008) 1057ff.

ance with article 36 § 2[54] of the Statute of the ICJ. In contrast to domestic courts, the Court does not have a compulsory jurisdiction, independent of the will of the States being judged.

As has been said, the Court can only give judgment on legal disputes. The distinction between *legal and non-legal (political or technical) disputes* is difficult to draw. There is no line that could be drawn objectively, according to the subject-matter: any question of international relations has its political and its legal aspects, even if it may be largely leaning to the one or the other of these poles. Montesquieu[55] is right when he speaks of international law as the 'political law among nations', underlining the very close interrelationship between law and politics in international public relations. A matter that comes to be considered as impinging on vital interests of a State at any given moment will automatically be considered largely political by the State involved, but may not be seen as such by other States. If it ceased to be related to vital questions, it will more easily be considered again simply a legal dispute suitable for adjudication. Conversely, a purely technical dispute on questions of meteorology or sanitary measures in some international organisation may hardly be legal at all at any time. Moreover, it will always be possible to give a legal answer to any question put to a judge, however political or however technical. Some general principle of law will always be found as a guiding star (prohibition of abuse of rights, good faith, equity, proportionality, etc) which could be applied to the facts at hand, even if there are no precise legal rules applicable. Moreover, if a plaintiff brings a claim against a defendant, the judge will always be able to reject the claim in legal terms by affirming that in the absence of a rule constraining the defendant to adopt a specific attitude, the claim is not well founded in law. Since such behaviour is not prohibited, it remains permitted. If the parties confront the judge with a joint special agreement, a rejection of the claim is no longer possible since there is no claimant and no defendant in any technical sense. But the judge could, in substance, declare once more that there is no rule prohibiting a specific attitude in dispute and that the law cannot therefore censor this course of conduct. This is a legal answer and it would settle the case by affirming a legal freedom to act. Sometimes, such a course is not open to the judge: if he is asked to draw a boundary, he cannot answer by affirming any 'freedom' of action for any party to the dispute. He will then have recourse to equity to draw a proper boundary. If he cannot find any clue as to how to draw this line, he could at the very extreme end declare a *non liquet*. In this way he gives a legal answer in affirming that there is no legal principle applicable to that particular dispute; this means that the parties have first themselves to create the applicable law.

At the end of the day, the only way to draw a distinction between legal and political disputes is to consider how the claimant in a unilateral suit or the parties to the dispute proceeding through a special agreement themselves frame the dispute (subjective approach). Do they ask the judge to consider it on the basis of legal

---

[54] 'The States parties to the present Statute may at any time declare that they recognize as compulsory *ipso facto* and without special agreement, in relation to any other state accepting the same obligation, the jurisdiction of the Court in all legal disputes . . .'. This article thus provides an interactive fabric of unilateral declarations that activate the compulsory jurisdiction of the Court between States that have made such declarations.

[55] CL Montesquieu, 'Le droit des gens, qui est la loi politique des nations, considérées dans le rapport qu'elles ont les unes avec les autres' in *De l'esprit des lois* book X, ch I.

rights and legal arguments put forward by them? Or do they not found their claim on legal provisions and arguments? In the first case, the dispute is technically speaking legal, notwithstanding how 'political' it looks. In the second case, the dispute is political, even if it occurs in the sphere of the law. Thus, for example, State A may claim that State B should change its foreign policy. If it produces a treaty and affirms that State B had therein committed itself to a specific conduct it now breached, the dispute is legal. The same would also be true if State A based itself on some general principle of law, however vague this could be, for example, that a particular foreign policy constitutes an abuse of rights or is infringing a substantive estoppel. If conversely State A claims that State B should change its foreign policy because of considerations of bloc solidarity, of moral duty, of appropriateness and so on, the dispute is political. Similarly, if State A claims that the treaty-provision on the relevant foreign policy is no longer satisfactory in a new international environment and should be changed, this is a political dispute. This plea is manifestly geared towards a modification of the law and not towards an application of the law. Thus, the dispute is not legal (application of the law) but political (new legislation).

2. *Advisory function*. To render advisory opinions that are not binding but are of legal importance, following a request by one of the principal political organs of the United Nations (except the Secretariat) or an affiliated organisation that is authorised by the General Assembly to request an advisory opinion of the Court (articles 65ff of the Statute of the ICJ and article 96 of the Charter).[56] These opinions permit United Nations organs to clarify any legal aspect of a question that arises in the scope of their activities.

§ 94 Execution of Judgments

The Security Council ensures the execution of the judgments of the Court in specific instances. The Council may decide to enforce the execution of a judgment by imposing sanctions or even by undertaking military action, without first having to establish the existence of a threat to the peace, a breach of the peace, or an act of aggression under article 39 of the Charter.[57] Indeed, the Court can directly base itself on article 94 § 2: 'If any party to a case fails to perform the obligations incumbent upon it under a judgment rendered by the Court, the other party may have recourse to the Security Council, which may, if it deems necessary, make recommendations *or decide* upon measures to be taken to give effect to the judgment' (emphasis added). It is rare, however, that a judgment of the Court will not be honoured. The opinion of the average person on the street is erroneous in this respect. Even the Permanent Court of International Justice (PCIJ), the predecessor of the current Court in the inter-war period, had surprising results in this respect. All its judgments were, without exception, spontaneously executed by the parties despite the troubled times in which they were

---

[56] Article 96: '1. The General Assembly of the Security Council may request the International Court of Justice to give an advisory opinion on any legal question. 2. Other organs of the United Nations and specialized agencies, which may at any time be so authorized by the General Assembly, may also request advisory opinions of the Court on legal questions arising within the scope of their activities'.

[57] This interpretation of is not generally accepted.

handed down. The consensual character of the jurisdiction of the Court has a positive impact in this regard: as States must express agreement to submit to the jurisdiction of the Court, they do so only after careful consideration of the pros and cons; consequently, they are generally ready to assume the outcome of adverse judgments and to honour their obligations. There are some cases where the execution of a judgment was, however, refused. One example is particularly interesting with respect to article 94.[58] Nicaragua requested the Security Council to enforce the execution of the judgment of the Court against the United States of America in *Military and Paramilitary Activities in and against Nicaragua* (Merits, 1986). The United States exercised its right of veto. The General Assembly was subsequently seized of the question, and it called on the United States to execute the judgment. The United States responded by exerting pressure on the new Nicaraguan government (led by Ms Chamorro) who, in order to normalise relations with its powerful neighbour, renounced its call for execution of the judgment. In some cases, it may take a long time before a judgment is executed. In the *Corfu Channel* case of 1949, Albania refused to honour the award of damages made by the Court in favour of the United Kingdom. However, the outstanding debt was finally paid as a result of an agreement (memorandum of understanding of 8 May) concluded in 1992.[59] Rather than the long time that had elapsed, what is remarkable here is that the judgment was, at the end of the day, executed.

§ 95 Activity of the Court

The Court has, overall, rendered a remarkable service in the settlement of disputes and in the progressive development of international law. It has established a well-developed jurisprudence that has clarified a number of uncertainties and lacunae in international law. In 60 years of activity, from 1947 to April 2007, the Court rendered 93 contentious judgments and 25 advisory opinions. The Court's judgments and opinions constitute required reading for States, international law experts and students. The Court is undoubtedly the most eminent judicial authority in international relations. A series of great cases and opinions cement its place in international law and the peaceful settlement of disputes: *Admission of new members to the United Nations* (1948); *Reparation for Damages* (1949); *Corfu Channel* case (1949); *Certain Expenses* (1962); *Nicaragua* (1986); *Legality of the Threat of Use of Nuclear Weapons* (1996), etc. The jurisprudence of the Court has sometimes been very progressive, particularly in the advisory opinions prior to 1960. This was the phase of internationalism, where faith in international cooperation was still notable. Following the stalemate phase of 1966 to 1986, the Court has again returned to the stage and is more and more solicited by States. Its recent judgments are conspicuous because of the many disputes that concern very serious and politically highly sensitive matters, such as the use of force (for example, *Armed Activities on the Territory of the Congo*, 2005) or acts of genocide (notably, *Application of the Convention on the Prevention and Punishment of the Crime of*

---

[58] See A Tanzi, 'Problems of Enforcement of Decisions of the International Court of Justice and the Law of the United Nations'(1995) 6 *European Journal of International Law* 539ff.

[59] See (1992) 63 *BYIL* 781–82 or (1993) 97 *RGDIP* 168.

Genocide, Bosnia and Herzegovina v. Serbia and Montenegro, 2007). There is here a certain danger that the Court is, and will be, solicited for reasons of embarrassing the opponent rather than for seeking to really solve a dispute on the merits[60]. Moreover, the execution of such judgments in highly sensitive matters could result severe difficulties for and lessen the excellent record of the Court in this respect. On the other hand, it is not unwelcome that the Court is no longer concerned only with minor legal disputes, but that it can contribute the strengthening the rule of law in crucial areas of international life.[61]

§ 96 Proposals for Reform

Various proposals have circulated concerning the possibility of optimising the work of the ICJ. One such proposal suggests asking the Court to exercise supervisory jurisdiction for the numerous international tribunals that have since been created (Tribunal for the law of the sea, criminal tribunals, appeals panels, etc). The aim of such a proposal is to ensure that the 'proliferation' of tribunals does not lead to an incoherent multiplication of interpretations of international law. In the wake of such a possibility, it is proposed that certain questions of law should be directly referred to the ICJ.[62] We have already addressed the referral by domestic courts to the ICJ of questions concerning the validity of Security Council actions.[63] The chances of the establishment of such a mechanism are very uncertain.

F. Secretariat

§ 97 General Aspects

The activities of the Secretariat of the United Nations are governed by Chapter XV of the Charter, articles 97–101. The Secretariat is composed of personnel that execute the daily work of the organisation. They are headed by the Secretary-General, who is elected by the General Assembly on the recommendation of the Security Council, for a renewable term of five years. The applicability of the right of veto to this voting procedure means that the five permanent members must agree on the nomination of the same person for the position. Politically, this means that the nomination of a person who is not supported by one of the five permanent members will result in that person not being elected. The right of veto also limits the margin of manoeuvre for the elected

[60] L Caflisch, 'Cent Ans de règlement pacifique des différends interétatiques' (2001) 288 *RCADI* 357 and 441.
[61] M Bedjaoui, 'L'humanité en quête de paix et de développement, Cours général de droit international public' (2006) 325 *RCADI* 90–92.
[62] A domestic court would not determine the validity of Security Council actions but would refer such questions to the ICJ for its decision and suspend in the meantime the procedure at the domestic level.
[63] See above, § 88.

Secretary-General, if he or she wishes to be re-elected. Every initiative proposed by the Secretary-General that is opposed by one of the five permanent members may cost the Secretary-General his or her re-election. Thus Boutros Boutros-Ghali, who was too independent in the eyes of the United States of America, was not re-elected. Article 97 provides: 'The Secretariat shall comprise a Secretary-General and such staff as the Organization may require. The Secretary-General shall be appointed by the General Assembly upon the recommendation of the Security Council. He shall be the chief administrative officer of the Organization'.

The Secretariat serves various United Nations organs. It prepares plans, statistics and the necessary documentation for their activities and the conferences that they organise. It also executes their decisions, for example, by putting into practice the maintenance of peace through a peacekeeping force or the temporary civil administration of a territory like Kosovo after 1999. The Secretariat comprises approximately 7300 staff members.

§ 98 Secretary-General

The Secretary-General has missions that are notably much more political in character than his predecessor in the League of Nations. The second United Nations Secretary-General and perhaps the greatest, Dag Hammarskjöld[64] of Sweden, enlarged even further the scope of the Secretary-General's activities and increased the diplomatic nature of the position. Hence, he promoted, for example, peacekeeping operations that were a purely praetorian invention not foreseen in the Charter. The current Secretary-General is Ban Ki-Moon from South Korea, who is elected for a mandate from 2006 to 2011. Previous Secretaries-General were Trygve Lie (Norway, 1946–52); Dag Hammarskjöld (Sweden, 1953–61); U Thant (Burma, 1961–71); Kurt Waldheim (Austria, 1972–81); Javier Perez de Cuéllar (Peru, 1982–91); Boutros Boutros-Ghali (Egypt, 1992–96); Kofi Annan (Ghana, 1997–2006). The Secretary-General is the window and the motor of the organisation symbolising the United Nations like no other person. He is able to seize the organisation as an entity distinct from States members; he or she is a subject endowed with its own personality and following its own particular policy.

Article 98 of the Charter highlights the 'servant' quality of the Secretary-General: 'The Secretary-General shall act in that capacity in all meetings of the General Assembly, of the Security Council, of the Economic and Social Council, and of the Trusteeship Council, and shall perform such other functions as are entrusted to him by these organs. The Secretary-General shall make an annual report to the General Assembly on the work of the Organization'. Thus, the Secretary-General has been entrusted with the most varied tasks, ranging from establishing commissions on particular topics to dispatching missions to some area in crisis. Article 99, in contrast, stresses the autonomous nature of the role: 'The Secretary-General may bring to the attention of the Security Council any matter which in his opinion may threaten the maintenance of international peace and security'. The Secretary-General is here

[64] See the very thorough study of M Fröhlich, *Dag Hammarskjöld und die Vereinten Nationen* (Paderborn, Munich; Vienna; Zurich, 2002).

considered a sort of watchdog on guard for situations that might lead to instability, violence or armed conflict. Subsequently, under the Rules of Procedure of the Assembly, he was also given the right to put an item on the agenda of this organ and to 'make either oral or written statements to the General Assembly concerning any question under consideration by it'. However, the Secretary-General has not limited his function to signalling crises to the main organs or to provide them with written statements or reports. He also deployed an intense diplomatic activity of his own, living up to the word of FD Roosevelt who saw in the highest official of the United Nations a sort of 'World's Moderator'. Thus, the various Secretary's-General have become involved in mediation work in almost every important conflict or crisis, ranging from Berlin (1948) to the Middle East (1948), from the US airmen held captive in China (1955), to Suez (1956), to Lebanon and Jordan (1958) and Laos (1959); from Cyprus (1964 onwards), to the Middle East (since 1967) or Namibia (in the seventies); from Iran/Iraq to Afghanistan in the 1980s; and finally to the various crises in the near and Middle East since the 1990s. In this area of 'political' work, consolidated through the subsequent practice of the organisation, the Secretary-General has stamped his mark in particular in the following activities:

—*Creation, management and control of peacekeeping operations.* These operations were thought up by the Canadian Minister for Foreign Affairs, Lester Pearson, and put into practice through the tenacity of Dag Hammarskjöld in order to put an end to the Suez crisis (1957).
—*Providing the Security Council with information.* The Secretary-General may bring any affair (dispute or situation) to the attention of the Security Council that could endanger international peace and security (article 99). Such an initiative has been taken by the Secretary-General on a number of occasions, such as during the Congo crisis (1960), or in relation to the hostage crisis in Tehran (1980). Sometimes information was provided in an informal way, such as the Greek crisis (1946).
—*Mediation and good offices.* This is a constant function of the Secretary-General, not provided for in the Charter. Examples include the lengthy involvement of the United Nations in trying to find peaceful solutions to the Palestinian or Cypriot crises. The mediation success of the Secretary-General in finding a solution to the Berlin crisis should also be recalled.[65]
—*Prevention.* The Secretary-General promotes early warning in order to address, as soon as possible, the first signs of crises. The Secretary-General has also contributed to peace by more general proposals, such as that made by Boutros Boutros-Ghali in his report entitled 'An Agenda for Peace' (1992). This report deals with the functions of the organisation in the new world that emerged from the Cold War.

§ 99 Independence of United Nations Personnel

United Nations personnel exercise an international function in the service of the world organisation. To this end they must enjoy full independence from the activities and judg-

[65] See Luard, *A History of the United Nations* vol I, above n 9 at 220–21.

ment of the States of origin.[66] They cannot receive instructions nor act out of loyalty to their national government. This would damage their international functions, call into question the independence of the United Nations and jeopardise the collective interests they have been called upon to serve. This is the reason why article 100 states:

> In the performance of their duties the Secretary-General and the staff shall not seek or receive instructions from any government or from any other authority external to the Organization. They shall refrain from any action which might reflect on their position as international officials responsible only to the Organization.

> Each Member of the United Nations undertakes to respect the exclusively international character of the responsibilities of the Secretary-General and the staff and not to seek to influence them in the discharge of their responsibilities.

This requirement of independence for international civil servants was, at the time of the League of Nations, a very important part of the *ethos* of such a career. Many staff members were strongly attached to this idea. There are famous instances where civil servants reacted to situations that threatened their independence. In this vein, a number of civil servants with United States nationality refused to respond to questionnaires that were sent to them by their national government in 1950. These questionnaires were an attempt to determine whether or not United Nations employees sympathised with communists. The initiator of the questionnaires was the famous Senator McCarthy. Resistance by a number of American employees to answering the questionnaires resulted in the non-renewal of their work contracts, following pressure from the United States of America. However, the employees commenced proceedings in the United Nations Administrative Tribunal (UNAT), which eventually upheld their claim. The Tribunal held that the non-renewal of the employees' contracts was unwarranted because it was unrelated to their professional qualities. Not having the power to reinstate the employees to their former positions, the Tribunal awarded reparation. Pressure from the United States on the General Assembly for these amounts not to be paid failed following the rendering of an advisory opinion by the ICJ, which affirmed that the finding that the Assembly should pay out the sums allocated by the UNAT in its judicial decision was final.[67] On this point, the UNAT thus made a decisive contribution to the rule of law within the United Nations.

The United Nations has also had to frequently intervene in order to protect the independence of its agents, notably its special rapporteurs in whom the State of origin has lost trust, or who has become the object of attack from a State member.[68] It is not usually employees with normal work contracts who experience these difficulties, but persons undertaking a United Nations mission. Article VI, section 22, of the Convention of the Privileges and Immunities of the United Nations (1946) applies in these cases.

---

[66] On this problem more generally, see the good commentary of C Schreuer and C Ebner, 'Article 100' in B Simma (ed), *The Charter of the United Nations: A Commentary*, above n 8 at 1230ff.

[67] *Effect of Awards of Compensation Made by the United Nations Administrative Tribunal* (Advisory Opinion) [1954] ICJ Reports 50ff.

[68] See, in particular, *Difference Relating to Immunity from Legal Process of a Special Rapporteur of the Commission on Human Rights* (Advisory Opinion) [1999] ICJ Rep 62ff; and *Applicability of Article VI, Section 22, of the Convention on the Privileges and Immunities of the United Nations* (Advisory Opinion) [1989] ICJ Rep 177. This latter case concerned an agent of the United Nations who fell into disgrace with the communist Romanian government at the time.

G. Subsidiary Organs

§ 100 General Aspects

Subsidiary organs have already been examined in relation to each of the principal organs discussed. In this section, the fundamental legal rules that apply to subsidiary organs will be discussed. The most important general rule is that all Unite Nations organs— whether principal organs or not—can create their own subsidiary organs. These are mainly commission and committees that are assigned special tasks by the organ that created them. For principal organs, this power is contained in the Charter in articles 7 § 2[69] (general rule); 22 (General Assembly); 29 (Security Council); 68 (Economic and Social Council). For all other organs, the power is contained in an unwritten rule of international organisations. This rule is legally derived from the doctrine of implied powers. Such was the interpretation given to the law of international organisations and in subsequent practice without objections since the time of the League of Nations.

The principal organ does not always delegate its own powers to a subsidiary organ. It can sometimes create powers for the subsidiary organ that lie outside its own domain by basing itself directly on the constituent instrument of the Organisation. This was the case when the General Assembly created the United Nations Administrative Tribunal even though the Assembly does not itself have any judicial powers.[70]

As a general rule, the subsidiary organ, as a subordinate organ, must follow orders given by the principal organ. These orders take the form of resolutions and may address formal questions (composition, procedure, voting in the subsidiary organ) or substantial questions (requirements concerning the manner with which to exercise the assigned functions). This power to order is nevertheless limited if the subsidiary organ enjoys a degree of independence, as is the case for the UNAT. The General Assembly cannot give the Tribunal an order with respect to its jurisprudence.

In a strict legal sense, a subsidiary organ is one which has the power to adopt decisions on its own behalf. Organs that must report back to the principal organ (the plenary) to decide a question are not strictly speaking subsidiary organs, even if they are referred to as such. This is merely an additional sign of the enormous flexibility and plurality that is present in this area of the law.

§ 101 Importance in Practice

Subsidiary organs are of enormous practical value. It is within these organs that a large and important part of the formal work of the United Nations is accomplished. Without the support of these additional organs, the United Nations would not be able to function adequately. The tasks it must accomplish are too great and require too

---

[69] 'Such subsidiary organs as may be found necessary may be established in accordance with the present Charter'.

[70] See above, § 82.

much diverse expertise for them to be carried out in the plenary assemblies. Law thus provides considerable flexibility for the creation, functioning and dissolution of subsidiary organs. These organs are legally tied to the need to accomplish the aims of the organisation, as determined by the principal organs at any given moment.

United Nations practice shows that a great number of subsidiary organs have been created (more than 1000). Their creation was either based on an express provision of the Charter, or they were created in accordance with the doctrine of implied powers. Some of these organs, and organs that created them, include:

—*General Assembly*. The six permanent committees; Committee on the Peaceful Uses of Outer Space; International Law Commission; Human Rights Committee; United Nations Administrative Tribunal; Disarmament Commission; United Nations Commission on International Trade Law (UNCITRAL); Special Committee on the Charter of the United Nations and on the Strengthening of the Role of the Organisation, etc.

—*Security Council*. Sanctions Committees; The United Nations Special Commission on Iraq (UNSCOM); the two ad hoc tribunals for the former Yugoslavia and Rwanda; various peace missions, etc.

—*Economic and Social Council*. Commission for Social Development; Commission on Narcotic Drugs; Commission on Sustainable Development; Commission on Crime Prevention and Criminal Justice; Statistical Commission; the former Human Rights Commission, dissolved in order to create the new Human Rights Council that is directly attached to the General Assembly. There are also regional commissions, such as the Economic and Social Commission for Asia and the Pacific, etc.

The ICJ also has the power to establish subsidiary organs. Until now, the Court has not however made use of this power. The Court has of course created a Budgetary and Administrative Committee, a Rules Committee and a Library Committee. However, these organs do not enjoy any autonomy and are therefore not, strictly speaking, subsidiary organs. They report back to the plenary Court, which then makes the decisions.

There may also be conjointly established subsidiary organs. For example, the General Assembly and the Economic and Social Council created the Committee for Programme and Coordination of the United Nations. Its activities include planning, programming and coordination of United Nations activities and budgeting for the organisation. There are also subsidiary organs common to the United Nations and affiliated organisations. For example, the United Nations and FAO created the Intergovernmental Committee, the aim of which is to establish the main policy guidelines for the World Food Program created in 1965 and which has been subject to subsequent reforms. Legally, such an organ must obey orders given by both its creator organs. These must in turn reach agreement in order to transmit to the subsidiary organ clear instructions and supervise its work. A duty of cooperation thus applies. In the absence of such understanding, the subsidiary organ would not be governable.

[71] UNGA Res 60/180 (20 December 2005) UN Doc A/RES/60/180.

[72] UNGA Res 1645 UN Dos S/RES/1645 (2005).

[73] Five members are the five permanent Security Council members; seven members are elected by the General Assembly on the basis of their participation in post-conflict operations and activities; seven members are elected by the Economic and Social Council; five members are elected on the basis of the financial contributions they make to the United Nations budgets; and lastly, five other members are selected from those States that provide the United Nations with the most blue helmets and police personnel.

§ 102 Peacebuilding Commission

The Peacebuilding Commission was established on 20 December 2005 in two resolutions adopted by the United Nations General Assembly,[71] and the Security Council respectively,[72] following a recommendation for its creation in the Brahimi Report (2000). The Commission is a subsidiary organ of both the Assembly and the Council. It is composed of 31 members.[73] Its purpose is to come to the aid of failing States or States that have become weak following years of internal armed conflict. It thus tries to either prevent States falling into armed conflict or to help them through the difficult post-conflict period of transition towards sustainable peace. To this end, the Commission must put into place a two-fold strategy of attacking the root causes of the crisis in addressing both pre-conflict and post-conflict situations. Thus, the Commission is notably called on to facilitate and coordinate efforts to maintain peace (international presence, legislative changes, free elections, etc) as well as addressing the economic and social situation (loans, debt management, legislative changes, etc). The Commission is able to provide the General Assembly, Security Council, Economic and Social Council and the Secretary-General with its opinion in its area of expertise. This area is extremely broad as it includes the whole spectrum of possible 'positive peace' measures. For this reason, conflicts of jurisdiction or overlapping action with other principal organs of the United Nations are not excluded.

The Commission is involved in long-term work: once the acute phase of a conflict has passed, it must strengthen peace bit by bit in States whose structures are weak. It is at this moment that an international response is crucial to prevent such States from oscillating once again towards instability and conflict. In this way, the Commission has spearheaded a new branch of international law, the *ius post bellum*. To date the Commission has dealt with situations in the African continent. At present, Burundi, the Central African Republic, Guinea-Bissau and Sierra Leone are on the agenda of the Commission.

10

United Nations 'Family':
Specialised Affiliated Organisations

§ 103 General Aspects

A whole series of areas of 'functional cooperation' has not been centralised within the United Nations. These areas are left to specialised agencies that have their own legal personality, as well as their own membership and a separate budget. The acronyms of these organisations are well known: the World Trade Organisation (WTO); the International Atomic Energy Agency (IAEA); the International Labour Organisation (ILO); the Food and Agriculture Organisation of the United Nations (FAO); the United Nations Educational, Scientific and Cultural Organization (UNESCO); the World Health Organisation (WHO); the International Bank for Reconstruction and Development (IBRD); the International Monetary Fund (IMF); the International Civil Aviation Organisation (ICAO); the International Maritime Organisation (IMO); the International Telecommunication Union (ITU); the Universal Postal Union (UPU); the World Meteorological Organisation (WMO); the World Intellectual Property Organization (WIPO); the United Nations Industrial Development Organisation (UNIDO), etc. Why is there such a decentralised system? There are four reasons:

1. *Fear of excessive centralisation.* There was a concern in 1945, of over-extending the reach of the United Nations to cover the numerous and quite different functional activities. A certain degree of decentralisation promised better results. This decentralisation would moreover result in the affiliated organisations enjoying a substantial amount of autonomy, to such an extent that the Secretary-General of the United Nations has often tried to curb the excessive expressions of independence in favour of maintaining a coordinated system.
2. *Experience of the League of Nations.* Practice with respect to article 24 of the Covenant of the League of Nations showed that previously independent organisms attempted to resist being placed under the direction of the League. This desire for independence was also due to the fact that members of specialised bodies were not also members of the League. Due regard was paid to the useful indicators of this earlier lesson to avoid creating potential problems with respect to the Charter.
3. *Risk of 'politicisation'.* The maintenance of an organic distance between the political world organisation and specialised organisations has always been felt as a way of distancing functional cooperation from politics and thus avoiding the 'politicisation' of the work of these entities. This useful 'separation of functions' was thus maintained.

4. *Question of membership*. Since 1945, various States have wanted to cooperate with the functional organisations, without, however, becoming a member of the United Nations. This was the case for a long time for Switzerland and also other States. It should be recalled that the United Nations has not always grouped together all the States in the world. Maintaining separate membership in the organisations permitted non-member States to become members of the specialised organisations without at the same time having to become members of the United Nations. Thus their important participation in functional matters was secured.

The Charter tries to ensure that the activities of all its affiliated organisations are coordinated with those of the United Nations. The work of the Economic and Social Council is important in this respect. The principal aim of the provisions of the Charter (articles 58, 60, 62 and following) is to coordinate the activities of all the organisations working in the area of functional cooperation at the universal level in order to guarantee maximum effectiveness and coherence, whilst guaranteeing reciprocal institutional independence. The United Nations family is thus built on a union of independence and diversity, rather than on fusion and centralisation.

§ 104 Affiliation Mechanism

The link of affiliation between a specialised organisation and the United Nations is created by agreement between the organisation and the Economic and Social Council. This agreement establishes the conditions of cooperation. It is submitted to the General Assembly for approval and constitutes an international treaty. In this respect, article 63 § 1 provides: 'The Economic and Social Council may enter into agreements with any of the agencies referred to in Article 57, defining the terms on which the agency concerned shall be brought into relationship with the United Nations. Such agreements shall be subject to approval by the General Assembly'. Paragraph 2 of Article 57 clarifies the nomenclature to be employed: 'Such agencies thus brought into relationship with the United Nations are hereinafter referred to as specialized agencies'.

The conditions that may be envisaged for such an affiliation are threefold . They are:

1. That intergovernmental organisations are created on the basis of a treaty (this would exclude, for example, the GATT).
2. That they are universal organisations (regional organisations can only have a consultative status but cannot be affiliated as the United Nations only deals with universal cooperation).
3. That the organisations are competent in one of the fields set out in article 57: 'The various specialised agencies, established by intergovernmental agreement and having wide international responsibilities, as defined in their basic instruments, in economic, social, cultural, educational, health, and related fields, shall be brought into relationship with the United Nations in accordance with Article 63'. The list of areas is thus very broad, as the residual clause evinces: 'and related fields'. The scope thus spans functional cooperation, that is, cooperation as defined at the time of the League of Nations as 'non-political cooperation'. It is this negative criterion that determines the fields covered. Only political cooperation, in the narrow

understanding of the term, is excluded as it forms part of the United Nations (the political wing) and not the specialised organisations (the technical wing).

§ 105 Effects of Affiliation

The effects of affiliation are regulated by the treaty of affiliation and, to a less extent, by the constitution of the specialised organisation. The effects thus differ case by case. There are nevertheless some typical characteristics found in all cases:

1. *Duty to cooperate.* The duty to cooperate with the United Nations and other specialised organisations in the network is assumed by the organisation when it becomes affiliated with the United Nations system. This coordination of activities takes place under the direction of the Economic and Social Council. The General Assembly also has powers in this respect, but normally defers to ECOSOC. Article 58 provides: 'The Organisation shall make recommendations for the coordination of the policies and activities of the specialised agencies'. To this article 60 adds: 'Responsibility for the discharge of the functions of the Organization set forth in this Chapter shall be vested in the General Assembly and, under the authority of the General Assembly, in the Economic and Social Council, which shall have for this purpose the powers set forth in Chapter X'.
2. *Duty to take notice, and to respect, United Nations resolutions.* A duty to take notice is generally stipulated. In some cases, a duty to respect United Nations resolutions is also included. This is often the case for Security Council resolutions taken under Chapter VII. This duty is stipulated in the affiliation agreements of the ILO, the WHO and IBRD. Coordination is not, however, always flawless, due to the fact that the specialised organisations remain autonomous entities composed of State members that are not necessarily the same as those in the United Nations. Instances have occurred where the voting behaviour of the member States in the United Nations and in a specialised organisation diverged. Resolution 33/119 (1978) of the General Assembly addresses such situations.
3. *Exchange of information and documents.* Specialised organisations must furnish the organs of the United Nations with information and documents concerning their particular field of activity.
4. *Membership coordination.* In some instances, members of the United Nations can automatically become members of a specialised organisation, without having to fulfil any admission requirements. This is the case for UNESCO, WHO and ICAO.
5. *Budgetary coordination.* The United Nations General Assembly controls the budgets of the specialised organisations. Article 17 § 3 provides: 'The General Assembly shall consider an approve any financial and budgetary arrangements with specialized agencies referred to in Article 57 and shall examine the administrative budgets of such specialized agencies with a view to making recommendations to the agencies concerned'. Additionally, the United Nations collects the financial contributions from members States and distributes them to the affiliated organisations.

6. *Other*. For example, there are shared rules relating to staff. The employment of personnel is provided for with respect to the United Nations system as a whole. Moreover, the different organisations share the principal administrative tribunals that are based in Geneva, namely the United Nations Administrative Tribunal (UNAT) and the International Labour Organisation Administrative Tribunal (ILOAT). These tribunals are competent to hear any claim brought by a member of staff relating to their contract.

§ 106 Panorama of Affiliated Organisations

For an overview of these organisations, please refer to the diagram provided by the United Nations (at pp 122–3). There are currently 16 autonomous specialised organisations affiliated with the United Nations. This number does not include the Foundations,[1] Institutions,[2] Conferences,[3] or Programmes.[4] The following 14 organisations can first be mentioned: Food and Agriculture Organisation (FAO); International Monetary Fund (IMF); International Fund for Agricultural Development (IFAD); International Labour Organisation (ILO); United Nations Educational, Scientific and Cultural Organisation (UNESCO); World Health Organisation (WHO); International Civil Aviation Organisation (ICAO); International Maritime Organisation (IMO); International Telecommunication Union (ITU); Universal Postal Union (UPU); World Meteorological Organisation (WMO); World Intellectual Property Organisation (WIPO); United Nations Industrial Development Organisation (UNIDO); and the world bank group including the International Bank for Reconstruction and Development (IBRD) and the International Centre for the Settlement of Investment Disputes (ICSID). In addition to these two organisations are the World Trade Organisation (WTO) and the International Atomic Energy Agency (AIEA). The WTO has a special status with greater autonomy. Both the WTO and the AIEA are directly related to the General Assembly. It should be noted that a number of these special organisations were granted the right—by the United Nations General Assembly—to request an advisory opinion of the International Court of Justice on any legal question arising out of their activities, namely within their area of competence. This is the case for the following organisations: AIEA, IBRD, FAO, IMF, ICAO, ITU, IMP, WMO, WIPO, WHO, UNIDO, ILO, and UNESCO. The WHO has had recourse to this right on more than one occasion in *Interpretation of the Agreement of 25 March 1951 between the WHO and Egypt* (1980),[5] and *Legality of the Use by a State of Nuclear Weapons in Armed Conflicts* (1996).[6]

---

[1] Such as UNICEF, the United Nations Children's Fund.

[2] Such as UNU, the United Nations University.

[3] Such as the Conference on disarmament.

[4] Such as the Joint United Nations Programme on HIV/AIDS (ONUAIDS), or the World Food Programme (WFP).

[5] *Interpretation of the Agreement of 25 March 1951 between the WHO and Egypt* (Advisory Opinion) [1980] ICJ Rep 73ff.

[6] *Legality of the Use by a State of Nuclear Weapons in Armed Conflicts* (WHO) (Advisory Opinion) [1996] ICJ Rep 66ff.

11

Article 103 of the Charter

§ 107 General Aspects

What should United Nations members do when faced with a number of incompatible obligations, some of which emanate from the Charter and others which are found in international law (especially treaty-law) outside the Charter? If States had a choice as to which obligation they would choose to respect, then even binding Security Council decisions taken under Chapter VII could be circumvented by some States on the pretext of conflicting treaty obligations. In this particular case, the efficiency of maintaining peace would be put at risk. This is the reason why article 103 provides that Charter obligations take priority over all other treaty-based obligations. Jurisprudence has applied this provision on numerous occasions.[1] The text of the article provides as follows: 'In the event of a conflict between the obligations of the Members of the United Nations under the present Charter and their obligations under any other international agreement, their obligations under the present Charter shall prevail'.

§ 108 Obligations Envisaged

The text of article 103 contains the term 'obligations'. It is obligations on the side of the Charter and obligations under treaty law outside the Charter that come into conflict. First, there must be an obligation under the Charter, flowing either from one of its provisions (for example, article 2 § 5) or from a binding resolution (for example, under Chapter VII). Secondly, it is in effect the obligations that a member has entered into outside the Charter that threaten the application of the latter instrument. What about 'rights'? Could it not be argued that the right of self-defence under article 51 of the Charter (a 'right' under the Charter) should prevail over all other treaty obligations by virtue of article 103 of the Charter? According to a teleological approach, this

---

[1] With respect to the ICJ, see in particular the *Lockerbie* case, [1992] ICJ Rep 15 (status of protective measures); [1998] ICJ 23–24 (jurisdiction and admissibility). In relation to other jurisdictions, see, eg, the judgment of the Court of First Instance of the European Communities (CFI) in the *Ahmed Ali Yusuf and Al Barakaat International Foundation v Council of the European Union and Commission of the European Communities*, judgment of 21 September 2005, § 231, where the Court held that obligations under the Charter trump (with the exception of *jus cogens* norms) even obligations contained in the European Convention on Human Rights and the European Communities Treaty. The Court of Justice of the European Communities in the meantime reversed this reasoning on appeal: judgment dated 3 September 2008.

question should probably be answered in the negative. Article 103 was included in order to preserve the integrity of the Charter, notably in the area of the maintenance of peace and not to protect the interests of States taken individually. One can, however, recall the case of Bosnia-Herzegovina, which argued that the embargo on weapons that applied to the whole of the territory of the former Yugoslavia deprived it of the possibility of defending itself as the weapons of the former federal army were almost all in the hands of Serb forces and the embargo prevented it from stocking up on the weapons it needed. In this case, obligations under Chapter VII prevailed over the right to exercise self-defence. If, however, article 103 had also applied to self-defence, there would have been a clash between two rules arising under the Charter. It is, therefore, not under article 103, but rather in the text of article 51 that an answer to this question has to be sought. According to the text of article 51, collective measures by the Security Council take precedence over individual or collective measures of self-defence:

> Nothing in the present Charter shall impair the inherent right of individual or collective self-defence [. . .] until the security Council has taken measures necessary to maintain international peace and security. [Self-defence measures] shall not in any way affect the authority and the responsibility of the Security Council under the present Charter to take at any time such action as it deems necessary in order to maintain or restore international peace and security.

There is thus here a clear subordination of action under self-defence to action under Chapter VII. In legal terms, this means that a State could not oppose Chapter VII injunctions by self-defence arguments. The only question that remains relates to the status of self-defence as *jus cogens* under general international law: if self-defence forms at least partially a *jus cogens* norm (this may be doubtful), the Council could not derogate its peremptory component under a Chapter VII resolution. This question cannot be explored here.

The obligations covered under article 103 are the substantive ones which the Charter imposes on member States, for example, the prohibition of using force under article 2 § 4. What about the *authorisations* given to State members to use force under article 42 of the Charter as modified by subsequent practice? The majority opinion is that the application of article 103 hinges on a teleological interpretation. The Council could not effectively act without such authorisation, which is a substitutive but primary measure for the maintenance of peace; to hold otherwise would mean that collective action would fail because of the different treaty obligations each State participating in such actions would be forced to respect. However, we can think of limiting the privilege of article 103 to only those States that act on the basis of such a Security Council authorisation and, eventually, only to the extent that they act within the granted mandate. Article 103 should not apply to those actions that are not undertaken in the collective interest, but only for the particular interests of one State. To this end, it is necessary to always clarify the mandate granted to States by the Council and to develop rules of 'delegation' of powers. In the absence of such a mechanism, there is far too great a risk of legal insecurity and excessive influence by political interests. Alternatively, it could be argued that article 103 does not apply to authorisations of the use of force, but that States acting on the basis of such authorisations could claim that these authorisations are circumstances precluding wrongfulness under the law of State responsibility, or raise the permissive effect of recommendations addressed by an organisation to its members. Should authorisations or eventual recommendations (not decisions, which are much more frequent), which bring into play article 41, for example with respect to economic sanctions, be treated analogically to those of article 42 that apply to uses of force? In light of the fact that they are also actions concerning the maintenance or re-establishment of international peace, by virtue of Chapter VII, it is possible for article 103 to apply in such instances. The character of public order of Chapter VII and the desire to give Council action the maximum amount of flexibility and efficiency is determinative of this choice. Alternatively, it could be argued once again that these are circumstances precluding any wrongfulness, or that the doctrine of permissive effects applies.

Article 103 provides that Charter obligations prevail only over other *treaty* obligations, for example treaties of alliance. What about customary law? The text does not cover these since it was believed in 1945 that only the particular law arising from treaties could meaningfully hamper enforcement measures of the Council and not the general norms of international law, probably inapplicable to Council action. The general response is that normally the obligations under the Charter will prevail over customary rules, to the extent required. Otherwise, the limitations imposed on Council action would be too great. And, in effect, the system of Chapter VII is founded on the idea of the priority of Chapter VII obligations with respect to custom: military action entails encroaching upon the territorial integrity of a State; it does not respect the prohibition on the use of force that exists in general international law; peaceful sanctions in the absence of a prior violation of international law by the targeted State (for example, a threat to the peace) also set aside customary rules relating to counter-measures; authorisation to intercept a vessel on the high seas in order to search their cargo departs from the rules governing the freedom of the seas and the exclusive powers of a State sailing under its flag, etc. However, derogations with respect to the aforementioned rules can only be exercised insofar as they are necessary for the exercise of the prerogatives under Chapter VII. Further, fundamental customary rules, notably those that have a *jus cogens* character,[2] cannot be trumped obligations under the Charter. In this particular context, article 103 does not permit derogation of the general rules of international law. This can cause delicate problems, for instance with respect to a conflict of norms that may arise between self-determination of peoples on the one side and a decision taken by the Council under Chapter VII on the other. Finally, it must be stressed that article 103 does not cover the relationship between international law and internal law. To this situation the general rule of international law may be applied, which provides that internal law is subordinate to international law (see, for example, article 27 of the Vienna Convention on the Law of Treaties, 1969).

The substantive obligations at the heart of the Charter today reflect customary law and sometimes form peremptory norms, such as article 2 § 4. These rules are not simply treaty-based, in contrast to what Angelo Piero Sereni continued to argue in the early 1960s.[3] The Charter has, in modern international law, influenced custom to the point that its substantive provisions have the double quality of treaty and customary norms. In this vein, article 103 also constitutes part of customary law. It can thus be said that the mechanism for granting priority in article 103 is itself customary.

---

[2] See art 53 of the Vienna Convention of the law of treaties, 1969.
[3] AP Sereni, *Diritto internazionale* vol IV (Milan, 1965) 1757ff, particularly at 1803.

In practice, interesting problems have arisen in respect of article 103. At the beginning of the 1950s, the Soviet Union and other socialist States argued that the creation of NATO, based on collective self-defence, was contrary to the system of collective security under the Charter (Chapter VII), as it introduced a sub-system that threatened the functioning of the general system. NATO would thus have been contrary to the Charter and the obligations under the latter would have prevailed under article 103. The conclusion of the Warsaw Treaty put an end to this argument. Then a conflict with the Charter occurred in relation to the Brezhnev doctrine on armed intervention in order to save the gains of the socialist system, just as with the Reagan doctrine of intervention justified on the basis of the human rights cause. Both doctrines were contrary to article 2 § 4 of the Charter. As this incompatibility was permanent and non-curable, article 103 should have produced an effect of making any contrary legal act void. Lastly, the Cyprus Treaty of Guarantee, insofar as it was interpreted by Turkey (an interpretation that permitted the use of force by Turkey to unilaterally intervene on Cyprus to help the Turkish community that it subjectively determined needed its support), is also incompatible with article 2 § 4 of the Charter. Here article 103 should have the effect of influencing the interpretation of this treaty clause in the sense of *in dubio pro validitate*: ie the treaty should be interpreted in such a way as not to produce an incompatibility with article 2 § 4, namely by rejecting the Turkish argument.

The priority of Charter obligations according to article 103 also extends to *other subjects of international law*. The Vienna Convention on the law of treaties between States and international organisations or between international organisations (1986) confirms in its article 30 § 6 that obligations by virtue of the United Nations Charter take priority over other treaties concluded by international organisations. By analogy, the same principles also apply to other subjects of international law.

§ 109 Scope *Ratione Personae*

What is the effect of article 103 on treaties among member States and non-member States or non-member States of the United Nations? If article 103 is not considered to be customary international law (and thus applicable to all States, members and non-members alike), then the following three hypotheses can be made:

1. *Treaty between a member State and another member State incompatible with a Charter obligation.* The treaty is void or suspended. It is void by any practical means if the conflict with the Charter is permanent and irremediable (or alternatively permanently suspended, which in effect is tantamount to admit voidness); it is suspended if the conflict with the Charter is temporary, for example, if a commercial treaty conflicts with obligations under Chapter VII sanctions or measures. See below, § 110.

2. *Treaty between a member State and a non-member State.* For the member State, the treaty is suspended if the Charter rule is a decision of the Council taken under Chapter VII. The third State may request reparation from the United Nations member for breach of the treaty, except for the execution of public order and *erga*

omnes norms to which all States have an interest and against which no State can complain. Could the member State void the treaty if it irreconcilably conflicted with the Charter? If the provisions of the treaty conflicted with *jus cogens* norms contained in the Charter, then the answer should be affirmative. In all other cases, the treaty can be denounced. United Nations member States would have an obligation to denounce in such situations. According to the wording of article 56 of the Vienna convention on the law of treaties (1969), such a treaty could be considered to be denounceable on the basis of its 'nature'.

3. *Treaty between a non-member State and another non-member State.* Article 103 of the Charter does not apply. A provision of the other treaty will be void if it is contrary to a *jus cogens* norm of general international law. This *jus cogens* rule of general international law may be identical to a rule also contained in the Charter, such as the prohibition of the use of force.

If article 103 is customary law, then the priority mechanism applies to all States. According to a minority of authors, article 103 is moreover an *erga omnes* rule because the Charter reflects international constitutional law.

§ 110 Legal Effect

Article 103 does not specify the effect of its application. It limits itself to providing that obligations under the Charter 'prevail'. Does this mean that conflicting obligations are void, inapplicable, suspended, inopposable or unable to be executed? The majority opinion is that there is a temporary suspension of such conflicting treaty or customary obligations. There is thus a simple temporary priority given to Charter obligations and not a general invalidity of incompatible obligations. The purpose of article 103 is, according to the majority of authors, to ensure the application of sanctions decided by the organisation. It would be excessive to declare a treaty void as the effectiveness of sanctions does not require such a disproportional move. The minority opinion, however, claims that in some circumstances conflicting treaties must be declared void. How can these differences of opinion be reconciled? By drawing the following distinction:

—*Conflicts between substantive obligations.* If a treaty obligation is irreversibly in conflict with a substantive obligation contained in the Charter, then it will be void (or permanently suspended, which is practically speaking much the same). In effect, in such circumstances there is a permanent clash of obligations with those of the Charter, which would entail permanent violation of the Charter. The treaty provision must thus be voided. This result flows legally from the priority rule of article 103 which binds all members. Moreover, such substantive obligations under the Charter will often have a *jus cogens* character, as is the case for the prohibition of the use of force. Voiding (rather than permanent suspension) could then follow from the peremptory character of the provision. Would the whole treaty be void or only the provision incompatible with the Charter? If the Turkish interpretation of the aforementioned Cyprus Treaty of Guarantee is correct, then only the invoked provision is incompatible with the Charter and with *jus cogens*, not the other provisions.

There is thus an issue of being able or not to separate the clause concerned from the rest of the treaty: either the clause is separable from the rest of the treaty and the other provisions would thus remain in force; or the clause is not separable from the rest of the treaty, which would then be entirely void. The issue must be resolved by applying the customary rules contained in article 44 of the Vienna Convention on the law of treaties (1969). In a situation where there is a clash with a *jus cogens* norm, the whole treaty is declared void (§ 5). If the rule is only incompatible with the Charter but not with *jus cogens*, a good argument for separation could be made on the basis of a narrow interpretation of the exceptional rule in article 44 § 5 of the VCLT, and of *in dubio pro validitate* and *in dubio minus*. Another question may be raised: what if there is a customary rule that is irreversibly in conflict with a rule under the Charter? This could be the case with respect to local custom, which would in such circumstances be void, for example the Brezhnev doctrine. On the other hand, it is difficult to see how such a situation could arise with respect to a rule of universal custom. If such a situation did arise, it would mean there is a fatal break-down of the Charter, or even of a *jus cogens* rule, through the effective practice and *opinio juris* of States. The Charter must prevent such a rule of custom developing as far as is possible. But if it did not succeed in this, the Charter, including article 103, would have become itself obsolete.

—*Concrete measures of an organ.* If a decision of the Council under Chapter VII (or under some other legal basis) affects a treaty that is not otherwise incompatible with the Charter, then the treaty is simply temporarily suspended. It will apply again once the measures imposed by the Council have been lifted or expire. The reapplication of the treaty here is automatic and need not be particularly stated. This was the case for the Montreal Convention on civil aviation (1972) following the termination of sanctions against Libya in the context of the *Lockerbie* case.

Amendment and Revision of the Charter

§ 111 General Aspects

It was never intended that the Charter would be etched in stone for eternity. The Charter simply constitutes a way of organising international activities in the collective interest at a particular moment in history. To this end, it provides for some institutional arrangements. Such an effort must be constantly renewed and adapted if it is to keep pace with events. Consequently, the Charter contains mechanisms for the revision of its text. Articles 108 and 109 regulate these modalities. Article 108 addresses the modalities for an ordinary revision, namely the procedure to follow in order modify a particular Charter provision. Article 109 addresses the modalities for an extraordinary revision of the Charter, namely the procedure to follow in order to profoundly change the Charter text by through a general revision conference. These two modalities only differ in a matter of degree with respect to the extent of the proposed changes. Thus, article 108 may be used to amend a number of different provisions of the Charter and this may merge into a general revision. But the two provisions also differ qualitatively with respect to the procedure to be followed. Article 109 stipulates that a general conference of United Nations members must be held to effect the proposed revision, whereas article 108 permits ordinary amendments to be decided in the General Assembly and the Security Council.

The most important common feature of these two procedures is that they both require a significant degree of approval in order to be accepted. In both cases, in article 108 as in article 109, the amendments must be approved by two-thirds of General Assembly members *and* the amended text must be ratified by two-thirds of United Nations members, including the five permanent members of the Security Council, in order to become applicable. Once adopted by fulfilling these stringent requirements, the amendments apply to all member States. Those that oppose the amendments have no other choice but to try to win over the qualified majority during the voting stage, to accept the amendment or later to withdraw from the organisation. Such a procedure of amendments accepted by a majority (however qualified) and binding on all member States, was revolutionary in 1945. It comes as no surprise that the bar to their success was thus placed very high. For successful amendments, the bar is indeed placed so high that the organisation has only been able to effect minor amendments to the Charter. For that which cannot be amended, the necessary changes are obtained by techniques of informal modification. These rest on the subsequent practice of organs, informally accepted by the member States.

§ 112 Ordinary Amendments under Article 108

Article 108 provides as follows: 'Amendments to the present Charter shall come into force for all Members of the United Nations when they have been adopted by a vote of two thirds of the members of the General Assembly and ratified in accordance with their respective constitutional processes by two thirds of the Members of the United Nations, including all the permanent members of the Security Council'. Each State member can propose an amendment. Proposed amendments are included in the programme for the next session of the Assembly by a vote by the simple majority. Other principal organs of the United Nations can also propose amendments, for example the Security Council or the Secretary-General. The process is identical in both situations. The proposed amendment is put to a vote in the Assembly. The vote is carried if two-thirds of the Assembly is in favour. The permanent members of the Security Council need not vote in its favour; they may also abstain from the voting procedure. However, the vote for an amendment is not conducted according to the normal voting procedure of all members 'present and voting'. It takes into account the total number of States represented in the Assembly. States that have been suspended from the organisation under article 5 of the Charter are not counted and during the period of suspension they cannot vote.

Following the vote in the General Assembly, a second phase takes place in which the voted-on amendment must be ratified by each State member. It is controversial whether the Assembly can stipulate a temporary limitation within which ratification must take place, whereby an amendment that does not receive the required amount of ratifications by a specific date does not inter into force. There is, however, no proper reason why this right should be refused the Assembly. At the same time, such a right should only be exercised with prudence, in order not to excessively limit the period of free deliberation by States. The Assembly might, however, consider an amendment to be urgent. If it failed to be ratified by a sufficient number of States by a particular date, it would be deprived of its effect. When ratifying an amendment, no reservations in the sense of articles 19 to 23 of the 1969 Vienna Convention on the law of treaties may be made. This conclusion is based on the fact that the Charter provides that an approved amendment binds all State members. Moreover, reservations may not freely be entered when the treaty is the constitutive instrument of an international organisation.[1] The amendment enters into force the moment the last instrument of ratification is deposited with the Depositary for the required number of States. The Depositary is in this case the Secretary-General.

Once adopted, an amendment binds all State members, even those that voted against and/or did not ratify the amendment. State parties to the Charter thus renounced an important aspect of their sovereignty. It could not be otherwise with respect to an institutional treaty of such importance as the Charter. The majority necessary for an amendment to be approved is so difficult to attain that States that oppose the proposed amendments are nevertheless more than sufficiently protected. Further, it was accepted at the San Francisco conference that a disagreement concerning an amendment was a legitimate reason for a State to denounce the Charter and withdraw its membership.

---

[1] See art 20 § 3 of the Vienna Convention on the law of treaties, 1969.

To date, there have only been three formal amendments of the Charter. They have all been effected by virtue of article 108.

1. *The 1963–65 amendments.* The proposal was made to modify the representation of States in some organs because the number of members of the organisation had considerably increased. Consequently, the number of non-permanent members in the Security Council was increased from 6 to 10, thereby increasing the number of Council members from 11 to 15 (article 23). The majority vote in the Council was thus adjusted from 7 to 9 votes (article 27 §§ 2 and 3). The number of members on the Economic and Social Council was also increased from 18 to 27 (article 61 § 1, of 1965). These amendments were adopted by the General Assembly on 17 December 1963 and entered into force on 31 August 1965.

2. *The 1965–68 amendments.* These amendments followed the first and addressed a point that had been overlooked. In effect, during the campaign for the 1963 modifications, the Assembly had forgotten to adjust the majority required by article 109 § 1 taking into account the new members of the Security Council. The figure of 'nine' instead of 'seven' was thus inserted in the mentioned provision. This amendment was adopted by the General Assembly on 20 December 1965, and entered into force on 12 June 1968.

3. *The 1971–73 amendments.* These amendments concerned an increase in the number of members represented in the Economic and Social Council. They were increased from 27 to 54 (article 61). This amendment was the result of a significant increase in the number of member States owing to the process of decolonisation. This amendment was adopted by the General Assembly on 20 December 1971 and entered into force on 24 September 1973.

Other proposed amendments were not successful. The discussions and current difficulties concerning reform of the organisation are well known.

§ 113 Extraordinary Amendments under Article 109

Article 109 provides as follows:

1. A General Conference of the Members of the United Nations for the purpose of reviewing the present Charter may be held at a date and place to be fixed by two-thirds vote of the members of the General Assembly and by a vote of any nine members of the Security Council. Each Member of the United Nations shall have one vote in the conference.

2. Any alteration of the present Charter recommended by a two-thirds vote of the conference shall take effect when ratified in accordance with their respective constitutional processes by two thirds of the Members of the United Nations including all the permanent members of the Security Council.

3. If such a conference has not been held before the tenth annual session of the General Assembly following the coming into force of the present Charter, the proposal to call such a conference shall be placed on the agenda of that session of the General Assembly, and the conference shall be held if so decided by a majority vote of the members of the General Assembly and by a vote of any seven members of the Security Council.

This provision provides for a general modification of the Charter, akin to a rewriting of the text, rather than a limited alteration. The fundamental legal difference between this article and article 108 is one of procedure. Whereas the General Assembly is the organ that adopts an amendment under article 108, article 109 requires a revision conference of all State members. This conference acts as a sort of a 'constituent assembly'. The conference is convoked by parallel decisions taken by the General Assembly and the Security Council. According to § 3, a revision conference should have automatically taken place ten years after the coming into force of the Charter in 1945. This was a mechanism introduced at the San Francisco conference to quell the concerns of small and medium States that had accepted heavy compromises, thereby offering them an opportunity to have any remaining concerns addressed in the future. However, such a conference has not subsequently been convoked and indeed never took place. In a resolution of 21 November 1955, the General Assembly decided 'that a General Conference to review the Charter shall be held at an appropriate time'.[2] The question was left buried and there was no reason to exhume the issue as article 108 provided the basis for any necessary amendments. Practice thus demonstrates that article 109 does not respond to a real need of the United Nations. It has remained a dead letter.

§ 114 Informal Modifications

Like all international treaties, the Charter may be modified by subsequent practice that is informally accepted by State members, or in relation to which they do not object. One here speaks of a 'constitutional practice' of the organisation and its members. The fact that a formal modification of the Charter is so difficult to obtain—due to the great number of States that need to approve it—explains that other ways were sought for obtaining the indispensable changes needed by a political organisation situated at the core of a constantly changing international environment.

This informal process of changing a constituent text had already been developed in the era of the Covenant of the League of Nations.[3] Formal modification of the Covenant was no easier to effect than for the Charter. The following are some examples of changes made by subsequent practice. Article 1 § 2 of the Covenant was reinterpreted to mean that States that did not govern themselves freely (non-democratic States) could be admitted as members, thereby opening the door of membership to Siam and Abyssinia. Article 16 was weakened by resolutions of the Assembly which provided that each State was free to qualify itself the *casus foederis vel garantiae*. The Council gradually obtained predominance in the organisation by reducing the role of the Assembly. The right of the organisation to conclude treaties (*jus tractatus*) was permitted in practice, for example in the context of the mandate agreements or the treaty between the League and Switzerland concerning League personnel (1926). The right of the organisation to enter into diplomatic relations was also admitted in practice. Consequently, a diplomatic mission was sent by the League to Mossul and the Åland islands.

---

[2] UNGA Res 992 (X) (20 November 1955).
[3] See W Schücking, 'Le développement du Pacte de la Société des Nations' (1927) 20(5) *RCADI* 359ff.

In the Charter, one finds the same propensity to effect changes by a subsequent prac-tice informally accepted to be law. One can cite the voting procedure in the Security Council (article 27 § 3), where the abstention of a permanent member was not counted as a veto.[4] Similarly, peacekeeping operations, with the specific rules that applied thereto, were introduced into the Charter in an informal manner.[5] One often speaks with some humour about Chapter VI½ of the Charter, as these operations constituted a sort of hybrid between the peaceful settlement of disputes (Chapter VI) and concrete action taken to maintain and re-establish peace (Chapter VII). There was also a new interpretation given to article 42 in practice as authorising member States to use force under a sort of 'mandate' of the United Nations.[6] The powers of the General Assembly by virtue of Resolution 377 (V), called 'Uniting for Peace' or 'Dean Acheson', rebalanced the domains of action between the Assembly and the Council. A constitutional practice thus developed as nowhere in the Charter is the mechanism 'Uniting for Peace' found. Article 12 § 1 of the Charter, subordinating the General Assembly to the Security Council when the latter organ is seized of a dispute, has also been the object of exceptions and flexible interpretation. The Assembly indeed more than once took position on a crisis notwithstanding that the Council was still formally seized of the question or even acting upon it.[7] The extent of decolonisation also affected United Nations practice in the 1950s. It modified the Charter in a profound way, notably in Chapter XI relative to non-autonomous territories. A more recent example is a re-evaluation of human rights law, including the 'responsibility to protect' individuals against grave and systematic violations against their physical integrity. Among the aims of the Charter, human rights law has thus gained more weight than it enjoyed in the drafting era of the Charter. Constitutional practice has also enriched the Charter in relation to other important issues and not only with respect to specific matters.

[4] Above, ch 9, § 84.
[5] Above, ch 7, § 58.
[6] *Ibid*, § 55.
[7] Especially since the 1960s: racial policies in South Africa; the situation in Angola, Southern Rhodesia, Tunisia, Cyprus, etc. See K Hailbronner and E Klein, 'Article 12' in B Simma (ed), *The Charter of the United Nations: A Commentary* vol I, 2nd edn (Oxford; New York, OUP, 2002) 290. There have in most cases been no notable objections to this practice.

13

Effectiveness of the United Nations

§ 115 How Effective is the United Nations?

Is the United Nations effective? Does it properly serve its fundamental purposes? Could we manage without it? There are several answers to these questions, many of them not devoid of passion, lack of knowledge or prejudice, either favourable or unfavourable. If it can be said that every human creation could be made better, it can also be said that every international organisation is only a reflection of the international environment in which it operates. In the complex world of today, a world organisation that provides a forum in which common problems can be explained, explored, discussed and eventually channelled into partial solutions is essential. The effectiveness of the United Nations is not an issue that will be discussed here in depth, since it is not a legal question. Rather, we will simply reproduce below a passage as a basis for discussion and an incitement for further reflection.

Has the United Nations Failed[1]?

Governments in all countries and of all political persuasions continually affirm, in as many as possible of their public statements, their undying devotion to the United Nations and all its purposes and principles. They continually express, as often as they decently can, as they have done for the past half-century, their determination to uphold its objectives, to strengthen its effectiveness and to love, cherish and preserve it in every possible way.

But there has sometimes been a tone of desperation in such statements. The words become an act of faith, an incantation which all feel obliged to pronounce, but in which they no longer feel any great confidence. The paying of such obeisance is regarded as a necessary formality, but there is little inclination to take them too seriously: still less to act on them. The underlying presumption has been that the UN is 'ineffective'. It has contributed little to the solution of the major problems in recent years. In a word, it has 'failed'. It must continue to exist, of course, like the House of Lords, the Daughters of the American Revolution and other decaying institutions; but little account need any longer be taken of it in the everyday policies of governments.

In some ways this general attitude of indifference, even contempt, was more disturbing in the 1970s and 1980s than the hostility which prevailed in earlier years. Previously there was,

---

[1] E Luard and D Heater, *The United Nations, How it Works and What it Does* 2nd edn (New York, 1994) 1–4.

among some, downright hostility to the UN and a wish to see it destroyed altogether. But there were at least many others who retained a burning faith in its potential, and were therefore prepared to give it a significant part in policy making. Recently, until the revival of support in the late 1980s, there have been fewer in either category: few who retained any faith in its capacity to forge a substantial change in the traditional conduct of international relations among states; just as there were few who wished to abolish it—for why abolish the totally impotent? It has been regarded not so much as the sinister instrument of hostile and seditious forces, as the feeble mouthpiece of ineffective busybodies; not as a threat, but as an irrelevance. The main exception to this prevailing attitude has been the Heritage Foundation in the US. This body, bitterly antipathetic to the UN, had considerable influence with the Reagan government.

These feelings derived from a number of sources. Partly they were the result of wholly unrealistic expectations. The child who expects her new doll not merely to talk but to answer all her questions correctly, the driver who expects his new car not merely to go at 100 miles an hour but to turn all corners automatically will (unless they have bought unusually advanced models) inevitably feel cheated and disillusioned. Similarly, those who have traditionally regarded the UN as the modern manifestation of divine providence, a holy and impeccable supreme being, which can be called down from the skies to wave its magic wand and produce peace at a moment's notice, are inevitably disillusioned when they discover it is composed of frail and mortal human beings, representing conventional and conflicting states, with the same weaknesses and inconsistencies as their predecessors over generations. Those who thought it only required the Security Council to meet and pronounce on every act of violence in any part of the world to produce instant concord have felt deceived and tricked when they find that even the most skillfully-worded resolution is invariably not instantaneous in effect. The syllogism is simple if crude: the UN was created to assure peace; peace has not been assured; therefore the UN has failed.

Even among those whose standards are somewhat less exacting, the sense of being let-down remains. Consciousness that the UN has failed to bring solutions to many of the main conflicts of recent years (the Middle East and Vietnam, Bangladesh and Biafra, the Dominican Republic and Yugoslavia, Ethiopia and Rhodesia) creates a feeling that it is an increasingly marginal force in modern world politics. The real solutions, the serious negotiations, it is felt (on these, as on East–West relations, strategic weapons or monetary and trade policy) are undertaken elsewhere, between the great powers. The UN, on all these matters, seems ineffective and irrelevant. It provides, it is said, only words but not deeds; it is a focus for propaganda rather than for serious discussion and debate; it is dominated by a majority of very small, irresponsible nations who use their votes to steamroller through unrealistic resolutions; it flounders in endless and insuperable financial difficulties; it is a costly, inefficient and time-consuming bureaucracy.

Some of these criticisms are downright untruths. It is not the case that the UN provides only words but not deeds. Even in the peacekeeping field, the most difficult of all, the UN has established several major peace forces, which have done much to maintain or restore peace in four important conflict areas (the Middle East, the Congo, Cyprus and south-western Africa), has established observer forces in a number of other cases, and has, elsewhere, successfully mediated in disputes which might otherwise have led to war. In the economic and social field, the deeds are even more manifest. Leaving aside the World Bank, which has $78 billion of loans outstanding in 1989, leaving aside other specialised agencies (a vitally important and growing part of the United Nations system, which spend over $2 billion a year in essential services), extensive programmes of economic and technical assistance are provided by the UNations proper. The United Nations Development Programme (UNDP) which is run and organised under the UN, spends about $700 million a year on worthwhile programmes. More important still, the UN is now increasingly called on to perform a whole range of new and important programmes, in areas where worldwide action is essential: on the environment, population, disaster relief, refugees, narcotic control and many others. These practical programmes have in many cases been outstandingly successful. Though sometimes ignored altogether in the assessments of its activities, these are the areas of United Nations activity which today are developing the fastest and are perhaps most valuable.

Some of the other criticisms contain a core of truth. The UN has a cumbersome and some-times irresponsible Assembly; is bureaucratic; has financial problems. The fact that the criti-cisms are made at all, however, and that so much is made of them, again shows the unrealistic standards which have been set for the UN, and for the UN alone. It is recognised that national parliaments waste much time in idle debate, childish antics and sterile altercation; but this causes little more reaction than a shrug of the shoulders and the assumption that this is a nor-mal fact of life. It is accepted that in almost every national administration in the world there is inefficient and wasteful bureaucracy (and in many, dishonesty and corruption as well, hap-pily virtually unknown in the United Nations system); and this too is taken for granted. It is known that national and municipal governments have their financial problems; and this is regarded as inevitable. It is only because many people have, if only subconsciously, a concep-tion of the UN as something above and beyond reality, as a mythical Utopian entity that should be free of all mortal failings, that they condemn, with such violence, inadequacies which elsewhere they would accept as inescapable.

The UN, indeed, as has often been pointed out, can never be anything but a mirror of the world as it is. It merely gathers together the multiplicity of individual nation states with all their imperfections. If the states are bellicose, the UN will be full of bellicosity. If the world is a world of cold war, the UN will be a system of cold war (as in the first fifteen years). If the world is one of rich–poor confrontation (as today), so will the UN be also. If the world is beset with nationalism, so must the UN be. If there are conflicts and disagreements among continents, races or ideologies, these will be manifest in the UN as well. It is no use blaming the UN, therefore, for deficiencies which are those of the world it reflects. The UN is as good or as bad as the nations which compose it.

14

United Nations, the Forum and the Oracle

How can an organisation with a modest yearly budget of a little more than $3.5 million (in 1999 still $2.5 million) face all the world's problems? The work of the United Nations covers cooperation in the field of development; support for political processes, such as *nation building* and democratisation and economic development (including the lending of money from its financial institutions); development aid and technology transfer; peace operations and the transitional administration of territories; human rights and humanitarian affairs; the settlement of disputes and mediation; jurisdictional activities and the development of international law, etc. There are hundreds of open fronts, and within each of them the United Nations must painfully progress and attempt to make small advances in a global context of enormous complexity and in a jumble of divergent interests held by independent sovereigns. The organisation must often respond to sudden upheavals and face the ordinary turmoil of human affairs. It must feel its way along in unexplored territory where imagination and will must often supplement experience.

Perhaps the best conclusion consists in setting out as an epigraph the only two functions that make the United Nations indispensable in the world today. What does the United Nations do that no other entity is capable of doing? In relation to which roles is the organisation irreplaceable? On reflection, it seems that the United Nations performs two functions that evince the heart of its raison d'être: its role as a forum and as an oracle in the international community.

1. *Forum.* The world organisation is the place of international cooperation at the universal level. Such cooperation is indispensable in the interdependent world in which we live. It is the only place where all States and other universal actors meet; it is the only permanent place of debate for all; it is the only place where the coordination of action can occur; it is the only place where a State can know the position of all other States, even if it does not agree with them. Information and the exchange of information are valuable assets for all political persuasions, whether these are communitarian in their tendency to position themselves in line with the aims of the United Nations, or whether they are unilateral insofar as they pander to the egoistic interests of a particular State, or whether they are both these different approaches at one and the same time in an exercise of the syncretism that States so enjoy practising. Any judgement of the organisation must always have two facets. The first judgement is 'positive'. It concerns the work of the organisation. What has it achieved with what means and in what space of time? The second judgement is 'negative'. It concerns the value of the organisation's existence as it currently stands. The question is the following: what would change if the organisation *did not* exist?

It is only by considering this second judgement that one can sufficiently penetrate the fundamental character of the organisation. It is this *sine qua non* that gives full weight to its importance. In many areas we would be helpless in the absence of the *forum* of communication and expertise of the world organisation. How would we survive if we had to manage the complex world of today with the primitive forms of exchange of the nineteenth century?

2. *Oracle*. The world organisation is also the international community's sole legitimate 'oracle'. It is sometimes capable of federating in spirit and more rarely in practice, positions transcending the individual interests of States, trying to lead them along the road of common concerns of humanity. This is not to suggest that the different positions taken by the United Nations habitually represent the common vision of a 'community', which remains more often an aspiration than a fact. This, however, means that the United Nations is the only place where, following discussions and debates, an opinion that represents the common will of universal society can possibly crystallise, be formulated and eventually be put into practice in certain concrete cases. Common values are able to be presented and can take on tangible forms. International legitimacy can be built up. Measures envisaged in order to put such values into practice can be canvassed by a great or small number of States. The law concerning decolonisation, forged by a number of States in the United Nations, demonstrates this momentum in a very tangible way. The protection of the natural environment is an important recent example. Despite the weaknesses and uncertainties that national idiosyncrasies and particular positions can bring to this process of progressive and complex crystallising of common values, these do not affect the core role of the United Nations as the only potential 'universal oracle'. At times too selective and too discreet, and providing us with only a rough outline, it cannot however be ignored.

The following words, proffered by the professor and diplomat Maurice Bourquin, some sixty years ago, when the Second World War reached its end, remain pertinent:

> It is not long since international institutions saw the emptiness surrounding them. Fate overwhelmed them. It has been said that the small flame that flickered inside of them was on the verge of extinguishment. They had fallen into disrepute. Those that received them with scepticism were considered clairvoyants. Others did almost apologise for having being cast under their spell. However, at the depths of the abyss we are now calling on them for help [. . .] Without them it is impossible for us to climb up the divide and find sustainable peace [. . .] The development of international collaboration has become a need so imperative that it would be absurd to consider it negatively.[2]

This pragmatic conclusion applies with full weight to the world political organisation, the 'organisation of organisations'.

As an ideal of world cooperation, the United Nations is immortal; as an institution, indispensable; as a human construction, faulty. In each case, the United Nations is no different from any other political entity, nor any other human enterprise.

Annex

COVENANT OF THE LEAGUE OF NATIONS
28 April 1919

THE HIGH CONTRACTING PARTIES,

In order to promote international co-operation and to achieve international peace and security

by the acceptance of obligations not to resort to war,

by the prescription of open, just and honourable relations between nations,

by the firm establishment of the understandings of international law as the actual rule of conduct among Governments, and

by the maintenance of justice and a scrupulous respect for all treaty obligations in the dealings of organised peoples with one another,

Agree to this Covenant of the League of Nations.

ARTICLE 1

The original Members of the League of Nations shall be those of the Signatories which are named in the Annex to this Covenant and also such of those other States named in the Annex as shall accede without reservation to this Covenant. Such accession shall be effected by a Declaration deposited with the Secretariat within two months of the coming into force of the Covenant. Notice thereof shall be sent to all other Members of the League.

Any fully self-governing State, Dominion or Colony not named in the Annex may become a Member of the League if its admission is agreed to by two-thirds of the Assembly, provided that it shall give effective guarantees of its sincere intention to observe its international obligations, and shall accept such regulations as may be prescribed by the League in regard to its military, naval and air forces and armaments.

Any Member of the League may, after two years' notice of its intention so to do, withdraw from the League, provided that all its international obligations and all its obligations under this Covenant shall have been fulfilled at the time of its withdrawal.

ARTICLE 2

The action of the League under this Covenant shall be effected through the instrumentality of an Assembly and of a Council, with a permanent Secretariat.

ARTICLE 3

The Assembly shall consist of Representatives of the Members of the League.

The Assembly shall meet at stated intervals and from time to time as occasion may require at the Seat of the League or at such other place as may be decided upon.

The Assembly may deal at its meetings with any matter within the sphere of action of the League or affecting the peace of the world. At meetings of the Assembly each Member of the League shall have one vote, and may have not more than three Representatives.

ARTICLE 4

The Council shall consist of Representatives of the Principal Allied and Associated Powers, together with Representatives of four other Members of the League. These four Members of the League shall be selected by the Assembly from time to time in its discretion. Until the appointment of the Representatives of the four Members of the League first selected by the Assembly, Representatives of Belgium, Brazil, Spain and Greece shall be members of the Council.

With the approval of the majority of the Assembly, the Council may name additional Members of the League whose Representatives shall always be members of the Council; the Council, with like approval may increase the number of Members of the League to be selected by the Assembly for representation on the Council.

The Council shall meet from time to time as occasion may require, and at least once a year, at the Seat of the League, or at such other place as may be decided upon.

The Council may deal at its meetings with any matter within the sphere of action of the League or affecting the peace of the world.

Any Member of the League not represented on the Council shall be invited to send a Representative to sit as a member at any meeting of the Council during the consideration of matters specially affecting the interests of that Member of the League.

At meetings of the Council, each Member of the League represented on the Council shall have one vote, and may have not more than one Representative.

ARTICLE 5

Except where otherwise expressly provided in this Covenant or by the terms of the present Treaty, decisions at any meeting of the Assembly or of the Council shall require the agreement of all the Members of the League represented at the meeting.

All matters of procedure at meetings of the Assembly or of the Council, including the appointment of Committees to investigate particular matters, shall be regulated by the Assembly or by the Council and may be decided by a majority of the Members of the League represented at the meeting.

The first meeting of the Assembly and the first meeting of the Council shall be summoned by the President of the United States of America.

ARTICLE 6

The permanent Secretariat shall be established at the Seat of the League. The Secretariat shall comprise a Secretary General and such secretaries and staff as may be required.

The first Secretary General shall be the person named in the Annex; thereafter the Secretary General shall be appointed by the Council with the approval of the majority of the Assembly.

The secretaries and staff of the Secretariat shall be appointed by the Secretary General with the approval of the Council.

The Secretary General shall act in that capacity at all meetings of the Assembly and of the Council.

The expenses of the League shall be borne by the Members of the League in the proportion decided by the Assembly.

ARTICLE 7

The Seat of the League is established at Geneva.

The Council may at any time decide that the Seat of the League shall be established elsewhere.

All positions under or in connection with the League, including the Secretariat, shall be open equally to men and women.

Representatives of the Members of the League and officials of the League when engaged on the business of the League shall enjoy diplomatic privileges and immunities.

The buildings and other property occupied by the League or its officials or by Representatives attending its meetings shall be inviolable.

ARTICLE 8

The Members of the League recognise that the maintenance of peace requires the reduction of national armaments to the lowest point consistent with national safety and the enforcement by common action of international obligations.

The Council, taking account of the geographical situation and circumstances of each State, shall formulate plans for such reduction for the consideration and action of the several Governments. Such plans shall be subject to reconsideration and revision at least every ten years.

After these plans shall have been adopted by the several Governments, the limits of armaments therein fixed shall not be exceeded without the concurrence of the Council.

The Members of the League agree that the manufacture by private enterprise of munitions and implements of war is open to grave objections. The Council shall advise how the evil effects attendant upon such manufacture can be prevented, due regard being had to the necessities of those Members of the League which are not able to manufacture the munitions and implements of war necessary for their safety.

The Members of the League undertake to interchange full and frank information as to the scale of their armaments, their military, naval and air programmes and the condition of such of their industries as are adaptable to war-like purposes.

ARTICLE 9

A permanent Commission shall be constituted to advise the Council on the execution of the provisions of Articles 1 and 8 and on military, naval and air questions generally.

ARTICLE 10

The Members of the League undertake to respect and preserve as against external aggression the territorial integrity and existing political independence of all Members of the League. In case of any such aggression or in case of any threat or danger of such aggression the Council shall advise upon the means by which this obligation shall be fulfilled.

ARTICLE 11

Any war or threat of war, whether immediately affecting any of the Members of the League or not, is hereby declared a matter of concern to the whole League, and the League shall take any action that may be deemed wise and effectual to safeguard the peace of nations. In case any such emergency should arise the Secretary General shall on the request of any Member of the League forthwith summon a meeting of the Council.

It is also declared to be the friendly right of each Member of the League to bring to the attention of the Assembly or of the Council any circumstance whatever affecting international relations which threatens to disturb international peace or the good understanding between nations upon which peace depends.

ARTICLE 12

The Members of the League agree that, if there should arise between them any dispute likely to lead to a rupture they will submit the matter either to arbitration or judicial settlement or to enquiry by the Council, and they agree in no case to resort to war until three months after the award by the arbitrators or the judicial decision, or the report by the Council. In any case under this Article the award of the arbitrators or the judicial decision shall be made within a reasonable time, and the report of the Council shall be made within six months after the submission of the dispute.

ARTICLE 13

The Members of the League agree that whenever any dispute shall arise between them which they recognise to be suitable for submission to arbitration or judicial settlement and which cannot be satisfactorily settled by diplomacy, they will submit the whole subject-matter to arbitration or judicial settlement.

Disputes as to the interpretation of a treaty, as to any question of international law, as to the existence of any fact which if established would constitute a breach of any international obligation, or as to the extent and nature of the reparation to be made for any such breach, are declared to be among those which are generally suitable for submission to arbitration or judicial settlement.

For the consideration of any such dispute, the court to which the case is referred shall be the Permanent Court of International Justice, established in accordance with Article 14, or any tribunal agreed on by the parties to the dispute or stipulated in any convention existing between them.

The Members of the League agree that they will carry out in full good faith any award or decision that may be rendered, and that they will not resort to war against a Member of the League which complies therewith. In the event of any failure to carry out such an award or decision, the Council shall propose what steps should be taken to give effect thereto.

ARTICLE 14

The Council shall formulate and submit to the Members of the League for adoption plans for the establishment of a Permanent Court of International Justice. The Court shall be competent to hear and determine any dispute of an international character which the parties thereto submit to it. The Court may also give an advisory opinion upon any dispute or question referred to it by the Council or by the Assembly.

ARTICLE 15

If there should arise between Members of the League any dispute likely to lead to a rupture, which is not submitted to arbitration or judicial settlement in accordance with Article 13, the Members of the League agree that they will submit the matter to the Council. Any party to the dispute may effect such submission by giving notice of the existence of the dispute to the Secretary General, who will make all necessary arrangements for a full investigation and consideration thereof.

For this purpose the parties to the dispute will communicate to the Secretary General, as promptly as possible, statements of their case with all the relevant facts and papers, and the Council may forthwith direct the publication thereof.

The Council shall endeavour to effect a settlement of the dispute, and if such efforts are successful, a statement shall be made public giving such facts and explanations regarding the dispute and the terms of settlement thereof as the Council may deem appropriate.

If the dispute is not thus settled, the Council either unanimously or by a majority vote shall make and publish a report containing a statement of the facts of the dispute and the recommendations which are deemed just and proper in regard thereto.

Any Member of the League represented on the Council may make public a statement of the facts of the dispute and of its conclusions regarding the same.

If a report by the Council is unanimously agreed to by the members thereof other than the Representatives of one or more of the parties to the dispute, the Members of the League agree that they will not go to war with any party to the dispute which complies with the recommendations of the report.

If the Council fails to reach a report which is unanimously agreed to by the members thereof, other than the Representatives of one or more of the parties to the dispute, the Members of the League reserve to themselves the right to take such action as they shall consider necessary for the maintenance of right and justice.

If the dispute between the parties is claimed by one of them, and is found by the Council, to arise out of a matter which by international law is solely within the domestic jurisdiction of that party, the Council shall so report, and shall make no recommendation as to its settlement.

The Council may in any case under this Article refer the dispute to the Assembly. The dispute shall be so referred at the request of either party to the dispute, provided that such request be made within fourteen days after the submission of the dispute to the Council.

In any case referred to the Assembly, all the provisions of this Article and of Article 12 relating to the action and powers of the Council shall apply to the action and powers of the Assembly, provided that a report made by the Assembly, if concurred in by the Representatives of those Members of the League represented on the Council and of a majority of the other Members of the League, exclusive in each case of the Representatives of the parties to the dispute, shall have the same force as a report by the Council concurred in by all the members thereof other than the Representatives of one or more of the parties to the dispute.

ARTICLE 16

Should any Member of the League resort to war in disregard of its covenants under Articles 12, 13 or 15, it shall ipso facto be deemed to have committed an act of war against all other Members of the League, which hereby undertake immediately to subject it to the severance of all trade or financial relations, the prohibition of all intercourse between their nationals and the nationals of the covenant-breaking State, and the prevention of all financial, commercial or personal intercourse between the nationals of the covenant-breaking State and the nationals of any other State, whether a Member of the League or not.

It shall be the duty of the Council in such case to recommend to the several Governments concerned what effective military, naval or air force the Members of the League shall severally contribute to the armed forces to be used to protect the covenants of the League.

The Members of the League agree, further, that they will mutually support one another in the financial and economic measures which are taken under this Article, in order to minimise the loss and inconvenience resulting from the above measures, and that they will mutually support one another in resisting any special measures aimed at one of their number by the covenant-breaking State, and that they will take the necessary steps to afford passage through their territory to the forces of any of the Members of the League which are co-operating to protect the covenants of the League.

Any Member of the League which has violated any covenant of the League may be declared to be no longer a Member of the League by a vote of the Council concurred in by the Representatives of all the other Members of the League represented thereon.

ARTICLE 17

In the event of a dispute between a Member of the League and a State which is not a Member of the League, or between States not Members of the League, the State or States not Members of the League shall be invited to accept the obligations of membership in the League for the purposes of such dispute, upon such conditions as the Council may deem just. If such invitation is accepted, the provisions of Articles 12 to 16 inclusive shall be applied with such modifications as may be deemed necessary by the Council.

Upon such invitation being given the Council shall immediately institute an inquiry into the circumstances of the dispute and recommend such action as may seem best and most effectual in the circumstances.

If a State so invited shall refuse to accept the obligations of membership in the League for the purposes of such dispute, and shall resort to war against a Member of the League, the provisions of Article 16 shall be applicable as against the State taking such action.

If both parties to the dispute when so invited refuse to accept the obligations of membership in the League for the purposes of such dispute, the Council may take such measures and make such recommendations as will prevent hostilities and will result in the settlement of the dispute.

ARTICLE 18

Every treaty or international engagement entered into hereafter by any Member of the League shall be forthwith registered with the Secretariat and shall as soon as possible be published by it. No such treaty or international engagement shall be binding until so registered.

ARTICLE 19

The Assembly may from time to time advise the reconsideration by Members of the League of treaties which have become inapplicable and the consideration of international conditions whose continuance might endanger the peace of the world.

ARTICLE 20

The Members of the League severally agree that this Covenant is accepted as abrogating all obligations or understandings inter se which are inconsistent with the terms thereof, and solemnly undertake that they will not hereafter enter into any engagements inconsistent with the terms thereof.

In case any Member of the League shall, before becoming a Member of the League, have undertaken any obligations inconsistent with the terms of this Covenant, it shall be the duty of such Member to take immediate steps to procure its release from such obligations.

ARTICLE 21

Nothing in this Covenant shall be deemed to affect the validity of international engagements, such as treaties of arbitration or regional understandings like the Monroe doctrine, for securing the maintenance of peace.

ARTICLE 22

To those colonies and territories which as a consequence of the late war have ceased to be under the sovereignty of the States which formerly governed them and which are inhabited by peoples not yet able to stand by themselves under the strenuous conditions of the modern world, there should be applied the principle that the well-being and development of such peoples form a sacred trust of civilisation and that securities for the performance of this trust should be embodied in this Covenant.

The best method of giving practical effect to this principle is that the tutelage of such peoples should be entrusted to advanced nations who by reason of their resources, their experience or their geographical position can best undertake this responsibility, and who are willing to accept it, and that this tutelage should be exercised by them as Mandatories on behalf of the League.

The character of the mandate must differ according to the stage of the development of the people, the geographical situation of the territory, its economic conditions and other similar circumstances.

Certain communities formerly belonging to the Turkish Empire have reached a stage of development where their existence as independent nations can be provisionally recognized subject to the rendering of administrative advice and assistance by a Mandatory until such time as they are able to stand alone. The wishes of these communities must be a principal consideration in the selection of the Mandatory.

Other peoples, especially those of Central Africa, are at such a stage that the Mandatory must be responsible for the administration of the territory under conditions which will guarantee freedom of conscience and religion, subject only to the maintenance of public order and morals, the prohibition of abuses such as the slave trade, the arms traffic and the liquor traffic, and the prevention of the establishment of fortifications or military and naval bases and of military training of the natives for other than police purposes and the defence of territory, and will also secure equal opportunities for the trade and commerce of other Members of the League.

There are territories, such as South-West Africa and certain of the South Pacific Islands, which, owing to the sparseness of their population, or their small size, or their remoteness from the centres of civilisation, or their geographical contiguity to the territory of the Mandatory, and other circumstances, can be best administered under the laws of the Mandatory as integral portions of its territory, subject to the safeguards above mentioned in the interests of the indigenous population.

In every case of mandate, the Mandatory shall render to the Council an annual report in reference to the territory committed to its charge.

The degree of authority, control, or administration to be exercised by the Mandatory shall, if not previously agreed upon by the Members of the League, be explicitly defined in each case by the Council.

A permanent Commission shall be constituted to receive and examine the annual reports of the Mandatories and to advise the Council on all matters relating to the observance of the mandates.

ARTICLE 23

Subject to and in accordance with the provisions of international conventions existing or hereafter to be agreed upon, the Members of the League:

(a) will endeavour to secure and maintain fair and humane conditions of labour for men, women, and children, both in their own countries and in all countries to which their commercial and industrial relations extend, and for that purpose will establish and maintain the necessary international organisations;

(b) undertake to secure just treatment of the native inhabitants of territories under their control;

(c) will entrust the League with the general supervision over the execution of agreements with regard to the traffic in women and children, and the traffic in opium and other dangerous drugs;

(d) will entrust the League with the general supervision of the trade in arms and ammunition with the countries in which the control of this traffic is necessary in the common interest;

(e) will make provision to secure and maintain freedom of communications and of transit and equitable treatment for the commerce of all Members of the League. In this connection, the special necessities of the regions devastated during the war of 1914–1918 shall be borne in mind;

(f) will endeavour to take steps in matters of international concern for the prevention and control of disease.

ARTICLE 24

There shall be placed under the direction of the League all international bureaux already established by general treaties if the parties to such treaties consent. All such international bureaux and all commissions for the regulation of matters of international interest hereafter constituted shall be placed under the direction of the League. In all matters of international interest which are regulated by general convention but which are not placed under the control of international bureaux or commissions, the Secretariat of the League shall, subject to the consent of the Council and if desired by the parties, collect and distribute all relevant information and shall render any other assistance which may be necessary or desirable.

The Council may include as part of the expenses of the Secretariat the expenses of any bureau or commission which is placed under the direction of the League.

ARTICLE 25

The Members of the League agree to encourage and promote the establishment and co-operation of duly authorised voluntary national Red Cross organisations having as purposes the improvement of health, the prevention of disease and the mitigation of suffering throughout the world.

ARTICLE 26

Amendments to this Covenant will take effect when ratified by the Members of the League whose Representatives compose the Council and by a majority of the Members of the League whose Representatives compose the Assembly.

No such amendments shall bind any Member of the League which signifies its dissent therefrom, but in that case it shall cease to be a Member of the League.

CHARTER OF THE UNITED NATIONS

INTRODUCTORY NOTE

The Charter of the United Nations was signed on 26 June 1945, in San Francisco, at the conclusion of the United Nations Conference on International Organization, and came into force on 24 October 1945. The Statute of the International Court of Justice is an integral part of the Charter.

Amendments to Articles 23, 27 and 61 of the Charter were adopted by the General Assembly on 17 December 1963 and came into force on 31 August 1965. A further amendment to Article 61 was adopted by the General Assembly on 20 December 1971, and came into force on 24 September 1973. An amendment to Article 109, adopted by the General Assembly on 20 December 1965, came into force on 12 June 1968.

The amendment to Article 23 enlarges the membership of the Security Council from eleven to fifteen. The amended Article 27 provides that decisions of the Security Council on procedural matters shall be made by an affirmative vote of nine members (formerly seven) and on all other matters by an affirmative vote of nine members (formerly seven), including the concurring votes of the five permanent members of the Security Council.

The amendment to Article 61, which entered into force on 31 August 1965, enlarged the membership of the Economic and Social Council from eighteen to twenty-seven. The subsequent amendment to that Article, which entered into force on 24 September 1973, further increased the membership of the Council from twenty-seven to fifty-four.

The amendment to Article 109, which relates to the first paragraph of that Article, provides that a General Conference of Member States for the purpose of reviewing the Charter may be held at a date and place to be fixed by a two-thirds vote of the members of the General Assembly and by a vote of any nine members (formerly seven) of the Security Council. Paragraph 3 of Article 109, which deals with the consideration of a possible review conference during the tenth regular session of the General Assembly, has been retained in its original form in its reference to a "vote, of any seven members of the Security Council", the paragraph having been acted upon in 1955 by the General Assembly, at its tenth regular session, and by the Security Council.

PREAMBLE

WE THE PEOPLES OF THE UNITED NATIONS DETERMINED

- to save succeeding generations from the scourge of war, which twice in our lifetime has brought untold sorrow to mankind, and
- to reaffirm faith in fundamental human rights, in the dignity and worth of the human person, in the equal rights of men and women and of nations large and small, and
- to establish conditions under which justice and respect for the obligations arising from treaties and other sources of international law can be maintained, and
- to promote social progress and better standards of life in larger freedom,

AND FOR THESE ENDS

- to practice tolerance and live together in peace with one another as good neighbours, and
- to unite our strength to maintain international peace and security, and

- to ensure, by the acceptance of principles and the institution of methods, that armed force shall not be used, save in the common interest, and
- to employ international machinery for the promotion of the economic and social advancement of all peoples,

HAVE RESOLVED TO COMBINE OUR EFFORTS TO ACCOMPLISH THESE AIMS

Accordingly, our respective Governments, through representatives assembled in the city of San Francisco, who have exhibited their full powers found to be in good and due form, have agreed to the present Charter of the United Nations and do hereby establish an international organization to be known as the United Nations.

CHAPTER I: PURPOSES AND PRINCIPLES

Article 1

The Purposes of the United Nations are:

1. To maintain international peace and security, and to that end: to take effective collective measures for the prevention and removal of threats to the peace, and for the suppression of acts of aggression or other breaches of the peace, and to bring about by peaceful means, and in conformity with the principles of justice and international law, adjustment or settlement of international disputes or situations which might lead to a breach of the peace;
2. To develop friendly relations among nations based on respect for the principle of equal rights and self-determination of peoples, and to take other appropriate measures to strengthen universal peace;
3. To achieve international co-operation in solving international problems of an economic, social, cultural, or humanitarian character, and in promoting and encouraging respect for human rights and for fundamental freedoms for all without distinction as to race, sex, language, or religion; and
4. To be a centre for harmonizing the actions of nations in the attainment of these common ends.

Article 2

The Organization and its Members, in pursuit of the Purposes stated in Article 1, shall act in accordance with the following Principles.

1. The Organization is based on the principle of the sovereign equality of all its Members.
2. All Members, in order to ensure to all of them the rights and benefits resulting from membership, shall fulfill in good faith the obligations assumed by them in accordance with the present Charter.
3. All Members shall settle their international disputes by peaceful means in such a manner that international peace and security, and justice, are not endangered.
4. All Members shall refrain in their international relations from the threat or use of force against the territorial integrity or political independence of any state, or in any other manner inconsistent with the Purposes of the United Nations.
5. All Members shall give the United Nations every assistance in any action it takes in accordance with the present Charter, and shall refrain from giving assistance to any state against which the United Nations is taking preventive or enforcement action.

6.   The Organization shall ensure that states which are not Members of the United Nations act in accordance with these Principles so far as may be necessary for the maintenance of international peace and security.
7.   Nothing contained in the present Charter shall authorize the United Nations to intervene in matters which are essentially within the domestic jurisdiction of any state or shall require the Members to submit such matters to settlement under the present Charter; but this principle shall not prejudice the application of enforcement measures under Chapter VII.

CHAPTER II: MEMBERSHIP

Article 3

The original Members of the United Nations shall be the states which, having participated in the United Nations Conference on International Organization at San Francisco, or having previously signed the Declaration by United Nations of 1 January 1942, sign the present Charter and ratify it in accordance with Article 110.

Article 4

1.   Membership in the United Nations is open to all other peace-loving states which accept the obligations contained in the present Charter and, in the judgment of the Organization, are able and willing to carry out these obligations.
2.   The admission of any such state to membership in the United Nations will be effected by a decision of the General Assembly upon the recommendation of the Security Council.

Article 5

A Member of the United Nations against which preventive or enforcement action has been taken by the Security Council may be suspended from the exercise of the rights and privileges of membership by the General Assembly upon the recommendation of the Security Council. The exercise of these rights and privileges may be restored by the Security Council.

Article 6

A Member of the United Nations which has persistently violated the Principles contained in the present Charter may be expelled from the Organization by the General Assembly upon the recommendation of the Security Council.

CHAPTER III: ORGANS

Article 7

1.   There are established as the principal organs of the United Nations: a General Assembly, a Security Council, an Economic and Social Council, a Trusteeship Council, an International Court of Justice, and a Secretariat.
2.   Such subsidiary organs as may be found necessary may be established in accordance with the present Charter.

Article 8

The United Nations shall place no restrictions on the eligibility of men and women to participate in any capacity and under conditions of equality in its principal and subsidiary organs.

COMPOSITION ➤

Article 9

1. The General Assembly shall consist of all the Members of the United Nations.
2. Each Member shall have not more than five representatives in the General Assembly.

FUNCTIONS and POWERS ➤

Article 10

The General Assembly may discuss any questions or any matters within the scope of the present Charter or relating to the powers and functions of any organs provided for in the present Charter, and, except as provided in Article 12, may make recommendations to the Members of the United Nations or to the Security Council or to both on any such questions or matters.

Article 11

1. The General Assembly may consider the general principles of co-operation in the maintenance of international peace and security, including the principles governing disarmament and the regulation of armaments, and may make recommendations with regard to such principles to the Members or to the Security Council or to both.
2. The General Assembly may discuss any questions relating to the maintenance of international peace and security brought before it by any Member of the United Nations, or by the Security Council, or by a state which is not a Member of the United Nations in accordance with Article 35, paragraph 2, and, except as provided in Article 12, may make recommendations with regard to any such questions to the state or states concerned or to the Security Council or to both. Any such question on which action is necessary shall be referred to the Security Council by the General Assembly either before or after discussion.
3. The General Assembly may call the attention of the Security Council to situations which are likely to endanger international peace and security.
4. The powers of the General Assembly set forth in this Article shall not limit the general scope of Article 10.

Article 12

1. While the Security Council is exercising in respect of any dispute or situation the functions assigned to it in the present Charter, the General Assembly shall not make any recommendation with regard to that dispute or situation unless the Security Council so requests.
2. The Secretary-General, with the consent of the Security Council, shall notify the General Assembly at each session of any matters relative to the maintenance of international peace and security which are being dealt with by the Security Council and shall similarly notify the General Assembly, or the Members of the United Nations if the General Assembly is not in session, immediately the Security Council ceases to deal with such matters.

Article 13

1. The General Assembly shall initiate studies and make recommendations for the purpose of: a. promoting international co-operation in the political field and encouraging the progressive development of international law and its codification; b. promoting international co-operation in the economic, social, cultural, educational, and health fields, and assisting in the realization of human rights and fundamental freedoms for all without distinction as to race, sex, language, or religion.
2. The further responsibilities, functions and powers of the General Assembly with respect to matters mentioned in paragraph 1 (b) above are set forth in Chapters IX and X.

Article 14

Subject to the provisions of Article 12, the General Assembly may recommend measures for the peaceful adjustment of any situation, regardless of origin, which it deems likely to impair the general welfare or friendly relations among nations, including situations resulting from a violation of the provisions of the present Charter setting forth the Purposes and Principles of the United Nations.

Article 15

1. The General Assembly shall receive and consider annual and special reports from the Security Council; these reports shall include an account of the measures that the Security Council has decided upon or taken to maintain international peace and security.
2. The General Assembly shall receive and consider reports from the other organs of the United Nations.

Article 16

The General Assembly shall perform such functions with respect to the international trusteeship system as are assigned to it under Chapters XII and XIII, including the approval of the trusteeship agreements for areas not designated as strategic.

Article 17

1. The General Assembly shall consider and approve the budget of the Organization.
2. The expenses of the Organization shall be borne by the Members as apportioned by the General Assembly.
3. The General Assembly shall consider and approve any financial and budgetary arrangements with specialized agencies referred to in Article 57 and shall examine the administrative budgets of such specialized agencies with a view to making recommendations to the agencies concerned.

VOTING ▶

Article 18

1. Each member of the General Assembly shall have one vote.

2. Decisions of the General Assembly on important questions shall be made by a two-thirds majority of the members present and voting. These questions shall include: recommendations with respect to the maintenance of international peace and security, the election of the non-permanent members of the Security Council, the election of the members of the Economic and Social Council, the election of members of the Trusteeship Council in accordance with paragraph 1 (c) of Article 86, the admission of new Members to the United Nations, the suspension of the rights and privileges of membership, the expulsion of Members, questions relating to the operation of the trusteeship system, and budgetary questions.
3. Decisions on other questions, including the determination of additional categories of questions to be decided by a two-thirds majority, shall be made by a majority of the members present and voting.

Article 19

A Member of the United Nations which is in arrears in the payment of its financial contributions to the Organization shall have no vote in the General Assembly if the amount of its arrears equals or exceeds the amount of the contributions due from it for the preceding two full years. The General Assembly may, nevertheless, permit such a Member to vote if it is satisfied that the failure to pay is due to conditions beyond the control of the Member.

PROCEDURE ➤

Article 20

The General Assembly shall meet in regular annual sessions and in such special sessions as occasion may require. Special sessions shall be convoked by the Secretary-General at the request of the Security Council or of a majority of the Members of the United Nations.

Article 21

The General Assembly shall adopt its own rules of procedure. It shall elect its President for each session.

Article 22

The General Assembly may establish such subsidiary organs as it deems necessary for the performance of its functions.

CHAPTER V: THE SECURITY COUNCIL

COMPOSITION ➤

Article 23

1. The Security Council shall consist of fifteen Members of the United Nations. The Republic of China, France, the Union of Soviet Socialist Republics, the United Kingdom of Great

Britain and Northern Ireland, and the United States of America shall be permanent members of the Security Council. The General Assembly shall elect ten other Members of the United Nations to be non-permanent members of the Security Council, due regard being specially paid, in the first instance to the contribution of Members of the United Nations to the maintenance of international peace and security and to the other purposes of the Organization, and also to equitable geographical distribution.

2. The non-permanent members of the Security Council shall be elected for a term of two years. In the first election of the non-permanent members after the increase of the membership of the Security Council from eleven to fifteen, two of the four additional members shall be chosen for a term of one year. A retiring member shall not be eligible for immediate re-election.

3. Each member of the Security Council shall have one representative.

FUNCTIONS and POWERS ➤

Article 24

1. In order to ensure prompt and effective action by the United Nations, its Members confer on the Security Council primary responsibility for the maintenance of international peace and security, and agree that in carrying out its duties under this responsibility the Security Council acts on their behalf.

2. In discharging these duties the Security Council shall act in accordance with the Purposes and Principles of the United Nations. The specific powers granted to the Security Council for the discharge of these duties are laid down in Chapters VI, VII, VIII, and XII.

3. The Security Council shall submit annual and, when necessary, special reports to the General Assembly for its consideration.

Article 25

The Members of the United Nations agree to accept and carry out the decisions of the Security Council in accordance with the present Charter.

Article 26

In order to promote the establishment and maintenance of international peace and security with the least diversion for armaments of the world's human and economic resources, the Security Council shall be responsible for formulating, with the assistance of the Military Staff Committee referred to in Article 47, plans to be submitted to the Members of the United Nations for the establishment of a system for the regulation of armaments.

VOTING ➤

Article 27

1. Each member of the Security Council shall have one vote.

2. Decisions of the Security Council on procedural matters shall be made by an affirmative vote of nine members.

3. Decisions of the Security Council on all other matters shall be made by an affirmative vote of nine members including the concurring votes of the permanent members; provided that, in decisions under Chapter VI, and under paragraph 3 of Article 52, a party to a dispute shall abstain from voting.

PROCEDURE ➤

Article 28

1. The Security Council shall be so organized as to be able to function continuously. Each member of the Security Council shall for this purpose be represented at all times at the seat of the Organization.
2. The Security Council shall hold periodic meetings at which each of its members may, if it so desires, be represented by a member of the government or by some other specially designated representative.
3. The Security Council may hold meetings at such places other than the seat of the Organization as in its judgment will best facilitate its work.

Article 29

The Security Council may establish such subsidiary organs as it deems necessary for the performance of its functions.

Article 30

The Security Council shall adopt its own rules of procedure, including the method of selecting its President.

Article 31

Any Member of the United Nations which is not a member of the Security Council may participate, without vote, in the discussion of any question brought before the Security Council whenever the latter considers that the interests of that Member are specially affected.

Article 32

Any Member of the United Nations which is not a member of the Security Council or any state which is not a Member of the United Nations, if it is a party to a dispute under consideration by the Security Council, shall be invited to participate, without vote, in the discussion relating to the dispute. The Security Council shall lay down such conditions as it deems just for the participation of a state which is not a Member of the United Nations.

CHAPTER VI: PACIFIC SETTLEMENT OF DISPUTES

Article 33

1. The parties to any dispute, the continuance of which is likely to endanger the maintenance of international peace and security, shall, first of all, seek a solution by

negotiation, enquiry, mediation, conciliation, arbitration, judicial settlement, resort to regional agencies or arrangements, or other peaceful means of their own choice.
2. The Security Council shall, when it deems necessary, call upon the parties to settle their dispute by such means.

Article 34

The Security Council may investigate any dispute, or any situation which might lead to international friction or give rise to a dispute, in order to determine whether the continuance of the dispute or situation is likely to endanger the maintenance of international peace and security.

Article 35

1. Any Member of the United Nations may bring any dispute, or any situation of the nature referred to in Article 34, to the attention of the Security Council or of the General Assembly.
2. A state which is not a Member of the United Nations may bring to the attention of the Security Council or of the General Assembly any dispute to which it is a party if it accepts in advance, for the purposes of the dispute, the obligations of pacific settlement provided in the present Charter.
3. The proceedings of the General Assembly in respect of matters brought to its attention under this Article will be subject to the provisions of Articles 11 and 12.

Article 36

1. The Security Council may, at any stage of a dispute of the nature referred to in Article 33 or of a situation of like nature, recommend appropriate procedures or methods of adjustment.
2. The Security Council should take into consideration any procedures for the settlement of the dispute which have already been adopted by the parties.
3. In making recommendations under this Article the Security Council should also take into consideration that legal disputes should as a general rule be referred by the parties to the International Court of Justice in accordance with the provisions of the Statute of the Court.

Article 37

1. Should the parties to a dispute of the nature referred to in Article 33 fail to settle it by the means indicated in that Article, they shall refer it to the Security Council.
2. If the Security Council deems that the continuance of the dispute is in fact likely to endanger the maintenance of international peace and security, it shall decide whether to take action under Article 36 or to recommend such terms of settlement as it may consider appropriate.

Article 38

Without prejudice to the provisions of Articles 33 to 37, the Security Council may, if all the parties to any dispute so request, make recommendations to the parties with a view to a pacific settlement of the dispute.

CHAPTER VII: ACTION WITH RESPECT TO THREATS TO THE PEACE, BREACHES OF THE PEACE, AND ACTS OF AGGRESSION

Article 39

The Security Council shall determine the existence of any threat to the peace, breach of the peace, or act of aggression and shall make recommendations, or decide what measures shall be taken in accordance with Articles 41 and 42, to maintain or restore international peace and security.

Article 40

In order to prevent an aggravation of the situation, the Security Council may, before making the recommendations or deciding upon the measures provided for in Article 39, call upon the parties concerned to comply with such provisional measures as it deems necessary or desirable. Such provisional measures shall be without prejudice to the rights, claims, or position of the parties concerned. The Security Council shall duly take account of failure to comply with such provisional measures.

Article 41

The Security Council may decide what measures not involving the use of armed force are to be employed to give effect to its decisions, and it may call upon the Members of the United Nations to apply such measures. These may include complete or partial interruption of economic relations and of rail, sea, air, postal, telegraphic, radio, and other means of communication, and the severance of diplomatic relations.

Article 42

Should the Security Council consider that measures provided for in Article 41 would be inadequate or have proved to be inadequate, it may take such action by air, sea, or land forces as may be necessary to maintain or restore international peace and security. Such action may include demonstrations, blockade, and other operations by air, sea, or land forces of Members of the United Nations.

Article 43

1. All Members of the United Nations, in order to contribute to the maintenance of international peace and security, undertake to make available to the Security Council, on its call and in accordance with a special agreement or agreements, armed forces, assistance, and facilities, including rights of passage, necessary for the purpose of maintaining international peace and security.
2. Such agreement or agreements shall govern the numbers and types of forces, their degree of readiness and general location, and the nature of the facilities and assistance to be provided.
3. The agreement or agreements shall be negotiated as soon as possible on the initiative of the Security Council. They shall be concluded between the Security Council and Members or between the Security Council and groups of Members and shall be subject to ratification by the signatory states in accordance with their respective constitutional processes.

Article 44

When the Security Council has decided to use force it shall, before calling upon a Member not represented on it to provide armed forces in fulfilment of the obligations assumed under Article 43, invite that Member, if the Member so desires, to participate in the decisions of the Security Council concerning the employment of contingents of that Member's armed forces.

Article 45

In order to enable the United Nations to take urgent military measures, Members shall hold immediately available national air-force contingents for combined international enforcement action. The strength and degree of readiness of these contingents and plans for their combined action shall be determined within the limits laid down in the special agreement or agreements referred to in Article 43, by the Security Council with the assistance of the Military Staff Committee.

Article 46

Plans for the application of armed force shall be made by the Security Council with the assistance of the Military Staff Committee.

Article 47

1. There shall be established a Military Staff Committee to advise and assist the Security Council on all questions relating to the Security Council's military requirements for the maintenance of international peace and security, the employment and command of forces placed at its disposal, the regulation of armaments, and possible disarmament.
2. The Military Staff Committee shall consist of the Chiefs of Staff of the permanent members of the Security Council or their representatives. Any Member of the United Nations not permanently represented on the Committee shall be invited by the Committee to be associated with it when the efficient discharge of the Committee's responsibilities requires the participation of that Member in its work.
3. The Military Staff Committee shall be responsible under the Security Council for the strategic direction of any armed forces placed at the disposal of the Security Council. Questions relating to the command of such forces shall be worked out subsequently.
4. The Military Staff Committee, with the authorization of the Security Council and after consultation with appropriate regional agencies, may establish regional sub-committees.

Article 48

1. The action required to carry out the decisions of the Security Council for the maintenance of international peace and security shall be taken by all the Members of the United Nations or by some of them, as the Security Council may determine.
2. Such decisions shall be carried out by the Members of the United Nations directly and through their action in the appropriate international agencies of which they are members.

Article 49

The Members of the United Nations shall join in affording mutual assistance in carrying out the measures decided upon by the Security Council.

Article 50

If preventive or enforcement measures against any state are taken by the Security Council, any other state, whether a Member of the United Nations or not, which finds itself confronted with special economic problems arising from the carrying out of those measures shall have the right to consult the Security Council with regard to a solution of those problems.

Article 51

Nothing in the present Charter shall impair the inherent right of individual or collective self-defence if an armed attack occurs against a Member of the United Nations, until the Security Council has taken measures necessary to maintain international peace and security. Measures taken by Members in the exercise of this right of self-defence shall be immediately reported to the Security Council and shall not in any way affect the authority and responsibility of the Security Council under the present Charter to take at any time such action as it deems necessary in order to maintain or restore international peace and security.

CHAPTER VIII: REGIONAL ARRANGEMENTS

Article 52

1. Nothing in the present Charter precludes the existence of regional arrangements or agencies for dealing with such matters relating to the maintenance of international peace and security as are appropriate for regional action provided that such arrangements or agencies and their activities are consistent with the Purposes and Principles of the United Nations.
2. The Members of the United Nations entering into such arrangements or constituting such agencies shall make every effort to achieve pacific settlement of local disputes through such regional arrangements or by such regional agencies before referring them to the Security Council.
3. The Security Council shall encourage the development of pacific settlement of local disputes through such regional arrangements or by such regional agencies either on the initiative of the states concerned or by reference from the Security Council.
4. This Article in no way impairs the application of Articles 34 and 35.

Article 53

1. The Security Council shall, where appropriate, utilize such regional arrangements or agencies for enforcement action under its authority. But no enforcement action shall be taken under regional arrangements or by regional agencies without the authorization of the Security Council, with the exception of measures against any enemy state, as defined in paragraph 2 of this Article, provided for pursuant to Article 107 or in regional arrangements directed against renewal of aggressive policy on the part of any such state, until such time as the Organization may, on request of the Governments concerned, be charged with the responsibility for preventing further aggression by such a state.
2. The term enemy state as used in paragraph 1 of this Article applies to any state which during the Second World War has been an enemy of any signatory of the present Charter.

Article 54

The Security Council shall at all times be kept fully informed of activities undertaken or in contemplation under regional arrangements or by regional agencies for the maintenance of international peace and security.

CHAPTER IX: INTERNATIONAL ECONOMIC AND SOCIAL CO-OPERATION

Article 55

With a view to the creation of conditions of stability and well-being which are necessary for peaceful and friendly relations among nations based on respect for the principle of equal rights and self-determination of peoples, the United Nations shall promote:

a.   higher standards of living, full employment, and conditions of economic and social progress and development;
   b. solutions of international economic, social, health, and related problems; and international cultural and educational cooperation; and
   c. universal respect for, and observance of, human rights and fundamental freedoms for all without distinction as to race, sex, language, or religion.

Article 56

All Members pledge themselves to take joint and separate action in co-operation with the Organization for the achievement of the purposes set forth in Article 55.

Article 57

   1. The various specialized agencies, established by intergovernmental agreement and having wide international responsibilities, as defined in their basic instruments, in economic, social, cultural, educational, health, and related fields, shall be brought into relationship with the United Nations in accordance with the provisions of Article 63.
   2. Such agencies thus brought into relationship with the United Nations are hereinafter referred to as specialized agencies.

Article 58

The Organization shall make recommendations for the co-ordination of the policies and activities of the specialized agencies.

Article 59

The Organization shall, where appropriate, initiate negotiations among the states concerned for the creation of any new specialized agencies required for the accomplishment of the purposes set forth in Article 55.

Article 60

Responsibility for the discharge of the functions of the Organization set forth in this Chapter shall be vested in the General Assembly and, under the authority of the General Assembly, in the Economic and Social Council, which shall have for this purpose the powers set forth in Chapter X.

CHAPTER X: THE ECONOMIC AND SOCIAL COUNCIL

COMPOSITION ➤

Article 61

1. The Economic and Social Council shall consist of fifty-four Members of the United Nations elected by the General Assembly.
2. Subject to the provisions of paragraph 3, eighteen members of the Economic and Social Council shall be elected each year for a term of three years. A retiring member shall be eligible for immediate re-election.
3. At the first election after the increase in the membership of the Economic and Social Council from twenty-seven to fifty-four members, in addition to the members elected in place of the nine members whose term of office expires at the end of that year, twenty-seven additional members shall be elected. Of these twenty-seven additional members, the term of office of nine members so elected shall expire at the end of one year, and of nine other members at the end of two years, in accordance with arrangements made by the General Assembly.
4. Each member of the Economic and Social Council shall have one representative.

FUNCTIONS and POWERS ➤

Article 62

1. The Economic and Social Council may make or initiate studies and reports with respect to international economic, social, cultural, educational, health, and related matters and may make recommendations with respect to any such matters to the General Assembly to the Members of the United Nations, and to the specialized agencies concerned.
2. It may make recommendations for the purpose of promoting respect for, and observance of, human rights and fundamental freedoms for all.
3. It may prepare draft conventions for submission to the General Assembly, with respect to matters falling within its competence.
4. It may call, in accordance with the rules prescribed by the United Nations, international conferences on matters falling within its competence.

Article 63

1. The Economic and Social Council may enter into agreements with any of the agencies referred to in Article 57, defining the terms on which the agency concerned shall be brought into relationship with the United Nations. Such agreements shall be subject to approval by the General Assembly.
2. It may co-ordinate the activities of the specialized agencies through consultation with and recommendations to such agencies and through recommendations to the General Assembly and to the Members of the United Nations.

Article 64

1. The Economic and Social Council may take appropriate steps to obtain regular reports from the specialized agencies. It may make arrangements with the Members of the United Nations and with the specialized agencies to obtain reports on the steps taken to give effect to its own recommendations and to recommendations on matters falling within its competence made by the General Assembly.
2. It may communicate its observations on these reports to the General Assembly.

Article 65

The Economic and Social Council may furnish information to the Security Council and shall assist the Security Council upon its request.

Article 66

1. The Economic and Social Council shall perform such functions as fall within its competence in connection with the carrying out of the recommendations of the General Assembly.
2. It may, with the approval of the General Assembly, perform services at the request of Members of the United Nations and at the request of specialized agencies.
3. It shall perform such other functions as are specified elsewhere in the present Charter or as may be assigned to it by the General Assembly.

VOTING ➤

Article 67

1. Each member of the Economic and Social Council shall have one vote.
2. Decisions of the Economic and Social Council shall be made by a majority of the members present and voting.

PROCEDURE ➤

Article 68

The Economic and Social Council shall set up commissions in economic and social fields and for the promotion of human rights, and such other commissions as may be required for the performance of its functions.

Article 69

The Economic and Social Council shall invite any Member of the United Nations to participate, without vote, in its deliberations on any matter of particular concern to that Member.

Article 70

The Economic and Social Council may make arrangements for representatives of the specialized agencies to participate, without vote, in its deliberations and in those of the commissions established by it, and for its representatives to participate in the deliberations of the specialized agencies.

Article 71

The Economic and Social Council may make suitable arrangements for consultation with non-governmental organizations which are concerned with matters within its competence. Such arrangements may be made with international organizations and, where appropriate, with national organizations after consultation with the Member of the United Nations concerned.

Article 72

1. The Economic and Social Council shall adopt its own rules of procedure, including the method of selecting its President.
2. The Economic and Social Council shall meet as required in accordance with its rules, which shall include provision for the convening of meetings on the request of a majority of its members.

CHAPTER XI: DECLARATION REGARDING NON-SELF-GOVERNING TERRITORIES

Article 73

Members of the United Nations which have or assume responsibilities for the administration of territories whose peoples have not yet attained a full measure of self-government recognize the principle that the interests of the inhabitants of these territories are paramount, and accept as a sacred trust the obligation to promote to the utmost, within the system of international peace and security established by the present Charter, the well-being of the inhabitants of these territories, and, to this end:

a.   to ensure, with due respect for the culture of the peoples concerned, their political, economic, social, and educational advancement, their just treatment, and their protection against abuses;
   b.   to develop self-government, to take due account of the political aspirations of the peoples, and to assist them in the progressive development of their free political institutions, according to the particular circumstances of each territory and its peoples and their varying stages of advancement;
   c.   to further international peace and security;
   d.   to promote constructive measures of development, to encourage research, and to co-operate with one another and, when and where appropriate, with specialized international bodies with a view to the practical achievement of the social, economic, and scientific purposes set forth in this Article; and
   e.   to transmit regularly to the Secretary-General for information purposes, subject to such limitation as security and constitutional considerations may require, statistical and other information of a technical nature relating to economic, social, and educational conditions in the territories for which they are respectively responsible other than those territories to which Chapters XII and XIII apply.

Article 74

Members of the United Nations also agree that their policy in respect of the territories to which this Chapter applies, no less than in respect of their metropolitan areas, must be based on the general principle of good-neighbourliness, due account being taken of the interests and well-being of the rest of the world, in social, economic, and commercial matters.

CHAPTER XII: INTERNATIONAL TRUSTEESHIP SYSTEM

Article 75

The United Nations shall establish under its authority an international trusteeship system for the administration and supervision of such territories as may be placed thereunder by subsequent individual agreements. These territories are hereinafter referred to as trust territories.

Article 76

The basic objectives of the trusteeship system, in accordance with the Purposes of the United Nations laid down in Article 1 of the present Charter, shall be:

a. to further international peace and security;
   b. to promote the political, economic, social, and educational advancement of the inhabitants of the trust territories, and their progressive development towards self-government or independence as may be appropriate to the particular circumstances of each territory and its peoples and the freely expressed wishes of the peoples concerned, and as may be provided by the terms of each trusteeship agreement;
   c. to encourage respect for human rights and for fundamental freedoms for all without distinction as to race, sex, language, or religion, and to encourage recognition of the interdependence of the peoples of the world; and
   d. to ensure equal treatment in social, economic, and commercial matters for all Members of the United Nations and their nationals, and also equal treatment for the latter in the administration of justice, without prejudice to the attainment of the foregoing objectives and subject to the provisions of Article 80.

Article 77

1. The trusteeship system shall apply to such territories in the following categories as may be placed thereunder by means of trusteeship agreements:

    a. territories now held under mandate;
    b. territories which may be detached from enemy states as a result of the Second World War; and
    c. territories voluntarily placed under the system by states responsible for their administration.
2. It will be a matter for subsequent agreement as to which territories in the foregoing categories will be brought under the trusteeship system and upon what terms.

Article 78

The trusteeship system shall not apply to territories which have become Members of the United Nations, relationship among which shall be based on respect for the principle of sovereign equality.

Article 79

The terms of trusteeship for each territory to be placed under the trusteeship system, including any alteration or amendment, shall be agreed upon by the states directly concerned, including the mandatory power in the case of territories held under mandate by a Member of the United Nations, and shall be approved as provided for in Articles 83 and 85.

Article 80

1. Except as may be agreed upon in individual trusteeship agreements, made under Articles 77, 79, and 81, placing each territory under the trusteeship system, and until such agreements have been concluded, nothing in this Chapter shall be construed in or of itself to alter in any manner the rights whatsoever of any states or any peoples or the terms of existing international instruments to which Members of the United Nations may respectively be parties.
2. Paragraph 1 of this Article shall not be interpreted as giving grounds for delay or postponement of the negotiation and conclusion of agreements for placing mandated and other territories under the trusteeship system as provided for in Article 77.

Article 81

The trusteeship agreement shall in each case include the terms under which the trust territory will be administered and designate the authority which will exercise the administration of the trust territory. Such authority, hereinafter called the administering authority, may be one or more states or the Organization itself.

Article 82

There may be designated, in any trusteeship agreement, a strategic area or areas which may include part or all of the trust territory to which the agreement applies, without prejudice to any special agreement or agreements made under Article 43.

Article 83

1. All functions of the United Nations relating to strategic areas, including the approval of the terms of the trusteeship agreements and of their alteration or amendment shall be exercised by the Security Council.
2. The basic objectives set forth in Article 76 shall be applicable to the people of each strategic area.
3. The Security Council shall, subject to the provisions of the trusteeship agreements and without prejudice to security considerations, avail itself of the assistance of the Trusteeship Council to perform those functions of the United Nations under the trusteeship system relating to political, economic, social, and educational matters in the strategic areas.

Article 84

It shall be the duty of the administering authority to ensure that the trust territory shall play its part in the maintenance of international peace and security. To this end the administering authority may make use of volunteer forces, facilities, and assistance from the trust territory in carrying out the obligations towards the Security Council undertaken in this regard by the administering authority, as well as for local defence and the maintenance of law and order within the trust territory.

Article 85

1. The functions of the United Nations with regard to trusteeship agreements for all areas not designated as strategic, including the approval of the terms of the trusteeship agreements and of their alteration or amendment, shall be exercised by the General Assembly.
2. The Trusteeship Council, operating under the authority of the General Assembly shall assist the General Assembly in carrying out these functions.

CHAPTER XIII: THE TRUSTEESHIP COUNCIL

COMPOSITION ➤

Article 86

1. The Trusteeship Council shall consist of the following Members of the United Nations:

   a. those Members administering trust territories;

   b. such of those Members mentioned by name in Article 23 as are not administering trust territories; and

   c. as many other Members elected for three-year terms by the General Assembly as may be necessary to ensure that the total number of members of the Trusteeship Council is equally divided between those Members of the United Nations which administer trust territories and those which do not.
2. Each member of the Trusteeship Council shall designate one specially qualified person to represent it therein.

FUNCTIONS and POWERS ➤

Article 87

The General Assembly and, under its authority, the Trusteeship Council, in carrying out their functions, may:

a.   consider reports submitted by the administering authority;
   b. accept petitions and examine them in consultation with the administering authority;
   c. provide for periodic visits to the respective trust territories at times agreed upon with the administering authority; and
   d. take these and other actions in conformity with the terms of the trusteeship agreements.

Article 88

The Trusteeship Council shall formulate a questionnaire on the political, economic, social, and educational advancement of the inhabitants of each trust territory, and the administering authority for each trust territory within the competence of the General Assembly shall make an annual report to the General Assembly upon the basis of such questionnaire.

VOTING ➤

Article 89

1. Each member of the Trusteeship Council shall have one vote.
2. Decisions of the Trusteeship Council shall be made by a majority of the members present and voting.

PREOCEDURE ➤

Article 90

1. The Trusteeship Council shall adopt its own rules of procedure, including the method of selecting its President.
2. The Trusteeship Council shall meet as required in accordance with its rules, which shall include provision for the convening of meetings on the request of a majority of its members.

Article 91

The Trusteeship Council shall, when appropriate, avail itself of the assistance of the Economic and Social Council and of the specialized agencies in regard to matters with which they are respectively concerned.

CHAPTER XIV: THE INTERNATIONAL COURT OF JUSTICE

Article 92

The International Court of Justice shall be the principal judicial organ of the United Nations. It shall function in accordance with the annexed Statute, which is based upon the Statute of the Permanent Court of International Justice and forms an integral part of the present Charter.

Article 93

1. All Members of the United Nations are *ipso facto* parties to the Statute of the International Court of Justice.
2. A state which is not a Member of the United Nations may become a party to the Statute of the International Court of Justice on conditions to be determined in each case by the General Assembly upon the recommendation of the Security Council.

Article 94

1. Each Member of the United Nations undertakes to comply with the decision of the International Court of Justice in any case to which it is a party.
2. If any party to a case fails to perform the obligations incumbent upon it under a judgment rendered by the Court, the other party may have recourse to the Security Council, which may, if it deems necessary, make recommendations or decide upon measures to be taken to give effect to the judgment.

Article 95

Nothing in the present Charter shall prevent Members of the United Nations from entrusting the solution of their differences to other tribunals by virtue of agreements already in existence or which may be concluded in the future.

Article 96

a.   The General Assembly or the Security Council may request the International Court of Justice to give an advisory opinion on any legal question.
b.   Other organs of the United Nations and specialized agencies, which may at any time be so authorized by the General Assembly, may also request advisory opinions of the Court on legal questions arising within the scope of their activities.

CHAPTER XV: THE SECRETARIAT

Article 97

The Secretariat shall comprise a Secretary-General and such staff as the Organization may require. The Secretary-General shall be appointed by the General Assembly upon the recommendation of the Security Council. He shall be the chief administrative officer of the Organization.

Article 98

The Secretary-General shall act in that capacity in all meetings of the General Assembly, of the Security Council, of the Economic and Social Council, and of the Trusteeship Council, and shall perform such other functions as are entrusted to him by these organs. The Secretary-General shall make an annual report to the General Assembly on the work of the Organization.

Article 99

The Secretary-General may bring to the attention of the Security Council any matter which in his opinion may threaten the maintenance of international peace and security.

Article 100

1. In the performance of their duties the Secretary-General and the staff shall not seek or receive instructions from any government or from any other authority external to the Organization. They shall refrain from any action which might reflect on their position as international officials responsible only to the Organization.
2. Each Member of the United Nations undertakes to respect the exclusively international character of the responsibilities of the Secretary-General and the staff and not to seek to influence them in the discharge of their responsibilities.

Article 101

1. The staff shall be appointed by the Secretary-General under regulations established by the General Assembly.
2. Appropriate staffs shall be permanently assigned to the Economic and Social Council, the Trusteeship Council, and, as required, to other organs of the United Nations. These staffs shall form a part of the Secretariat.
3. The paramount consideration in the employment of the staff and in the determination of the conditions of service shall be the necessity of securing the highest standards of efficiency, competence, and integrity. Due regard shall be paid to the importance of recruiting the staff on as wide a geographical basis as possible.

CHAPTER XVI: MISCELLANEOUS PROVISIONS

Article 102

1. Every treaty and every international agreement entered into by any Member of the United Nations after the present Charter comes into force shall as soon as possible be registered with the Secretariat and published by it.
2. No party to any such treaty or international agreement which has not been registered in accordance with the provisions of paragraph 1 of this Article may invoke that treaty or agreement before any organ of the United Nations.

Article 103

In the event of a conflict between the obligations of the Members of the United Nations under the present Charter and their obligations under any other international agreement, their obligations under the present Charter shall prevail.

Article 104

The Organization shall enjoy in the territory of each of its Members such legal capacity as may be necessary for the exercise of its functions and the fulfilment of its purposes.

Article 105

1. The Organization shall enjoy in the territory of each of its Members such privileges and immunities as are necessary for the fulfilment of its purposes.
2. Representatives of the Members of the United Nations and officials of the Organization shall similarly enjoy such privileges and immunities as are necessary for the independent exercise of their functions in connexion with the Organization.
3. The General Assembly may make recommendations with a view to determining the details of the application of paragraphs 1 and 2 of this Article or may propose conventions to the Members of the United Nations for this purpose.

CHAPTER XVII: TRANSITIONAL SECURITY ARRANGEMENTS

Article 106

Pending the coming into force of such special agreements referred to in Article 43 as in the opinion of the Security Council enable it to begin the exercise of its responsibilities under Article 42, the parties to the Four-Nation Declaration, signed at Moscow, 30 October 1943, and France, shall, in accordance with the provisions of paragraph 5 of that Declaration, consult with one another and as occasion requires with other Members of the United Nations with a view to such joint action on behalf of the Organization as may be necessary for the purpose of maintaining international peace and security.

Article 107

Nothing in the present Charter shall invalidate or preclude action, in relation to any state which during the Second World War has been an enemy of any signatory to the present Charter, taken or authorized as a result of that war by the Governments having responsibility for such action.

CHAPTER XVIII: AMENDMENTS

Article 108

Amendments to the present Charter shall come into force for all Members of the United Nations when they have been adopted by a vote of two thirds of the members of the General Assembly and ratified in accordance with their respective constitutional processes by two thirds of the Members of the United Nations, including all the permanent members of the Security Council.

Article 109

1. A General Conference of the Members of the United Nations for the purpose of reviewing the present Charter may be held at a date and place to be fixed by a two-thirds vote of the members of the General Assembly and by a vote of any nine members of the Security Council. Each Member of the United Nations shall have one vote in the conference.
2. Any alteration of the present Charter recommended by a two-thirds vote of the conference shall take effect when ratified in accordance with their respective constitutional processes by two thirds of the Members of the United Nations including all the permanent members of the Security Council.
3. If such a conference has not been held before the tenth annual session of the General Assembly following the coming into force of the present Charter, the proposal to call such a conference shall be placed on the agenda of that session of the General Assembly, and the conference shall be held if so decided by a majority vote of the members of the General Assembly and by a vote of any seven members of the Security Council.

CHAPTER XIX: RATIFICATION AND SIGNATURE

Article 110

1. The present Charter shall be ratified by the signatory states in accordance with their respective constitutional processes.
2. The ratifications shall be deposited with the Government of the United States of America, which shall notify all the signatory states of each deposit as well as the Secretary-General of the Organization when he has been appointed.

3. The present Charter shall come into force upon the deposit of ratifications by the Republic of China, France, the Union of Soviet Socialist Republics, the United Kingdom of Great Britain and Northern Ireland, and the United States of America, and by a majority of the other signatory states. A protocol of the ratifications deposited shall thereupon be drawn up by the Government of the United States of America which shall communicate copies thereof to all the signatory states.

4. The states signatory to the present Charter which ratify it after it has come into force will become original Members of the United Nations on the date of the deposit of their respective ratifications.

Article 111

The present Charter, of which the Chinese, French, Russian, English, and Spanish texts are equally authentic, shall remain deposited in the archives of the Government of the United States of America. Duly certified copies thereof shall be transmitted by that Government to the Governments of the other signatory states.

IN FAITH WHEREOF the representatives of the Governments of the United Nations have signed the present Charter. DONE at the city of San Francisco the twenty-sixth day of June, one thousand nine hundred and forty-five.

Select Bibliography*

1. United Nations Documentation: Research Guide

- *www.un.org*

  United Nations Website. Access to the United Nations Treaty Collection.

- *Official Documents System (ODS)*: www.documents.un.org/

  ODS covers all types of official United Nations documentation, beginning in 1993. Older UN documents are, however, added to the system on a daily basis. ODS also provides access to the resolutions of the General Assembly, Security Council, Economic and Social Council and the Trusteeship Council from 1946 onwards.

- *Yearbook of the United Nations* (New York, Lake Success, United Nations Department of Public Information, 1947–).

  Arranged by broad subjects, with a detailed index. An excellent source to start gathering references to and UN document symbols for the most important UN resolutions, reports and meetings on a topic and for situating a topic in the context of other UN action.

  Also available online (1946–2005): www.unyearbook.un.org/

- *Repertory of Practice of United Nations Organs* (New York, United Nations, 1955).

  The Repertory is a legal publication containing analytical studies of the decisions of the principal organs of the United Nations under each of the Articles of the Charter of the United Nations.

  Also available online: www.un.org/law/repertory/

- *Annual Review of United Nations Affairs* (Dobbs Ferry, New York, Oceana Publications, 1949–).

  This Review presents the key UN documents that highlight the work of the principal United Nations organs each year, focusing annually on one theme of particular relevance.

  * Prepared by Anne-Laurence Brugère, University of Geneva. March 2009.

• *Max Planck Yearbook of United Nations Law/Max-Planck-Institut für ausländisches öffentliches Recht und Völkerrecht* (The Hague, Kluwer Law International; Leiden, Martinus Nijhoff, 1997–).

This publication, edited by the directors of the Max Planck Institute for Comparative Public Law and International Law in Heidelberg, Germany, is a scholarly periodical focusing on activities of the United Nations in the field of international law.

• *United Nations Conference on International Organization, San Francisco 1945* (Selected Documents) (Washington, 1946); *United Nations Conference on International Organization, San Francisco 1945* (Conference Proceedings: texts of documents adopted by the conference) (London, 1945).

Preparatory Works ('Travaux Préparatoires') of the United Nations Charter.

• *Acronyms and Abbreviations covering the United Nations System and other International Organizations* (New York, United Nations, 1981).

List of abbreviations covering the United Nations System.

• *Yearbook of the League of Nations* (Boston, World Peace Foundation, 1924–29).

• *Other Research Guides*:

United Nations Dag Hammarskjöld Library: www.un.org/Depts/dhl/resguide/
Columbia University: www.library.law.columbia.edu/guides/United_Nations
Chamberlain, W and Carter Moor, C, *How to Use United Nations Documents* (New York University Occasional Papers No 1, New York University Press, 1953).
Chamberlain, W and Hartley Clark, W, 'Materials for Undergraduate Study of the United Nations' (March 1954) 48(1) *The American Political Science Review* 204–11.
Winton, HNM (ed), *Publications of the UN System: A Reference Guide* (New York; London, RR Bowker, 1972).

2. Origins of the United Nations

Ago, R, 'L'organizzazione internazionale dalla Società delle Nazioni alle Nazioni Unite' (2004) 59(3) *La Comunità Internazionale* 5–23.
Drakidis, P, *La Charte de l'Atlantique 1941, La Déclaration des Nations Unies 1942 sauvegardées par la Charte des Nations Unies, arsenal prioritaire de paix et de sécurité mondiales* (Besançon, Centre de recherche et d'information politique et sociale, 1995).
Gerbet, P, Ghebali V-Y and Mouton, MR, *Le Rêve d'un ordre mondial: de la SDN à l'ONU* (Paris, Imprimerie nationale, 1996).
Ghebali, VY, 'La transition de la Société des Nations à l'Organisation des Nations Unies', in: *The League of Nations in Retrospect* (Walter de Gruyter, Berlin/New York, 1983) 73–92.
Goodrich, LM, 'From League of Nations to United Nations' (1947) 1 *International Organization* 3–21.
Guggenheim, P, *L'organisation de la société internationale* (Neuchâtel, édition de la Baconnière, 1944).
Hilderbrand, RC, *Dumbarton Oaks: The Origins of the UN and the Search for Postwar Security* (Chapel Hill, University of North Carolina Press, 1990).
Luard E, *A History of the United Nations, The Years of Western Domination, 1945–1955* (London, MacMillan, 1982).
—— *The Age of Decolonization, 1995–1965* (London, MacMillan, 1989).

Marbeau, M, *La Société des Nations* (Paris, Presses Universitaires de France, 2001).

Murray, G, *From the League to the UN* (London, OUP, 1948).

Myres, DP, 'Representation in the League of Nations Council' (1926) 20(4) *AJIL* 689–713.

—— 'The League of Nations Covenant: 1939 Model' (1939) 33(2) *American Political Science Review* 193–218.

—— 'Liquidation of League of Nations Functions' (1948) 42(3) *AJIL* 320–54.

Russell, RB, *A History of the United Nations Charter: The Role of the United States* (1940–1945) (Washington, The Brookings Institution, 1958).

Schlesinger, S, *Act of Creation: The Untold Story of the Founding of the United Nations* (Colorado, Westview Press, 2003).

Walters, FP, *A History of the League of Nations* (London/New York/ Toronto, OUP, 1960).

Webster, CK (with some chapters written by Herbert, S), *The League of Nations in Theory and Practice* (London, G Allen and Unwin, 1933).

3. General

Abi-Saab, G (ed), *Le concept d'organisation internationale* (Paris, UNESCO, 1980).

Archer, C, *International Organizations* (New York, Routledge, 2001).

Baehr, PR and Gordenker, L, *The United Nations: Reality and Ideal* (New York, Palgrave, Macmillan Press, 2005).

Bailey, SD, *The United Nations: A Short Political Guide* (Hampshire; London, Macmillan Press, 1989).

Bennett, AL and Oliver, JK, *International Organizations: Principles and Issues* (Englewood Cliffs, Prentice Hall, 2002).

Bentwick, N and Martin A, *A Commentary on the Charter of the UN* (London, Routledge; New York, Kraus Reprint, 1969).

Berridge, GR and Jennings, A (eds), *Diplomacy at the UN* (Houndmills, Basingstoke, Macmillan Press, 1987).

Bertrand, M, *L'ONU* (Paris, La Découverte, 2007).

Bettati, M, *Le droit des organisations internationales* (Paris, Presses Universitaires de France, 1987).

Brierly, JL, *The Law of Nations. An Introduction to International Law of Peace* (Oxford, Clarendon Press, 1981).

Cede, F and Sucharipa-Behrmann, L (eds), *The United Nations: Law and Practice* (The Hague, Kluwer Law International, 2001).

Chemain, R and Pellet, A (eds), *La Charte des Nations Unies, constitution mondiale?* (Paris, Pedone, 2006).

Chesterman, S, Franck, T and Malone, DM, *Law and Practice of the United Nations, Documents and Commentary* (New York; Oxford, OUP, 2008).

Cohen, BV, *The United Nations: Constitutional Developments, Growth and Possibilities* (Cambridge, MA, Harvard University Press, 1961).

Conforti, B, *Le Nazioni Unite* (Padova, CEDAM, 2005).

—— *The Law and Practice of the United Nations* (Leiden, Martinus Nijhoff, 2005).

Cot, J-P, Pellet, A and Forteau, M (eds), *La Charte des Nations Unies: Commentaire article par article* (Paris, Economica, 2005).

Coyle, DC, *The United Nations and How it Works* (New York, Columbia University Press, 1969).

Diez de Velasco Vallejo, M, *Les organisations internationales* (Paris, Economica, 2002).

Dijkzeul, D and Beigbeder, Y (eds), *Rethinking International Organizations: Pathology and Promise* (Oxford, Berghahn Books, 2003).

Elmandjra, M, *The United Nations System. An Analysis* (London, Faber and Faber, 1973).

Emmerij, L, Jolly, R and Weiss, TG, *Ahead of the Curve? UN Ideas and Global Challenges* (Bloomington, Indiana University Press, 2001).

Escher, R, *Friedliche Erledigung von Streitigkeiten nach dem System der Vereinten Nationen* (Zurich, Schulthess, 1985).

Evatt, HV, *The United Nations* (Cambridge, MA, Harvard University Press, 1948).

—— *The Task of Nations* (New York, Duell, Sloan and Pearce, 1949).

Falk, RA and Mendlovitz, SH (eds), *The Strategy of World Order, Volume III: The United Nations* (New York, World Law Fund, 1966).

Fasulo, L, *An Insider's Guide to the UN* (New Haven, Yale University Press, 2004).

Feller, AH, *United Nations and World Community* (Boston, Little, Brown, 1952).

Foot, R, MacFarlane, SN and Mastanduno, M (eds), *US Hegemony and International Organizations* (Oxford, OUP, 2003).

Ghebali, V-Y, *La crise du système des Nations Unies* (Paris, La Documentation française, 1988).

Goodrich, LM and Hambro, E, *Charter of the UN, Commentary and Documents* (London, Stevens and Sons Ltd, 1949)

Goodrich, LM, Hambro, E and Simons, AP, *Charter of the UN, Commentary and Documents* 3rd edn (New York; London, Columbia University Press, 1969).

Gutierrez Baylon, J de D, *Sistema jurídico de las Naciones Unidas* (Mexico, Editorial Porrúa, 2007).

Heinbecker, P and Goff, P (eds), *Irrelevant or Indispensable? The United Nations in the 21st Century* (Waterloo, Wilfrid Laurier University Press, 2005).

Hoffmann, S, *Organisations internationales et pouvoirs politiques des Etats* (Paris, A Colin, 1954).

Jenks, CW, *The World beyond the Charter in Historical Perspective: A Tentative Synthesis of Four Stages of World Organization* (London, G Allen and Unwin, 1969).

Joyner, CC (ed), *The United Nations and International Law* (Cambridge, CUP, 1997).

Kelsen, H, *The Law of the United Nations: A Critical Analysis of its Fundamental Problems* (London, Stevens & Sons, 1950).

Kopelmanas, L, *L'organisation des Nations Unies, Volume I, L'organisation constitutionnelle des Nations Unies* (Paris, Sirey, 1947).

Lie, T, *In the Cause of Peace: Seven Years with the United Nations* (New York, Macmillan Press, 1954).

Luard, E, *A History of the United Nations, Volume I, The Years of Western Domination 1945–1955* (London; Basingstoke, Macmillan Press, 1989).

—— *A History of the United Nations, Volume II, The Age of Decolonization 1955–1965* (London; Basingstoke, Macmillan Press, 1989).

—— *The United Nations: How it Works and What it Does* (Houndmills, Basingstoke, Macmillan Press, 1994).

Marchisio, S, *L'ONU: il diritto delle Nazioni Unite* (Bologne, Il Mulino, 2003).

Meisler, S, *United Nations: The First Fifty Years* (New York, Atlantic Monthly Press, 1995).

Mestre-Lafay, F, *L'Organisation des Nations Unies* (Paris, Presses Universitaires de France, 2003).

Padelford, NJ and Goodrich, LM (eds), *The United Nations in the Balance (Accomplishments and Prospects)* (New York; Washington, FA Praeger, 1965).

Patterson, EM (ed), *Progress and Prospects of the United Nations, Volume 252* (Philadelphia, The American Academy of Political and Social Science, July 1947).

Pellet, A, *Les Nations Unies: textes fondamentaux* (Paris, Presses Universitaires de France, 1995).

Reinalda, B and Verbeek, B (eds), *Decision Making Within International Organisations* (London, Routledge, 2004).

Roosevelt, E and Witt, WA, *United Nations: Today and Tomorrow* (New York, Harper & Brothers Publishers, 1953).

Ross, A, *The United Nations: Peace and Progress* (New York, The Bedminster Press, 1966).

Schachter, O, 'United Nations Law' (1994) 88(1) *AJIL* 11–23.

Schachter, O and Joyner, CC (eds), *United Nations Legal Order* (Cambridge, Grotius Publications Limited/CUP, 1995).

Schermers, HG, 'We the People of the Nations' (1997) 1 *Max Planck UNYB* 111–28.

Schorlemer, S (von) (ed), *Praxishandbuch UNO. Die Vereinten Nationen im Lichte globaler Herausforderungen* (Heidelberg, Springer Verlag, 2003).

Simma, B (ed), *Charta der Vereinten Nationen. Kommentar* (München, CH Beck, 1991).

—— *The Charter of the United Nations: A Commentary* Volume 2, 2nd edn (Oxford; New York, OUP, 2002).

Smith, CB, *Politics and Process at the United Nations: The Global Dance* (Boulder, Lynne Rienner Publishers, 2006).

Smouts, M-C, *Les organisations internationales* (Paris, A Colin, 1995).

Sohn, LB, *Cases on United Nations Law* (Brooklyn, The Foundation Press, 1967).

Taylor, P and Groom, AJR (eds), *The United Nations at the Millennium: The Principal Organs* (London; New York, Continuum International Publishing Group, 2001).

Tomuschat, C (ed), *The United Nations at Age Fifty: A Legal Perspective* (The Hague, Kluwer Law International, 1995).

Virally, M, *L'Organisation Mondiale* (Paris, A Colin, 1972).

Vismara, M, *L'azione politica delle Nazioni Unite*, 1946–1976, 2 volumes (Padova, CEDAM, 1983).

Volger, H, *A Concise Encyclopedia of the United Nations* (The Hague, Kluwer Law International, 2002).

Waters, M, *The United Nations (International Organization and Administration)* (New York; London, MacMillan Press, 1967).

Weiss, P, *Les organisations internationales* (Paris, A Colin, 2005).

Weiss, TG and Daws, S (eds), *The Oxford Handbook on the United Nations* (Oxford; New York, OUP, 2007).

Wolfrum, R (ed), *Handbuch Vereinte Nationen*, 2 volumes (München, CH Beck, 1991).

—— *United Nations: Law, Policies and Practice*, 2 volumes (Munich, CH Beck; Dordrecht, Martinus Nijhoff, 1995).

Zyss, W, 'Le régime commun des Nations Unies' (1987) 91(2) *RGDIP* 341–478.

4. Specific Issues

Arangio-Ruiz, G, 'The Establishment of the International Criminal Tribunal for the Former Territory of Yugoslavia and the Doctrine of Implied Powers of the United Nations' in FSE Lattanzi (ed), *Dai tribunali penali internazionali ad hoc a une corte permanente: atti del Convegno,* Roma 15–16 dicembre 1995 (Naples, Editoriale scientifica, 1996) 31–45.

Berlia, G, 'Admission d'un Etat aux Nations Unies' (1949) 53 *RGDIP* 481–502.

Bindschedler, RL, 'La délimitation des compétences des Nations Unies' (1963) 108(1) *RCADI* 307–422.

Blum, YZ, *Eroding the United Nations Charter* (Dordrecht; Boston; London, Martinus Nijhoff, 1993).

Cadoux, C, 'La supériorité du droit des Nations Unies sur le droit des Etats membres' (1959) 63(4) *RGDIP* 649–80.

Castaneda, J, 'Valeur juridique des résolutions des Nations Unies' (1970) 129(1) *RCADI* 205–331.

Chaumont, C, 'Nations Unies et neutralité' (1956) 89(1) *RCADI* 1–59.

Conforti, B, 'Le rôle de l'accord dans le système des Nations Unies' (1974) 142(2) *RCADI* 203–88.

—— 'Prolifération organique, prolifération normative et crise des Nations Unies: réflexions d'un juriste' in *L'adaptation des structures et méthodes des Nations Unies*. Workshop: The Adaptation of Structures and Methods at the United Nations, The Hague, 4–6 November 1985 (Dordrecht, Martinus Nijhoff, 1986)153–69.

Dagory, J, *Les rapports entre les institutions spécialisées et l'Organisation des Nations Unies* (Paris, Pedone, 1969).

Distefano, G, 'Observations éparses sur les caractères de la personnalité juridique internationale' (2007) 53 *AFDI* 105–28

Dominicé, C, 'The International Responsibility of the United Nations for Injuries Resulting from Non-Military Enforcement Measures' in M Ragazzi (ed), *International Responsibility Today: Essays in Memory of Oscar Schachter* (Leiden; Boston, Martinus Nijhoff, 2005) 363–70.

Dupuy, P-M, 'The Constitutional Dimension of the Charter of the United Nations Revisited' (1997) 1 *Max Planck UNYB* 1–34.

Etienne, G, 'L'article 2, paragraphe 7, de la Charte des Nations Unies: une lecture à la lumière de la pratique récente de l'Assemblée générale et du Conseil de sécurité des Nations Unies' (2003) 11 *African Yearbook of International Law* 217–62.

Fitschen, T, 'Inventing the Rule of Law for the United Nations' (2008) 12 *Max Planck UNYB* 347–80.

Flauss, J-F, 'Les réserves aux résolutions des Nations Unies ' (1981) 85(1) *RGDIP* 5–37.

Franck, TM, 'The "Powers of Appreciation": Who is the Ultimate Guardian of the UN Legality?' (July 1992) 86(3) *AJIL* 519–23.

—— 'Is the UN Charter a Constitution?' in JA Frowein *et al* (eds), *Verhandeln für den Frieden— Negotiating for Peace: Liber Amicorum Tono Eitel* (Berlin, Springer, 2003) 95–106.

Halderman, JW, *The United Nations and the Rule of Law* (New York, Oceana Publications, 1966).

Kaeckenbeeck, G, 'La Charte de San-Francisco dans ses rapports avec le droit international' (1947) 70(1) *RCADI* 109–330.

Kahng, TL, *Law, Politics and the Security Council: An Inquiry into the Handling of Legal Questions Involved in International Disputes and Situations* (The Hague, Martinus Nijhoff, 1969).

Kasme, B, *La capacité de l'Organisation des Nations Unies de conclure des traités* (Paris, Librairie générale de droit et de jurisprudence, 1960).

Kelsen, H, 'The Preamble of the Charter. A Critical Analysis' (1946) 8 *The Journal of Politics* 134–59.

—— 'Du droit de se retirer de l'Organisation des Nations Unies' (1948) 52 *RGDIP* 5–19.

Klein, P, *La responsabilité des organisations internationales dans les ordres juridiques internes et en droit des gens* (Bruxelles, Bruylant, 1998).

—— 'Responsibility for Serious Breaches of Obligations Deriving from Peremptory Norms of International Law and the United Nations' (2002) 13(5) *EJIL-JEDI* 1241–55.

Kolb, R, 'Does Article 103 of the Charter of the United Nations apply only to Decisions or also to Authorizations adopted by the Security Council?' (2004) 64(1) *Zeitschrift für ausländisches öffentliches Recht und Völkerrecht* 21–35.

Lauterpacht, E, 'The Legal Effect of Illegal Acts of International Organisations' in RJ Jennings (ed), *International Law. Essays in Honour of Lord McNair* (London, Stevens & Sons, 1965) 88–121.

Lavieille, J-M, 'La procédure de suspension des droits d'un Etat membre des Nations Unies' (1977) 81(2) *RGDIP* 431–65.

MacFarlane, SN, and Khong, YF, *Human Security and the UN: A Critical History* (Bloomington, Indiana University Press, 2006).

Nemours, A, *La Charte des Nations Unies: étude comparative de la Charte avec les propositions de Dumbarton Oaks, le Covenant de la Société des Nations, les Conventions de la Haye, les propositions et doctrines interaméricaines* (Port-au-Prince, H Deschamps, 1945) 17–188.

Niemelä, P, 'A Cosmopolitan World Order? Perspectives on Francisco de Vitoria and the United Nations' (2008) 12 *Max Planck UNYB* 301–44.

Öberg, MD, 'The Legal Effects of Resolutions of the UN Security Council and General Assembly in the Jurisprudence of the ICJ' (2005) 17(5) *EJIL-JEDI* 879–906.

Pançarci, V, *De la Charte des Nations Unies à une meilleure organisation du monde* (Paris, Pedone, 1962).

Perez Gonzalez, M, 'Les Organisations Internationales et le droit de la responsabilité' (1988) 92(1) *RGDIP* 63–102.

Philippe, X, 'Les Nations Unies et la justice transitionnelle: bilan et perspectives' (2006) 20(21) *Observateur des Nations Unies* 169–91.

Picone, P (ed), *Interventi delle Nazioni Unite e diritto internazionale* (Padova, CEDAM, 1995).

Preuss, L, 'Article 2, paragraph 7 of the Charter of the United Nations and Matters of Domestic Jurisdiction' (1949) 74(1) *RCADI* 547–653.

Raman, KV (United Nations Institute for Training and Research, UNITAR), *Dispute Settlement through the United Nations* (New York, Oceana Publications, 1977).

Reisman, M, 'The Constitutional Crisis in the United Nations' (1993) 87 *AJIL* 83–100.

Rosenne, S, 'United Nations Treaty Practice' (1954) 86(2) *RCADI* 275–444.

Ruiz Fabri, H and Sorel, J-M (eds), *La motivation des décisions des juridictions internationals* (Paris, Pedone, 2008).

Saba, H, 'Les accords régionaux dans la Charte de l'ONU' (1952) 80(1) *RCADI* 635–720.

Schachter, O, 'The Relation of Law, Politics and Action in the United Nations' (1963) 109(3) *RCADI* 165–256.

Schrijver, NJ, 'The Future of the Charter for the United Nations' (2006) 10 *Max Planck UNYB* 1–34.

Simma, B, 'Does the UN Charter Provide an Adequate Legal Basis for Individual or Collective Responses to Violations of Obligations *Erga Omnes*?' in J Delbrück (ed), *The Future of International Law Enforcement. New Scenarios. New Law?* Proceedings of an International Symposium of the Kiel Institute of International Law, 25–27 March 1992 (Duncker & Humblot, 1993) 125–46.

Tavernier, P, 'L'année des Nations Unies – Problèmes juridiques' (2008) 54 *AFDI* 285–304; (2007) 53 *AFDI* 535–54; (2006) 52 *AFDI* 285–304; (2005) 51 *AFDI* 319–39; (2004) 50 *AFDI* 545–63; (24 December 2001–20 December 2002) (2002) 48 *AFDI* 531–52; (2 December 2000–24 December 2001) (2001) 47 *AFDI* 329–48; (23 December 1999–22 December 2000) (2000) 46 *AFDI* 380–402; (23 December 1997–18 December 1998) (1998) 44 *AFDI* 472–93; (20 December 1996–22 December 1997) (1997) 43 *AFDI* 500–20; (1996) 42 *AFDI* 552–75; (1995) 41 *AFDI* 537–60; (1994) 40 *AFDI* 555–74; (1993) 39 *AFDI* 684–716; (1992) 38 *AFDI* 683–718; (1991) 37 *AFDI* 617–46; (1990) 36 *AFDI* 536–65.

Thierry, H, 'Les résolutions des organes internationaux dans la jurisprudence de la Cour internationale de Justice' (1980) 167(2) *RCADI* 385–450.

Toublanc, A, 'L'article 103 et la valeur juridique de la Charte des Nations Unies' (2004) 108(2) *RGDIP* 439–62.

Tunkin, GI, 'The Legal Nature of the United Nations' (1966) 119(3) *RCADI* 1–68.

Valticos, N, 'Et si l'on faisait revenir le siège des Nations Unies en Europe?' (2003) 107(3) *RGDIP* 529–33.

Vellas, P, *Le régionalisme international et l'Organisation des Nations Unies* (Paris, Pedone, 1948).

Verdross, A, 'Idées directrices de l'Organisation des Nations Unies' (1953) 83(2) *RCADI* 1–77.

Villani, U, 'Les rapports entre l'ONU et les organisations régionales dans le domaine du maintien de la paix' (2001) 290 *RCADI* 225–436.

Virally, M, 'Les actes unilatéraux des organisations internationales' in M Bedjaoui (ed), *Droit international, Bilan et perspectives*, volume 1 (Paris, Pedone, 1991) 253–76.

Wolfrum, R, 'The Protection of Regional or Other Interests as Structural Element of the Decision-Making Process of International Organizations' 1 (1997) *Max Planck UNYB* 259–82.

5. Particular Organs

General Assembly

Asamoah, OY, *The Legal Significance of the Declarations of the General Assembly of the United Nations* (The Hague, Martinus Nijhoff, 1966).

Bailey, SD, *The General Assembly of the United Nations: A Study of Procedure and Practice* (Westport, Greenwood Press, 1978).

Brugiere, PF, Les résolutions amendant les pouvoirs de l'Assemblée générale des Nations Unies pour la sécurité collective' (1953) 57 *RGDIP* 453–76.

—— *Les pouvoirs de l'Assemblée générale des Nations Unies en matière de politique et de sécurité* (Paris, A Pedone, 1955).

Finley, B, *The Structure of the UN General Assembly (its Committees, Commissions and Others Organisms 1946–77)* 2 volumes (New York, Dobbs Ferry, 1990).

Goodwin, G, 'The General Assembly of the United Nations' in E Luard (ed), *The Evolution of International Organizations* (New York, Washington, FA Praeger, 1966) 42–67.

Jung-Gun, K, 'La validité des résolutions de l'Assemblée générale des Nations Unies' (1971) 75(1) *RGDIP* 92–104.

Ladame, PA, *L'Assemblée générale des Nations Unies* (Paris, Antares, 1949).

Lujân Flores, M (del), 'The Role of Law in the UN Decision-making Process of the Sixth Committee of the General Assembly' (1995) 27(3) *JILP* 611–18.

Mindaoudou, DA, 'La notion de majorité comme preuve de démocratie à l'Assemblée générale des Nations Unies' (1996) 8(2) *African Journal of International and Comparative Law* 447–55.

Morris, V, 'The Work of the Sixth Committee at the Fiftieth Session of the UN General Assembly' (1996) 90(3) *AJIL* 491–500.

Peterson, MJ, *The UN General Assembly* (London, Routledge, 2006).

Queneudec, J-P, 'Le président de l'Assemblée générale des Nations Unies' (1966) 70(4) *RGDIP* 878–915.

Rauschning, D, Wiesbrock, K and Lailach, M (eds), *Key Resolutions of the United Nations General Assembly 1946–1996* (Cambridge, CUP, 1997).

Sloan, B, *United Nations General Assembly Resolutions in our Changing World* (Ardsley-on-Hudson, New York, Transnational Publishers, 1991).

Sohn, LB, 'Enhancing the Role of the General Assembly of the United Nations in Crystallizing International Law' in J Makarczyk (ed), *Theory of International Law at the Threshold of the 21st Century: Essays in Honour of Krzystof Skubiszewski* (The Hague; Boston, Kluwer Law International, 1996) 549–61.

Vallat, F, 'The General Assembly and the Security Council of the United Nations' (1952) 29 *BYIL* 63–105.

—— 'The Competence of the UN General Assembly' (1959) 97(2) *RCADI* 203–92.

The Secretary-General and the Secretariat

Alexandrowicz, CH, 'The Secretary-General of the United Nations' (1962) 11 *International and Comparative Law Quarterly* 1109–130.

Annan, K, 'In Larger Freedom: Decision Time at the UN' (May–June 2005) 84(3) *Foreign Affairs* 63–74.

Bailey, SD, *The Secretariat for the United Nations* (New York, Carnegie Endowment for International Peace, 1962).

Baratta, JP, 'The Secretary-General: Should his Role be Abolished?' in W Hoffmann (ed), *A New World Order: Can it Bring Security to the World's People?: Essays on Restructuring the United Nations* (Washington DC, World Federalist Association, 1991).

Boudreau, TE, *Sheathing the Sword: The UN Secretary-General and the Prevention of International Conflict* (New York, Westport, Greenwood Press, 1991).

Bourloyannis, MC, 'Fact-finding by the Secretary-General of the United Nations' (1990) 22 *JILP* 641–69.

Boutros-Ghali, B, 'Le Secrétaire général des Nations Unies: entre l'urgence et la durée' (Summer 1996) 61(2) *Politique étrangère* 407–14.

—— *Mes années à la maison de verre* (Paris, Fayard, 1999).

Boven, TC (van), 'The Role of the United Nations Secretariat in the Area of Human Rights' (1991) 24 *JILP* 69–107.

Brehio, A, 'Good Offices of the Secretary-General as Preventive Measures' (1998) 30 *JILP* 589–643.

Buza, L, 'The Position of the Secretary-General of the United Nations in International Law' G Haraszti (ed), *Questions of International Law* (Budapest, International Law Association, Hungarian Branch, 1962) 5–23.

Chesterman, S (ed), *Secretary or General? The UN Secretary-General in World Politics* (Cambridge, CUP, 2007).

Cordier, AW, 'The Role of the Secretary-General' (1960) 10 *Annual Review of United Nations Affairs* 1–14.

Cordier, AW and Foote, W (eds), *Public Papers of the Secretaries-General of the United Nations* (New York, Columbia University Press, 1969–1977).

Cox, RW, 'The Executive Head: An Essay on Leadership in International Organization' (1969) 23(2) *International Organization* 205–30.

Crocker, WR, 'Some Notes on the United Nations Secretariat' (1950) 4 *International Organization* 598–613.

Elaraby, NA, 'The Office of the Secretary-General and the Maintenance of International Peace and Security' (1986) 42 *Revue Egyptienne de Droit International* 1–83.

Fischer, G, 'Les compétences du Secrétaire Général des Nations Unies' (1955) 1 *AFDI* 345–48.

Franck, TM, 'The Secretary-General's Role in Conflict Resolution: Past, Present and Pure Conjecture' (1995) 6 *EJIL-JEDI* 360–87.

—— 'Finding a Voice: How the Secretary-General makes himself heard in the Councils of the Nations' in J Makarczyk (ed), *Essays in International Law in Honour of Judge Manfred Lachs* (The Hague, Martinus Nijhoff, 1984) 481–91.

Franck, TM and Nolte, G, 'The Good Offices Function of the UN Secretary General' in A Roberts and B Kingsbury (eds), *United Nations, Divided World: The UN's Roles in International Relations* (Oxford, Clarendon Press, 1993) 143–82.

Fröhlich M, *Dag Hammarskjöld und die Vereinten Nationen* (Paderborn/Munich/Vienna/Zurich, F Schöningh, 2002).

Goodrich, L, 'The Political Role of the Secretary-General' (1962) 16 *International Organization* 720–35.

Goodrich, L, 'Hammarskjöld, the UN and the Office of the Secretary-General' (1974) 28 *International Organization* 467–83.

Gordenker, L, U Thant and the Office of UN Secretary-General' (1966) 22 *International Journal* 1–16.

—— *The UN Secretary-General and the Maintenance of Peace* (New York, Columbia University Press, 1967).

—— *The UN Secretary-General and Secretariat* (London, Routledge, 2005).

Goulding, M, 'The UN Secretary-General' in DM Malone (ed), *The UN Security Council: From the Cold War to the 21st Century* (Boulder, Lynne Rienner, 2004) 267–80.

Hammarskjöld, D, 'The International Civil Servant in Law and in Fact' (lecture delivered to Congregation at Oxford University, 30 May 1961) in W Foote (ed), *Servant of Peace: A Selection of the Speeches and Statements of Dag Hammarskjöld, Secretary-General of the United Nations 1953–1961* (New York, Harper & Row, 1962) 329–49.

Han, HH, 'The UN Secretary-General's Treaty Depositary Function: Legal Implications' (1988) 14 *Brooklyn Journal of International Law* 549–72.

Hill, C (ed), The Papers of United Nations Secretary-General Boutros Boutros-Ghali (New Haven, Yale University Press, 2003).

Johnstone, I, 'The Role of the UN Secretary-General: The Power of Persuasion based on Law' (2003) 9 *Global Governance* 441–58.

Meisler, S, *Kofi Annan: A Man of Peace and a World of War* (Hoboken, NJ, J Wiley, 2007).

Masland, JW, 'Secretariat of the United Nations' (1945) 5 *Public Administration Review* 364–72.

Meron, T, *The United Nations Secretariat: The Rules and Practice* (Lexington, MA, Lexington Books, 1977).

Newman, E, *The UN Secretary-General from the Cold War to the New Era: A Global Peace and Security Mandate* (New York, Palgrave Macmillan, 1998).

Perez de Cuellar, J, 'Le rôle du Secrétaire général des Nations Unies' (1985) 89(2) *RGDIP* 233–42.

—— 'The Role of the UN Secretary-General' in A Roberts and B Kingsbury (eds), *United Nations, Divided World: The UN's Roles in International Relations* (Oxford, Clarendon Press, 1993) 125–42.

Ramcharan, BG, *Humanitarian Good Offices in International Law: The Good Offices of the United Nations Secretary-General in the Field of Human Rights* (The Hague, Martinus Nijhoff, 1983).

Rivlin, B and Gordenker, L (eds), 'The Challenging Role of the UN Secretary-General: Making the "Most Impossible Job in the World" Possible' (London, Praeger Publishers, 1993).

Schwebel, SM, 'The Origins and Development of Article 99 of the Charter: The Powers of the Secretary-General of the UN' (1951) 28 *BYIL* 371–82.

—— *The Secretary-General of the United Nations: His Political Powers and Practice* (Cambridge, MA, Harvard University Press, 1952).

Sciora, R (ed), *A la maison de verre: l'ONU et ses secrétaires généraux* (Paris, Saint-Simon, 2006).

Smouts, M-C, *Le secrétaire général des Nations Unies: son rôle dans la solution aux conflits internationaux* (Paris, A Colin, 1971).

Szasz, PC, 'The Role of the UN Secretary-General: Some Legal Aspects' (1991) 24 *JILP* 161–98.

Thant, M-U and Scott, A, *The UN Secretariat: A Brief History* (New York, International Peace Academy, 2007).

Security Council

Repertoire of the Practice of the Security Council, 1946– (New York, Columbia University Press).

Alvarez, JE, 'The Once and Future Security Council' (Spring 1995) 18(2) *Washington Quarterly* 5–20.

—— 'Judging the Security Council' (1996) 90(1) *AJIL* 1–39.

—— 'What's the Security Council for?' (Winter 1996) 17(2) *Michigan Journal of International Law* 221–28.

American Society of International Law, 'The Security Council: Its Authority and Legitimacy' (Proceedings of the 87th Annual Meeting of the American Society of International Law, 31 March– 3 April 1993, Washington DC) 300–20.

Aston, JD, 'Die Bekämpfung abstrakter Gefahren für den Weltfrieden durch legislative Massnahmen des Sicherheitsrat–Resolution 1373 (2001) im Kontext' (2002) 62(1–2) *Zeitschrift für ausländisches öffentliches Recht und Völkerrecht* 257–91.

Bailey, SD, 'The UN Security Council: Evolving Practice' (March 1978) 34(3) *The World Today (The Royal Institute of International Affairs)* 100–06.

—— *The Procedure of the UN Security Council* (Oxford, OUP, 1998).

Balmond, L, 'Le Conseil de sécurité contre la paix?' (1993) 14(5) *Arès* 9–27.

Bedjaoui, M, *The New World Order and the Security Council: Testing the Legality of its Acts* (Bruxelles, Bruylant, 1994).

Berdal, M, 'The UN Security Council: Ineffective but Indispensable' (Summer 2003) 45(2) *Survival* 27–30.

Berman, EG, 'The Security Council's Increasing Reliance on Burden-Sharing: Collaboration or Abrogation?' (Spring 1998) 4(1) *International Peacekeeping* 1–21.

Bothe, M 'Les limites des pouvoirs du Conseil de Sécurité' in *Le développement du rôle du Conseil de sécurité*. Workshop: Peace-keeping and Peace-building: The Development of the Role of the Security Council, The Hague, 21–23 July 1992 (Dordrecht, Martinus Nijhoff, 1993) 67–81.

Boyd, A, Fifteen *Men in a Powder Keg—A History of the United Nations Security Council* (London, Methuen &Co Ltd, 1971).

Brugiere, P, *La règle de l'unanimité des membres permanents au Conseil de Sécurité: 'droit de veto'* (Paris, Pedone, 1952).

Bruha, T, 'Security Council' in R Wolfrum (ed), *United Nations: Law, Policies and Practice* volume 1 (Munich, CH Beck; Dordrecht, Martinus Nijhoff, 1995) 1147–61.

Cannizzaro, E, 'A Machiavellian Moment?: The UN Security Council and the Rule of Law' (2006) 3(2) *International Organizations Law Review* 189–224.

Caron, DD, 'The Legitimacy of the Collective Authority of the Security Council' (1993) 87(4) *AJIL* 552–88.

Chai, FY, *Consultation and Consensus in the Security Council* (New York, UNITAR, 1971).

Conforti, B, 'Le pouvoir discrétionnaire du Conseil de sécurité en matière de constatation d'une menace contre la paix, d'une rupture de la paix ou d'un acte d'aggression' in *Le développement du rôle du Conseil de sécurité*. Workshop: Peace-keeping and Peace-building: The Development of the Role of the Security Council, The Hague, 21–23 July 1992 (Dordrecht, Martinus Nijhoff, 1993) 51–60.

Cryer, R, 'The Security Council and International Humanitarian Law' in SC Breau *et al* (eds), *Testing the Boundaries of International Humanitarian Law* (London, British Institute of International and Comparative Law (BIICL), 2006) 245–75.

Day, G, *Le droit de veto dans l'Organisation des Nations Unies* (Paris, Pedone, 1952).

Delon, F, 'La concertation entre les membres permanents du Conseil de sécurité' (1993) 39 *AFDI* 53–64.

Distefano, G, 'Le Conseil de sécurité et la validation des traités conclus par la menace ou l'emploi de la force' in C-A Morand (ed), *La crise des Balkans de 1999, les dimensions historiques, politiques et juridiques* (Bruxelles, Bruylant; Paris, Librairie générale de droit et de jurisprudence, 2000) 167–92.

Doehring, K, 'Unlawful Resolutions of the Security Council and their Legal Consequences' (1997) 1 *Max Planck UNYB* 91–110.

Dominicé, C, 'Le Conseil de sécurité et l'accès aux pouvoirs qu'il reçoit du chapitre VII de la Charte des Nations Unies (1995) 5(4) *Revue suisse de droit International et de droit européen* 417–39.

Fassbender, B, 'Uncertain Steps into a Post-Cold War World: The Role and Functioning of the UN Security Council after a Decade of Measures against Iraq' (2002) 13(1) *EJIL-JEDI* 273–303.

Fenton, N, *Understanding the UN Security Council: Coercion or Consent?* (Aldershot, Ashgate Publishing, 2004).

Feuerle, L, 'Informal Consultations: A Mechanism in Security Council Decision-Making' (1985) 18(1) *JILP* 267–308.

Foy, L, 'Trop d'ombre autour du Conseil de sécurité' (1993) 965 *Revue politique et parlementaire* 67–68.

Freudenschuss, H, 'Article 39 of the UN Charter Revisited: Threats to the Peace and the Recent Practice of the UN Security Council' (1993) 46(1) *Austrian Journal of Public and International Law* 1–39.

Fry, JD, 'The UN Security Council and the Law of Armed Conflict: Amity or Enmity?' (2006) 38(2) *George Washington International Law Review* 327–47.

Gaja, G, 'Réflexions sur le rôle du Conseil de Sécurité dans le nouvel ordre mondial' (1993) 97(2) *RGDIP* 297–320.

Gardam, JG, 'Legal Restraints on Security Council Military Enforcement Action' (1996) 17(2) *Michigan Journal of International Law* 285–332.

Gill, TD, 'Legal and Some Political Limitations on the Power of the UN Security Council to Exercise its Enforcement Powers under Chapter VII of the Charter' (1995) 26 *Netherlands Yearbook of International Law* 33–138.

Gowlland-Debbas, V, 'Security Council Enforcement Action and Issues of State Responsibility' (1994) 43(1) *International and Comparative Law Quarterly* 55–98.

—— 'The Functions of the United Nations Security Council in the International Legal System' in M Byers (ed), *The Role of Law in International Politics* (Oxford, OUP, 2000) 277–313.

Green, LC, *Gentlemen's Agreements and the Security Council* (London, Stevens & Sons, 1960).

Happold, M, 'Security Council Resolution 1373 and the Constitution of the United Nations' in P Eden and T O'Donnell (eds), *September 11, 2001: A Turning Point in International and Domestic Law* (Ardsley, NY, Transnational Publishers, 2005) 617–45.

Harper, K, 'Does the United Nations' Security Council have the Competence to Act as Court and Legislature?' (1994) 27(1) *JILP* 103–57.

Herndl, K, 'Reflections on the Role, Functions and Procedures of the Security Council of the United Nations' (1987) 206(4) *RCADI* 289–395.

—— 'The "Forgotten" Competences of the Security Council' in A Mock and H Schambeck (eds), *Verantwortung in unserer Zeit: Festschrift für Rudalf Kirchschläger* (Österreichische, Staatsdruckerei, 1990) 83–91.

Hilaire, M, *United Nations Law and the Security Council* (Aldershot; Burlington, VT, Ashgate, 2005).

Kochler, H, *The Voting Procedure in the United Nations Security Council: Examining a Normative Contradiction in the UN Charter and its Consequences on International Relations* (Vienna, International Progress Organization, 1991).

Jensen, E, 'The United Nations Security Council: Action and Inaction' (1994) 8(1) *Cambridge Review of International Affairs* 8–22.

Jimenez de Arechaga, E, 'Le traitement des différends internationaux par le Conseil de Sécurité (1954) 85(1) *RCADI* 1–105.

Kelsen, H, 'Organization and Procedure of the Security Council' (1946) 59(7) *Harvard Law Review* 1087–1121.

Kerbrat, Y, *La référence au chapitre VII de la Charte des Nations Unies dans les résolution à caractère humanitaire du Conseil de sécurité* (Paris, Librairie générale de droit et de jurisprudence, 1995).

Kirgis, F, 'The Security Council's First Fifty Years' (1995) 89(3) *AJIL* 506–39.

Koskenniemi, M, 'The Police in the Temple. Order, Justice and the UN: A Dialectical View' (1995) 6(2) *EJIL-JEDI* 325–48.

Lailach, M, 'Die Wahrung des Weltfriedens und der internationalen Sicherheit als Aufgabe des Sicherheitsrates der Vereinten Nationen' ('The Jurisdiction of the United Nations Security Council with regard to the Maintenance of International Peace and Security') (Doctoral thesis, University of Göttingen, 1997).

Lamb, S, 'Legal Limits to United Nations Security Council Powers' in SG Goodwin-Gill and S Talmon (eds), *The Reality of International Law. Essays in Honour of Ian Brownlie* (Oxford, Clarendon Press, 1999) 361–88.

Leprette, J, 'Le rôle de la France au Conseil de sécurité comme organe de décision juridique' in *L'internationalité dans les institutions et le droit: convergences et défis. Etudes offertes à Alain Plantey* (Bordeaux, Pedone, 1995) 133–43.

Lobel, J and Ratner, M, 'Bypassing the Security Council: Ambiguous Authorizations to Use Force, Cease-fires, and the Iraqi Inspection Regime' (1999) 93(1) *AJIL* 124–54.

Lopez-Jacoiste Diaz, E, *Actualidad del consejo de seguridad de las naciones unidas: La legalidad de sus decisiones y el problema de su control* (Madrid, Editorial Civitas, 2003).

Lowe, V, Roberts, A, Welsh, J and Zaum, D (eds), *The United Nations Security Council and War* (Oxford, OUP, 2008).

Malone, DM (ed), *Decision-Making in the UN Security Council. The Case of Haiti, 1990–1997* (Oxford, Clarendon Press, 1998).

—— *The UN Security Council: From the Cold War to the 21st Century* (Boulder, Lynne Rienner Publishers, 2004).

—— *The International Struggle for Iraq: Politics in the UN Security Council 1980–2005* (Oxford, OUP, 2006).

Marschik, A, 'The Security Council as World Legislator? Theory, Practice and Consequences of an Expanding World Power' (Working Paper) (2005) 18 *IILJ* Working Paper, http://iilj.org/publications/documents/2005.18Marschik.pdf.

Momtaz, D, 'La délégation par le Conseil de sécurité de l'exécution de ses actions coercitives aux organisations régionales'(1997) 63 *AFDI* 105–15.

Nicol, D, *The United Nations Security Council: Towards Greater Effectiveness* (New York, UNITAR, 1982).

Novosseloff, A, 'Le processus de décision au sein du Conseil de sécurité des Nations Unies: une approche historique' (1995) 3 *Revue d'Histoire diplomatique* 273–304.

—— *Le Conseil de sécurité des Nations Unies et la maîtrise de la force armée* (Bruxelles, Bruylant, 2003).

Papa, MI, *I rapporti fra la Corte internazionale di giustizia e il Consiglio di sicurezza* (Padova, CEDAM, 2006).

Patil, AV, *The Veto: A Historical Necessity, 1946–2001—A Comprehensive Record of the Use of the Veto in the UN Security Council* (New York, In-house Inc, 2001).

Preux, J (de), *Le droit de veto dans la Charte des Nations Unies* (Paris, Société d'exploitation de l'Imprimerie Bellenand, 1949).

Quéneudec, J-P, 'A propos de la composition du Conseil de sécurité' (1995) 99(4) *RGDIP* 955–60.

Quigley, J, 'The "Privatization" of Security Council Enforcement Action: A Threat to Multilateralism' (1996) 17(2) *Michigan Journal of International Law* 249–84.

Rosand, E, 'The Security Council as "Global Legislator": *ultra vires* or ultra innovative?' (2005) 28(3) *Fordham International Law Journal* 542–90.

Rossman, JE, 'Article 43: Arming the UN Security Council' (1994) 21(1) *New York University Journal of International Law and Politics* 227–63.

Rudzinsk, AW, 'The So-Called Double Veto: Some Changes in the Voting Practice of the Security Council' (1951) 43(3) *AJIL* 443–62.

Salomon, A, *Le Conseil de Sécurité et le règlement pacifique des différends* (Genève; Paris, Les Editions Internationales, 1948).

Schäfer, A, *Der Begriff der 'Bedrohung des Friedens' in Artikel 39 der Charta der Vereinten Nationen: die Praxis des Sicherheitsrates* (Frankfurt am Main, P Lang Europäischer Verlag der Wissenschaften, 2006).

Schmitz, K, *Durchgriffswirkung von Maßnahmen der UN und ihrer Sonderorganisationen unter besonderer Berücksichtigung von Resolutionen des UN-Sicherheitsrates: Die Entwicklung supranationaler Strukturen* (Frankfurt, Peter Lang, 2003).

Sicilianos, L-A, 'L'autorisation par le Conseil de sécurité de recourir à la force: une tentative d'évaluation' (2002) 106(1) *RGDIP* 5–50.

Société Française pour le Droit International, *Le chapitre VII de la Charte des Nations Unies*, Colloque de Rennes (Paris, Pedone, 1995).

Sonnenfeld, R (ed), *Resolutions of the United Nations Security Council* (Dordrecht, Martinus Nijhoff, 1988).

Sur, S, Le Conseil de sécurité dans l'après 11 septembre (Paris, Librairie générale de droit et de jurisprudence, 2004).

Suy E, 'Some Legal Questions Concerning the Security Council, in I Münch (Von) (ed), *Staatsrecht, Völkerrecht, Europarecht: Festschrift für Hans-Jürgen Schlochauer zum 75. Geburtstag am 28. März 1981* (Berlin; New York, W de Gruyter, 1981) 677–89.

Szasz, PC, 'The Security Council Starts Legislating' (2002) 96(4) *AJIL* 901–05.

Talmon, S, 'The Security Council as World Legislature' (2005) 99(1) *AJIL* 175–93.

Tavernier, P, 'Les déclarations du Président du Conseil de sécurité' (1993) 39 *AFDI* 86–104.

Teixeira, P, *Le Conseil de sécurité à l'aube du XXIe siècle—Quelle volonté et quelle capacité a-t-il de maintenir la paix et la sécurité internationales?* (Genève, UNIDIR/IFRI, 2002).

Thome, N, *Les pouvoirs du Conseil de sécurité au regard de la pratique récente du chapitre VII par le Conseil de Sécurité* (Aix-en-Provence, Presses universitaires d'Aix-Marseille, 2005).

Ubertazzi, GM, *Contributo alla teoria della conciliazione delle controversie internazionali davanti al Consiglio di sicurezza* (Milan, Giuffrè, 1958).

Voina-Motoc, I, 'Le pouvoir interprétatif du Conseil de sécurité' (juillet–décembre 1996) 7(2) *Revue roumaine des sciences juridiques* 165–82.

Weckel, P, 'Le Conseil de sécurité des Nations Unies et l'arme nucléaire' (2006) 52 *AFDI* 178–97.

Weiss, W, 'Security Council Powers and the Exigencies of Justice after War' (2008) 12 *Max Planck UNYB* 45–112.

Wellens, KC, *Résolutions et déclarations du Conseil de sécurité (1946–1992): recueil thématique* (Bruxelles, Bruylant, 1993).

—— *Resolutions and Statements of the United Nations Security Council (1946–2000): A thematic guide* (The Hague, Kluwer Law International, 2001).

—— 'The Security Council and New Threats to the Peace: Back to the Future' (2003) 8 *Journal Conflict & Security Law* 15–70.

Weston, BH, 'Security Council Resolution 678 and Persian Gulf Decision Making: Precarious Legitimacy' (1991) 85(3) *AJIL* 516–35.

Wet, E (de), *The Chapter VII Powers of the United Nations Security Council* (Oxford, Hart Publishing, 2004).

Wheatley, S, 'The Security Council, Democratic Legitimacy and Regime Change in Iraq' (2006) 17(3) *EJIL-JEDI* 531–51.

Winkelmann, I, 'Bringing the Security Council into a New Era' (1997) 1 *Max Planck UN YB* 35–90.

—— 'Security Council' in H Volger (ed), *A Concise Encyclopedia of the United Nations* (The Hague, Kluwer Law International, 2002) 497–505.

Wood, M, 'Security Council Working Method and Procedure: Recent Developments' (1996) 45(1) *International and Comparative Law Quarterly* 150–61.

Zambelli, M, 'La souveraineté étatique au sein des Nations Unies: quelques réflexions au sujet de la portée normative des mesures du chapitre VII de la Charte' in *La souveraineté au XXIe siècle* (Fribourg, Ed. interuniversitaires suisses, 2003) 71–89.

—— *La constatation des situations de l'article 39 de la Charte des Nations Unies par le Conseil de Sécurité: le champ d'application des pouvoirs prévus au chapitre VII de la Charte des Nations Unies* (Bâle; Genève, Helbing & Lichtenhahn, 2002).

—— 'Les relations entre la Cour pénale internationale et le Conseil de sécurité: la nécessaire conciliation entre justice et paix internationales' (2006) 20(21) *Observateur des Nations Unies* 197–222.

Zemanek, K, 'Is the Security Council the Sole Judge of its Own Legality?' in E Yakpo and T Boumedra (eds), *Liber Amicorum Judge Mohammed Bedjaoui* (The Hague, Kluwer Law International, 1999) 629–45.

International Court of Justice

Ago, R, 'Les avis consultatifs obligatoires de la Cour internationale de justice, problème d'hier et d'aujourd'hui' in *Mélanges Michel Virally, Le droit international au service de la paix, de la justice et du développement* (Paris, Pedone, 1991) 9–24.

Bedjaoui, M, 'La place de la Cour internationale de justice dans le système général de maintien de la paix institué par la charte des Nations Unies' (September 1996) 8(3) *African Journal of International and Comparative Law* 541–48.

Chappez, J, 'Questions d'interprétation et d'application de la Convention de Montréal de 1971 résultant de l'incident aérien de Lockerbie (Jamahiriya libyenne c. Royaume-Uni) (Jamahiryia libyenne c. Etats-Unis). Mesure conservatoires, ordonnances du 14 avril 1992' (1992) 38 *AFDI* 468–79.

Daniele, L, L'ordonnance sur la demande d'examen de la situation dans l'affaire des essais nucléaires et le pouvoir de la Cour internationale de Justice de régler sa propre procédure' (1996) 100(3) *RGDIP* 653–71.

Distefano, G, 'La demande reconventionnelle au fil des textes régissant le fonctionnement de la Cour de La Haye et de sa jurisprudence' (2008) 1(2) *Revue suisse de droit international et de droit européen* 45–67.

Dubisson, M, *La Cour internationale de Justice* (Paris, Librairie générale de droit et de jurisprudence, 1964).

Guillaume, G, 'La Cour internationale de Justice: quelques propositions concrètes à l'occasion du cinquantenaire' (1996) 100(2) *RGDIP* 323–33.

Gowlland-Debbas, V, 'The Relationship between the International Court of Justice and the Security Council in the Light of the Lockerbie Case' (1994) 88(4) *AJIL* 643–77.

Jouannet, E, 'Le principe de l'or monétaire à propos de l'arrêt de la Cour du 30 juin 1995 dans l'affaire du Timor oriental, Portugal c. Australie' (1996) 100(3) *RGDIP* 673–714.

Lowe, V and Fitzmaurice, M (eds), *Fifty years of the International Court of Justice: Essays in Honour of Sir Robert Jennings* (Cambridge; New York, CUP, Grotius Publications, 1996).

Papa, MI, *I rapporti fra la Corte internazionale di giustizia e il Consiglio di sicurezza* (Padova, CEDAM, 2006).

Petculescu, I, 'The Review of the United Nations Security Council Decisions by the International Court of Justice' (2005) 52 *Netherlands International Law Review* 167–95.

Rosenne, S, *Procedure in the International Court: A Commentary on the 1978 Rules of the International Court of Justice* (The Hague, Martinus Nijhoff, 1983).

—— *The World Court. What it is and How it Works* (Dordrecht, Martinus Nijhoff, 1989).

—— 'The General List of the International Court of Justice' in in J Makarczyk (ed), *Theory of International Law at the Threshold of the 21st Century: Essays in Honour of Krzystof Skubiszewski* (The Hague; Boston, Kluwer Law International, 1996) 805–16.

—— *The Law and Practice of the International Court 1920–2005, Volume I–III* (Leiden, Brill Academic Publishers, 2005).

Schwebel, SM, 'Relations between the International Court of Justice and United Nations' in *Mélanges Michel Virally, Le droit international au service de la paix, de la justice et du développement* (Paris, Pedone, 1991) 431–44.

Schweigman, D, *The Authority of the Security Council under Chapter VII of the UN Charter: Legal Limits and the Role of the International Court of Justice* (The Hague, Kluwer Law International, 2001).

Shahabuddeen, M, *Precedent in the World Court* (Cambridge; New York, CUP, 1996).

Shaw, NM, 'The Security Council and the International Court of Justice: Judicial Drift and Judicial Function' in SA Muller, D Raic and JM Thuránsky (eds), *The International Court of Justice: Its Future Role after Fifty Years* (The Hague, Martinus Nijhoff, 1997) 219–59.

Skubiszewski, K, 'The International Court of Justice and the Security Council' in V Lowe and M Fitzmaurice (eds), *Fifty Years of the International Court of Justice: Essays in Honour of Sir Robert Jennings* (Cambridge; New York, CUP, Grotius Publications , 1996) 606–29.

Thirlway, HWA, 'The Law and Procedure of the International Court of Justice, 1960–1989' (1996) 67(8) *BYIL* 1–73.

Weil, P, 'Compétence et saisine: un nouvel aspect du principe de la juridiction consensuelle' in J Makarczyk (ed), *Theory of International Law at the Threshold of the 21st Century: Essays in Honour of Krzystof Skubiszewski* (The Hague; Boston, Kluwer Law International, 1996) 833–48.

Wellens, K, *Economic Conflicts and Disputes before the World Court, 1922–1995: A Functional Analysis* (The Hague; Boston, Kluwer Law International, 1996).

Zimmermann, A, Tomuschat, C and Oellers-Frahm, K (eds), *The Statute of the International Court of Justice: A Commentary* (Oxford, OUP, 2006).

6. Maintenance of Peace

Use of Force

'A more secure world. Our shared responsibility'. Report of the Secretary's General's High-Level Panel on Threats, Challenges and Changes (2 December 2004), http://www.un.org/secureworld/report.pdf

Allan, P and Keller A (eds), *What is a Just Peace?* (Oxford, OUP, 2006).

Arntz, J, *Der Begriff der Friedensbedrohung in Satzung und Praxis der Vereinten Nationen* (Berlin, Duncker und Humblot, 1975).

Bennouna, M, 'The United Nations, Guarantor of International Peace and Security' in C Tomuschat (ed), *The United Nations at Age Fifty: A Legal Perspective* (The Hague, Kluwer Law International, 1995) 3–7.

Berlia, G, *Le maintien de la paix: doctrine et problèmes* (1919–1976) (Paris, Montchrestien, 1976).

Bourquin, M, 'Règles générales du droit de la paix' (1931) 35(1) *RCADI* 5–229.

Chesterman, S, *Just War or Just Peace? Humanitarian Intervention and International Law* (Oxford, OUP, 2001).

Corten, O, 'Operation *Iraqi Freedom*: peut-on admettre l'argument de l'"autorisation implicite" du Conseil de sécurité?' (2003) 36(1) *Revue belge de droit international* 205–47.

—— *Le droit contre la guerre. L'interdiction du recours à la force en droit international contemporain* (Paris, Pedone, 2008).

Corten, O and Dubuisson, F, 'L'hypothèse d'une règle émergente fondant une intervention militaire sur une "autorisation implicite" du Conseil de sécurité' (2000) 104(4) *RGDIP* 873–910.

Coulon, J (ed), *Guide du maintien de la paix* (Outremont, Athena et CEPES, 2007).

Diallo, A, *Les Nations Unies face aux nouveaux enjeux de la paix et de la sécurité internationales* (Paris, L'Harmattan, 2006).

Dinh, N-Q, 'La légitime défense d'après la Charte des Nations Unies' (1948) 52 *RGDIP* 223–54.

Fenwick, CG, 'When is there a Threat to the Peace? Rhodesia' (1967) 61(3) *AJIL*, 61/3 753–55.

Fletcher, GP and Ohlin, JD, *Defending Humanity: When Force is Justified and Why* (New York City, OUP, 2008).

Franck, TM, 'Who Killed Article 2 paragraph 4, or Changing Norms Governing the Use of Forces by States' (1970) 64(4) *AJIL* 809–37.

—— 'The United Nations as Guarantor of International Peace and Security: Past, Present and Future' in C Tomuchat (ed), *The United Nations at Age Fifty: A Legal Perspective* (The Hague, Kluwer Law International, 1995) 25–38.

Gaja, G, 'Use of Force Made or Authorized by the United Nations' in C Tomuschat (ed), *The United Nations at Age Fifty: A Legal Perspective* (The Hague, Kluwer Law International, 1995) 39–58.

Giraud, E, 'L'interdiction du recours à la force; la théorie et la pratique des Nations Unies' (1963) 34(3) *RGDIP* 501–544.

Graefrath, B and Mohr, M, 'Legal Consequences of an Act of Aggression: The Case of the Iraqi Invasion and Occupation of Kuwait (1992) 43(2–3) *Austrian Journal of Public International Law* 109–38.

Gray, C, *International Law and the Use of Force* (Oxford, OUP, 2008).

Hampson, O and Malone D (eds), *From Reaction to Conflict Prevention: Opportunities for the UN System, A Project of the International Peace Academy* (Boulder; London, Lynne Rienner Publishers, 2002).

Higgins, R, 'The United Nations Role in Maintaining International Peace: The Lessons of the First Fifty Years' (1996) 2 *New York Law School Journal of International and Comparative Law* 135–49.

Kolb, R, *Le droit relatif au maintien de la paix internationale: évolution historique, valeurs fondatrices et tendances actuelles* (Paris, Pedone, 2005).

Kolb R, *Ius contra bellum, Le droit international relatif au maintien de la paix* 2nd edn (Basle/Brussels, Helbing & Lichtenhahn/Bruylant, 2009).

Liu, F-T, *The Evolving Role of the United Nations in the Maintenance of International Peace and Security: An Outline* (International Peace Academy, 28 October 1996).

Makinda, SM, 'Sovereignty and International Security: Challenges for the United Nations' (May/August 1996) 2 *Global Governance* 149–68.

Petit, Y, *Droit international du maintien de la paix* (Paris, Librairie générale de droit et de jurisprudence, 2000).

Qizhi, HE, 'The Crucial Role of the United Nations in Maintaining International Peace and Security' in C Tomuschat (ed), *The United Nations at Age Fifty: A Legal Perspective* (The Hague, Kluwer Law International, 1995) 77–90.

Schachter, O, 'The Right of States to Use Armed Force' (1984) 82 *Michigan Law Review* 1620–46

—— 'United Nations Law in the Gulf Conflict' (1991) 85(3) *AJIL* 452–73.

Simma, B, 'NATO, the UN and the Use of Force: Legal Aspects' (1999) 10(1) *EJIL-JEDI* 1–22.

Stahn, C and Kleffner, JK (eds), *Jus Post Bellum: Towards a Law of Transition From Conflict to Peace* (The Hague, TMC Asser Press, 2008).

Stürchler, N, *The Threat of Force in International Law* (Cambridge, CUP, 2007).

Sur, S, 'Les Nations Unies et le désarmement' (Spring/Summer 1998) 4 *Observateur des Nations Unies* 77–98.

Unitar, *The UN and the Maintenance of International Peace and Security* (Dordrecht; Boston, Martinus Nijhoff,1987).

Collective Security

Arcari, M, 'Responsabilité de l'Etat pour violations graves du droit international et système de sécurité collective' (2005) 21 *Anuario de derecho internacional* 415–47.

Bancroft, HF, 'United Nations as a Collective Security Organization' (1951) 163(45) *American Society of International Law Proceedings* 159–64.

Barrea, J, *La Sécurité Collective: ses origines, ses fondements et son institutionnalisation* (Bruxelles, Artel / CIACO, 1991).

Bourquin, M, 'Le problème de la sécurité internationale ' (1934) 49(3) *RCADI* 473–541.

Chaumont, C, *La sécurité des Etats et la sécurité du monde* (Paris, Librairie générale de droit et de jurisprudence, 1948).

—— *Analyse de certains aspects concernant la sécurité collective dans le monde contemporain* (Nancy, Presses Universitaires de Nancy, 1972).

Colard, D and Guilhaudis, J-F, *Le droit de la sécurité internationale* (Paris, Masson, 1987).

Colard, D, Guilhaudis, J-F and Labaye H (eds), *Paix et sécurité internationales* (Lyon, Grenoble, SDEDSI, CEDSI, 1988).

David, C-P (ed), *Repenser la sécurité: nouvelles menaces, nouvelles politiques* (Montréal, Fidès, 2002).

Delbrück, J, 'Collective Security' (1982) 3 *Encyclopedia of Public International Law* 104–12.

Dupuy, P-M, 'Sécurité collective et organisation de la paix' (1993) 97(3) *RGDIP* 617–27.

—— 'Sécurité collective et construction de la paix dans la pratique contemporaine du Conseil de sécurité' in *Recht zwischen Umbruch und Bewahrung* (Berlin; New York, Springer, 1995) 41–56.

Forteau, M, *Droit de la sécurité collective et droit de la responsabilité internationale de l'Etat* (Paris, Pedone, 2006).

Frangulis, A, 'Une Ligue des Nations comme garantie d'une paix durable est-elle possible?' (1917) 24 *RGDIP* 437–52.

Freudeuschuss, H, 'Between Unilateralism and Collective Security: Authorizations of the Use of Force by the Security Council' (1994) 5 *EJIL-JEDI* 492–531.

Frowein, AJ, 'Collective Enforcement of International Obligations' (1987) 47(1) *Zeitschrift für ausländisches öffentliches Recht und Völkerrecht* 67–79.

—— 'Unilateral Interpretation of Security Council Resolutions—A Threat to Collective Security?' in V Götz *et al* (eds), *Liber Amicorum Günther Jaenicke zum 85. Geburtstag* (Berlin, Springer, 1998) 97–111.

Graefrath, B, 'International Crimes and Collective Security' in K Wellens (ed), *International Law: Theory and Practice. Essays in Honour of Eric Suy* (The Hague, Martinus Nijhoff, 1998) 237–52.

Henrikson, AK, 'The United Nations and Regional Organizations: "King Links" of a "Global Chain"' (Fall 1996) 7(1) *Duke Journal of Comparative and International Law* 35–70.

Kelsen, H, 'Collective Security and Collective Self-defence under the Charter of the United Nations' (1948) 42(4) *AJIL* 783–96.

—— *Collective Security under International Law* (Newport Rhode Island; Naval War College, Washington, Government Printing Office, 1957).

Koskenniemi, M, 'The Place of Law in Collective Security' (1995–96) 17 *Michigan Journal of International Law* 456–90.

Krisch, N, 'Unilateral Enforcement of the Collective Will: Kosovo, Iraq, and the Security Council' (1999) 3 *Max Planck UNYB* 59–103.

Lorenz, JP, *Peace, Power, and the United Nations: The Uses and Limits of Collective Force* (Harper Collins Canada, Westview Press, 1998).

Manin, P, *L'Organisation des Nations Unies et le maintien de la paix* (Paris, Librairie générale de droit et de jurisprudence, 1971).

Muracciole, J-F, *L'ONU et la sécurité collective* (Paris, Ellipses, 2006).

Price, R and Zacher, M (eds), *United Nations and Global Security* (New York, Palgrave MacMillan, 2004).

Sarooshi, D, *The United Nations and the Development of Collective Security: The Delegation by the UN Security Council of its Chapter VII Powers* (New York, OUP, 1999).

Société Française pour le Droit International, *Les métamorphoses de la sécurité collective, Droit, pratique et enjeux stratégiques* (Paris, Pedone, 2005).

Sur, S, 'Sécurité collective et rétablissement de la paix : la résolution 687 (3 avril 1991) dans l'affaire du Golfe' in *Le développement du rôle du Conseil de sécurité*. Workshop: Peace-keeping and Peace-building: The Development of the Role of the Security Council, The Hague, 21–23 July 1992 (Dordrecht, Martinus Nijhoff, 1993) 13–40.

—— Sécurité collective in T (de) Montbrial and J Klein (eds), *Dictionnaire de stratégie* (Paris, PUF, 2000) 305–09.

Sutterlin, JS, *The United Nations and the Maintenance of International Security: A Challenge to be Met* (Westport, Praeger Publishers, 2003).

Thakur, R, *The United Nations, Peace and Security: From Collective Security to the Responsibility to Protect* (Cambridge, CUP, 2006).

Türsan, H, 'La sécurité collective: chimère, éphémère ou mutante?' (1994) 36(1) *Res publica* 67–84.

Van Logenhove, F, *La crise du système de sécurité collective des Nations Unies: 1946–1957* (The Hague, Martinus Nijhoff, 1958).

White, ND (ed), *Collective Security Law* (Dartmouth, Ashgate, 2003).

United Nations Forces

Carnegie Commission, 'Preventing Deadly Conflict' (Final Report) (Carnagie Corporation, New York, 1997).

UN Department of Public Information, *The Blue Helmet: A Review of United Nations Peace-keeping*, 3rd edn (United Nations, New York, 1996).

Abi-Saab, G, *The United Nations Operations in the Congo 1960–1964* (Oxford, OUP, 1978).

—— 'La deuxième génération des opérations de maintien de la paix: quelques réflexions prélim-inaires' (1996) 34 *Le Trimestre du Monde* 87–97.

Aksu, E, *The United Nations, Intra-state Peacekeeping and Normative Change* (Manchester, Manchester University Press, 2003).

Azimi, N and In, CL (eds), *The United Nations Transitional Administration in East Timor (UNTAET)* (Leiden, Brill Academic Publishers, 2003).

Ballaloud, J, *L'ONU et les Opérations de maintien de la paix* (Paris, Pedone, 1971).

—— 'L'opération des Nations Unies à Chypre' (1976) 80(1) *RGDIP* 130–62.

Bernadotte, F, *To Jerusalem* (London, Hodder and Stoughton, 1951).

Biermann, W, *'Old' UN Peacekeeping Principles and 'New' Conflicts: Some Ideas to Reduce the Troubles of Post-cold War Peace Missions* (Copenhagen, Centre for Peace and Conflict Research, 1994).

Boyd, JM, *United Nations Peace Keeping Operations: A Military and Political Appraisal* (New York, Praeger Publishers, 1971).

Cassese, A (ed), *United Nations Peace-keeping. Legal Essays* (The Hague, Martinus Nijhoff, 1978).

Cellamare, G, *Le operazioni di peace-keeping multifunzionali* (Torino, G Giappichelli, 1999).

Chesterman, S, *You, The People: The United Nations, Transitional Administration, and State-Building* (Oxford, OUP, 2004).

Claude, I, 'The Peace-Keeping Role of the United Nations' in BE Tompkins, *The United Nations in Perspective* (Stanford University, Hoover Institution Press, 1972).

Coulon, J, *Les casques bleus* (Québec, éditions Fides, 1994).

Daillier, P, 'La fin des opérations de maintien de la paix des Nations Unies' (1996) 42 *AFDI* 62–78.

Damrosch, LF, 'From Keeping the Peace to Making It: The Changing Role of UN Security Forces' (Proceedings, 88th meeting, American Society of International Law, 1994) 328–53.

Daniel, DCF and Hayes, BC (eds), *Beyond Traditional Peacekeeping* (Basingstoke, Macmillan, 1995).

Dupuy, R-J, *The Development of the Role of the Security Council. Peace-keeping and Peace-building* (Dordrecht, Martinus Nijhoff, 1993).

Durch, WJ, *The Evolution of UN Peace-Keeping: Case Studies and Comparative Analysis* (New York, St Martin's Press, 1993).

Engdahl, O, 'The Status of Military Personnel in United Nations Peace Operations: Interplay between the Laws of Peace and War' in *Peace and Security: Current Challenges in International Law* (Lund, Studentlitteratur, 2004) 53–84.

Fabian, LL, *Soldiers without Enemies: Preparing the United Nations for Peacekeeping* (Washington, The Brookings Institution, 1971).

Fetherston, AB, *Towards a Theory of United Nations Peacekeeping* (New York, Saint Martin's Press, 1994).

Frechette, L, 'United Nations Peace-Keeping at Fifty: Looking Back, Looking Forward' International Relations Studies United Nations Occasional Reports and Papers 3 (The Academic Council on the United Nations System, Yale University, 1998).

Fröhlich, M, 'Keeping Track of UN Peace-keeping: Suez, Srebrenica, Rwanda and the Brahimi Report' (2001) 5 *Max Planck UNYB* 185–248.

Goebel, CM, 'Population Transfer, Humanitarian Law, and the Use of Ground Force in UN Peacemaking: Bosnia and Herzegovina in the Wake of Iraq' (1993) 25(3) *JILP* 627–98.

Hegelsom, GJ (van), 'The Law of Armed Conflict and UN Peace-keeping and Peace-enforcing Operations' (1993) 6 *Hague Yearbook of International Law* 45–58.

Higgins, R, *United Nations Peacekeeping: 1946–1967. Documents and Commentary* Volume I: The Middle East (1969); Volume II: Asia (1970); Volume III: Africa (1980) (Royal Institute of International Affairs, OUP).

—— *United Nations Peacekeeping: 1946–1979. Documents and Commentary* Volume IV: Europe (Royal Institute of International Affairs, OUP, 1981).

Irmscher, TH, 'The Legal Framework for Activities of the United Nations Interim Administration Mission in Kosovo: the Charter, Human Rights, and the Law of Occupation' (2002) 44 *German Yearbook of International Law* 353–95.

Khan, R, United Nations Peace-keeping in International Conflicts: Problems and Perspectives' (2000) 4 *Max Planck UNYB* 543–81.

Kolb, R, Porretto, G and Vite, S, *L'application du droit international humanitaire et des droits de l'homme aux organisations internationales: forces de paix et administrations civiles transitoires* (Bruxelles, Bruylant, 2005).

Kouassi, EK, 'Rôles respectifs du Conseil de sécurité et de l'Assemblée générale dans le traitement des opérations de maintien de la paix. Approche juridique et historique' in *Le développement du rôle du Conseil de sécurité*. Workshop: Peace-keeping and Peace-building: The Development of the Role of the Security Council, The Hague, 21–23 July 1992 (Dordrecht, Martinus Nijhoff, 1993) 425–61.

Lagrange, E, *Les opérations de maintien de la paix et le chapitre VII des Nations Unies* (Paris, Montchrestien, 1999).

Lavoyer, J-P, 'Perspectives for a UN Modus Operandi in the 21st Century: International Intervention: Some Legal Challenges'. United Nations as Peacekeeper and Nation-Builder: Continuity and Change: What Lies Ahead? (Report of the 2005 Hiroshima Conference) (Leiden, Martinus Nijhoff, 2006)185–96.

Lehmann, T, 'Some Legal Aspects of the United Nations of Peace-keeping Operations' (1985) 54 *Nordisk tidsskrift for international ret* 11–18.

Leininger, J, 'Democracy and UN Peace-Keeping—Conflict Resolution through State-Building and Democracy Promotion in Haiti' (2006) 10 *Max Planck UNYB* 465–530.

Lepper, SJ, 'The Legal Status of Military Personnel in United Nations Peace Operations; One Delegate's Analysis' (Winter 1996) 18(2) *Houston Journal of International Law* 359–464.

Liegeois, M, *Maintien de la paix et diplomatie coercitive: l'organisation des Nations-Unies à l'épreuve des conflits de l'après-guerre froide* (Bruxelles, Bruylant, 2003).

Liu, F-T, 'United Nations Peace-keeping Operations: their Importance and their Limitations in a Polarized World' speech delivered on 8 May 1987 (1987) 201(1) *RCADI* 385–400; also in (1987) 42(3) *Comunità internazionale* 336–46.

—— *History of the UN Peace Keeping Operations in the Post Cold War Era: 1988–1997* (UNITR, Programme of Correspondence Instruction in Peace-Keeping Operations, New York, 1998).

MacQueen, N, *Peacekeeping and the International System* (New York, Routledge, 2006).

McCoubrey, H, *The Blue Helmets: Legal Regulation of United Nations Military Operations* (Aldershot, Brookfield, Dartmouth, 1996).

Murphy, R, *UN Peacekeeping in Lebanon, Somalia and Kosovo, Operational and Legal Issues in Practice* (Cambridge, CUP, 2007).

Mustapha, MY, 'Historique et évaluation des opérations de maintien de la paix de l'ONU au Moyen-Orient' (1976) 13(4) *Revue algérienne des sciences juridiques, économiques et politiques* 919–53.

Opie, R, 'United Nations' Responsibility for United Nations Mandated Peace Operations—A Necessary Contribution to the Efficacy of International Humanitarian Law' (2003) 18 *New Zealand Armed Forces Review*.

Orakhelashvili, A, 'The Legal Basis of the United Nations Peace-keeping Operations (Winter 2003) 43(2) *Virginia Journal of International Law* 485–524.

Palwankar, UY, 'L'applicabilité du droit international humanitaire aux Forces des Nations Unies pour le maintien de la paix' (1993) 801 *Revue Internationale de la Croix-Rouge* 245–87.

Peck, J, 'The UN and the Laws of War: How can the World's Peacekeepers be Held Accountable?'(1995) 21 *Syracuse Journal of International Law and Commerce* 283–310.

Pouligny, B, *Ils nous avaient promis la paix. Opérations de l'ONU et populations locales* (Paris, Presses de Sciences-Po, 2004).

Schachter, O, 'United Nations Law in the Gulf Conflict' (1991) 85(3) *AJIL* 452–73.

Siekmann, RCR, 'The Multinational Peace-keeping Force in the Sinai in the Light of United Nations Practice on Peace-keeping Forces' (October/December 1984) 24(4) *Indian Journal of International Law* 504–24.

—— 'The Development of the United Nations Law Concerning Peace-keeping Operations' (October 1992) 5(2) *Leiden Journal of International Law* 273–81.

Stern, B, 'L'évolution du rôle des Nations Unies dans le maintien de la paix et de la sécurité internationales' United Congress on Public International Law Towards the Twenty First Century (International Law as a Language for International Relations, 13–17 March 1995, New York).

Suy, E, 'United Nations Peace-keeping System' in R Bernhardt (ed), *Encyclopedia of Public International Law* Volume IV (Amsterdam, Elsevier, 1982) 1143–49.

Suy, E, 'Peace-keeping Operations' in R-J Dupuy (ed), *Manuel sur les organisations internationals* (Dordrecht, Martinus Nijhoff, 1988) 379–96.

—— 'Legal aspects of UN Peace-keeping Operations' (1988) 35(3) *Netherlands International Review* 318–20.

Tardy, T, 'Le discrédit du maintien de la paix' in V-Y Ghebali, *L'ONU et les conflits de l'après-guerre froide* (Paris, Bruylant, 1999).

Tavernier, P, *Les casques bleus* (Paris, PUF, 1996).

Warner, D, *New Dimensions of Peace-keeping* (Dordrecht, Martinus Nijhoff, 1995).

Werner, S and Yuen, A, 'Making and Keeping Peace' (Spring 2005) 59(2) *International Organization* 261–92.

White, ND, *Keeping the Peace: the United Nations and the Maintenance of International Peace and Security* (Manchester, England; New York, Manchester University Press, 1990).

Yanamoto, R, 'Legal Issues Concerning Japan's Participation in United Nations Peace-Keeping Operations (1991–2003)' (2004) 47 *Japanese Annual of International Law* 136–67.

Sanctions

Abi-Saab, G, 'The Concept of Sanctions in International Law' in V Gowlland-Debbas (ed), *United Nations Sanctions and International Law* (The Hague, Kluwer Law International, 2001) 29–41.

Bennouna, M, 'Les sanctions économiques des Nations Unies' (2002) 300 *RCADI* 9–77.

Beyerlin, U, 'Sanctions' in R Wolfrum (ed), *United Nations: Law, Policies and Practice*, volume 2 (Munich, CH Beck; Dordrecht, Martinus Nijhoff, 1995) 1111–28.

Bruderlein, C, 'The UN Security Council at the Crossroads: Toward More Humane and Better Targeted Sanctions' in K Boustany and D Dormoy (eds), *Perspectives humanitaires entre conflits, droit(s) et action* (Bruxelles, Bruylant, edn de l'Université de Bruxelles, 2002) 233–50.

Caron, DD and Morris, B, 'The UN Compensation Commission: Practical Justice, not Retribution' (2002) 13(1) *EJIL-JEDI* 183–99.

Cavaré, L, 'Les sanctions dans le cadre de l'ONU' (1952) 80(1) *RCADI* 191–291.

Combacau, J, *Le pouvoir de sanction de l'ONU, Etude théorique de la coercition non militaire* (Paris, Pedone, 1974).

Condorelli, L, 'La compatibilité des sanctions du Conseil de sécurité avec le droit international humanitaire: commentaire' in V Gowlland-Debbas (ed), *United Nations Sanctions and International Law* (The Hague, Kluwer Law International, 2001) 233–40.

Cortright, D and Lopez, GA, *The Sanction Decade: Assessing UN Strategies in the 1990s. A Project of the International Peace Academy* (Boulder, Lynne Rienner Publishers, 2000).

Crawford, J, 'The Relationship between Sanctions and Countermeasures' in V Gowlland-Debbas (ed), *United Nations Sanctions and International Law* 57–68.

Doxey, M, 'International Sanctions in Practice' (1983) 15 *Case Western Reserve Journal of International Law* 273–88.

Dugard, J, 'Judicial Review of Sanctions' in V Gowlland-Debbas (ed), *United Nations Sanctions and International Law* 83–92.

Eisemann, P-M, *Les sanctions contre la Rhodésie* (Paris, Pedone, 1972).

Forlati, LP and Sicilianos, L-A (eds), *Les sanctions économiques en droit international* (Académie de droit international de la Haye) (Leiden, Martinus Nijhoff, 2004).

Frigessi di Rattalma, M, 'Le régime de responsabilité internationale institué par le Conseil d'administration de la Commission de compensation des Nations Unies' (1997) 100(1) *RGDIP* 45–90.

Gowlland-Debbas, V, *Collective Responses to Illegal Acts in International Law—United Nations Action in the Question of Southern Rhodesia* (Dordrecht; Boston, Martinus Nijhoff, 1990).

—— 'Sanctions Regimes under Article 41 of the UN Charter' in *National Implementation of United Nations Sanctions* (Leiden, Martinus Nijhoff, 2004) 3–31.

Horn, A, *Multilaterale ökonomische Sanktionsregime der Vereinten Nationen* (Frankfurt, Peter Lang, 2003).

Matam Farrall, J, *United Nations Sanctions and the Rule of Law* (Cambridge, CUP, 2007).

Mehdi, R (ed), *Les Nations Unies et les sanctions: quelle efficacité?* (Paris, Pedone, 2000).

O'Connell, ME, 'Debating the Law of Sanctions'(2002) 13(1) *EJIL-JEDI* 63–79.

Oette, L, *Die Vereinbarkeit der vom Sicherheitsrat nach Kapitel VII der UN-Charta verhängten Wirtschaftssanktionen mit den Menschenrechten und dem humanitären Völkerrecht* (Frankfurt, Peter Lang, 2003).

Reinisch, A, 'Developing Human Rights and Humanitarian Law Accountability of the Security Council for the Imposition of Economic Sanctions' (2001) 95(4) *AJIL* 851–72.

Reisman, WM and Stevick, LD, 'The Applicability of International Law Standards to United Nations Economic Sanctions Programmes' (1998) 9(1) *EJIL-JEDI* 86–141.

Sassoli, M, 'Sanctions and International Humanitarian Law—Commentary' in V Gowlland-Debbas (ed), *United Nations Sanctions and International* 241–48.

Schaller, C, 'Die Richtigen treffen: die Vereinten Nationen und die Probleme zielgerichteter Sanktionen' (2005) 53(4) *Vereinte Nationen* 132–38.

Tehindrazanarivelo, D, 'Le droit des Nations Unies et les limites au pouvoir de sanction du Conseil de sécurité' in LP Forlati and L-A Sicilianos (eds), *Les sanctions économiques en droit international* (Leiden, Martinus Nijhoff, 2004) 21–277.

—— *Les sanctions des Nations Unies et leurs effets secondaires: assistance aux victimes et voies juridiques de prevention* (Paris, Presses Universitaires de France, 2005).

International Terrorism

Academie de Droit International de la Haye, *Centre d'étude et de recherche de droit international et de relations internationales 2006: Terrorisme et droit international* (Leiden, Martinus Nijhoff, 2007).

Bianchi, A, (ed) *Enforcing International Law Norms Against Terrorism* (Oxford/Portland, Hart Publishing, 2004).

—— 'Security Council's Anti-terror Resolutions and their Implementation by Member States: an Overview' (2006) 4(5) *Journal of International Criminal Justice* 1044–73.

Boulden, J and Weiss, TG (eds), *Terrorism and the UN: Before and After September 11* (Bloomington, Indiana University Press, 2004).

Corten, O, 'Vers un renforcement des pouvoirs du Conseil de Sécurité dans la lutte contre le terrorisme?' in K Bannelier *et al* (eds.), *Le droit international face au terrorisme: après le 11 septembre 2001* (Paris, Pedone, 2002) 259–77.

Fassbender, B, 'The UN Security Council and International Terrorism' in A Bianchi (ed), *Enforcing International Law Norms against Terrorism* (Oxford, Hart Publishing, 2004) 83–102.

Gaja, G, 'Combating Terrorism: Issues of Jus ad Bellum and Jus in Bello: the Case of Afghanistan' in *Anti-terrorist Measures and Human Rights* (Leiden, Martinus Nijhoff, 2004) 161–70.

Gehr, W, 'The Counter-Terrorism Committee and Security Council Resolution 1373 (2001)' (2004) (4(1–2) *Forum on Crime and Society* 101–07.

Goldie, LF, 'Combating International Terrorism: The United Nations Developments' in *Readings on International Law from the Naval War College Review 1978–1994* (Newport, RI, Naval War College, 1995) 387–99.

Jonge Oudraat, C (de), 'Le Conseil de sécurité de l'ONU et la lutte contre le terrorisme' (2005) 6 *Annuaire Français de Relations Internationales* 116–27.

Klein P, 'Le droit international à l'épreuve du terrorisme' (2006) 321 *RCADI* 203–484.

Martin, J-C, *Les règles internationales relatives à la lutte contre le terrorisme* (Brussels, Bruylant, 2006).

Martin, J-C, 'Le Conseil de sécurité face au terrorisme islamiste: à propos des sanctions contre Al-Qaida, les Taliban et leurs associés' (2006) 20(21) *L'Observateur des Nations Unies* 145–66.

Nesi, G, *International Cooperation in Counter-Terrorism: The United Nations and Regional Organizations in the Fight against Terrorism* (Burlington, VT, Ashgate, 2006).

Olivier, C, 'Human Rights Law and the International Fight against Terrorism: How do Security Council Resolutions Impact on States' Obligations Under International Human Rights Law?' (2004) 73(4) *Nordic Journal of International Law* 399–419.

Rosand, E, 'Security Council Resolution 1373, the Counter-Terrorism Committee, and the Fight Against Terrorism' (2003) 97(2) *AJIL* 333–41.

—— 'Security Council Resolution 1373 and the Counter-terrorism Committee: The Cornerstone of the United Nations Contribution to the Fight against Terrorism' in *Legal Instruments in the Fight against International Terrorism: A Transatlantic Dialogue* (Leiden, Martinus Nijhoff, 2004) 603–31.

Rostow, N, 'Before and After: The Changed UN Response to Terrorism since September 11th' (2002) 35(3) *Cornell International Law Journal* 475–90.

Santori, V, 'The UN Security Council's (Broad) Interpretation of the Notion of the Threat to Peace in Counter-Terrorism' in *International Cooperation in Counter-Terrorism: The United Nations and Regional Organizations in the Fight against Terrorism*, (Aldershot, Ashgate, 2006) 89–111.

Saul, B, 'Definition of "Terrorism" in the UN Security Council: 1985–2004' (2005) 4(1) *Chinese Journal of International Law* 141–66.

Saura, J, 'Some Remarks on the Use of Force against Terrorism in Contemporary International Law and the Role of the Security Council' (2003) 26(1) *Loyola of Los Angeles International & Comparative Law Review* 27–30.

Sossai, M, 'La cooperazione multilaterale nella lotta al terrorismo internazionale: il Comitato contro il terrorismo del Consiglio di sicurezza delle Nazioni Unite' (2004) 1 *Pace diritti umani* 79–90.

Stromseth, JE, 'The Security Council's Counter-terrorism Role: Continuity and Innovation' (2003) 97 *American Society of International Law Proceedings* 41–45.

Subedi, SP, 'The War on Terror and UN Attempts to Adopt a Comprehensive Convention on International Terrorism' in *September 11, 2001: A Turning Point in International and Domestic Law* (Ardsley, NY, Transnational Publishers, 2005) 207–25.

Szurek, S, 'La lutte internationale contre le terrorisme sous l'empire du chapitre VII: un labora-
toire normatif' (2005) 109(1) *RGDIP* 5–49.

Tercinet, J, 'Le Conseil de sécurité et le terrorisme' in S Kirschbaum (ed), *Terrorisme et sécurité
internationale* (Bruxelles, Bruylant, 2004) 49–67.

Wagner, M, 'Die wirtschaftlichen Massnahmen des Sicherheitsrates nach dem 11 September 2001
im völkerrechtlichen Kontext: von Wirtschaftssanktionen zur Wirtschaftsgesetzgebung?' (2003)
63(4) *Zeitschrift für ausländisches öffentliches Recht und Völkerrecht* 879–920.

Walter, C, 'Zwischen Selbstverteidigung und Völkerstrafrecht: Bausteine für ein internationales
Recht der "präventiven Terrorismus-Bekämpfung"' in *Rechtsfragen der Terrorismusbekämpfung
durch Streitkräfte: Legal Issues of Military Counter-terrorist Operations with English Executive
Summary* (Baden-Baden, Nomos, 2004) 23–42.

Ward, CA, 'Building Capacity to Combat International Terrorism: The Role of the United
Nations Security Council' (2003) 8(2) *Journal of Conflict and Security Law* 289–305.

—— 'Convergence of International Law and International Relations in Combating International
Terrorism: The Role of the United Nations: Commentary' in *International Law and
International Relations: Bridging Theory and Practice* (London, Routledge, 2007) 127–37.

Wessel, R, 'Debating the "Smartness" of Anti-terrorism Sanctions: The UN Security Council
and the Individual Citizen' in *Legal Instruments in the Fight against International Terrorism:
a Transatlantic Dialogue* (Leiden, Martinus Nijhoff, 2004) 633–60.

Witschel, G and Brandes, M, 'Die Vereinten Nationen und die Bekämpfung des internationalen
Terrorismus' in *Globale Probleme und Zukunftsaufgaben der Vereinten Nationen* (Baden-
Baden, Nomos, 2006) 22–50.

Wood, MC, 'Towards New Circumstances in which the Use of Force may be Authorized?: The
Cases of Humanitarian Intervention, Counter-Terrorism, and Weapons of Mass Destruction'
in *The Security Council and the Use of Force: Theory and Reality: A Need for Change?* (Leiden,
Martinus Nijhoff, 2005) 75–90.

7. Law-Making

Abi-Saab, G, 'Diplomatie multilatérale et développement du droit international: le rôle des résolutions de l'Assemblée générale' in V-Y Ghebali and D Kappeler (eds), *Les multiples aspects
des relations internationales: études à la mémoire du professeur Jean Siotis* (Bruxelles, Bruylant,
1995) 83–99.

Arangio-Ruiz, G, 'The Normative Role of the General Assembly of the United Nations and the
Declaration of Principles of Friendly Relations' (1972) 137(3) *RCADI* 419–742.

—— 'On the Security Council's "Law-making"' (2000) 80(3) *Rivista di diritto internazionale*
609–725.

Boisson de Chazournes, L, 'Les résolutions des organes des Nations Unies, et en particulier
celles du Conseil de sécurité, en tant que source de droit international humanitaire' in
L Condorelli *et al* (eds), *Les Nations Unies et le droit international humanitaire* (Paris, Pedone,
1996) 149–73.

Cahin, G, *La coutume internationale et les organisations internationales. L'incidence de la dimension institutionnelle sur le processus coutumier* (Paris, Pedone, 2001).

Condorelli, L 'Le pouvoir législatif du Conseil de sécurité des Nations Unies vu à la 'loupe
Salmon' in N Angelet (ed), *Mélanges Salmon, Droit du pouvoir, pouvoir du droit* (Bruxelles,
Bruylant, 2007) 1229–240.

Corten, O, 'La participation du Conseil de sécurité à l'élaboration, à la cristallisation ou à la
consolidation de règles coutumières' (May 2005) 55(3) *Arès* 87–100.

David, E, 'Méthodes et formes de participation des Nations Unies à l'élaboration du droit inter-national humanitaire: rapport introductif' in L Condorelli *et al* (eds), *Les Nations Unies et le droit international humanitaire* (Paris, Pedone, 1996) 87–113.

Denis, C, *Le pouvoir normatif du Conseil de Sécurité: portée et limites* (Bruxelles, Bruylant, 2004).

Higgins, R, *The Development of International Law through the Political Organs of the United Nations* (London, OUP, 1963).

—— 'The Development of International Law by the Political Organs of the United Nations' (1965) 116 *American Society of International Law Proceedings* 116–124.

Lavalle, R, 'A Novel, if Awkward, Exercise in International Law-Making: Security Council Resolution 1540 (2004)' (2004) 51(3) *Netherlands International Law Review* 411–37.

McWhinney, E, *Les Nations Unies et la formation du droit: relativisme culturel et idéologique et formation du droit international pour une époque de transition* (Paris, Pedone UNESCO, 1986).

Pellet, A, 'La formation du droit international dans le cadre des Nations Unies' (1995) 6(3) *EJIL-JEDI* 401–25.

Saba, H, 'L'activité quasi-législative des institutions spécialisées des Nations Unies' (1964) 111(1) *RCADI* 603–90.

Skubiszewski, K, 'The Elaboration of General Multilateral Conventions and Non-Contractual Instruments having a Normative Function or Objective—Resolutions of the General Assembly of the United Nations' (Report) (1985) 61(1) *Annuaire de l'Institut de Droit International* 29–249.

8. Economic and Social Development

Bertrand, M, *The Role of the United Nations in the Economic and Social Fields* (New York, UNA-USA, 1987).

Boas, M and McNeill, D (eds), *Global Institutions and Development: Framing the World?'* (London, Routledge, 2004).

Comanescu, L, 'La contribution de l'Organisation des Nations Unies au renforcement de la coopération économique internationale' (July/August 1985) 19(4) *Revue roumaine d'études internationales* 353–61.

Daudet, Y (ed), *Les Nations Unies et le développement social international: cinquièmes rencontres internationales de l'I.E.P. d'Aix-en-Provence, colloque des 16 et 17 février 1996* (Paris, Pedone, 1996).

Fontanel, J, *Les organisations économiques internationales* (Paris, New York, Masson, 1981).

Rucz, C, *Le Conseil économique et social de l'ONU et la coopération pour le développement* (Paris, Economica, 1983).

Seynes, P (de), 'Quarante années . . . l'organisation des Nations Unies dans son rôle d'organisme économique et social' in *L'adaptation des structures et méthodes des Nations Unies. Workshop: The Adaptation of Structures and Methods at the United Nations, The Hague, 4–6 November 1985* (Dordrecht, Martinus Nijhoff, 1986) 47–61.

Sharp, WR, *The United Nations Economic and Social Council* (New York, Columbia University Press, 1969).

Sen, S, *United Nations in Economic Development: A Need for a New Strategy* (New York, Oceana Publications, 1969).

South Centre (South Commission), *Enhancing the Economic Role of the United Nations* (Geneva, Switzerland, South Centre, 1992).

Toye, J and Toye, R, *The UN and Global Political Economy: Trade, Finance and Development* (Bloomington, Indiana University Press, 2004).

Weiss, TG *et al., UN Voices: The Struggle for Development and Social Justice* (Bloomington, Indiana University Press, 2005).

World Commission on Environment and Development, *Our Common Future* (New York, OUP, 1987).

9. Human Rights

'In Larger Freedom: Towards Security, Development and Human Rights for all'. Report of the Secretary-General of the United Nations (New York, 24 March 2005): http://www.un.org/largerfreedom/

Alston, P and Megret, F (eds), *The United Nations and Human Rights: A Critical Appraisal* (Oxford, OUP, 2009).

Breen, C, 'Revitalising the United Nations Human Rights Special Procedures Mechanisms as a Means of Achieving and Maintaining International Peace and Security' (2008) 12 *Max Planck UNYB* 177–204.

Brunet, R, *La garantie internationale des droits de l'homme, d'après la Charte de San Francisco* (Genève, C Grasset, 1947).

Cardenas, EJ, 'The United Nations Role in the Future of Human Freedoms' (Spring/Summer 1996) 27(3) *University of Miami Inter-American Law Review* 441–52.

Cassin, R, *La Déclaration universelle des droits de l'homme de 1948* (Paris, Académie des sciences morales et politiques, 1958).

Chetail, V (ed), 'Le Conseil des droits de l'homme des Nations Unies: réformer pour ne rien changer?' in V Chetail (ed), *Mélanges en l'honneur du Professeur Victor-Yves Ghébali: conflits, sécurité et coopération* (Bruxelles, Bruylant, 2008) 125–68.

Clapham, A, 'Creating the High Commissioner for Human Rights: The Outside Story' (1994) 556 *EJIL-JEDI* 556–68.

Cohen-Jonathan, G, 'Les réserves dans les traités institutionnels relatifs aux droits de l'homme: nouveaux aspects européens et internationaux' (1996) 100(4) *RGDIP* 915–49.

—— 'Le Conseil de sécurité et les droits de l'homme' in J-F Flauss and P Wachsman (eds), *Le droit des organisations internationales : recueil d'études à la mémoire de Jacques Schwob* (Bruxelles, Bruylant, 1997) 19–70.

Colard, D, 'L'organisation des Nations Unies et les droits de l'homme'(November 1993) 49(11) *Défense nationale* 113–26.

Decaux, E (ed), *Les Nations Unies et les droits de l'homme: enjeux et défis d'une réforme* (Paris, Pedone, 2006).

Donnelly, J, 'Human Rights at the United Nations 1955–1985: the Question of Bias' (1988) 32 *International Studies Quarterly* 275–303.

Eudes, M, 'De la commission au conseil des droits de l'homme: vraie réforme ou faux-semblant?' (2006) *AFDI* 599–616.

Farer, T, 'The United Nations and Human Rights: More than a Whimper, Less than a Roar' (1987) 550(9) *Human Rights Quarterly* 550–86.

Guyomar, G, 'Nations Unies et organisations régionales dans la protection des droits de l'homme' (1964) 68(3) *RGDIP* 687–707.

Henkin, AH (ed), *Honoring Human Rights under International Mandates, Lessons from Bosnia, Kosovo and East Timor* (Washington DC, The Aspen Institute, 2003).

Henry, L, 'Les Nations Unies et le droit des peuples à disposer d'eux-mêmes' (2006) 20(21) *Observateur des Nations Unies* 225–60.

Humphrey, JP, *Human Rights & the United Nations: A Great Adventure* (New York, Transnational Publishers Inc, 1984).

Joinet, L, 'L'action des Nations Unies dans le domaine des droits de l'homme' (September/October 1990) 5 *Revue du droit public et de la science politique en France et à l'étranger* 1247–53.

Mbaye, K, 'L'Organisation des Nations Unies et les droits de l'homme' in *L'adaptation des structures et méthodes des Nations Unies.* Workshop: The Adaptation of Structures and Methods at the United Nations, The Hague, 4–6 November 1985 (Dordrecht, Martinus Nijhoff, 1986) 289–318.

Megret, F and Hoffman, F, 'The UN as a Human Rights Violator? Some Reflections on the United Nations Changing Human Rights Responsibilities' (2002) 25(2) *Human Rights Quarterly* 314–42.

Mertus , J, *The United Nations and Human Rights: A Guide for a New Era* (London, Routledge, 2005).

Schreiber, M, 'La pratique récente des Nations Unies dans le domaine de la protection des droits de l'homme' (1975) 145(2) *RCADI* 297–398.

Simma, B, 'Human Rights' in C Tomuschat (ed), *The United Nations at Age Fifty: A Legal Perspective* (The Hague, Kluwer Law International, 1995) 263–80.

Tavernier, P, 'L'ONU et l'affirmation de l'universalité des droits de l'homme' (1997) 31 *Revue Trimestrielle des Droits de l'Homme* 379–93.

Ténékidès, G, 'L'action des Nations Unies contre la discrimination raciale' (1980) 168(3) *RCADI* 269–487.

United Nations Centre for Human Rights (UNCHR), 'United Nations Action in the Field of Human Rights' (1994) UN Doc ST/HR/2/Rev. 4.

White, ND and Klaasen, D (eds), *The UN, Human Rights and Post-conflict Situations* (Manchester, Manchester University Press, 2005).

10. United Nations Reform

Alger, CF 'Thinking About the Future of the UN System' (1996) 2(3) *Global Gouvernance* 335–60.

—— (ed), *The Future of the United Nations System. Potential for the Twenty-first Century* (Tokyo; New York, United Nations University Press, 1998).

Arnold, T, 'Reforming the UN: Its Economic Role' discussion paper, no 57 (London, Royal Institute of International Affairs, 1995).

Beigbeder, Y, *United Nations Organizations. The Long Quest for Reform* (Houndmills; London, MacMillan Press, 1997).

Bertrand, M, 'A propos de la réforme du Conseil de sécurité' (1999) 30(2) *Etudes internationales* 413–22.

—— 'Les leçons des erreurs d'une réforme manquée. Le problème de la "mondialisation politique" in V Chetail (ed), *Mélanges Ghébali: conflits, sécurité et coopération* (Bruxelles, Bruylant, 2008) 35–50.

—— 'The Historical Development of Efforts to Reform the UN' in A Roberts and B Kingsbury (eds), *United Nations, Divided World: The UN's Roles in International Relations* 2nd edn (Oxford, Clarendon Press, 1993) 420–36.

Bertrand, M and Warner, D, *A New Charter for a Worldwide Organization* (The Hague, Kluwer International Law, 1996).

Blanc Altemir, A and Real, B, 'La réforme du Conseil de sécurité des Nations Unies: quelle structure et quels membres?' (2006) 110(4) *RGDIP* 801–25.

Boisson de Chazournes, L, 'Rien ne change, tout bouge, ou le dilemme des Nations Unies: propos sur le Rapport du Groupe de personnalités de haut niveau sur les menaces, les défis et le changement' (1995) 109(1) *RGDIP* 147–61.

Boutros Ghali, B, ?Empowering the United Nations? (Winter 1992/93) 71 *Foreign Affairs* 89?102.

Calvez, J-Y, 'Peut-on réformer l'ONU?' (2007) 406(4) *Etudes* 441–51.

Carlsson, I, 'The UN at Fifty: A Time to Reform' (Fall 1995) 100 *Foreign Policy* 3–18.

Chesterman, S, 'Reforming the United Nations: Legitimacy, Effectiveness, and Power after Iraq' (2006) 10 *Singapore Year Book of International Law* 1–28.

Childers, E and Urquhart, B, *Renewing the United Nations System* (New York, Uppsala, Ford Foundation & Dag Hammarskjöld Foundation, 1994).

Dicke, K, 'Reform of the United Nations' in R Wolfrum (ed), *United Nations: Law, Policies and Practice* volume 2 (Munich, CH Beck; Dordrecht, Martinus Nijhoff, 1995) 1012–24.

Dormoy, D, 'Les modalités de réforme de l'Organisation des Nations Unies' in V Chetail (ed), *Mélanges Ghébali: conflits, sécurité et coopération* (Bruxelles, Bruylant, 2008) 223–36.

Economides, CP, 'La révision de la Charte des Nations Unies' (1977) 30 *Revue Hellénique de Droit International* 20–41.

Eban, A, The UN Idea Revisited' (September/October 1995) 74(5) *Foreign Affairs* 39–55.

Fassbender, B, *UN Security Council Reform and the Right of Veto* (The Hague; Boston; London, Kluwer, 1998).

Fleurence, O, *La réforme du Conseil de sécurité. L'état du débat depuis la fin de la guerre froide* (Bruxelles, Bruylant, 2000).

Franck, TM, 'Collective Security and UN Reform: Between the Necessary and the Possible' (2006) 6 *Chicago Journal of International Law* 597–613.

Giraud, E, 'La révision de la Charte des Nations Unies' (1956) 90(2) *RCADI* 307–467.

Hilpold, P, 'The Duty to Protect and the Reform of the United Nations—A New Step in the Development of International Law?'(2006) 10 *Max Planck UNYB* 35–69.

Hüfner, K (ed), *Die Reform der Vereinten Nationen*: Die Weltorganisation zwischen Krise und Erneuerung (*The Reform of the United Nations: The World Organization between Crisis and Renewal*) (Opladen, Leske, Budrich, 1994).

Imber, M, *Environment, Security, and UN Reform* (New York, St Martin's Press, 1994).

Independent Commission of the South on Development Issues, *The Challenge to the South: The Report of the South Commission* (Oxford, Oxford University Press, 1990).

Independent Commission on Disarmament and Security Issues, *Common Security: A Blueprint for Survival* (New York, Simon and Schuster, 1982).

Independent Working Group on the Future of the United Nations, *The United Nations in its Second Half-Century* (New York, Ford Foundation, 1995).

International Symposium, 'Prospects for Reform of the United Nations System' (Rome, 15–17 May 1992 (Padova, CEDAM, 1993).

Jessup, PC, 'To Form a More Perfect United Nations'(1970) 129(1) *RCADI* 1–23.

Kanninen, T, *Leadership and Reform: The Secretary-General and the UN Financial Crisis of the Late 1980s. Legal Aspects of International Organization* volume 22 (The Hague, Kluwer Law International, 1995).

Kaufmann, J, Schrijver, N *et al. Changing Global Needs: Expanding Roles for the United Nations System* Reports and Papers, 1990–95 (Hanover, NH, Academic Council on the United Nations, 1990).

Kennedy, P, 'Will the UN Survive into the Next Century?' (1996) 13 *New Perspectives Quarterly* 35–38.

Kennedy, P and Russett, B, 'Reforming the United Nations' (September/October 1995) 74(5) *Foreign Affairs* 56–71.

Knight, AW, 'Success and Failure of the UN Adaptations and Reforms'. Paper presented to the International Studies Association Conference (Washington DC, April 1994).

Langhorne, R, 'Reforming the United Nations: The International and Institutional Contexts of Reform'. Wilton Park Paper (London, HMSO, 1995).

Laurenti, J, 'Reforming the Security Council: What American Interests?' UNA/USA, Occasional Paper Series, 1997.

Luck, CE, 'Reforming the United Nations: Lessons from a History in Progress, Editor Jean Krasno'. International Relations Studies and the United Nations Occasional Papers 1 (2002) (The Academic Council on the United Nations System, Yale University, 2003).

Malone, DM, 'The High Level Panel and the Security Council' (September 2005) 36(3) *Security Dialogue* 370–72.

Martin, A and Edwards, JBS, *The Changing Charter: A Study in the Reform of the United Nations* (London, Sylvan Press, 1955).

Matanle, E, *The UN Security Council: Prospects for Reform* (London, Royal Institute of International Affairs, 1995).

Muller, JW, 'The Reform of the UN. 1—Report' *Annual Review of United Nations Affairs* special volume (New York, 1992).

Novosseloff, A, 'La réforme des Nations Unies: Enjeux et Perspectives' (Spring/Summer 1998) 4 *L'Observateur des Nations Unies* 1–29.

Russett, B, 'Ten Balances for Weighing UN Reform Proposals' (1996) 111 *Political Science Quarterly* 259–69.

Saksena, KP, *Reforming the United Nations: The Challenge of Relevance* (New Delhi; Newbury Park, Sage Publications, 1993).

Seara-Vazquez, M, 'The UN Security Council at Fifty: Midlife Crisis or Terminal Illness?' (September/December 1995) 1(3) *Global Governance* 285–96.

Snyder, R, 'Reforming the Security Council for Post-Cold War World' (1997) 15(1) *International Journal of World Peace* 3–16.

Stanley Foundation, 'The United Nations and the Twenty-First Century: The Imperative for Change'. Report of the Thirty-first United Nations of the Next Decade Conference, 16–21 June 1996 (Muscatine, Iowa, Stanley Foundation, 1996).

Steele, D, *The Reform of the United Nations* (London; Wolfeboro, NH, Croom Helm, 1987).

Tavernier, P, 'Le processus de réforme des Nations Unies' (1988) 92(2) *RGDIP* 305–34.

Taylor, P, Daws, S and Adamczick-Gerteis, U (eds), *Documents on Reform of the United Nations* (Aldershot, Brookfield, Dartmouth, 1996).

Index